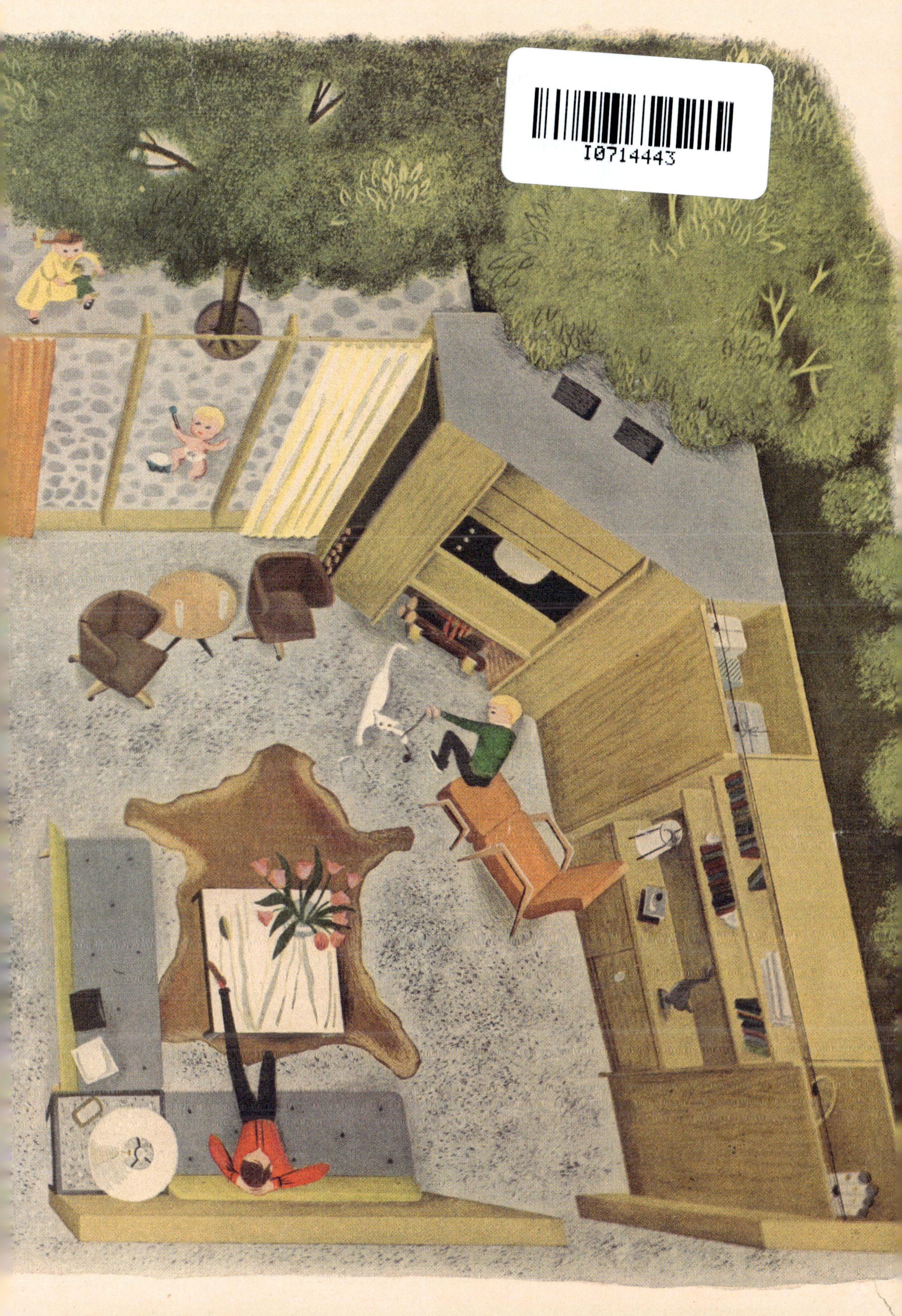

I0714443

Mid-Century
Modernism
and the
American Body

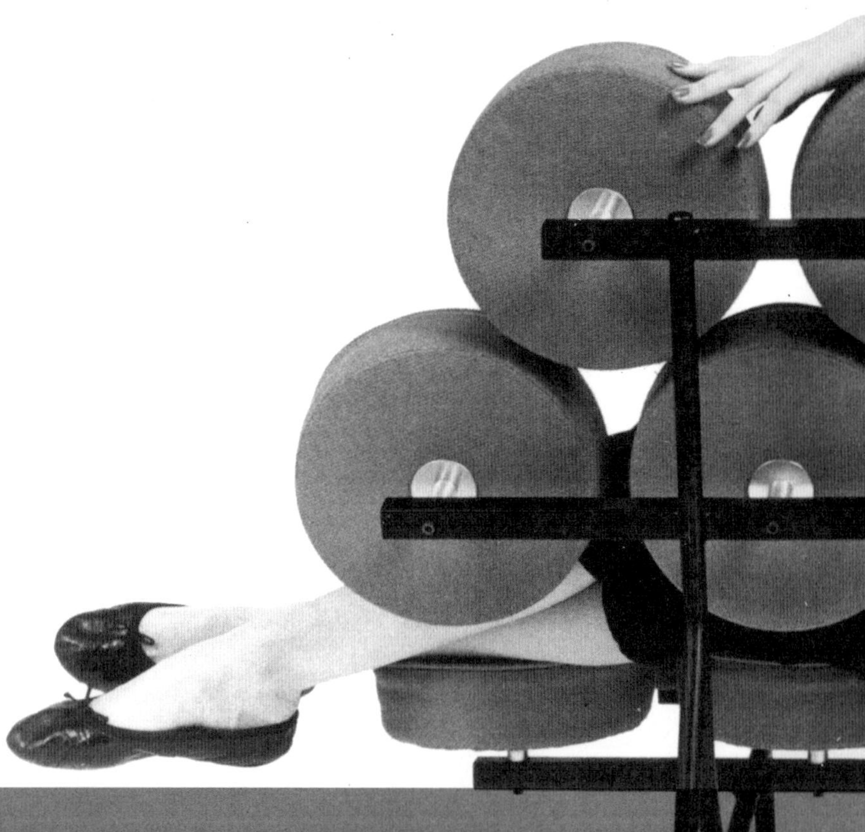

Mid-Century Modernism and the American Body

Race, Gender, and the Politics of Power in Design

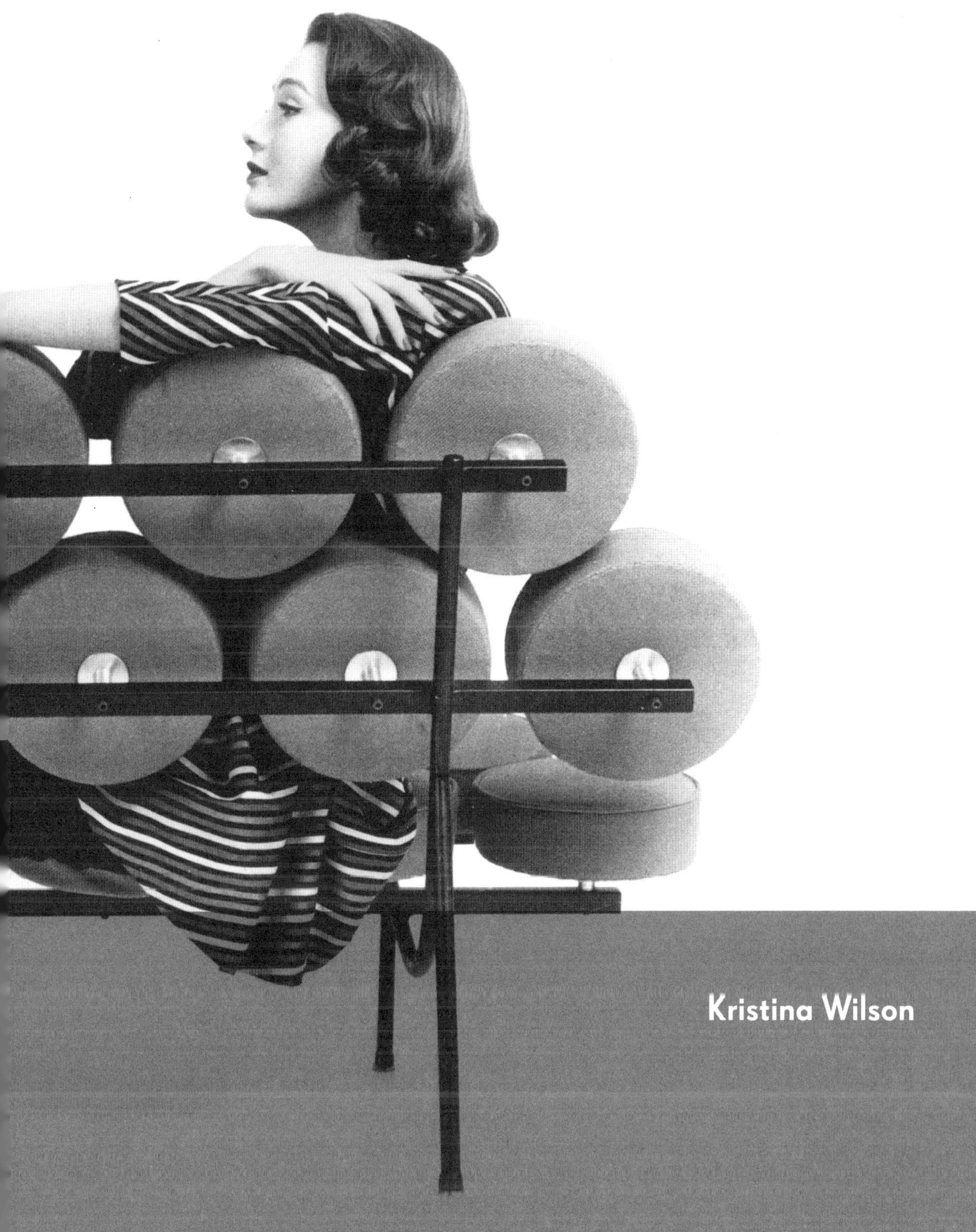

Kristina Wilson

Princeton University Press
Princeton and Oxford

Published by Princeton University Press, 41 William Street, Princeton, New Jersey 08540

In the United Kingdom: Princeton University Press, 6 Oxford Street, Woodstock, Oxfordshire OX20 1TR

press.princeton.edu

Cover illustration: Fashion Fair, *Ebony*, August 1953, 85. Christa, photographer. ©2020 Christa Zinner
Illustration in front matter: pp. ii–iii, reproduction of fig. 76
Illustrations at chapter openers: p. 20, reproduction of fig. 27; p. 160, detail of fig. 106
Illustrations in back matter: pp. 236–37, detail of fig. 102; p. 244, detail of fig. 146; p. 253, detail of fig. 70
Illustration on endpapers: reproduction of fig. 25

Library of Congress Cataloging-in-Publication Data

Names: Wilson, Kristina, author.
Title: Mid-century modernism and the American body : race, gender, and the politics of power in design / Kristina Wilson.
Description: First. | Princeton : Princeton University Press, 2021. | Includes bibliographical references and index.
Identifiers: LCCN 2020010430 | ISBN 9780691208190 (hardback) | ISBN 9780691213491 (ebook)
Subjects: LCSH: Design—Social aspects—United States—History—20th century. | Modernism (Aesthetics)—Social aspects—United States. | Decorative arts—United States—Marketing. | Power (Social sciences)—United States—History—20th century.
Classification: LCC NK1404 .W557 2021 | DDC 745.40973/0904—dc23
LC record available at https://lccn.loc.gov/2020010430

British Library Cataloging-in-Publication Data is available

Publication of this book has been aided by the Higgins School of Humanities, Clark University, and a Global Equity Grant, Princeton University Press

Designed by Roy Brooks, Fold Four, Inc.

This book has been composed in Avenir and Super Grotesk

Printed on acid-free paper. ∞

Printed in Italy

10 9 8 7 6 5 4 3 2

Contents

For David and Anya

Acknowledgments

There comes a time in one's career when life is so full that it takes an embarrassingly long time to complete a project such as this! I have been very fortunate to have great colleagues, collaborators, friends, and family who have supported and engaged this project at many different levels, and at wildly varying times in its progress and growth.

I'm extremely lucky to have spent most of my career at Clark University, where my fellow faculty members are unfailingly generous, intellectually curious, and funny, and my students challenge and inspire me in every class. The intellectual heart of this project began when I cotaught a seminar in fall 2013 with my friend and colleague in the Geography School, Deb Martin, titled Suburbia and the Rhetoric of Freedom. Our students bravely grappled with the interdisciplinary mix of readings we assigned; many of the ideas that arose in our thought-provoking classroom discussions, as well as the actual syllabus readings, appear throughout this book. As an interdisciplinary seminar, it was generously sponsored by the Higgins School of Humanities and supported by then-director Amy Richter. The Higgins School of Humanities at Clark is a fabulous gathering place for all sorts of illuminating conversations, and I am grateful to both Amy and her successor as director, Meredith Neuman, for considerable financial support toward the research and publication of this book. I have also found invigorating intellectual kinship with the members of the critical race theory faculty reading group, sponsored by associate provost and dean of the faculty Esther Jones. Within my home department, I especially thank Hugh Manon and John Garton, who read multiple drafts of multiple chapters; our conversations about this project profoundly shaped it. Frank Armstrong, renowned photographer, and Chris Ruble, resource librarian, provided essential support with the digital images for the book.

I explored many of the ideas in this book in a wide range of public talks, and I am thankful for the creative feedback I received in many different settings, including audiences at College of the Holy Cross; Clark University; Newberry Library Seminar in American Art and Visual Culture; Kansas State University; Washington University; University of Texas at Austin; Rhode Island College; Stanford University; Scriven Arts Colony; Ned Cooke's Material Culture Lunch Colloquium at Yale University; and the Smithsonian American Art Museum. My especial thanks to Mona Hadler, who invited me to participate in her session on the visual culture of *Mad Men* at College Art Association in 2013; and to Imogen Hart, who included me in her panel on arts and design at CAA in 2016. I've had stimulating conversations with many colleagues about this project, and I would like to thank Glenn Adamson, Bonnie Campbell Lilienfeld, Jennifer Greenhill, Carma Gorman, Camara Dia Holloway, Min Kyung Lee, Chris Long, Paula Lupkin, Victoria Pass, E. Carmen Ramos, Macushla Robinson, Elizabeth

Seaton, Toby Sisson, Abraham Thomas, Michelle Wilkinson, and Gail Windisch for their insights. I am very grateful that I got to know Ilana Harris-Babou and her art when she had an installation and exhibition at Recess in Brooklyn in the summer of 2018; studying her work, and several conversations with her, have helped me conceptualize the twenty-first-century part of this story. The short-term George Gurney Senior Fellowship at the Smithsonian American Art Museum in 2019 allowed me to wrap up important archival work in Washington, DC, and to benefit from the wonderful community in the Research and Scholars Center. I appreciate the perceptive comments of the anonymous reviewers for Princeton University Press; any infelicities of fact or idiosyncrasies of interpretation are purely my own. Part of chapter 3 appeared in an article in the *Journal of Design History* in 2015; and some of the research for chapter 4 was originally done for the RISD Museum's exhibition *Cocktail Culture* (2011) and for the Mariana Kistler Beach Museum of Art's exhibition on Associated American Artists, *Art for Every Home* (2015).

I would like to thank the many archivists and librarians at multiple different collections who have generously helped me: Andreas Nutz and Matthias Pühl, archivists, and Jochen Eisenbrand, curator, at the Vitra Design Museum; Amy Auscherman and Alexa Hagen, archivists, and Gloria Jacobs and Linda Baron at the Herman Miller Corporate Archives; the staff at the Department of Special Collections, Syracuse University Library, Syracuse, New York, which house the Russel Wright Papers; the staff at New School for Social Research Archives Collection, New York, which cares for the papers of Mary L. Brandt; the staff at the National Museum of American History, where Freda Diamond's papers are kept; and the accomplished, dedicated staff at the Archives of American Art. In addition, I am grateful to the John Hay Whitney Foundation, MS 1952, Manuscripts and Archives Collection, Yale University Library, for permission to quote from their archives. Finally, the research and interlibrary loan librarians at both Goddard Library, Clark University, and the Yale University Libraries have been incredible resources for me in this project, and I appreciate their help enormously.

At Princeton University Press, it has been a pleasure to work with Michelle Komie; her support for this project over many years has been invaluable, and I thank her for her help in bringing it, finally, to a larger audience. I have also appreciated the professionalism and sage advice of Lisa Black, Kenneth Guay, Lauren Lepow, and Steven Sears.

Anya has heard more about this book—she even sat through a lecture or two—than any thirteen-year-old needs to: thank you for reminding me when to put away the screen. David has been through this before; his patience, great sense of humor, and love make it all possible.

Mid-Century
Modernism
and the
American Body

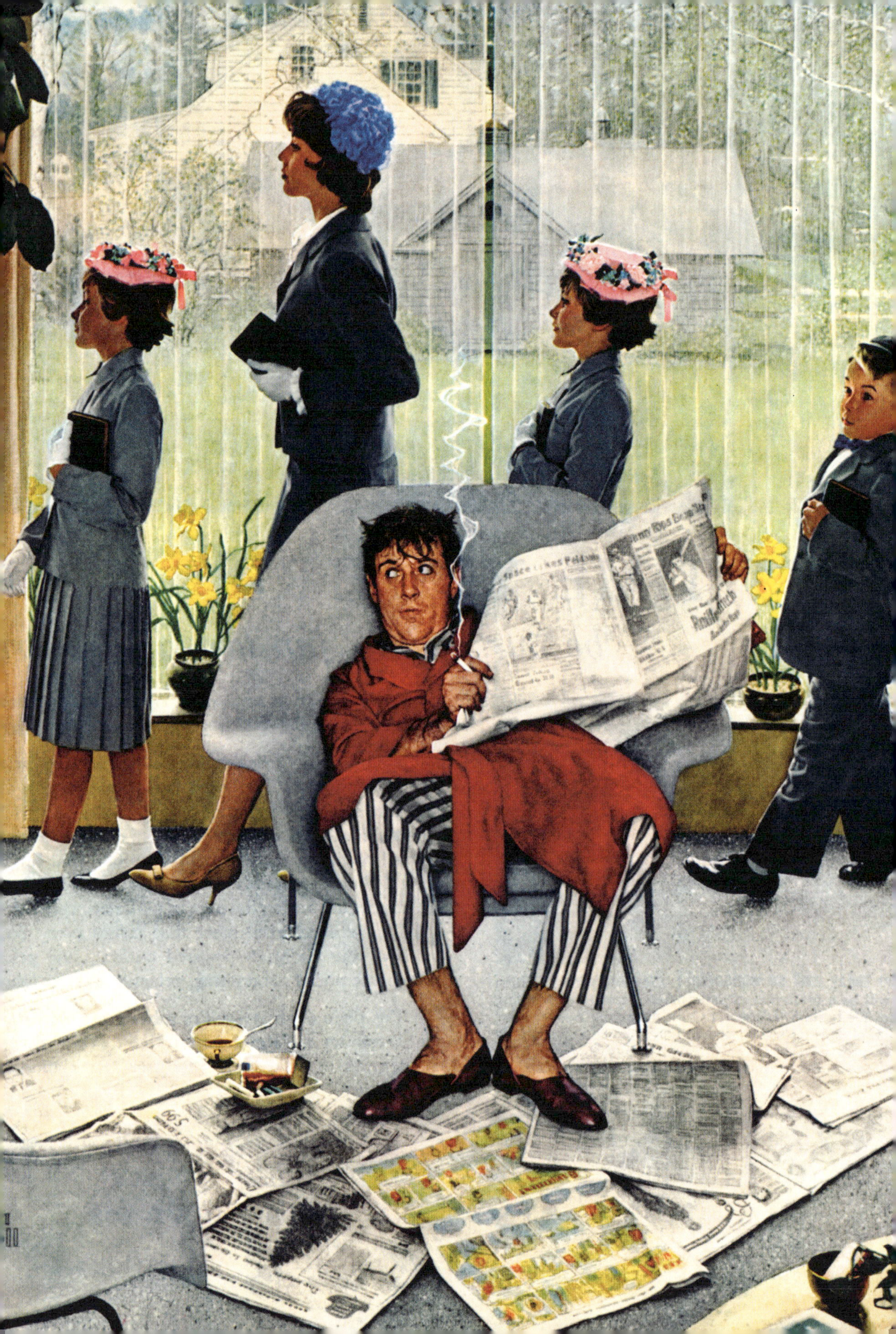

Introduction

The millions of subscribers to the *Saturday Evening Post* found an illustration by Norman Rockwell on the cover of their May 16, 1959, number (fig. 1). This issue—perhaps arriving in the mailboxes of suburban houses similar to the one depicted on its cover—was published at the end of the period studied in this book. As a widely seen image that features a White, male body slouching in a recognizably Modern chair, Rockwell's illustration is a thought-provoking introduction to many of the themes I engage in the coming chapters.

The cover depicts a White, upper-middle-class suburban family on a Sunday morning.[1] The mother, two daughters, and son, dressed for church and prayer books in hand, file out of the house in lockstep, ignoring their father, who is clearly not joining them. The father, hair comically disheveled and wearing pajamas, slippers, and a red robe, hides from his family's censure by slumping in Eero Saarinen's Womb Chair, first designed in 1946 and put into production about 1948.[2] Newspapers are strewn around his chair; he has been sitting there so long that the chair even steps on one section of the paper. The smoke of his cigarette trails off into the sheer window coverings behind him, one bit of its curlicue path just crossing the exposed opening to the plate-glass window itself.[3] The pink and blue hats on the girls and youthful mother contrast with their gray suits, much like the father's vibrant red robe against the gray upholstery of the Womb Chair.

How are we meant to read this image? At first glance, Modernism (in the form of Saarinen's chair) seems to be associated with nonconformity. The father is refusing to go to church, and his pose is excessively casual—especially in contrast to the marching-band formation of the mother and children, who not only walk in step but carry their

Fig. 1. Norman Rockwell, *Easter Morning* (also, *Sunday Morning*), 1959. Published as the cover of *Saturday Evening Post*, May 16, 1959. Printed by permission of the Norman Rockwell Family Agency.

prayer books in almost identical fashion. Although the stripes on his pajamas might suggest that the father is in prison, the chair acts as a shelter as much as a prison: the chair allows him to slouch and smoke, adopting a posture of defiance, and to escape his wife's control. The young boy is, notably, ambivalent about his location in this drama. He walks in step with his mother, but his eyes, if not precisely trained on his father, look in the same general direction as his father's eyes.

Rockwell's image is powerful to the extent that it calls upon several assumptions. The picture window references the surrounding neighborhood and the story of postwar suburban development. The characters set up a joke about gendered differences and the reign of the housewife in that suburban milieu. The house is clearly a Modernist one: elsewhere in the room we catch glimpses of the distinctive curves of the Eameses' fiberglass-reinforced plastic chairs, and the broad, low picture window is a defining feature of postwar Modernist domestic architecture. The family who disdains their father lives in this house seven days a week. While they may disapprove of his Sunday morning ritual, the house is the setting for all of their lives, and Modernism is thus, ironically, the agent for their orderly selves as much as the shelter for his defiance. Indeed, if the rest of the room appears both Modern and orderly, then perhaps the Modernist chair has imprisoned the sloppy husband, and Modernism is revealed as a force to combat the mess generated by his newspapers, coffee, and cigarettes: maybe the Womb Chair is trying to stamp out the disarray by marching across the newspapers.

While the husband is trapped, is he comfortable? The *Saturday Evening Post* argued not in its editorial narrative describing the scene: "Why is Papa not going to church—is he ill? No, his health is sound, except that he is suffering a momentary chill as his family coldly passes by. Is the poor man just hopelessly tired out? From what—yesterday's golf? … Papa may be an estimable man, but right now he has lapsed into a red-devil phase, and artist Norman Rockwell is quite warranted in equipping him with horns. May papa's chill last until he repents, until he resolves that sinning in this way is just too uncomfortable to be fun."[4] However, I propose a revised interpretation: in this image, Modernism is shielding and supporting the reclined White male body. Moreover, as Rockwell has used the chair to frame the father in the center of the image, it defines the space where the father can ultimately retain a sense of agency: in the chair, he can lurk, smoke, and read. The *Post*'s textual narrative scolds him, but it also focuses solely on him. He is the actor, and the rest of the family is mere background. We sympathize with the father—we wait for him to sigh, turn his head, and settle back into his sports page—not the mother. Modernism may be a force of order in this household, but it does ultimately cradle the body of the patriarch and encourage us to identify with him.

This vignette is a story about suburbia, Modernism, and gender. It is also, not least, a story about racial Whiteness. Just because there are no families of color in this Modernist living room does not mean that there were no families of color who lived in Modernist homes in the 1950s. It means only that in this imaginary—a field of cultural and commercial references constructed by an editorially conservative publication with a largely White readership—Whiteness was all that mattered. Images such as *Sunday Morning* reinforce an idea that postwar American suburbia just happened to be White, when in fact racial segregation was legislated through federal laws and private development practices that privileged White home buyers exclusively. Moreover, this cover promotes an idea that Modernism was a racially agnostic design language for a simply White community, when in fact, as I will argue in this book, Modernist design was a powerful tool for constructing Whiteness to White consumers in the postwar period. In Rockwell's painting, Modernism is equated with the White family: there are no other furnishing styles evident, just as there are no other races present. Modernism is positioned as a force to maintain rationality and cleanliness—stereotypes of the White suburbs—and constrain delinquency and mess, which were supposed characteristics of urban, racially diverse communities. The fact that disorder is embodied in the figure of the White patriarch is, ultimately, the punch line of the image.

Mid-Century Modernism and the American Body examines the broader social context from which Rockwell's cover emerges. In the chapters of this book, I explore multiple ways that American consumers encountered Modernist design (and, to a lesser extent, Modernist art) for their homes in the postwar years. In particular, I study domestic advice manuals and popular magazines—vehicles for selling objects and ideas—as well as the furniture objects and decorative accessories themselves. I have two major goals in the narrative that follows. The first is to illuminate the default Whiteness that undergirds the history of Modern design as it is most commonly studied in the United States. Manufacturers and advertisers encourage consumers to buy design objects as part of a process of self-fashioning: how we choose to furnish our homes broadcasts our sense of identity to our peers. However, the absence of any discussion of race in the academic literature on mid-century design reflects the White blindness of most of the design history establishment. Because the community of design scholars in the United States (up through the 2010s, at the time of this writing) is largely White, myself included, we tend not to notice the ways these objects were deployed to reinforce White power, and we have presumed—just as Rockwell's image suggests—that the designs are not about race in any way. This book argues that through forms that empower the bodies of some users while controlling others, through narratives of exclusion and discipline conjured in advertisements and popular images, and through the strategic use of allegedly "exotic" accessories in Modernist interiors, Modernism was consistently deployed for White audiences in the 1950s as a tool that established and reinforced the distinctiveness of racialized Whiteness. Whiteness as an identity—and the same must be said for any racial identity marker—is not fixed and was certainly not static in the postwar period.[5] Instead, in the years after

World War II, Whiteness was in a continual process of formation and negotiation, and its boundaries and qualities were forged and challenged through what White sociologist Herbert Blumer described in 1958 as "the public media," where "racial groups form images of themselves and others."[6] Modern design, I will demonstrate, was a popular tool in this media universe of White image-making for those consumers who thought of themselves as White. Why is it important to recognize this? Because the first step in dismantling power structures is to see them for what they are and call out their seeming naturalness and hidden biases. It is important to see this history of Modernist design as marked by specific racialized agendas.

This is not, however, the end of the story. Once we have understood that the history of mid-century Modernism is not a foregone conclusion, but rather the consequence of calculated decisions and passive blind spots, the scholarly community may be more open to looking for—and finding— parallel histories of Modernism. My second goal in *Mid-Century Modernism and the American Body* is to suggest that while Modernism may have underwritten White distinctiveness and superiority for White audiences in the 1950s, there were diverse audiences looking at Modern design in this period and using it. Following the model of media theorist John Fiske and the practices of critical race theory (CRT), I argue that there are "counter-histories" of Modern design in the postwar years that have been largely unstudied, and these open up the possibility that, as a tool of self-fashioning, Modern design resonated differently among different cultural groups.[7] In the chapters that follow, I examine the presence of Modernist design in African American professional and popular culture of the 1950s as one case study that provides evidence for a counter-history of Modernism. In contrast to Modernism's rhetorical role in magazines and ads targeting White audiences, where it was frequently deployed as a tool of distinction that demarcated Whiteness, in media intended for African American readers, Modernism was more commonly associated with bodily comfort and community sociability. While the Modernism of the African American media and that of the White media arenas are not mutually exclusive, the differing points of emphasis are meaningful, as I will discuss. Modernism's symbolic valence in the African American imaginary is hardly the sole "counter-history" of Modernism that we could explore: its resonances for Asian American, Latinx American, and Native American audiences, among others, remain to be studied. My hope is that this book will begin a scholarly conversation aimed at revealing the multiple counter-histories of Modernism that circulated in the middle decades of the twentieth century.

Postwar Suburbia: Development and Sociology

Postwar American culture is typically associated with the unprecedented scale of domestic dwelling construction: according to some statistics, eleven million single-family homes were built in the suburbs during the decade of the 1950s.[8] These homes were situated in developments of varying sizes across the country, built by local contractors who aimed to make a profit through economies of scale. By constructing the houses according to a few preset floor plans, with uniform systems and appliances, these builders could sell them at (mid-decade) prices that ranged from $10,000 to $12,500 in developments targeting working-class incomes, to $17,000–$18,000 for middle income, and above $30,000 for the most comfortable and expansive homes.[9] The multiple Levittown developments in New York and Pennsylvania have been the subject of significant scholarship, and Barbara Miller Lane's research has broadened our understanding of smaller-scale developers in the Northeast, Midwest, and California.[10] The most popular style of house in these developments throughout the 1950s was some variation on the "ranch," characterized by a single-story structure, usually with a combined living room and dining room. Although the plate-glass window in Rockwell's illustration may strike some viewers as a quintessential ranch-style window—especially with its low sill, which emphasizes the horizontality of the interior space—as Lane argues, "picture windows" were in fact a standard feature of suburban homes regardless of style throughout the 1950s.[11] Their appeal, as Sandy Isenstadt has shown, may have been twofold.[12] On the one hand, they promoted a connection to the outdoors, which was a selling point of suburbia. On the other hand, they created an illusion of spaciousness in homes that averaged between eight hundred and one thousand square feet.[13]

These houses cannot be separated from the broader racial politics that supported homeownership after World War II. Richard Rothstein is the most recent scholar to trace the impact of the Federal Housing Authority's "redlining" policies, and to argue that housing segregation was the product of federal law: the FHA would insure mortgages only for homes in racially homogeneous neighborhoods, which in practice translated into White neighborhoods.[14] Architectural historian Dianne Harris has examined how the very houses of suburbia—the close-to-identical ranches, split-levels, or Capes—could be read through the lenses of critical race theory. She has recently argued that postwar suburban architecture actually constructed and enforced an idea of Whiteness that was "so pervasive it [was] almost invisible."[15]

Historians such as Mary Pattillo-McCoy and Andrew Wiese have studied the experience of middle-class African Americans as they moved to the suburbs, and have helped to illuminate the complex, intertwined relationship of race and class in the United States. African Americans who moved to the suburbs in the postwar decades had attained a level of economic wealth that could be defined as middle-class. In real numbers, however, middle-class Black incomes were almost always lower than middle-class White incomes. In addition, Blacks were less likely to have achieved other middle-class status markers such as inherited wealth, a college education, or a white-collar job. For these reasons, Wiese, focusing on the postwar decades, and McCoy, who has studied African American culture in the 1990s, both argue for a culturally distinct experience among African Americans in suburbia.[16] Sociologist George Lipsitz helps to clarify this difference when he writes of a "white spatial imaginary" in the contemporary American landscape and a "black spatial imaginary." Based on the systemic racism of American society and its structural, economic inequalities, he writes that "struggles for racial justice require more than mere inclusion into previously excluded places. They also necessitate creation of a counter social warrant with fundamentally different assumptions about place than the white spatial imaginary allows."[17] His formulation reminds us that the embodied, suburban experience of Blacks and Whites in the postwar United States was structured with fundamental differences, even if some of the external trappings—lawn, picture-window, Modernist furniture—appeared to be the same.

The twenty-first-century histories that we write about the postwar suburbs are immeasurably enlivened by the voices of popular and academic sociologists from the period. "The appearance of the mass-produced suburbs has been seized upon by the media, mass and otherwise, as a *major phenomenon*," notes Bennett M. Berger in 1960: "Suburbia is something to *talk* about—everywhere from the pages of learned journals to best sellers, from academic halls to smoke-filled political rooms to suburban patios and picture-windowed living rooms."[18] From these writings, it is possible to identify cultural biases, preoccupations, and blind spots. For example, many articles and books take as their stated topic the question of class stratification in contemporary White American culture.[19] The comparative assessment of class was driven, in part, by a sense that the traditional status-based markers of American society were undergoing unprecedented change. Many young White veterans who had not expected to attend an institution of higher education received tuition assistance through the GI Bill, which ultimately fostered access to the middle class; similarly, those same men received Veterans' Association–sponsored mortgages, which allowed more families to move up the status ladder into homeownership than before. By contrast, African American veterans confronted layers of institutional racism in the administration of the GI and VA assistance that prevented them from benefiting, in as great numbers as White veterans, from this era of class mobility.[20] Material acquisitions for the suburban home, including refrigerators, televisions, and furniture, along with smaller items such as dinnerware, accessories, and artwork, became a part of the expression of homeownership. As sociologist Walter Goldschmidt comments in 1950, because Americans are reluctant to discuss financial concerns openly—details such as one's income, or the amount of savings in the bank—but yet live in a society where "the overwhelming importance of pecuniary considerations in everyday life" is inescapable, they turn instead to "symbolic" representations of "financial matters": "hence the importance of occupation (source of income) and expenditures (its public display)."[21]

These White sociologists and cultural critics also discuss the gender roles that they observe in suburbia. Some, like the popular writer John Keats, offer broad stereotypes of the limited world to which women are confined when they move to the suburbs. In *The Crack in the Picture Window*, his description of the life of his protagonist, Mary Drone, is unrelentingly domestic and miserable:

> Mary moodily gathered up the coffee cups and the saucers with their ground-out cigaret[te] butts, and piled the debris in the littered sink. She hadn't done the breakfast dishes because she'd picked up the children's room and had sorted the wash first thing after John left on his mile-long walk to the bus stop. She saw the washing machine lid open, started to close it from force of habit, and realized she hadn't taken the wash out to dry. Chip was making Kim cry in the living room, but Mary was beyond the point of caring much about it one way or another. The beds were unmade.[22]

In a more restrained tone, Harry Henderson describes for the readers of *Harper's* a similar routine. "The daily pattern of household life is governed by the husband's commuting schedule," he reports. "It is entirely a woman's day because virtually every male commutes. … This leaves the woman alone all day to cope with the needs of the children, her housekeeping, and shopping."[23] William H. Whyte, tellingly, does not devote sustained attention to the lives and experiences of women in the Illinois suburb of Park Forest in his influential 1956 study, *The Organization Man*. Rather, he presumes that they are the anchor of the home, and that their work is largely focused on the domestic sphere, in contrast to the men who work outside of the home. As he explains, suburbia can provide community to "fill a void in the life of the young wife that is not always filled elsewhere—and this is particularly important for the wife whose husband travels."[24]

The relentless emphasis on women's roles in the domestic sphere in many popular books and magazines of the period ultimately led Betty Friedan to write *The Feminine Mystique* (1963), in which she calls the misery expressed by Keats's character Mary "the problem that has no name."[25] Historians have argued, recently, that many women living in the postwar suburbs actually worked outside the home.[26] However, in popular literature of the time, the dominant myth presented to readers is that women are ultimately always responsible for the domestic sphere, even if they have professional success outside the home as well.[27] There is remarkably little evidence of popular literature that advises men to take on household tasks such as cleaning and cooking (with the possible exception of Russel Wright, discussed in chapter 1).

Given the invisibility of women's lives in literature of the period, it is unsurprising that White authors would devote relatively little room in their research to the experiences of the African American community, or to other nonmajority groups such as Asian Americans and Latinx Americans. For some, this is a product of how they constructed their studies. Whyte, for example, interviewed residents of a suburban community that excluded African Americans, but did not note this structural imbalance and thus shaped his research around a default of Whiteness. Similarly, Henderson's articles were based on interviews across six communities, none of which permitted homeownership to African Americans.[28] Henderson, however, calls out the explicit segregation of these communities: "What has been created here is therefore something abnormal and atypical of American life, that is, in deep conflict with democratic American ideals: large cities and towns without Negroes, something that cannot be found in either North or South. Levittown is now the largest community in America that has no Negro population."[29] His text also explores the varied, conflicting attitudes expressed by White suburbanites about the possible future racial integration of their neighborhoods. Ultimately, because of the limits of his study subjects, he is unable to shed light on the experiences of African Americans living in suburbia. Vance Packard describes the segregationist policies that guide suburban development, but his study recapitulates the biases of Whyte and Henderson: he offers a lengthy analysis of taste across various White ethnic groups and classes, but does not include African Americans—by ethnicity or class—as consumers of home goods.[30] Indeed, in 1960, sociologist W. Lloyd Warner may ultimately have provided the most honest assessment of how and why White sociologists ignored questions of taste, consumption patterns, and life in African American communities in the postwar period. He asserts, simply, that "color-caste in America is a separate problem" from the study of "social class." "Color-caste," he summarizes, "is a system of values and behavior which places all people who are thought to be white in a superior position and those who are thought of as black in an inferior status."[31] From this perspective, the study of a racially distinct group must always fall outside the purview of a scholar studying White society.

Warner's article builds on the concept, introduced by Blumer in 1958, of racial prejudice as a part of group identity rather than the product of individual biases. Blumer's structural assessment of racism resonates with the work of critical race theorists writing in the 1980s, 1990s, and 2000s, and provides a contemporaneous lens for understanding the structural racial identities that I will examine in the following chapters. He argues not only that racial prejudice is generated by group identity formation, but that racialized identity is constructed in relational terms: "To characterize another racial group is, by opposition, to define one's own group. This is equivalent to placing the two groups in relation to each other, or defining their positions *vis-à-vis* each other."[32] He then locates four "basic types of feeling that seem to be always present in race prejudice in the dominant group." These include a sense of superiority on the part of the dominant group and a concomitant sense of "intrinsic" difference and inferiority in another racial group. He describes, as well, the tendency for the dominant group to feel a "proprietary claim" to spaces, jobs, or "the display of the symbols and accoutrements" of "social prestige." And, finally, Blumer argues that the "feeling essential to race prejudice" is one of being "threatened" by a subordinate group, through that group's access to space or other objects of proprietary claim.[33] I will argue in subsequent chapters that Modernism, in the hands of White postwar authors, publications, and advertisers, is deployed as a force to keep dirt, mess, and outsiders at bay; with the gloss of Blumer's analysis, we can begin to see these examples as pieces in a larger "collective process" of White racialized group identity formation, establishing the space of White social privilege through the process of excluding racial others.[34]

Although White professional sociologists did not research the tastes and consumer trends of African Americans in the postwar years, African American sociologist E. Franklin Frazier published several studies of Black middle-class America after World War II. His 1957 book *Black Bourgeoisie* (originally published in French in 1955) is a polemical distillation of social criticism he had developed over the previous three decades as a cultural critic and professor at Howard University. As a young writer contributing to the New Negro movement in the interwar decades, Frazier had studied collective models of labor, and he retained throughout his life a profound skepticism toward the self-posturing and self-interest of the self-made middle class (of which he was avowedly a member).[35] In *Black Bourgeoisie*, he faults middle-class African Americans for blindly copying the standards of taste and consumption modeled by whites, and simultaneously faults them for having a poor sense of taste. He dismisses the homes that are pictured in *Ebony* magazine, in particular, as "reveal[ing] the most atrocious and childish tastes," and critiques the pervasive materialism of the Black middle class at large: "The homes of many middle-class Negroes have the appearance of museums for the exhibition of American manufactures and spurious art objects. The objects which they are constantly buying are always on display."[36] Historian Adam Green has refuted Frazier's interpretation of middle-class living in *Ebony*, arguing that the magazine promoted liberal models of agency and self-determination.[37] While my own reading of *Ebony* is more aligned with Green's, as will be evident in chapters 2 and 4, Frazier's scholarship does much to illuminate the diverse experiences of African Americans across a wide range of class positions. Moreover, his strongly critical view of postwar middle-class African American culture, and of the editorial and advertising agendas of the Johnson Publishing Company in particular, demonstrate that even within a single class—the broad middle class—there was considerable diversity of opinion about professional accomplishments, cultural products, and the expression of taste.

Even as Frazier accused African Americans of modeling their cultural tastes on White standards, Bernard Wolfe, a White cultural critic with a strong interest in jazz, wrote a trenchant essay in 1949 about the ways that White Americans appropriated African American art.[38] In his interpretation, Whites have designated Black Americans as a source of "unrestrained," "emotionally supercharged, spontaneous" aesthetic expression, and they look to Black performers of jazz and blues to find precisely these qualities. He ridicules White aesthetes who claim to possess "an uncanny sort of racial omniscience" and to understand " 'the Negro as he really is.' " "By a devious interracial irony," Wolfe asserts, "the 'creative' Negro, far from being his own spontaneous self, may actually be dramatizing the white man's image of the 'spontaneous' Negro 'as he really is.' "[39] Both Wolfe and Frazier, despite their different approaches and, ultimately, different sympathies, seem to argue one point: the distinctiveness of postwar middle-class African American culture is difficult to locate, and perhaps, even, to define, as it is continually shaped by the hegemonic power of White American middle-class culture. Their contemporary sociological view only reinforces the challenges in seeking a counter-history of Modernism in the postwar period: Is there a counter-narrative to find, if even those writing at the time thought not? What would it mean to argue that the resonance of Modernist design within the African American consumer imaginary differs from its resonance within the White American consumer imaginary? Could this actually be a "counter-Modernism," not just a counter-history of Modernism?

Modernisms

A brief discussion about the word "Modernism" and its role in *Mid-Century Modernism and the American Body* is in order. In this book, I capitalize "Modernism" and its variants ("Modern," "Modernistic," etc.) in order to designate Modernism as a specific movement, with loose temporal boundaries, in the worlds of art and design. In the decades around World War II, "modernism" was roughly synonymous with the contemporary moment, and its lower case appellation gave it a quality of inevitability and omnipresence: the modern was the apogee of all art, design, and architecture movements, and would not be surpassed. To argue that we have entered an era beyond Modernism is outside of the scope of this book, but as the succession of many artistic and design movements since the 1970s indicates, Modernism is no longer the presumed aesthetic sensibility of the contemporary day. Perhaps the strongest argument in favor of Modernism's past-ness is the fact that Modern designs from the middle decades of the twentieth century are routinely revived, in the twenty-first century, as historical signifiers in homes and corporate settings (a phenomenon I will discuss in my epilogue).

"Modernism" itself was a contested word in the postwar decades. Manufacturers such as Herman Miller, Knoll, and designer Paul McCobb produced furniture that they marketed as "modern," generally understood to have few historical references, no ornament, simple, geometric contours, and materials that were sometimes new (the Eames fiberglass-reinforced plastic chairs epitomized new materials; the predominance of wood in McCobb's Directional designs did not). Some critics expressed appreciation of the "lean, picked, bare-boned look" of some of the more minimalist designs, while also voicing concern that Modernist homes "had been swept so clean that there was no personality left either."[40] Other tastemakers, such as Elizabeth Gordon, editor of *House Beautiful* during the 1950s, promoted Modernist designs that openly emphasized natural materials—grained woods, nubbly fabrics, stone, and ceramics—that countered the tendency toward industrial coolness and lack of "personality" in some corners of the Modernist world. As design historian Monica Penick has documented, Gordon's "American Modernism" of the 1950s was closely allied, in fact, with the model of "organic modernism" that Frank Lloyd Wright had been promoting since the 1930s (fig. 2).[41] Countless advertisements in home-decorating magazines from the period reveal that manufacturers often promoted slightly simplified versions of their core stock as "Modern": as writ in a hope chest, bedroom suite, or a sectional sofa, these "stunning modern functional designs" had broad geometric contours and fewer passages of period-specific ornament, but were generally heavier and bulkier than the "bare-boned" strand of Modernist design (fig. 3).[42]

Within the professional world of designers, decorators, and magazine editors, the boundaries of "Modernism," and even its definition, were positions worth fighting over. However, for the broad public, it is unlikely that these distinctions were very important; the very multiplicity of examples of "Modern" design in period magazines suggests that many readers experienced a broad, variegated view of the style. In the chapters that follow, my embrace of Modernist design is similarly catholic, and I engage with a range of objects that generally have simplified, geometric or biomorphic contours; lack ornament or other historical references; tend to have lower, more horizontal profiles than period-designed furniture, and make use of modern materials such as metals and plastics. Where possible, I have identified the designs that appear as props in editorial and advertising photographs. However, given the countless manufacturers who were producing similarly designed upholstered lounge chairs (for example), it has not always been possible to verify the Modernist credentials of the object I will be analyzing. Instead, I have relied on the period sensibility that emerges from the magazines of the decade, collating together the manufacturers' designs that are recognizable or that remain in production today (such as those of Herman Miller, Knoll, and Dunbar); the aesthetic sensibility

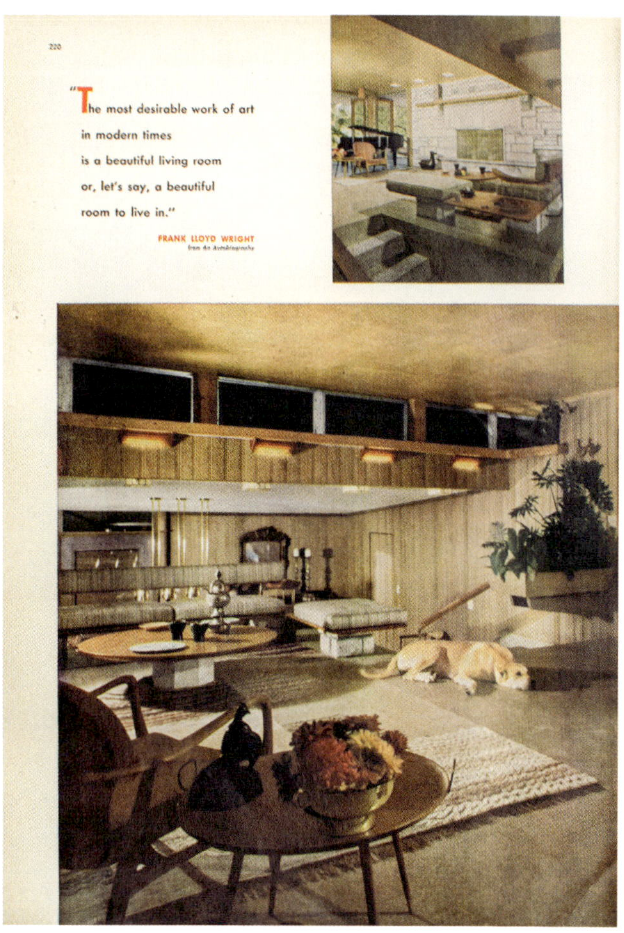

of the "organic" Modernism of *House Beautiful*; and the multiple-choice Modernism offered by many manufacturers.

No one, in the middle decades of the twentieth century, referred to the Modernist design that populated media, domestic, and corporate landscapes as "mid-century Modernism," of course. That specific label arose in the later twentieth century as a collecting term and is broadly applied today to many of the Modernist objects that survive (or continue to be reproduced) from that period. I chose to use the phrase in the title of my book for several reasons. First, it anchors my study chronologically. Second, its lack of ideological specificity—the term refers to both organic Modernist designs made of wood as well as the new-materials minimalism of the period—resonates with the "big-tent" view of Modernism that I describe here. Third, its familiarity may set up the expectation that the history traced in this book is familiar, but in fact my goal is to defamiliarize the conventional wisdoms about Modernist design in the middle decades of the twentieth century.

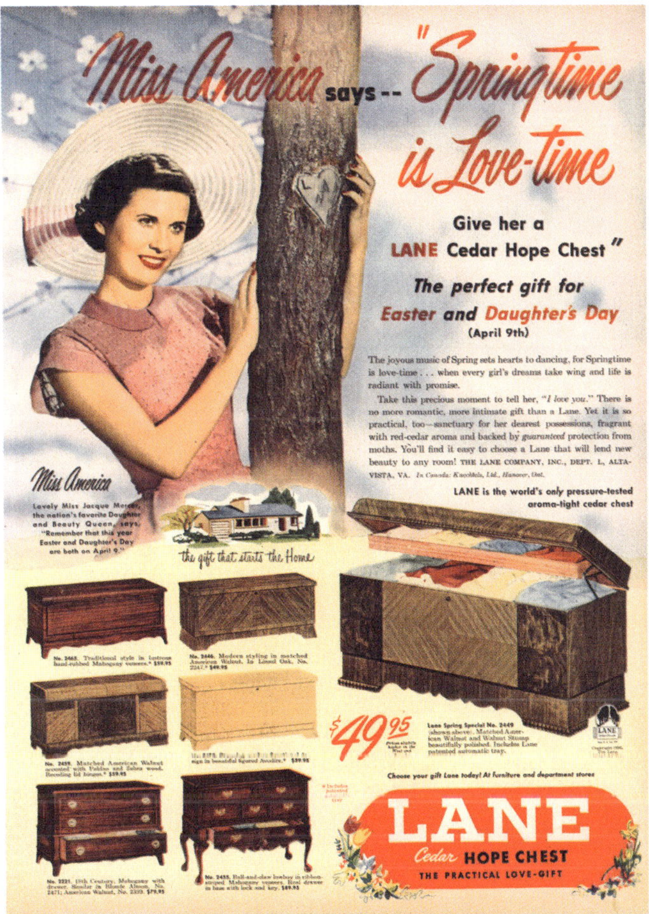

Methodologies

This book poses questions about how design objects engage with the work
of constructing racialized identities for consumers. I owe a debt to theorists
and historians of race and race in art history, including those conducting
research along the lines of critical race art history (CRAH) and those who
have established frameworks for understanding racialized Whiteness in art
history.[43] The starting place for many scholars — including historian David
Roediger, film theorist Richard Dyer, and art historian Martin Berger — is to
interrogate the presumed neutrality of White identity, or what sociologist
Ruth Frankenberg has called the "seeming normativity" of Whiteness and
its "structured invisibility."[44] Roland Barthes offers a useful term for describing the all-encompassing power of racialized Whiteness, *ex-nomination*.
Although he originally developed the concept as a political critique of
the massive, invisible power of the bourgeoisie, his description applies
to the power of racial Whiteness in the United States as well. In his analysis, the "bourgeoisie has some difficulty acknowledging itself," and as it

becomes the dominant cultural and political power in Western society, it "has obliterated its name."[45] Indeed, "the bourgeoisie is defined as *the social class which does not want to be named*."[46] The refusal to be named is the phenomenon that he calls "ex-nomination," and is what creates a landscape where power cannot be called out as such: "Bourgeois ideology can therefore spread over everything and in so doing lose its name without risk: no one here will throw this name of bourgeois back at it. It can without resistance subsume bourgeois theatre, art and humanity under their eternal analogues; in a word, it can ex-nominate itself without restraint when there is only one single human nature left: the defection from the name 'bourgeois' is here complete."[47] For White Americans, racialized Whiteness has frequently operated in just this way: it is a mode of existing in the world and a position of power that does not need to be interrogated, and, indeed, cannot be named as such. Dyer applies Barthes's ideas to race when he writes, "Moreover, the position of speaking as a white person is one that white people now almost never acknowledge and this is part of the condition and power of whiteness: white people claim and achieve authority for what they say by not admitting, indeed not realizing, that for much of the time they speak only for whiteness."[48]

Race is always, fundamentally, a relational concept: as Blumer argued in 1958, one has race because one is marked as different from someone else and yet like another. His observations have been echoed in subsequent decades, as in the writings of theorist Kalpana Seshadri-Crooks, who argues specifically that the relational position of Whiteness is always negotiated against another: "By Whiteness, I refer to a master signifier (without a signified) that establishes a structure of relations, a signifying chain that through a process of inclusions and exclusions constitutes a pattern for organizing human difference."[49] Architectural historian Dianne Harris, in her study of postwar architecture, *Little White Houses*, examines how Whiteness was defined both negatively and positively in the 1940s and 1950s, how "whiteness … depends on the ability of whites to identify what they are *not* in equal measure to deciding what they are."[50] In her analysis, the presence of White people—and the absence of non-Whites—in renderings or advertising literature is a part of how Whiteness was positively constructed. In addition, the open floor plans and emphasis on spaciousness in suburban homes, she argues, conveyed Whiteness through the implied contrast to their opposite: "dirt, crowding, trash, lack of privacy, and untidy spaces signalled poverty and insecure racial identities. In contrast, clutter-free and clean environments were construed as belonging to middle-class, white occupants." She continues, "The illusion of spaciousness was equally important. … cramped and crowded living conditions signalled ethnic origins and reminded Americans of a Depression-era past."[51] In this book, I analyze the ways that Modernist design participated in the constructions of race—for both White Americans and Black Americans—both positively and negatively.

These constructions were ongoing processes: designs and media representations coached consumers (implicitly and explicitly) about how to behave, what to expect, and what to fear. Racialized identities are performed and continually recalibrated, and I attempt to trace these shifting formations in the following history of revealed Whiteness and counter-history of African American Modernism.

Two philosophers have recently endeavored to establish a rigorous understanding of the ontological position of Whiteness. Shannon Sullivan argues, like Dyer, that Whiteness is a largely unconscious position, and describes the privilege of Whiteness as one that continually appropriates the objects, accomplishments, and spaces of non-Whites.[52] Linda Martín Alcoff raises the question of whether Whiteness can ever be understood in ways that are distinct from the trope of superiority: What is Whiteness beyond superiority, beyond its group position "*vis-à-vis* another," in Blumer's words? She proposes that Whiteness must ultimately be understood as a marked position, like any other racial identity, and suggests that in our twenty-first-century society, Whites take on a "double consciousness" similar to that originally theorized by W.E.B. Du Bois: a White person must simultaneously see herself as an individual and as a person whose race represents negative associations to others.[53] Throughout the narrative that follows, I have been challenged to be mindful of my own White biases and to note Whiteness as a marked position—even when articulated unconsciously—in historical texts.

My own engagement with these questions began when I read Harris's study of postwar architectural suburbia, and this project is inspired by many of the questions she posed. Harris, like Dyer, Sullivan, and many others, argues that "white Americans have tended not to see, think about, or acknowledge their unearned privileges, nor have they tended to examine the ways in which their white identities are socially constructed and culturally reinforced." And she notes, "If it seems to some readers that I see race everywhere in this study, perhaps my view can serve as a necessary corrective to the extensive body of architectural histories that have seen race nowhere."[54] Race has similarly been absent in almost all studies of postwar American design, and, when I read *Little White Houses*, I asked myself whether the popular postwar designs manufactured by companies such as Herman Miller could truly be understood as race-neutral. Was it possible that my own position as a White scholar had made me blind to the ways that the designs, in fact, spoke "only for whiteness"? To explore this has necessitated multiple avenues of inquiry. Some of my lines of research examine Modernism itself: How was Modernism discussed, by authors, critics, and designers in the postwar period? How were Modernist design objects presented in the marketplace of the 1950s? Other trajectories examine how Modernism was interpreted for presumed White audiences at the time, such as the readership of *Life* magazine and other shelter magazines such as *Better Homes and Gardens* or *House Beautiful*.

All of these research paths serve to illuminate the marked Whiteness of Modernism, and they help us to see how Modernism speaks for Whiteness when it speaks to White audiences in the postwar period. Indeed, to find Whiteness in mid-century Modernism is to discover how thoroughly it was embedded in the social landscape of its time. If large-scale housing developments—the suburbia that constituted the American imaginary of mid-century—legislated segregation by drawing clear boundary lines between White and non-White neighborhoods, then it is unsurprising to see Modernism presented to White consumers as a vigilant border guard for race. But, of course, White superiority was not the only racial dynamic in the United States after the war. African Americans returning home after fighting in World War II began the work of social organizing and protests that would ultimately become the civil rights movement of the 1960s. Over the decade of the 1950s, many high-profile events covered in the national media gathered momentum for the cause of racial equality, including the 1954 Supreme Court decision in *Brown v. Board of Education*, the murder of Emmett Till in 1955, the Montgomery, Alabama, bus boycott of 1955–56, and the Prayer Pilgrimage to Washington in 1957. These individual events pointed to a much larger movement that eventually brought about the end of Jim Crow restrictions on the African American body, de jure (if not de facto) segregation, and the Civil Rights and Voting Rights Acts of 1964 and 1965.[55] The complexity of postwar African American culture is represented in both Frazier's scholarship and the multiple publications of the Johnson Publishing empire (in addition to *Ebony* and *Jet*, John H. Johnson published the monthlies *Tan* and *Hue* in the 1950s). How did Modernism resonate for these audiences, growing in number as well as—slowly—in economic and political strength? Does Modernism still speak for Whiteness when it speaks to a non-White audience, such as the readers of African American monthly magazines?

To begin answering these questions, I have looked for Modernism in the hands and words of African American designers, as well as the popular representation of Modernism in *Ebony*, the magazine with the largest African American readership of the day. Cultural studies theorist Stuart Hall argues that popular culture is an "arena that is *profoundly* mythic … where we discover and play with the identifications of ourselves." According to his model, popular culture is best understood not as a series of essentializing binaries, but rather as an expressive arena that has the capacity for a "dialogic" relationship between image and reader.[56] In my examination of *Ebony*, I endeavor to look beyond Frazier's dismissal of its middle-class lifestyles as mere copies of White lifestyles—as a set of racial binaries—and to ask how Modernism might have been a tool for the formation of a distinctive, if "mythic," identity for its readers. If, in the hands of White advertisers, Modernism is a force that excludes, controls, and even occasionally owns bodies of color, I argue that, in the hands of African American designers, Modernism is presented as an agent that protects bodies of color, provides physical comfort, and fosters community. This history is suggested in the evidence in the chapters that follow, and I propose that it is one of possibly many "counter-histories" of Modernism that exist in mid-century America. As Blackhawk Hancock explains, John Fiske's model of "counter-history" has several components. It "counters traditional history through revealing the particularities of events and their socializing effects upon bodies (both individual bodies and the collective social body)" and also "emphasizes multiplicity and discontinuity over the homogenizing grand narrative trend of traditional history."[57]

This concept of a counter-history in Modernism studies has a deeper legacy in the field of critical race theory, which celebrates the "narrative voice" and the importance of "storytelling" — even "counter-storytelling" — as a tool for expressing "experiential knowledge … [as] legitimate, appropriate, and critical to understanding, analyzing and teaching about racial subordination."[58] *Mid-Century Modernism and the American Body* is by no means an exhaustive study of Modernist design in mid-century African American culture but rather is intended to suggest future avenues of scholarly inquiry. The counter-history of African American reception of Modernism that is opened up here should be viewed along-side extant historical narratives as well as the work of future scholars. "Counter-history is never as strong as the dominant history, nor does it seek to replace the dominant history as the only truth of the world," Hancock reminds us; "rather counter-history works to be 'effective' as it is con-structed and operates to provide documentation and testimony to subju-gated positions in society."[59] In keeping with Hancock's exegesis, I argue that what is valuable in this counter-history of Modernism is not its utter dif-ference from mainstream Modernism. Indeed, there are points of overlap between the two: White Modernists, for example, did discuss the physical comfort of their designs. However, what is significant is the prominence of certain themes — exclusion and control in White media arenas, sociability and comfort in African American discourses — and when we view them side by side, we see the persistent strength of the counter-narrative.

While race is relatively uncharted in the field of American design history, gender is a much more commonly used analytical lens. Gender is integral to the study of objects made for the home, as we consider who uses them, where in the house they are kept, and who is expected to clean them.[60] In this book, I attend to questions of both race and gender because they are two axes by which individual identity is defined. More importantly, they are both vectors of social power, and they frequently collide in ways that allow for an intersectional analysis, to use a framework introduced by CRT scholars.[61] When we look at a chair and admire its curves as we would those of a White woman's body (as I suggest in chapter 3) or when a White consumer unthinkingly uses a water pitcher modeled on the body of an African woman (as I argue in chapter 4) the objects themselves are revealed to be complicit in maintaining certain power dynamics. In these cases, it is not merely that gender places the female in a subordinate position, but that race allows the White woman to be seen and the woman of color to remain invisible. Ultimately, we use objects, but they also tell us how to use them. As they interact with our bodies in multiple ways over the course of any given day, they physically shape our expectations about what is possible in the world. They are props that we use to negotiate and perform identities of race and gender.

This book may be categorized as a work of design history, but the visual material I study moves far beyond the physical products of design. In addition to interrogating the forms, compositions, and textures of various functional design objects, I also apply close formal analysis to the photographs, architectural designs, drawings, and advertisements that presented design to consumers in the postwar years. These multidisciplinary artifacts are sources that allow us to trace the visual circulation of design in society. In order to tell the history of Modernist design in the postwar United States, I therefore conduct close readings of photographs that have designs in them; deconstruct texts that discuss design; and analyze actual design objects. At times in my research—as I have considered works through the lenses of the history of photography, architectural history, art history, and design history—this project has felt most like a multidisciplinary visual culture practice. Ultimately, Modernism was not limited to fine art, to design, or to architecture. As it became a mentality that pervaded visual expression in the middle of the twentieth century, it was available as a force to shape modes of behavior and ways of looking at the world. Its very breadth requires the art historian to look at diverse media, and to consider each object and image as a work intentionally crafted to make meaning.

In the chapters that follow, I argue that Modernism helped to forge racialized and gendered identities for consumers in the postwar period. I develop this argument by exploring a range of materials that brought Modernism to the broad public after World War II. In the first two chapters, I study texts that introduced Modernism to readers; in the latter two chapters, I examine the physical products of Modernist design that consumers were encouraged to put in their homes.

Chapter 1 analyzes a group of domestic advice manuals that frame the concept of Modernism in the home for consumers. In comparing the voices of Black and White male authors, I argue that Modernism was repeatedly deployed as a force for the control of women's bodies. For the White authors discussed in the chapter, Modernism was a tool to police racialized boundaries and exclude non-Whites, but in the words and designs of African American architect Paul R. Williams, Modernism was positioned as a force that could gather together and protect the residents of a house.

Chapter 2 continues the discussion of the print-based fantasy representation of Modernism by comparing Modernism in *Life* and *Ebony* magazines over the decade of the 1950s. Through a close analysis of photographs and advertisements in both publications, I argue that Modernism in *Life* was invested in defining racialized Whiteness, but that its presence in *Ebony* largely avoided any overt references to race and instead could be more explicitly linked to class status. Indeed, in *Life*, Modernism was a tool for asserting middle-class Whiteness, whereas in *Ebony*, it functioned to define elite wealth. In the pages of *Ebony*, Modernism became a prop that enabled the security, bodily comfort, and social confidence associated with upper-class communities of color.

In chapter 3, a case study of the designs manufactured by the Herman Miller Furniture Company provides a counterpoint to the print-based Modernism of chapters 1 and 2. I use this chapter as a space to explore the methodological implications of examining race in design objects. I analyze the furniture designed by George Nelson and Charles and Ray Eames as empathetic objects—as objects that anticipate users and, through their form, invite users to imagine what interaction with them will be like. Ultimately, such empathetic forms are also tools of control, as the biomorphic shapes constrain the body that sits on them. I then interpret the company's publicity materials, and Nelson's and the Eameses' strategic use of non-Western indigenous artifacts as "exotic" accessories in corporate showrooms, through the lenses of racialized identity formation.

Finally, chapter 4 continues the study of particular design objects with a discussion of the smaller-scale decorative accessories that were sold for the Modern postwar home. These include glassware, ceramic objects such as ashtrays and candy dishes, and two-dimensional art to be hung on the walls. These objects legislate social behaviors and, as such, can be interpreted as another example of Modernist control of the body. Moreover, they were especially invested with the power to give "personality" to a room, in the words of many critics, and should be understood as symbols that are consciously displayed to project a homeowner's identity. In this chapter, I continue the discussion of the display of non-Western artifacts, moving from the realm of commercial showroom to the domestic spaces illustrated in *Life* and *Ebony*. The tradition of displaying such objects—especially African art—in Black American homes as a statement of legacy and cultural pride contravenes the practice dominant in many White homes, and again suggests a counter-history of Modernism that emphasizes community and sociability over exclusion.

As I began my research on the designs and culture of mid-century American Modernism, one of the most challenging aspects was its enduring popularity in the twenty-first century. For much of the twentieth century, the most popular style of home furnishing for Americans was some kind of Colonial Revival, and I have come to think of "mid-century Modernism" as today's Colonial Revival. I explore this conundrum in my epilogue.

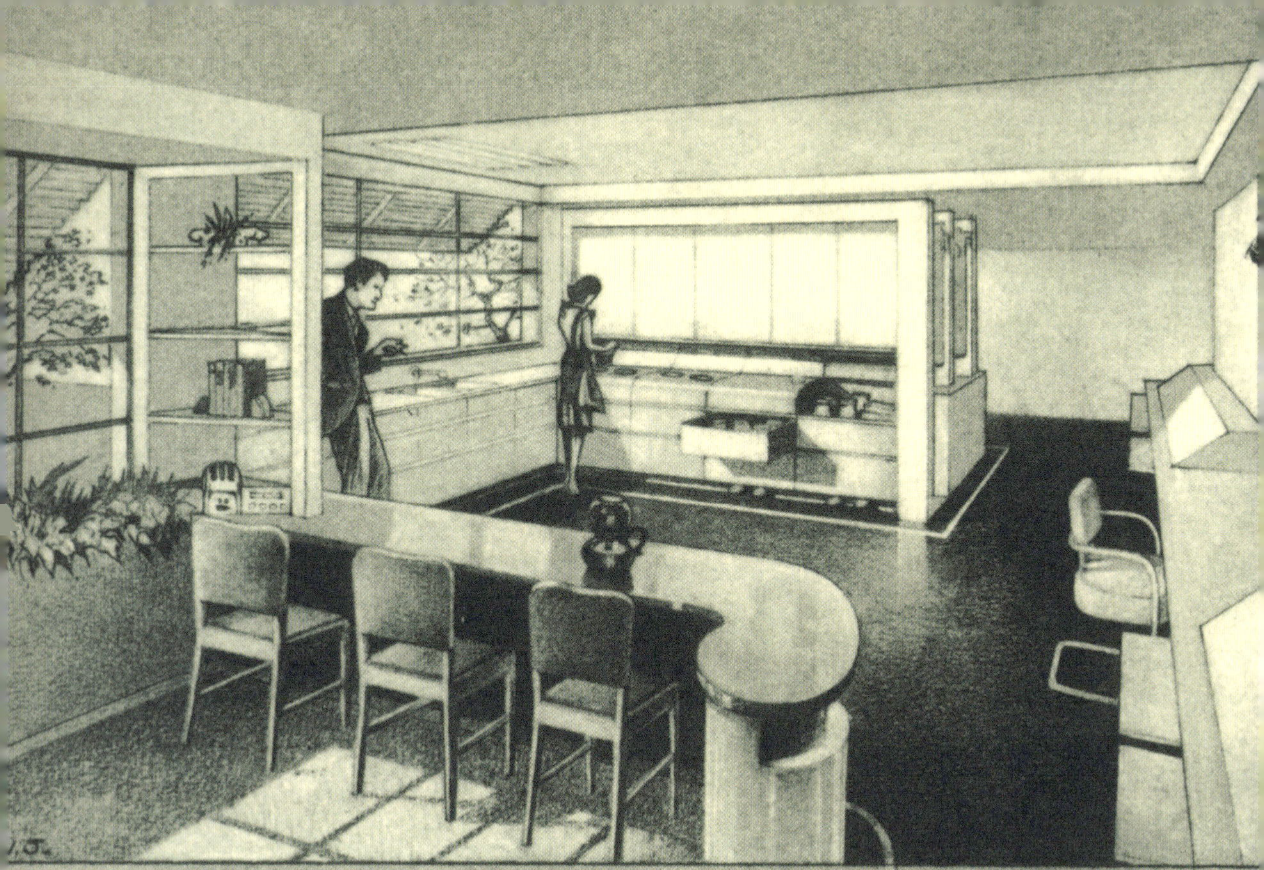

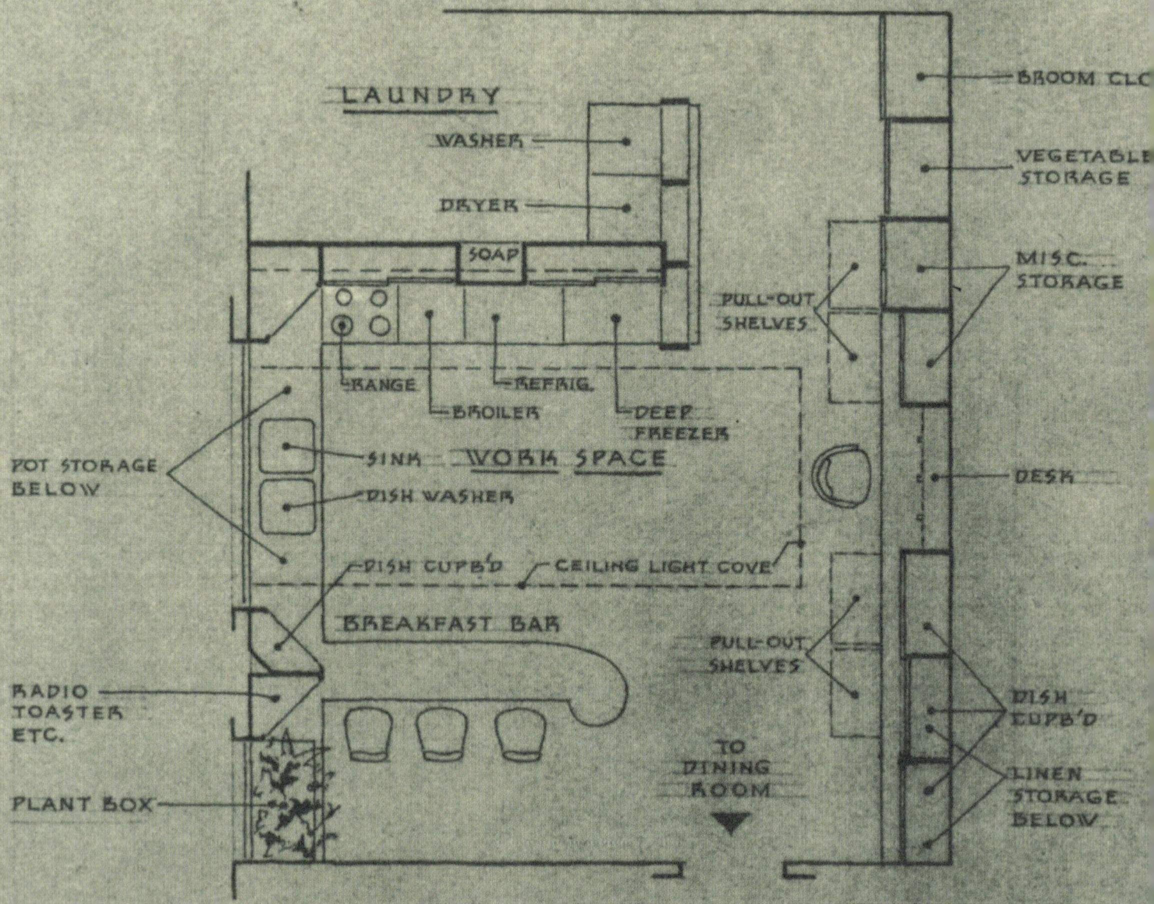

LAUNDRY

WASHER

DRYER

SOAP

PULL-OUT SHELVES

BROOM CLO[SET]

VEGETABLE STORAGE

MISC. STORAGE

RANGE

BROILER

REFRIG

DEEP FREEZER

POT STORAGE BELOW

SINK

WORK SPACE

DISH WASHER

DESK

DISH CUPB'D

CEILING LIGHT COVE

BREAKFAST BAR

PULL-OUT SHELVES

DISH CUPB'D

LINEN STORAGE BELOW

RADIO TOASTER ETC.

PLANT BOX

TO DINING ROOM

The Body in Control
Modernism and the Pursuit of Better Living

Numerous domestic advice books published in the five years following World War II celebrate the Modern American home and its beneficial effects on the nuclear family unit. Designers Russel and Mary Wright suggest, in their 1950 book *Guide to Easier Living*, that there should be one room in the Modern house where the entire family will find enjoyment. They present an "active" living room that includes barbells, a Ping-Pong table, an easel for painting, and an area for "lounging and drinking," thus creating a space of "real warmth and life" for the whole family to gather together (fig. 4).[1] Architect Paul R. Williams, in *New Homes for Today* (1946), also extolls the vision of family togetherness, although his unifying family room is outfitted in a Colonial Revival style rather than overt Modernism (fig. 5). "Here is a room designed around the informal way the average family lives," he explains. "The children can study at the dining table; the parents can be comfortable at the other end of the room and if a guest drops in the entire room extends friendly invitation to join the family group."[2] The idealized family unit, corralled into one of these model rooms, might be represented in an endearing sketch found in the opening pages of the 1950 *Decorate Your Home for Better Living*, by interior designer Mary I. Brandt (fig. 6). In this portrait, the five members are merged as a single entity, yet each pursues his or her own distinctive activities while smiling in harmony: the father reads the paper and listens to the radio; the mother sews; the older son reads and listens to records; the daughter talks on the phone; and the younger son is caught up in a game, perhaps of "Cowboys and Indians," judging from the feather affixed to his head and the toy rifle in his hand.

A closer examination of these illustrations and their accompanying texts reveals agendas that are, perhaps, a bit more complex than the mere celebration of the nuclear family unit. Each demonstrates a persistent

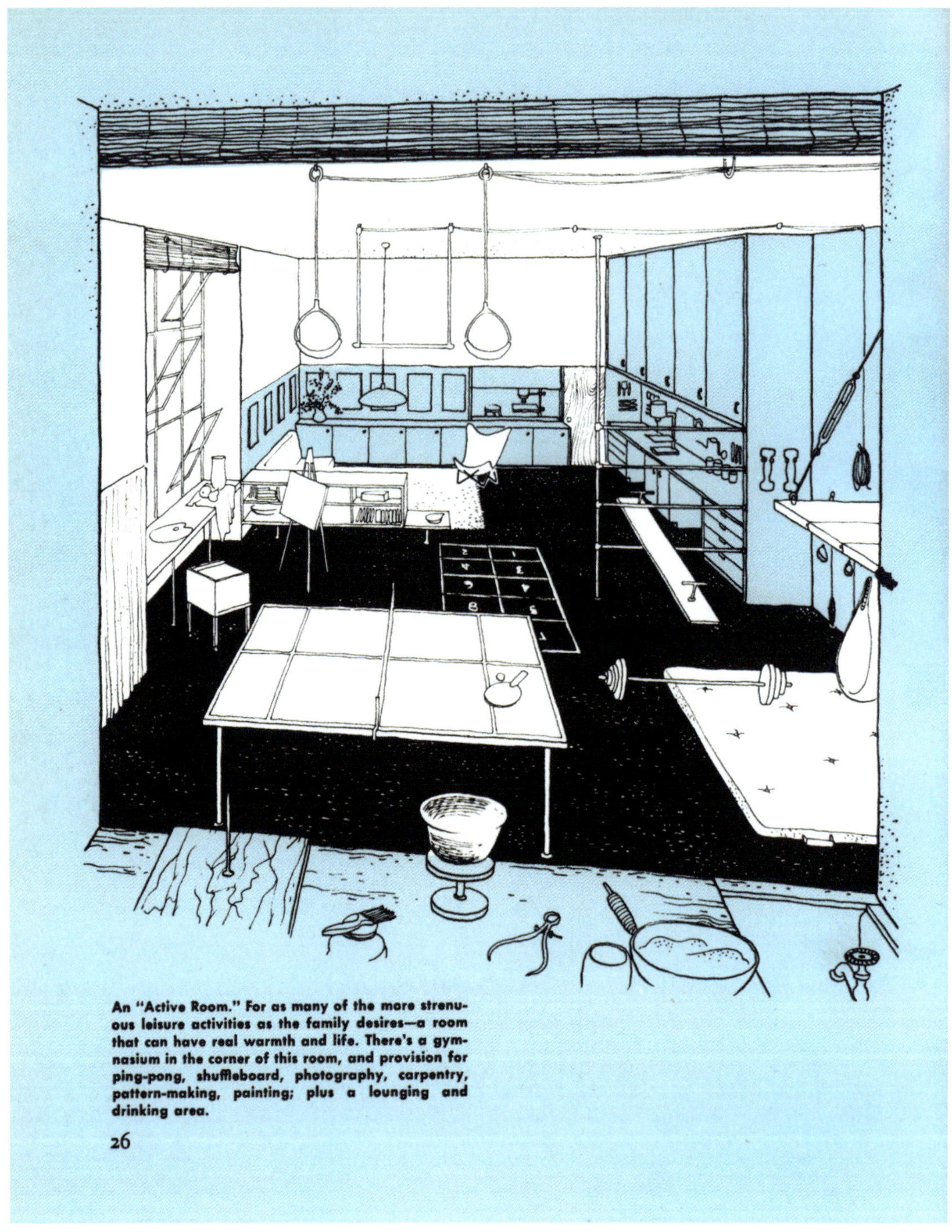

Fig. 4. James Kingsland, "An 'Active Room,'" p. 26. From *Guide to Easier Living* by Mary and Russel Wright (1950) reprinted in 2003 by Gibbs Smith Publisher; by permission of the publisher.

Fig. 5. Frank Jamison, "The Living-Dining Room," *New Homes for Today* (1946), p. 95.

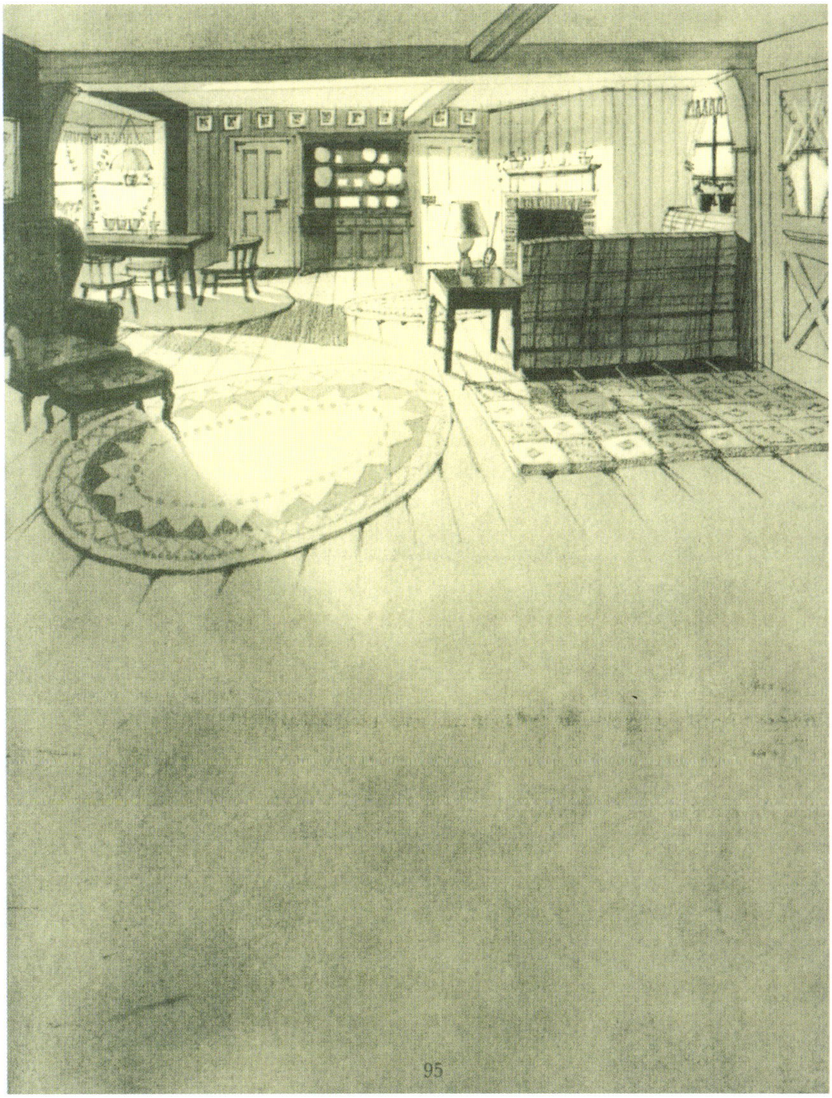

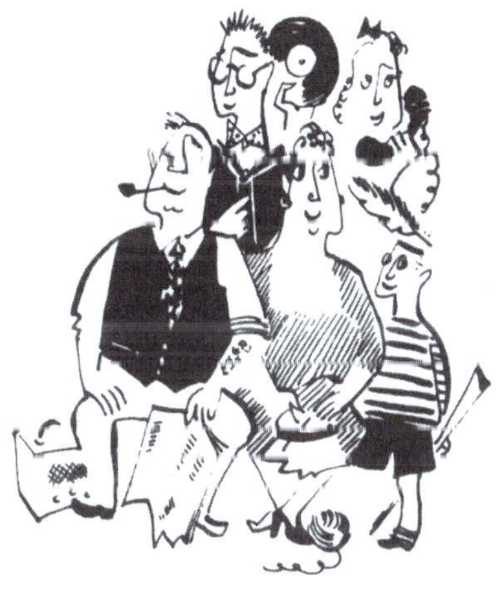

Fig. 6. Marylin Hafner, decorative spot, p. 7. From *Decorate Your Home for Better Living* by Mary L. Brandt. Charles Scribner's Sons, 1950. Courtesy of the estate of Marylin Hafner.

interest in how the Modern home can control that nuclear family, both socially and bodily. Brandt's family is as unified (and maybe as uncomfortable) as the portrait heads on Mount Rushmore. The father's body is the most complete of the group, as he extends his bent left elbow and knee across the wife's space, while she herself is surrounded on all sides by the heads (if not bodies) of her smiling children. Brandt describes the value of a room in the Modern home where this five-headed figure would reside, imploring her readers: "Have you a space apart from the living room where, if fixed up, the family could relax at games, hobbies, or for study and reading; like a basement room, an attic room, or an extra studio-room?"[3] They are bodily constrained and controlled by their pyramid mass, a metaphor for the social expectations that wrap them tightly together and prevent anyone from breaking away from the group. Really, who smiles happily with LPs, instruments, and telephones just inches from one's ears?

The Wrights' "active" living room likewise thrums with calibrated physical and social pressure (see fig. 4). Physical activity and the ideal of the healthy body are evoked in the gymnastics rings in the front of the room that serve as a pendant to the Modernist light fixture over the lounge area at the back; the misplaced barbells, lying halfway off the exercise mat in the foreground, suggest recent (or imminent) failure in strength. The room itself is perplexing. The light-blue wash of color applied throughout the sketch helps us to parse the layers of accessories gathered in this space, which we view as if through a window. We cannot see a path to enter the room, as if the family that gathers in it is actually trapped. To be frank, the fantasy it offers seems unattainable, perhaps even a bit unbelievable (whether we are readers in the twenty-first or the twentieth century).[4] But as the Wrights explain, the stakes for our houses are very high, and so perhaps the difficulty of achieving the social model established in this room is a struggle worth taking on:

> All too often, comfort, ease, and spontaneity are all sacrificed to an unrealistic dream that makes home life formal and unsatisfying. Far from drawing families together, our homes send adolescent children to the juke joints for their fun, lead husbands to prefer a movie or the local bar for their after-work relaxation, make entertaining friends an ordeal of drudgery. … There are in our times a multitude of complex motives for adolescents getting into trouble, or marriages breaking up, but it is not too far-fetched to say that our homes and the way we live in them must be listed among the important causes.[5]

Williams's Colonial Revival living-dining room, too, participates in a rhetoric of control (see fig. 5). The deep slant of the foreground rug, half cast in shadow, emerges fully formed from the void of empty space in the lower half of the page to pull us into a room that appears bathed in warm light emanating from the bay window at left. The great expanse between the bottom of the page and the room in the upper third creates a sense of drama, as does the back of the sofa that blocks our view of the warmth of the fireplace: Will we be able to physically traverse the yawning distance and enter this room? What will be required, in terms of class achievement, to be the guest that "drops by" or—better yet—the family group that extends the "friendly invitation"? The air of exclusivity fostered by the distant, sunlit space and aspirational fantasizing in its accompanying text give this image its controlling power: it sets the stage for a story about family togetherness that is performed for the family and guests alike. Furthermore, Williams assures us, this room that brings together living and dining in an open space, common in many new suburban homes, could be designed with "period or modern" furnishings.[6]

Each of these illustrations and texts connects the Modern postwar house—Modern in its open-floor-plan rooms and amenities, if not always in furnishings—with the bodily and physical control of the ideal nuclear family. Questions of gendered control and racialized control percolate through them as well, albeit not as obviously. The mother is the indubitable matriarch who bears the crushing responsibility of creating hospitality in each of these vignettes—surrounded by her husband and children, under threat that any of them might escape the house and run to a "juke joint." Race would seem not to be present at all. However, as this chapter will argue, it is more accurate to say that in these books, Whiteness is frequently a presumed cultural position of power, unnecessary to call out and almost unspeakable—that "which does not want to be named," or "ex-nominated" in Roland Barthes's terminology.[7] Most of these books coach readers to perform the cultural authority most commonly, if unconsciously, associated with Whiteness. The young boy who plays at being an "Indian" can assume his White superiority without even thinking about it, and then drop the game as he takes up a position playing Ping-Pong in the protection of the Wrights' room.

These books, with their illustrations that intrigue our imaginations and their engaging prose, are examples of domestic advice literature published in the half decade immediately following World War II.[8] Offering guidance on everything from floor plans and lighting technology to furnishing arrangements and household maintenance, they embody the aspirational rhetoric of the advice genre. They encourage the reader to construct an unfettered, optimistic view of her future self and life—in this case, her nuclear family, who share and enjoy pastimes together—even as they pointedly remind her of the inadequacies of her present circumstances (embodied in the lack of a room for family unity). In the logic of the self help world, awareness of one's current failures should provide the motivation to change, and the advice offered by the all-knowing author will reveal the path forward to achieve that change. Advice literature uses as its foundation the gossamer shimmer of fantasy—the illusion of a perfectly achieved goal—and might be understood as inhabiting a perpetual future. The reader of the book is seduced into spending much time envisioning her future self, with only occasional attention paid to the present (the site of failure), and very little to the past. The lack of clarity about present-day circumstances in this type of advice literature has led many scholars, correctly, to argue that these texts cannot be taken as practical, historical documents reflecting how daily life was, in fact, lived. Yet in their narratives, they demonstrate the fantasies and expectations that may have shaped how individuals imagined their lives. As historians, we cannot know how individual readers understood these texts, but we can interrogate the models that the texts give us. We can examine the attitudes, the blind spots, and the biases that these books represent in their approach to Modernism in domestic life in the immediate postwar years.[9]

As consumers and commercial interests alike anticipated the dramatic increase in domestic construction in 1945, and then swam in the tide of the growing market through the late 1940s and early 1950s, architects, designers, and critics weighed in on the housing boom in the form of thousands of pages of design advice. These appeared in magazines, newspaper columns, radio and eventually television programs, and an ever-growing shelf of domestic advice books. This chapter compares five books that offered advice on the design and care of the home in the years between 1945 and 1950: *Tomorrow's House*, by George Nelson and Henry Wright (New York: Simon and Schuster, 1945); *The Small Home of Tomorrow* and *New Homes for Today*, by Paul R. Williams (Hollywood, CA: Murray and Gee, 1945 and 1946); *Decorate Your Home for Better Living*, by Mary L. Brandt (New York: Charles Scribner's Sons, 1950); and *Guide to Easier Living*, by Mary and Russel Wright (New York: Simon and Schuster, 1950). I have selected these books because they were commercially successful: published, for the most part, by major presses and reviewed in popular and professional media outlets. I have also chosen them because of the diversity of lived and professional experiences represented by their authors. Nelson, Henry Wright, Brandt, and Russel and Mary Wright were all Euro-American, and Williams was African American. Nelson, Henry Wright, and Williams were architects, while Russel and Mary Wright were designers and Brandt was an interior designer (trained as an architect). Nelson, Henry Wright, and Williams were all men whose professional identities were independent of their marital status; Brandt was a professional woman who, like the men, did not mingle her married status with her work identity; Russel and Mary Wright built their narrative around their self-presentation as a heteronormative married couple.[10] Finally, I have kept my sample small in order to delve deeply into each of these texts and their illustrations. My intent in this chapter is a careful deconstruction of how these authors—using the commercial product of a book—teach their readers about Modernism.

In particular, this chapter interrogates how the authors of these books position Modernism as a tool for exercising domestic expectations and ultimately exerting control over the lives lived within the postwar home. In these texts, Modernism polices the boundaries of gendered identities and racialized identities as it attempts to shape and direct the comportment of those who live with it. My own narrative is premised on a comparative account of these five books. The monolithic—if stereotypical—voice promoting Modernism has tended to highlight its capacity for rational efficiency. When we listen to the multiple, distinctive voices in these books and put them in dialogue with one another—gathered around a metaphorical table, if you will—what we find, by contrast, is a complex, multifaceted view of Modernism that privileges some audiences and experiences over others. This comparative exercise suggests that there may have been alternative experiences with Modernism that have not hitherto been a part of the dominant academic history. Modernism may have been a rational, efficient servant for White men, in particular, but it set onerous standards of physical domestic labor for both White women and women of color. While the White authors studied here invoke Modernism as a style that demarcates implied racial boundaries, Williams—the sole author of color to publish a domestic advice manual in this period—is less apt to assign Modernism any specific cultural power, instead positioning it as one possible route, among several, for a homeowner's self-realization. The laborious Modernism of a gendered experience, and the less dogmatic, more pluralistic celebration of Modernism in Williams's texts, suggest "counterhistories" of Modernism, in the words of John Fiske, that take into account lived experiences.[11]

Because of their state of perpetual future, domestic advice literature makes an apt topic for the opening chapter to a book on design in the home. Just as the reader of an advice manual considers how to write the future narrative of her domestic setting, so too you, the reader of this book, contemplate the narrative that will unfold in these pages about postwar homes. My decision to position a chapter about advice literature at the start of my story has an additional agenda, however. Throughout this chapter, there are numerous, sometimes lengthy quotations from the books under discussion. These are important not only for their content, but for their intonation, rhythm, and attitude. They are, truly, voices from the period, and it is helpful to begin our study with an ear—as well as an eye—to how Modernism circulated through the fantasy world of postwar domesticity.

The Texts and Their Images

The five books that are the subject of this chapter are, at first glance, noticeably different. The latter part of the chapter analyzes the themes and arguments put forth in these books, and posits that meaningful points of resonance can be found across them. In this section, I introduce the publications, embracing the distinctive character of each. Their differences begin with the circumstances around the publication of each book.

Paul R. Williams was a highly successful architect based in Los Angeles with a thriving office; at the time he published his two books, he had completed over two thousand projects, including the Twenty-Eighth Street YMCA in Los Angeles and high-profile residences for magnates such as E. L. Cord and Jay Paley.[12] As one of the few African Americans to break into the insular, club-like world of professional architecture, between the late 1930s and late 1940s he was featured in national publications including *Life*, *Ebony*, *American Magazine*, and *Time*.[13] (The editorial context of *Ebony* and *Life* magazines will be examined in chapter 2.) He published *The Small Home of Tomorrow* and *New Homes for Today* with a California publisher, Murray and Gee, whose portfolio tended more toward Hollywood industry memoirs and fiction than architecture or interior design.[14] Both books were reviewed in *Architectural Record*.[15] Indeed, when *New Homes for Today* came out in 1946, its preface noted, "Many books designed for the prospective home-builder have been issued since the publication of Paul R. Williams' 'The Small Home of Tomorrow.' Several of those books are outstanding but none has wrested first place from 'The Small Home of Tomorrow,' just as none of them will surpass this new book by the same author."[16]

George Nelson and Henry Wright and Russel and Mary Wright published their books with one of the largest commercial publishers in the country, Simon and Schuster. As White professionals in the architecture and design fields based on the East Coast, their access to a major publishing house was made possible through various routes. Russel Wright's reputation as a designer of domestic wares had been established in the 1930s, when, with careful publicity work from Mary, he became nationally known as the maker of the informal, multicolored American Modern ceramic tablewares line. (The American Modern tablewares and 1950s glassware will be analyzed in chapter 4.) He and Mary worked through several drafts of the book manuscript in 1948 and 1949, originally thinking they would pitch it as a series of articles for a women's magazine; his name recognition was undoubtedly appealing to Simon and Schuster, and after the book's publication in late 1950, Russel appeared on numerous radio and television shows to promote the book.[17] In contrast to Williams's and Russel Wright's accomplished professional reputations, George Nelson, trained as an architect, had built only one private home by 1945, the year he coauthored *Tomorrow's House*. He had established himself as a writer about architecture, publishing in both professional venues (*Architectural Forum*) and, anonymously, in more mainstream journals (*Fortune*).[18] He held an editorial position at *Architectural Forum*, where he collaborated with Henry Wright, the journal's managing editor, on the book. The imprimatur of *Architectural Forum* must have helped bring their book to press, because the cover page of *Tomorrow's House* identifies each author prominently by

his position at that esteemed journal, and the book's preface is written by
Howard Myers, identified as the journal's publisher. (D. J. DePree, president
of the Herman Miller Furniture Company, read *Tomorrow's House* in 1945
and, on the strength of it, hired Nelson to be the company's design director, as will be discussed in chapter 3.)

Finally, Brandt, who had wanted to be a "lady architect" after college, built her career around her early professional experiences in interior
decorating.[19] In the 1940s, after her tenure as a decorator at Lord and
Taylor department store, she developed a curriculum for training sales
personnel in home goods departments. As a White professional, she had
access to several hundred retail establishments across the country; however, her position as a woman lecturing to buyers and salespeople who
were mostly men was occasionally challenging.[20] She branded her work
as the "Mary L. Brandt Home Furnishings Training Course," and her material became the rough draft of *Decorate Your Home for Better Living*.[21]
Her established authority in the retail world and presence as a writer
for magazines such as *Better Homes and Gardens* presumably helped
her secure her first book contract with Charles Scribner's Sons, the well-
regarded literary press.

If each book discussed here represents a distinctive publication
history, so, too, is each a unique commercial product with distinguishing
formats, address to reader, and illustrations. Nelson and Henry Wright cul
tivate a strongly opinionated tone of voice and do not hesitate to express
impatience with their readers. They begin their book with the following
warning: "This book has a point of view which may seem strange to you.
What it is will be made pretty clear in the first few pages of this introduction. If, after reading that far, the viewpoint seems not only strange, but
unpalatable as well, put this book aside and forget it, for what we have
to say will not be for you."[22] They are equally strident in their promotion
of Modernism as the preferred architectural mode for domestic building:
"We have included only modern houses in this book because in our time
they are the only way to carry on the great tradition. There is no possible
chance to turn the clock back. In designing houses today we have to be
ourselves—twentieth century people with our own problems and our own
technical facilities. *There is no other way to get a good house.* No other
way at all."[23] They explicitly refrain from offering sample floor plans, "no
catalogues of 'styles,' no orations on good taste."[24] Instead, this book, sub-
titled *A Complete Guide for the Home-Builder*, promotes a function-based
approach to the house: rather than a chapter on dining rooms, for example,
the reader finds a chapter titled "Where Shall We Eat?" The text positions
itself as a challenge to its readers, daring them to make the cut and persist
past page 3. Such pressure ultimately exerts its own kind of control, as the
text continually reminds readers to stay in line with its dogmatism.

For all its protestations against dictating taste, Nelson and Wright's
book uses illustrations to make a strong argument about that very topic.

The sections of text are interrupted by multipage "picture sections," laid out like a shelter magazine with large photographs, often in full bleed or across the gutter accompanied by minimal text (fig. 7). These images perform a type of photographic work that I call the rhetoric of interior space and will discuss again in chapter 2. With only five exceptions out of the 232 reproduced in the book, they depict rooms with no human inhabitants. The position of the camera is frequently at adult standing height with a moderately wide-angle lens, which maximizes the viewer's sensation of ownership and control: we look slightly down into each of these rooms, surveying the broad sweep of their contents from a position of physical superiority, as if we possess them and have the right to scrutinize everything in them (figs. 8, 9).[25] The rhetoric of the interior-space photograph does more than cultivate an intimate sense of possession, however. It emphasizes the spaciousness of the room captured on film by leaving open apparently large expanses of floor, thus encouraging the viewer to imagine walking unimpeded into the space; it might, alternatively, create an impression of spaciousness by including as many windows as possible. Windows present a challenge to the photographer because of the extreme contrast in light levels that usually exists between interior and exterior. Some

Fig. 7. Pages 32–33, with photographs by Robert M. Damora, Paul Davis, Philip Fein, Elmer L. Astleford. From *Tomorrow's House: A Complete Guide for the Home-Builder* by George Nelson and Henry Wright. Simon and Schuster, 1945.

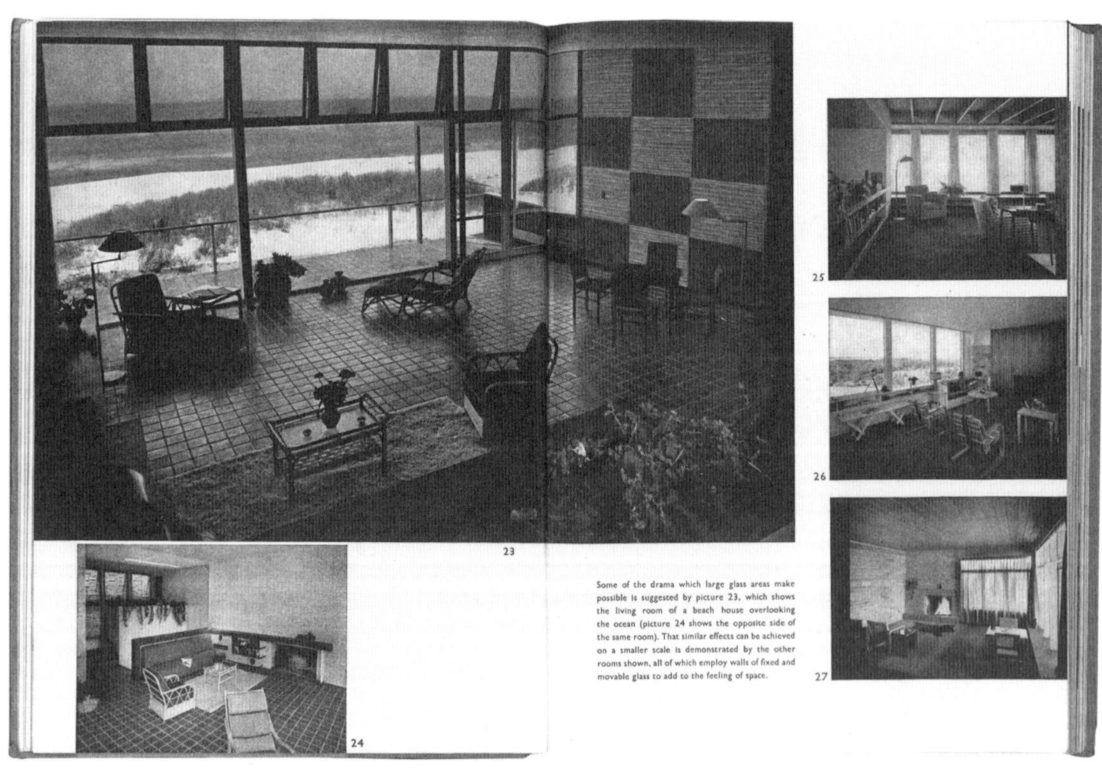

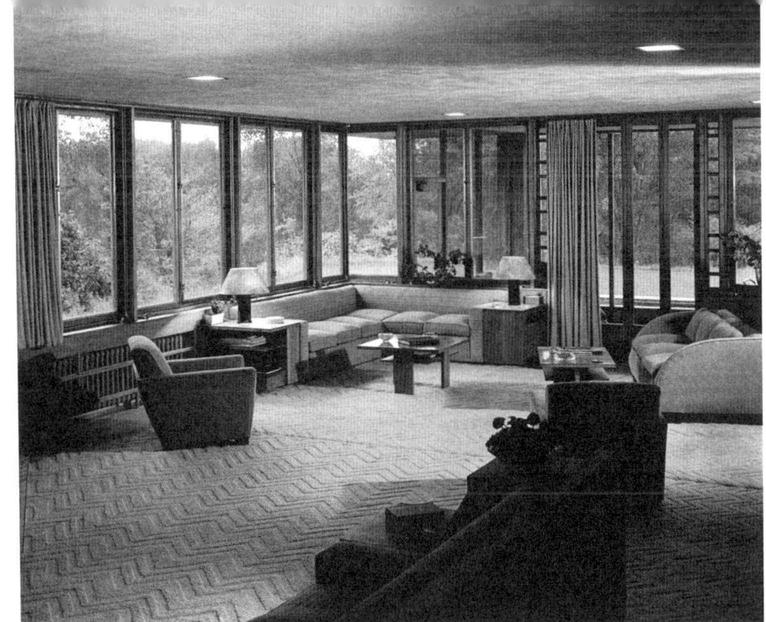

Fig. 8 (left). Interior view of the Kohler residence, Kohler, Wisc., 1938 (William F. Deknatel, architect). Hedrich-Blessing Studio, photographer. Published in *Tomorrow's House* (1945), p. 36. HB-04921-I, Chicago History Museum, Hedrich-Blessing Collection.

Fig. 9 (below). Interior view of Hagerty House, Cohasset, Mass., 1938 (Marcel Breuer, architect). Paul Davis, photographer. Published in *Tomorrow's House* (1945), p. 37. Marcel Breuer Papers, Special Collections Research Center, Syracuse University Libraries.

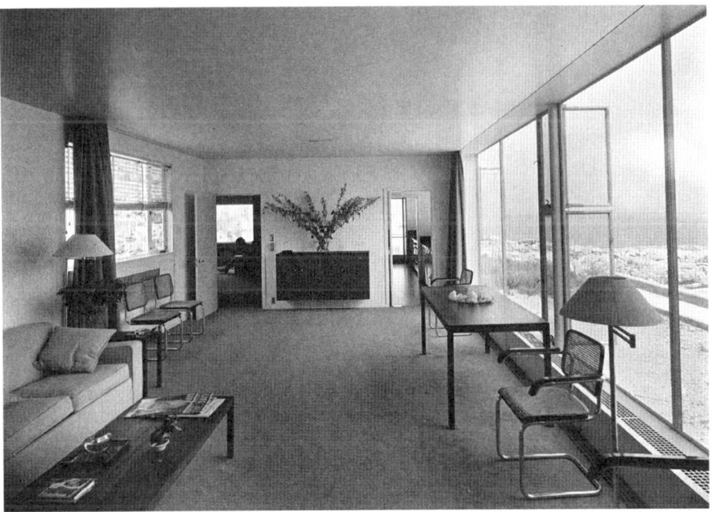

photographers, such as the Hedrich-Blessing Studio artist in fig. 8, exposed his negative so that our visual experience flows without interruption from the rug in the foreground to the table and sofa in the middle distance and on to the suburban wilderness outside. Others, such as Paul Davis, who created fig. 9, calibrated his printing to let us to see out the large plate-glass window on the right of the photograph but then apparently burned out the remaining three windows to create blinding blocks of white; while we can see the expanse of the landscape on the right, the otherworldliness of the white at the remaining windows creates a dramatic sensation of unfettered spaciousness surrounding this domestic structure.

Each object—large and small—is placed for maximal graphic effect in these interior-space photographs. The colossal spray of flowers on the end wall of Davis's photograph, for example, creates a sense of symmetry in the room where, in fact, none exists. The objects in the room create the drama in the absence of humans. Davis's photograph is one of the few in *Tomorrow's House* that includes a human figure: a woman sits in the back left room, a silhouette against the window. In this case, the hint of a human figure might help the reader to imagine living in the room depicted. For the most part, however, in photographs that follow the rhetoric of the interior-space image (and in the vast majority of the photographs in this book), the furniture objects seem content to be the actors on the stage. Although they frame a space—a clear expanse of floor or rug—where a human could enter, their compositions are so carefully constructed that the addition of a person actually threatens to send the room careening off its delicately balanced axis. In fig. 8, it might be the carefully placed identical table lamps, or the way the angled armchair on the left calls across to the rounded arc of the love seat on the right; in fig. 9, the two Breuer chairs are close together on the left and far apart on the right, as if the four of them are contemplating their ideal configuration. Just as Nelson and Wright's text insists that readers step up to its high ideals, so too these rooms demand respect and do not countenance interference.

The interior-space photographs are not the only illustrations in *Tomorrow's House*. In addition, the text-based chapters are peppered with line drawings by Nelson, most of which illustrate specific technical concepts such as where to hang acoustical tiles. A few drawings, however, render an entire room and provide an illuminating contrast to the interior-decorating photographs. In the "Where Shall We Eat?" chapter, Nelson and Wright begin with an account of late nineteenth-century dining rooms, which they contend were a "family social center." Nelson captures this dining room in a drawing that is full of character (fig. 10): he includes layers of patterns—from the marquetry on the china cabinet to the wallpaper and the finish on the door—as well as an abundance of extraneous objects, such as a chandelier over the table and a candelabra on the table, multiple forks and knives for the place settings, and tankards and jugs, clearly for display purposes only, on the plate rail. The drawing is congested, but at the same time Nelson's line is animated by slight irregularities that give the entire image a sense of quivering life. Even when compared against a photograph of a dining room by Frank Lloyd Wright filled with objects for eating and serving, reproduced a few pages later, the drawing possesses greater dynamism (fig. 11). The nineteenth-century dining room is meant to be hopelessly out of date, and yet in its layers of irregular lines it seems to welcome human intervention and action. The right angles of Wright's furniture in fig. 11, and the sharp dagger of light created by the geometric clerestory window, are, by contrast, inert and uncompromising, inhospitable to the human figure, despite the open expanse of floor in the foreground. We are meant to behold and admire the meticulous design of the space, even if it does not welcome us. As the reader balances the outmoded drawing and the

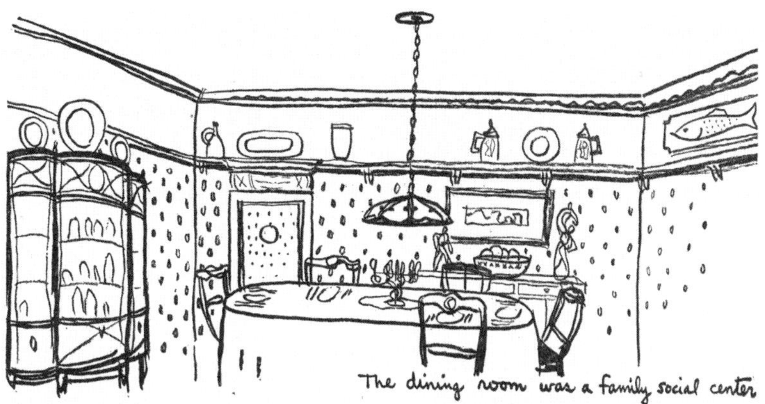

Fig. 10 (above). George Nelson, "The dining room was a family social center," p. 40. From *Tomorrow's House: A Complete Guide for the Home-Builder* by George Nelson and Henry Wright. Simon and Schuster, 1945.

Fig. 11 (right). Interior view of the dining area in the Malcolm E. Willey House, Minneapolis, Minn., 1934 (Frank Lloyd Wright, architect). Hedrich-Blessing Studio, photographer. Published in *Tomorrow's House* (1945), p. 57. HB-04414–4T2, Chicago History Museum, Hedrich-Blessing Collection and The Frank Lloyd Wright Foundation Archives (The Museum of Modern Art/Avery Architectural and Fine Arts Library, Columbia University, New York).

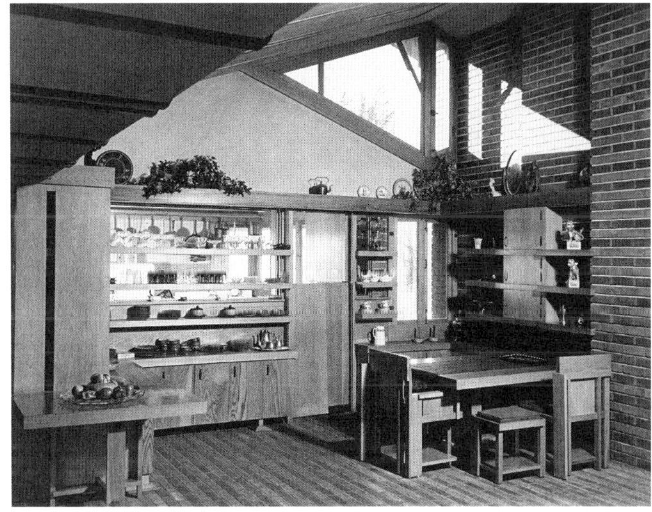

Modern photograph, she is reminded of the standards in taste, demeanor, and philosophical outlook that this book requires of her.

If Nelson and Wright's book constantly challenges the reader to live up to its expectations, *The Small Home of Tomorrow* and *New Homes for Today*, written by Paul R. Williams, offer a much more collaborative and encouraging message to their readers. Williams published *The Small Home of Tomorrow* in 1945, at the same time as *Tomorrow's House*, and opens his book with an optimistic assessment: "It is a foregone conclusion that there will be thousands of modern small homes built in the post-war world. An eager generation of young people coming out of the war is filled with the desire to have homes of their own—and homes of their own planning and building."[20] Both publications begin with several pages of general advice to readers, ranging from a discussion of new building technologies to brief interior-decorating guidelines, advice on selecting a building site, and an argument in favor of working with a professional architect.

Throughout, Williams offers his advice in an evenhanded tone, with relatively little judgment. He asserts, for example, that "Modern design is practical because it is less costly to build than a house of period design where traditional detail is a consideration," but then offers a less dogmatic vision of Modernism than Nelson and Wright's: "Let no one think however, that the postwar homes will all be in a modern style, or that all the fine period houses now standing the country over will be outmoded by any sudden landslide to Modern Architecture. … The best of the Modern probably will not be too streamlined or extreme in appearance. They may even retain much of the charm of the period houses and yet have a definite contemporary flare as do many of the fine small houses in this book."[27]

Williams positions his two books, as Nelson and Wright do their volume, as resources for the "home-builder"—the imagined husband and wife starting their housing search on a proverbial blank page of options—rather than devoting himself to the concerns of a preexisting, already inhabited house.[28] Both of Williams's books are predominantly catalogues of sample house designs, the very product Nelson and Wright pointedly avoided. In *The Small Home of Tomorrow* and *New Homes for Today*, Williams lays out the book as a sequence of spreads: as the reader turns each page, she discovers a new floor plan, accompanied by an artistic rendering (all of which were done by the chief renderer in Williams's office, Frank Jamison), all on one page, paired against a short written description of the design on the opposing page (fig. 12).[29] The styles of houses depicted in Williams's books vary widely. Some adhere to a commonly understood definition of Modernism with some combination of flat roofs, overhanging eaves, and horizontal bands of windows (see fig. 12); others combine a variety of period styles in a more conservative design, such as one house "influenced by the city homes of Mexico City," with a hip roof, symmetrical façade, central entrance framed by modest neoclassical moldings, and large pilasters at the corners (fig. 13). Jamison rendered almost all of these houses as if we are seeing them from the street as we walk up to them. This is not only the view that would most likely impress our neighbors and friends, but is also the view that would welcome us home every time we returned to the house, an intimate greeting. To reconcile the artistic rendering in the upper part of the page with the floor plan below frequently requires mental work on the part of the reader, as we puzzle out the relationship between the two images: we situate the orientation of the plan against the façade, matching up entrances, windows, or building masses, and slowly piece together the life of the house as the spaces unfurl behind the façade. The result is a sense of accomplishment—of having worked to comprehend the house—and for some readers that might inspire a feeling of ownership over the design.[30] Over the course of many pages, Williams builds up our confidence in our ability to read the images, and establishes a connection between us and him. Interestingly, he includes a few house designs by friends and colleagues in each volume,

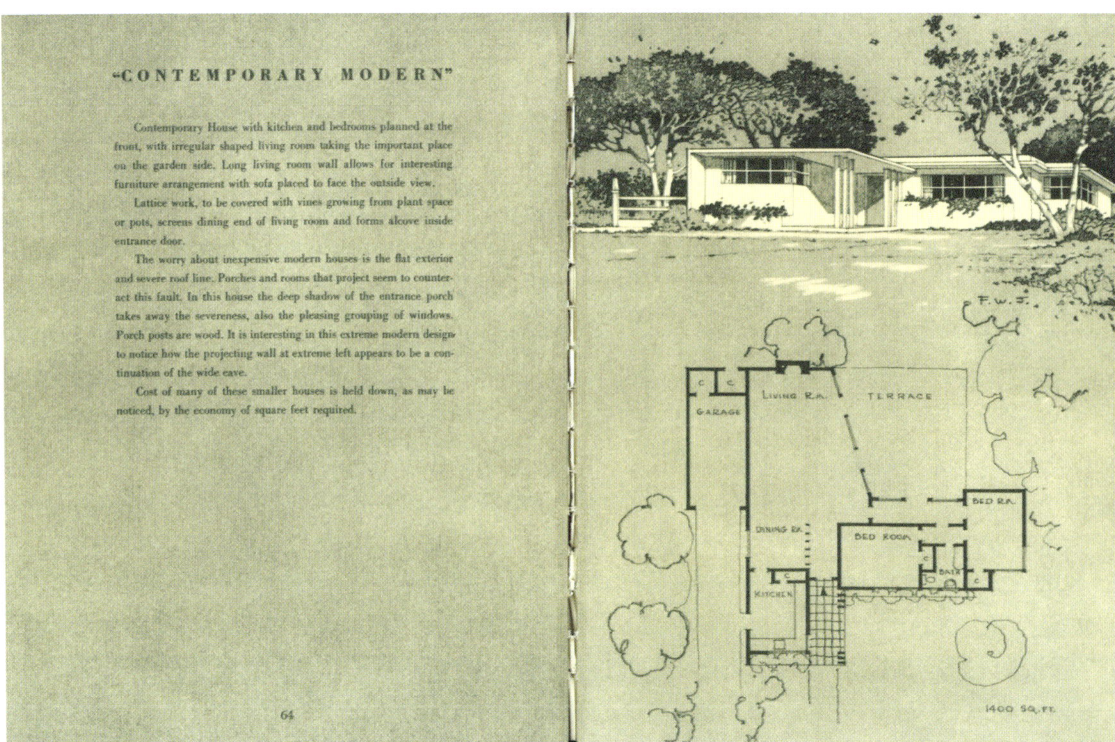

but he has these rendered from an aerial view, as, for example, "The Paul Thiry" (fig. 14). The aerial view gives us authority over the design—we can see more of it than in a street-front view of a house—but it also distances us physically from the house. Furthermore, the aerial house rendering echoes the floor plan so readily that we hardly need to work to understand it, and the connection to the design forged through our mental labor is lost.

Just as he provides some advice about interior decorating in his opening texts, Williams also includes a few page spreads that focus on specific room designs. These rooms are decorated in a variety of styles, mirroring his catholic approach to architectural style. In both publications he discusses the importance of an informal "rumpus room" for family activities and entertaining, and in each he offers a sample design (although neither is actually labeled "rumpus room"). In the 1945 book, the "Recreation Room" is decidedly modern, featuring a built-in radio and phonograph, horizontal windows, a streamlined bar, tubular steel chairs, and an indoor barbecue station, whereas the "Playroom" in 1946 is "most effective with period furnishings," with "plaid upholstered seat covers" on the chairs gathered around the "snack-bar with the television back-bar"[31] (figs. 15, 16). Both of these images adhere to the rhetoric of the interior-space photograph: the viewer is positioned high enough to have a sense of dominion

Fig. 12. Paul R. Williams, "Contemporary Modern," Frank Jamison, renderer, *The Small Home of Tomorrow* (1945), pp. 64–65.

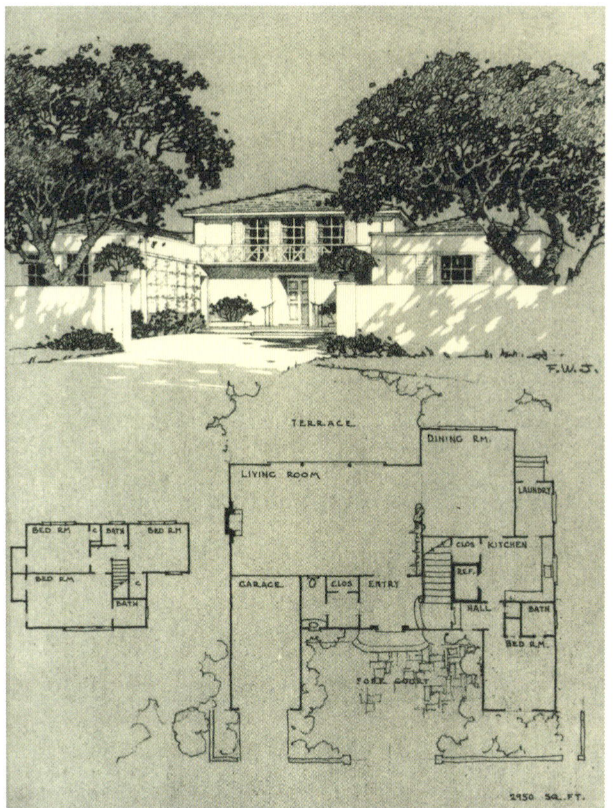

Fig. 13 (above). Paul R. Williams, "The Riviera," Frank Jamison, renderer, *The Small Home of Tomorrow* (1945), p. 31.

Fig. 14 (right). Frank Jamison, "The Paul Thiry," *The Small Home of Tomorrow* (1945), p. 61.

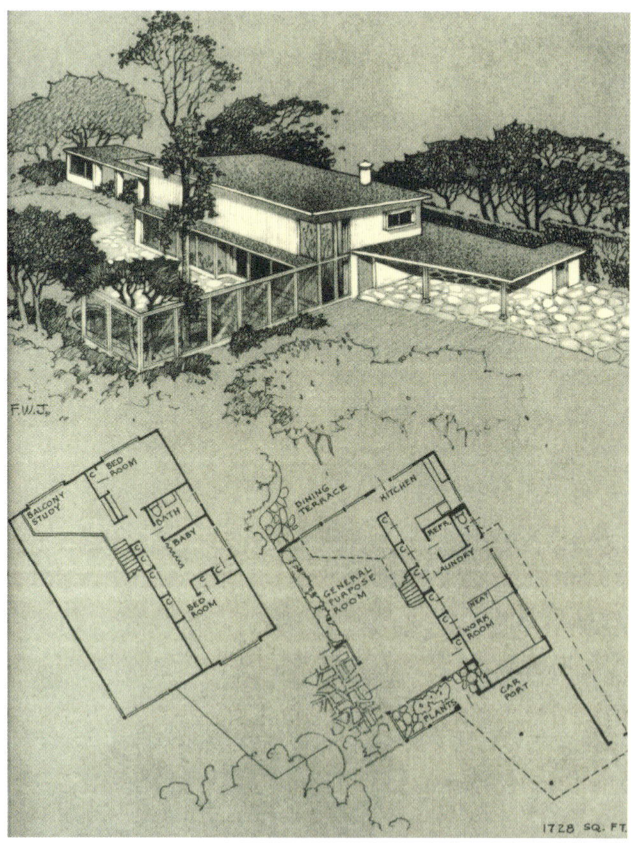

over the room, and the furnishings create dynamic relationships that do not really require humans. Yet because they are hand rendered, with expressive attention to shadows, patterns, and highlights, the images convey a greater sense of warmth and welcome to the viewer than does the typical interior-decorating photograph. These drawings grow out of the blank space of the tinted pages as if they are illustrations to a story, and invite imaginative projections. Indeed, these fully conceptualized rooms might be best understood as the visual embodiment of Williams's skill as a designer and salesman, which one journalist described in 1949: "Clients sometimes are amazed at how far Williams is ahead of them. He seems to see the home complete, with a well-laid fire glowing in the fireplace, while they still are trying to imagine their lot with all the weeds cleared off. While roughing out a sketch of their possible feature dream house … they may be astonished to hear him say … 'This room needs a brightly colored chintz sofa' or 'In here I'd like to see a large braided rug on a dark brown plank floor.' "[32]

While Williams and Nelson and Wright all write for the "home-builder," a gender-neutral persona that might include stereotypical male interests such as plumbing or financing as well as stereotypical female interests such as kitchen design and color schemes, Mary L. Brandt explicitly writes for the female "home-maker" in *Decorate Your Home for Better Living*. Published in 1950, *Decorate Your Home* was the first of four books Brandt authored during the 1950s, and is her magnum opus. It is a primer on interior decorating and provides information on everything from color schemes to fabrics and furniture styles. Unlike the architect-authors, Brandt assumes that her readers already have a home (or apartment) but need help decorating it; like Williams, she offers advice and information about a wide range of styles, including Modernism. The content and organization of the book are closely modeled on her retailing course, with some important changes. In her retailing course materials, written around 1946, she explains to her students that "Modern Design" is "Not Everyone's Dish," but by the time she publishes the book in 1950, she has clearly decided on a more emphatic endorsement and proclaims "Modern Is Here to Stay."[33] In addition, the factual information in the book is permeated by a strident, judgmental tone that is largely absent in her retailing course material.[34] For example, both her training course and *Decorate Your Home* include a chapter on "Provincial" styles of furniture. Where the training course text ends, the book continues with a lengthy warning about the perils of "so-called provincial furniture. … It is rustic all right, but the heavy wooden wings on the armchair and the heavy turnings on the legs, plus the orange shellac finish, give it a pretty grisly look." Lest the reader misunderstand the lowly status of this "so-called" furniture, she continues with admonishing advice: these "copies of a copy" are frequently accompanied by "spotty wallpaper in a quaint and diluted pattern … postage-stamp size hooked and rag rugs (that crumple into a ball every time you step on one) and a pair of dinky green bottles in the shape of violins with sprigs of ivy

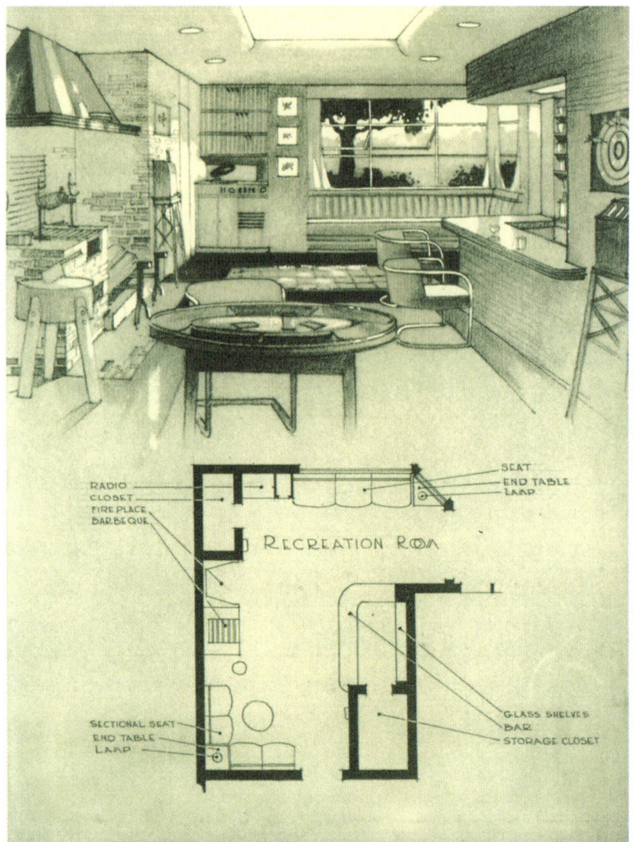

Fig. 15 (above). Frank Jamison, "Recreation Room," *The Small Home of Tomorrow* (1945), p. 84.

Fig. 16 (right). Frank Jamison, "The Playroom," *New Homes for Today* (1946), p. 93.

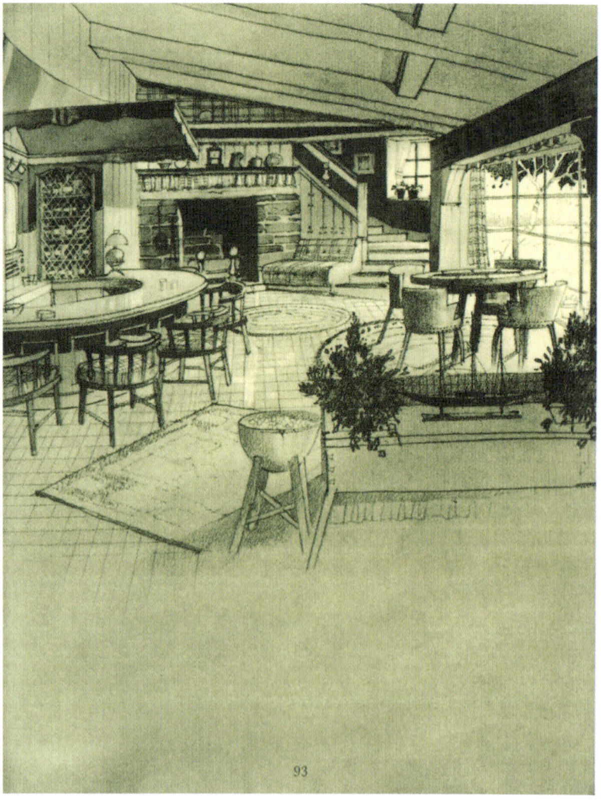

on the mantel. The effect of a room furnished like this is dull, practical, but not artistic and decidedly commonplace."[35] Whereas Nelson and Wright use condescension to pressure and control their readers, Brandt relies on the more direct strategy of shame: readers should follow her advice or risk social embarrassment.

Brandt illustrates her book with a few photographs in the interior-decorating mode reprinted courtesy of various shelter magazines (including *Bride's* and *Living for Young Homemakers*). However, these are less prominent in the publication than the frequent appearance, sprinkled throughout the text, of small line drawings by illustrator Marylin Hafner. Brandt first used Hafner's "decorative spots" in her training course materials from 1946, and in the book their function is varied.[36] In some passages, they humorously anthropomorphize the concepts discussed in Brandt's text, turning the book into a comic strip of interior decorating. In the chapter on color, for example, cans of paint relax in the sun, go skiing, and mix with other colors (fig. 17); when Brandt explains how you can connect rooms with color, Hafner gives us two happy rooms holding hands and chained together at the ankles (fig. 18). Hafner's illustrations sometimes seem to give voice to the anxieties that the reader may have in response to Brandt's forceful prose: alongside the injunction to consider the question "Is there a place where your children can keep their favorite swing records?" Hafner provides a vignette of two desultory teenagers, their albums strewn across the living room floor, as if channeling the guilty thought that crosses the reader's mind (fig. 19). The cartoons also dramatize Brandt's advice: beneath the query "If the laundry is a damp, dingy place in the basement, have you thought of making it into a cheerful, efficient place to work?" Hafner's sketch shows a beleaguered woman, hair in her face, leaning over a washtub in a basement whose small window is partially blocked by a spider web (fig. 20). Between text and image, the message is persuasive if relentless: no one can possibly enjoy doing laundry in a basement, and the reader's energy should be directed toward a future state of "cheerful," above-grade clothes washing.

In addition to the editorial cartoons, Brandt provides several bold, silhouette-style illustrations that serve to reinforce her pedagogical lessons. In the chapters on period decorations, Brandt creates charts of furniture styles that could almost be flashcards for the student learning her furniture history: using pen and a black ink wash, her drawings emphasize contours and compositional devices that distinguish one style from another (fig. 21). In another chapter, she uses black-and-white silhouettes to demonstrate "GOOD" and "BAD" examples of furniture balance (fig. 22). These illustrations are not intended to tickle the reader's imagination or to make her smile, as did the calligraphic, whimsical lines of Hafner's spots. Instead, these use bold graphics, stark black against the white page, to create the impression that the information they convey is a series of incontrovertible truths. Like her baldly judgmental rhetoric, Brandt's illustrations exhort

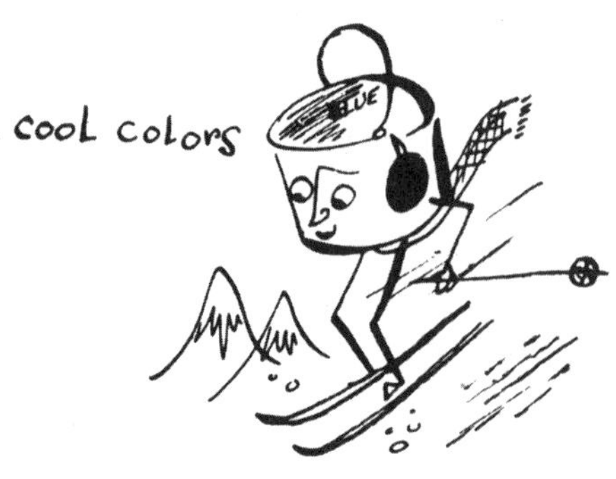

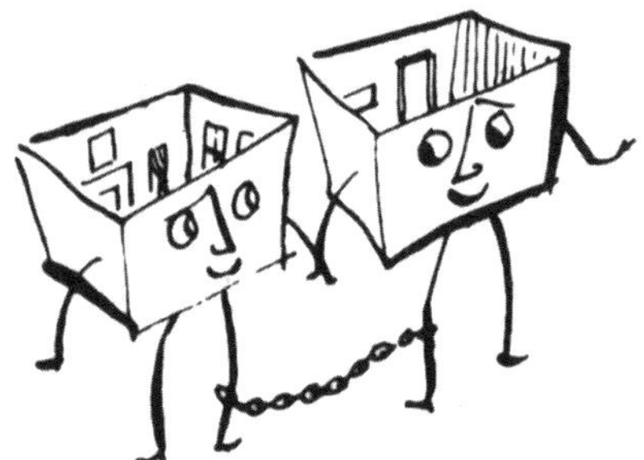

Fig. 17 (above). Marylin Hafner, decorative spot, p. 18. From *Decorate Your Home for Better Living* by Mary L. Brandt. Charles Scrbner's Sons, 1950. Courtesy of the estate of Marylin Hafner.

Fig. 18 (top right). Marylin Hafner, decorative spot, p. 41. From *Decorate Your Home for Better Living* by Mary L. Brandt. Charles Scribner's Sons, 1950. Courtesy of the estate of Marylin Hafner.

Fig. 19 (right middle). Marylin Hafner, decorative spot, p. 7. From *Decorate Your Home for Better Living* by Mary L. Brandt. Charles Scribner's Sons, 1950. Courtesy of the estate of Marylin Hafner.

Fig. 20 (bottom right). Marylin Hafner, decorative spot, p. 8. From *Decorate Your Home for Better Living* by Mary L. Brandt. Charles Scribner's Sons, 1950. Courtesy of the estate of Marylin Hafner.

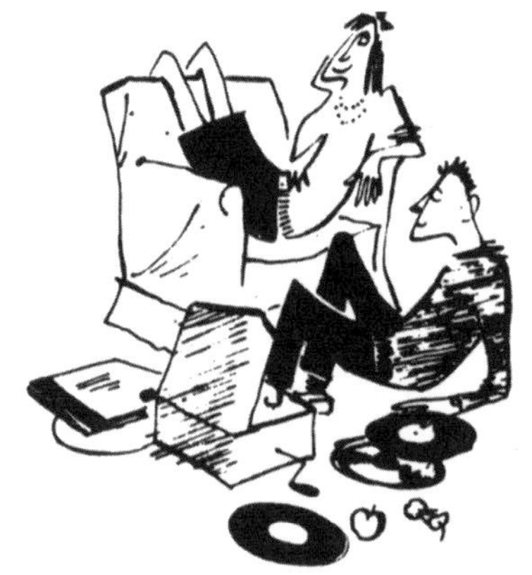

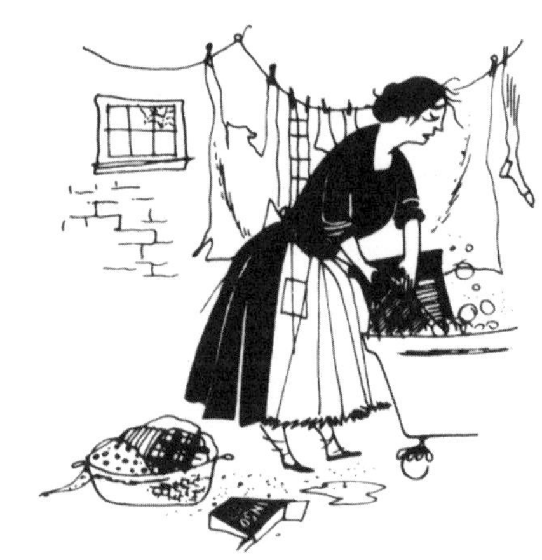

Fig. 21 (right). Mary L. Brandt, "Formal Traditional Styles," p. 68. From *Decorate Your Home for Better Living* by Mary L. Brandt. Charles Scribner's Sons, 1950.

Fig. 22 (below). Mary L. Brandt, "Informal Balance," p. 51. From *Decorate Your Home for Better Living* by Mary L. Brandt. Charles Scribner's Sons, 1950.

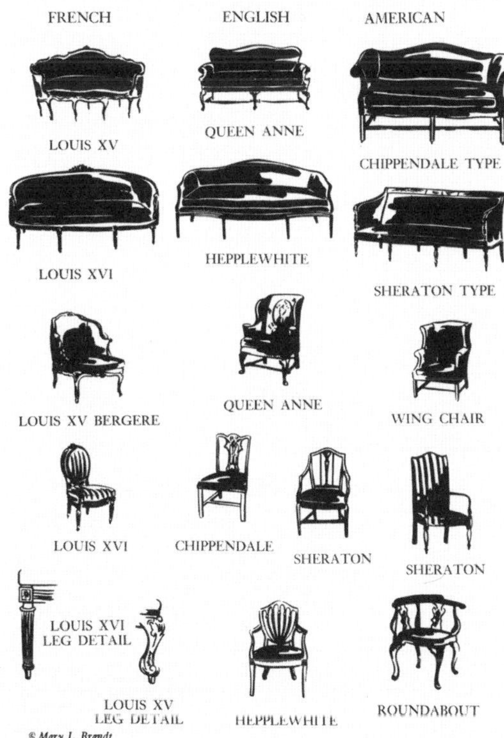

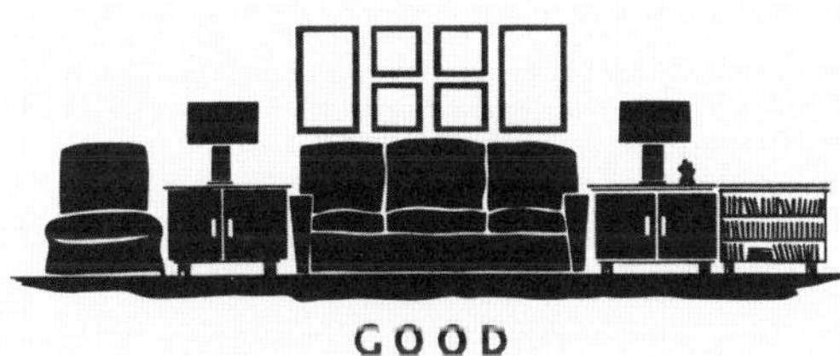

Do use related shapes and sizes that go together.

Do use informal balance for a friendly effect.

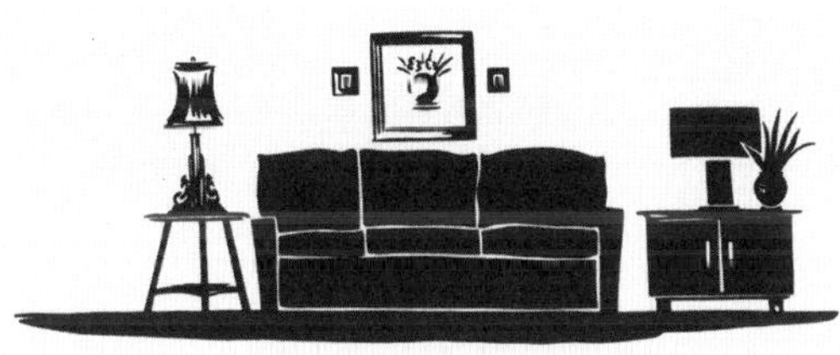

Don't use objects together that are too unrelated and badly scaled.

A combination of both FORMAL and INFORMAL balance makes a room more interesting and livable.

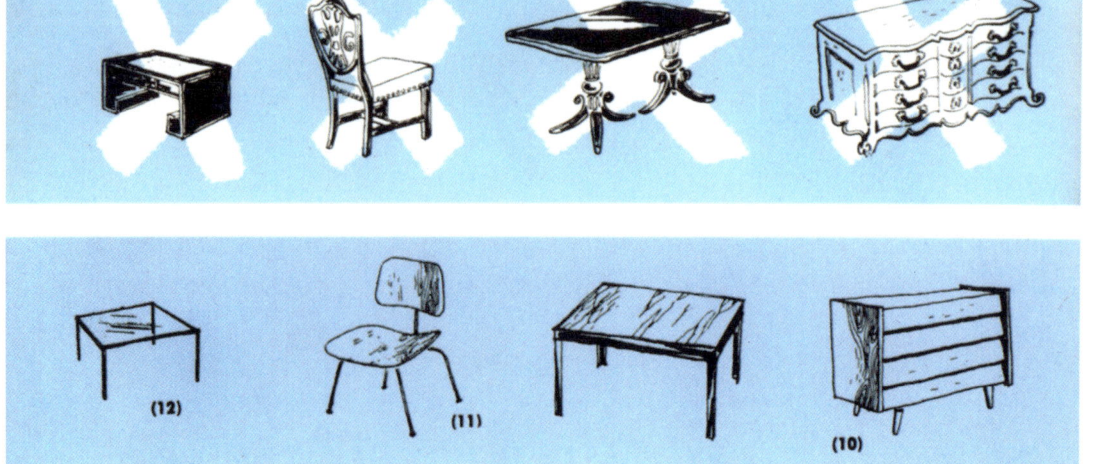

readers to follow rules and classifications or risk embarrassing mistakes.

The final book studied in this chapter, Mary and Russel Wright's *Guide to Easier Living*, was published the same year as Brandt's *Decorate Your Home for Better Living*. Whether in pursuit of "easier" or "better" living, the reader of both of these books is presumed to already have a house in need of better care, decoration, and management. Like Brandt and Williams, the Wrights provide advice on how to furnish the various rooms; however, their approach is driven entirely by function, rather than style, and their prose thus sounds more like the function-oriented design approach of Nelson and Henry Wright in *Tomorrow's House*. Although the Wrights repeatedly argue for the superiority of Modernism in their illustrations — as in one sequence where period designs are blotted out with large X marks, contrasted against intact Modern designs such as an Eames plywood chair and Knoll sideboard — they rarely call out Modern design by name (fig. 23). Unique among the five books discussed here, the Wrights' *Guide* provides extensive information about how to perform the maintenance tasks required to keep a house in acceptable condition for visitors. They assume that the housewife has traditionally been responsible for this work, and thus address their book primarily to her. However, throughout the book they make radical propositions, such as "Father may be the best interior decorator or pie-baker," and in their model of expanded, shared responsibility for housework, the book is ultimately addressed to male and female members of a household.[37] The text sets up a clear enemy in the outmoded etiquette standards of previous generations and seeks to empower its (female) readers by calling on them to recognize the enormous amount of their daily

Fig. 23. James Kingsland, Furniture for the "Room to Relax," pp. 22–23. From *Guide to Easier Living* by Mary and Russel Wright (1950), reprinted in 2003 by Gibbs Smith Publisher; by permission of the publisher.

work: "The entire fiction of 'gracious living' is a cruel charade, imposed on us by a set of standards we should have discarded long ago. We are victimized by the illusion of generations who had the kind of servants we do not have, afraid to change anything in the interest of comfort, work-saving, or better family living, hearing inside our very walls the scornful whisper that we can't afford, or don't know how, or haven't the taste to do things 'properly.' The Dear Old Dream dictatorship is a stifling influence in American life."[38]

The Wrights' book is illustrated exclusively with line drawings by James Kingsland.[39] Unusual among the illustrations in the books collected here, Kingsland's drawings capture the lives of people in their houses by showing them and their pets in rooms with casual, anecdotal accessories (rather than carefully curated objects). In a drawing of the "leisure area" of a bedroom, Kingsland includes open scissors and a trailing piece of fabric at a sewing machine, and a collection of records open on the sofa/bed (fig. 24).[40] Many of the rooms in the book are presented from a bird's-eye view, as in the open-plan room in fig. 25. Here, the mother works in the kitchen while the father relaxes, one foot on the coffee table, as his son teases the cat with a ball of yarn and the baby plays outside on the patio. Two casually placed glasses on the round side table in front of the patio suggest a prior configuration of humans—perhaps the parents sat in that pair of

Fig. 24. James Kingsland, "Bedroom designed for considerable daytime use," p. 65. From *Guide to Easier Living* by Mary and Russel Wright (1950). Russel Wright Papers, Special Collections Research Center, Syracuse University Libraries.

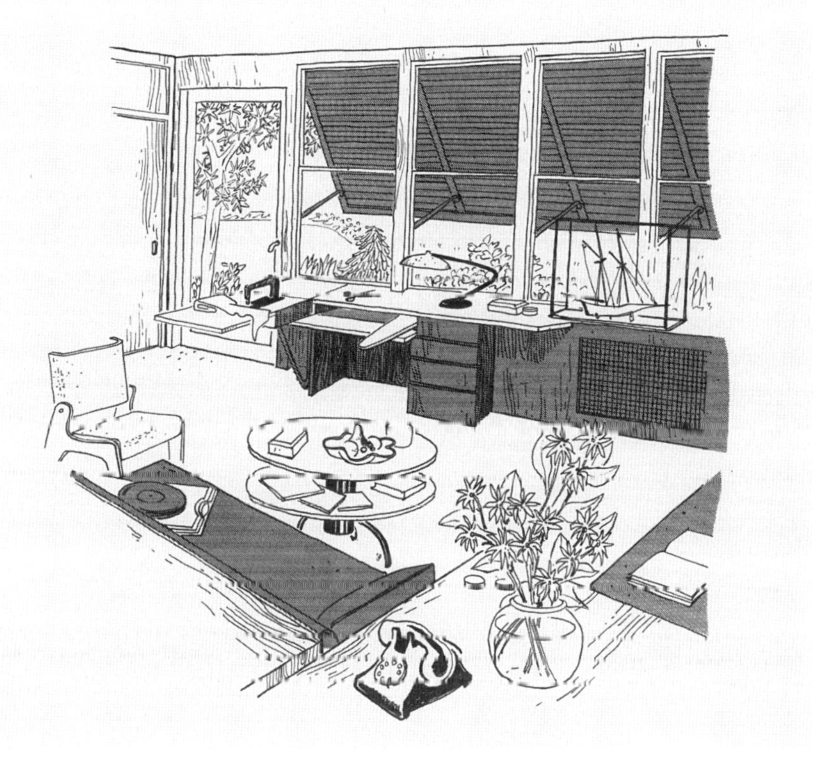

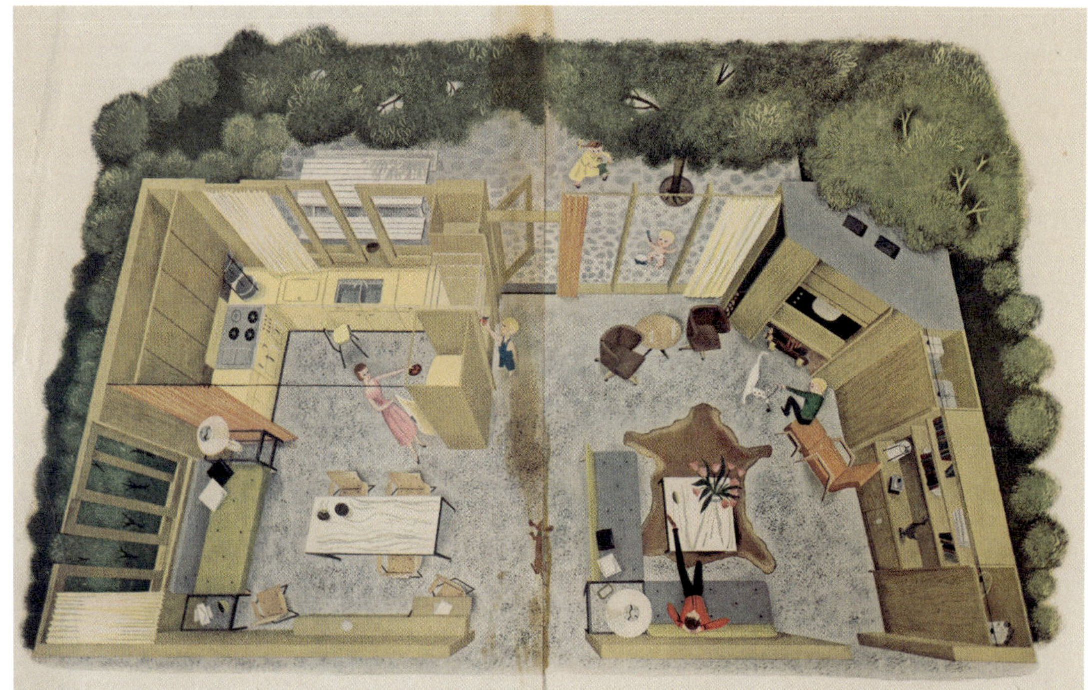

side chairs ten minutes earlier—while the desk chair in the dining area is left awkwardly askew. These small details, and the presence of actors in the space, help to humanize the rooms in the Wrights' book to a level not achieved in any other book discussed in this chapter. Yet, while the narratives conjured up are friendly, the bird's-eye viewpoint

Fig. 25. James Kingsland, "The all-in-one-room," color sketch for illustration published in *Guide to Easier Living* by Mary and Russel Wright (1950), pp. 48–49. Russel Wright Papers, Special Collections Research Center, Syracuse University Libraries.

has additional connotations: we can see every aspect of this White, suburban family's life, putting them, in effect, under our surveillance.[41] What's more, they seem to have internalized this power dynamic themselves: the wife is positioned to walk around the space and survey all activity, while the husband's eye is in line with the plate-glass window, watching the goings-on outside. If we take the advice of this book, do we submit our own lives to the potential for constant scrutiny from our neighbors and friends?

As this overview suggests, each of these books engages the postwar reader in a distinctive way. While the conceit of the domestic advice book is that the author speaks from a position of authority and even, occasionally, omniscience, in the analysis that follows in the second part of this chapter, I endeavor to limit my claims to the text and its author, mindful of the individual circumstances that led to the publication of each of these books. Williams, in particular, was caught in a publicity matrix during his lifetime where both White and non-White audiences tended to see him as representative of all Black professionals—or more insidiously, all Black men.

There is, too, a predisposition to examine a figure like Mary Brandt as representative of all White women who tried to establish independent professional success in the field of interior decoration in the mid-twentieth century. Mary and Russel Wright disclose a few details throughout their book about the choices they make in the maintenance of their home, but even as they try to model heteronormativity for their readers, we should be cognizant that it is the authors' strategic desire, not a transcendent model.[42] The comparison of these texts is productive both for the dissonance in their forms and history and for the consonance in their themes. In dialogue, they reveal larger pressure points in the field of Modernism in the postwar suburban home.

Modernism in the Postwar Imagined Home

All of the books discussed in this chapter explicitly embrace Modernism in architecture and design as a tool of efficiency and informal living. Many of the authors frame their views in an argument about functionality: Modernism responds directly to the reader's functional needs, has no conflicting allegiances to traditional forms and languages of ornament, and is thus able to maximize its effectiveness. Nelson and Henry Wright express this point of view in their closing pages.

> The difference between building an old-fashioned house and tomorrow's house is that the latter is a genuinely exciting and truly creative activity. The architect, instead of functioning as an arbiter of elegance — refusing to let you put the bathroom where it belongs because it would interfere with his symmetrical window arrangement, for instance — becomes the leading member of a team whose sole objective is to get a house that does everything a house could possibly do. With a conventional house, planning is done within a strait-jacket. Wherever one turns there are rules which, while meaningless, are all-powerful. … The planning is never free and the result could have been predicted in advance. With the modern house, no holds are barred.[43]

Williams, too, endorses the flexibility of Modernism in response to client preferences: "Modern design is practical because it is less costly to build than a house of period design where traditional detail is a consideration. It is more personal because it may indulge specific demands without thought of conforming to any accepted period framework."[44]

    These arguments in favor of Modernism have an almost legalistic quality to them, with little attention given to the possible aesthetic or emotional pleasure of the new style. Russel and Mary Wright suggest some behaviors that Modernism's efficiency and informality enable, and begin to forge an association between fun and the new style:

> Living in [the modern American home] will be based on an informal and improvised design, rather than on a formal, traditional pattern. Its etiquette will derive from modern democratic ideals.
>
> A new way of living, informal, relaxed, and actually more gracious than any strained imitation of another day could be, is in fact growing up, despite the etiquette despots and the die-hards. There is evidence all around that the hard shell of snobbish convention is cracking. Casual clothes invade many precincts once sacred to formal attire. The relaxed cocktail party or barbecue is a far more popular way of entertaining friends these days than the stiff dinner or the formal tea party.[45]

Brandt also discusses Modernism in terms of playful excitement: "Modern is a challenge to your imagination and your love of adventure."[46]

For all of these authors, Modernism was efficient and functional, and perhaps, more importantly, it promoted joyful lifestyles unconstrained by formal traditions and habits of behavior and appearance. A closer reading of these books, however, reveals limits to Modernism's revolutionary powers. The pursuit of efficiency, liberation, and happiness was predicated on a White, male, heteronormative social structure that relied on women's bodies as both the site of labor and the abject. Moreover, this worldview required the exclusion of bodies of color in order to maintain its White racial superiority.

Modernism and Gender

Gender structures the Modernist landscape of these books in both overt and unconscious ways. The texts studied here tackle the question of household responsibilities and the roles of individual family members, and in so doing they directly address gender expectations in postwar American society. These books also reveal a more deeply buried discourse of bodily control that takes as its object the unruly female body. Time and again, these books explain how Modernism can contain, direct, and restrain the female body. Indeed, the need to contain that body represents a chauvinism that structures both the household and the larger society.

All five of the books studied here describe household responsibilities that adhere, with few deviations, to the gendered stereotypes that have structured American society for most of its history. Mary L. Brandt was herself an extremely successful professional, and although there is some acknowledgment in her book and in Mary and Russel Wright's *Guide to Easier Living* of the prevalence of women who work outside the home, in general all five of these books presume that household maintenance work such as cooking, cleaning, laundry, child care, and hospitality are the responsibility of the woman of the house. The fictional men in these idealized accounts interact with their homes much the way the young husband does in the Wrights' illustration in fig. 25: they rest after their long workday conducted elsewhere, feet often propped up on furniture; they read, they listen to music, and they engage in productive, solitary hobbies such as stamp collecting. The gendered stereotypes routinely filter down to accounts of the children in these imagined homes, where boys' bedrooms always contain books and a desk for homework and the girls' bedrooms prioritize, instead, a dressing table where she can anticipate how her appearance will be evaluated by others.[47] Nelson and Wright sketched one such family in an opening chapter. The son's leisure activity is productive: with "his drums and his three music-loving companions … [they] weekly made the neighborhood air quiver with their uneasy efforts to achieve something new in contemporary music." The daughter, on the other hand, is defined by her desire to entertain others: she declares to her parents, "Isn't there going to be any place in this house where your children can carry on a normal social life?"[48]

Given Brandt's nationally recognized professional success in the male-dominated field of retail and merchandising, her treatment of gender merits closer attention. In an early chapter of her book, she explains clearly the gendered connotations of various period styles: "Through association, lines have assumed a character all their own. A sturdy Jacobean oak chair with its essentially straight lines expresses a masculine and substantial quality, while a fragile, Louis XVI chair with its delicately tapered legs, curved back and beautifully shaped arms suggests a graceful, feminine quality."[49] Yet as she moves into a discussion of "the horizontal lines of Modern furniture," her terms change. Below a series of cartoons that include a Herman Miller–style daybed and the distinctive legs of the Nelson platform bench, she declares, "Horizontal lines in tables, chairs, sofas, fabrics and even in rooms, express repose"[50] (fig. 26; see also chapter 3). The reader is confronted, momentarily, with the possibility that Modernism exists beyond the gendered binaries of period furniture, that its efficiency has allowed it to transcend gender—before Brandt once again anchors her analysis in the familiar references of masculine and feminine forms: "Curved lines are graceful and feminine and give an appearance of more relaxation than straight lines. … Even in some Modern furniture today, curved lines have been introduced to make the furniture more graceful and pleasing."[51] Modernism thus has the capacity to embody either gender, but in her lexicon it must always be one or the other.

Ultimately, Brandt's text reveals gendered assumptions that are unsurprising for postwar American society. She expects that her readers are female, and she encourages them to improve themselves by approaching their decorating projects like "a man," who "doesn't build a house without a definite plan worked out first."[52] She praises the housewife protagonist in one anecdote who has "been reading everything she could find on

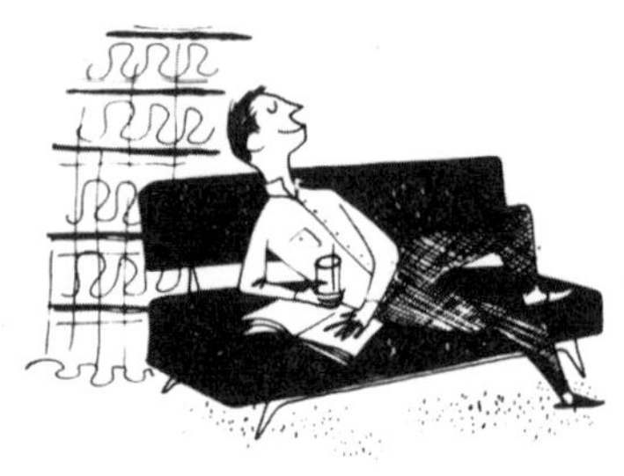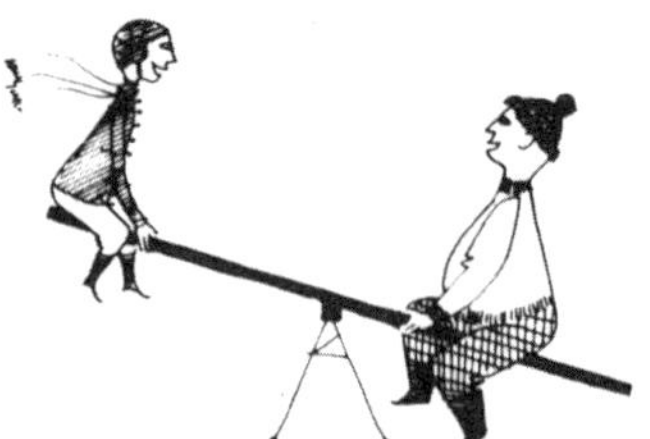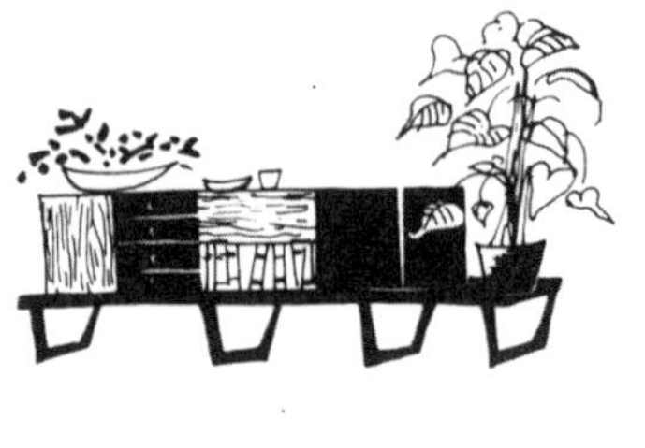

decorating" and is "completely absorbed, after the day's shopping, in trying little samples of wall color, wall papers and fabrics all over the apartment." This woman's redecoration is successful, finally, because she has "taken the time to learn about the principles of decorating." While her studiousness and planning skills may cast her in a masculine light, Brandt finishes the anecdote by firmly reinforcing the traditional role of the man in the house: "Her husband confessed to me that he soon forgot to complain about or remind her of the late dinners and the many inconveniences, because the newly decorated apartment was so much more comfortable and cheerful. He said he loved sitting in his favorite armchair with its gay cretonne, while listening to his favorite records, or lying on the blue upholstered sofa beside the crackling fire while he read, or just snoozed, before dinnertime."[53]

Fig. 26. Marylin Hafner, decorative spot, p. 44. From *Decorate Your Home for Better Living* by Mary L. Brandt. Charles Scribner's Sons, 1950. Courtesy of the estate of Marylin Hafner.

Both Russel and Mary Wright and Paul Williams celebrate Modernism as a style that lessens housework. Their attention to the real labor of the house, as well as interest in reducing it, demonstrates an awareness of the work of women and illustrates what might be called an incipient feminism. However, in none of these publications is the housewife ever fully empowered. In the Wrights' chapter titled "The Housewife-Engineer," they suggest that a woman's work in the house can be reduced by a modernized "simplification of methods" as well as by a more equitable sharing of responsibilities among the members of the household. They envision the housewife as CEO, convening a meeting of her vice presidents: "The mother, as household manager and chairman, brings her list of tasks to be done, and suggestions as to who is best suited by inclination, ability, and time to do the various jobs," although they stop short of giving her full executive authority, qualifying it with "but the family as a whole makes the decisions. It is important, if the rest of the family—particularly the children—are not to feel they're being imposed upon or coerced into drudgery, that the council unearth the special talents and interests of each member, and discover how to use these for the benefit of all."[54] Mother's housework is replaced by emotionally taxing parenting work as she figures out how to compel compliance without apparently upsetting anyone. Indeed, even as they radically assess housework from its very foundation levels, the authors are reluctant to completely free women of their burdens. The ideal kitchen for the Wrightian housewife includes furniture that simultaneously aids her in her tasks and traps her there for the entire day: a sofa where "Father stretches out with the evening paper before dinner, and Mother takes her ease during a free hour," a desk for "leisure reading, knitting bag, sewing basket," and "a radio (but *not* television; that's too much distraction)."[55] They also recommend "a small auxiliary make-up shelf and mirror in the kitchen [that] will help your morale," if the housewife has forgotten that she needs to remain made-up and attractive as she completes her endless to-do list.[56]

In Williams's introductory text in *The Small Home of Tomorrow*, he states that Modern design is valuable for its potential to reduce household labor. He writes, "Without resorting to any trickery, [in the modern house] there will be more recessed features, greater storage space, and many more built-ins which mean fewer free-standing pieces of furniture to move and clean beneath."[57] His choice of words vividly evokes the manual labor of cleaning. Moreover, Modernism is connected to honesty: in his formulation, no one will be "tricked" into thinking a modern house is less work to maintain, because it will actually be so. Nonetheless, the close reader of Williams's book suspects that responsibility for housework, no matter the amount, resides with the housewife. In a house design titled "The Conservative," he notes that "the kitchen is conveniently placed for answering front door bell," leaving us to assume that whoever occupies the kitchen is also responsible for greeting guests and door-to-door salesmen at the front door.[58] The question of the kitchen's occupant is answered in the illustration that accompanies his account of "The Kitchen of Tomorrow," the only interior rendering in the book that includes human inhabitants (fig. 27). In his kitchen, which features plenty of windows, a lengthy breakfast bar, and a desk for sundry tasks, the wife stands at the stove, in an elegant dress covered by an apron, stirring a pot. Next to her is an open drawer, which, we read in the accompanying description, is an element of the "horizontal refrigerated food space."[59] She is thus firmly placed inside a matrix of food preparation, even if the minimalist design of the kitchen appears to physically minimize her labor. She is accompanied by her husband, who, like Russel and Mary Wright's fictional husband, is enlightened enough to visit her in the kitchen — yet not so enlightened as to help with any chores. He stands, cigarette in hand, slouched against the counter at the farthest corner from his wife, as if closer proximity will draw him into the vortex of her work.

In the acknowledgments to *Tomorrow's House*, George Nelson and Henry Wright credited their wives, Frances Nelson and Dorothy Wright, with "deflat[ing] exaggerated ideas [and] correct[ing] certain masculine misconceptions about the business of running a home." However, their prose expresses an attitude toward household labor that differs from that informing any of the other books discussed here.[60] Whereas Williams, the Wrights, and

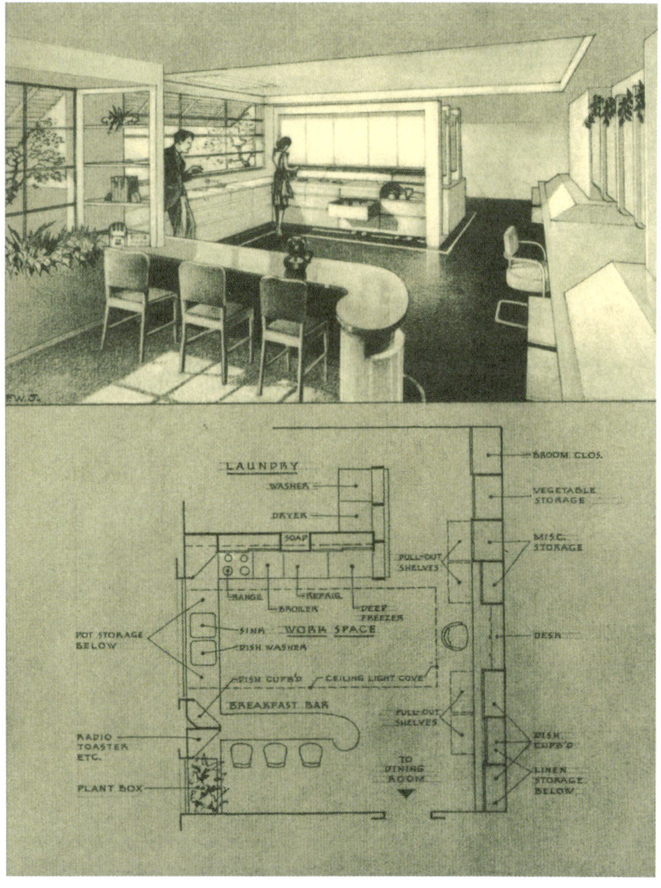

Fig. 27. Paul R. Williams,
"The Kitchen of Tomorrow,"
Frank Jamison, renderer,
The Small Home of Tomorrow
(1945), p. 91.

even Brandt recognize that a person residing in the house—most commonly the wife—performs its necessary maintenance, in *Tomorrow's House* the picture of labor is perpetually deferred. In numerous anecdotes, Nelson and Wright refer to servants who are separate from the family and literally work behind closed doors. In the chapter on dining, for example, they reminisce about cooking in the early twentieth century and the presence of "the hired girl—newly arrived, in all probability, from Sweden, Ireland, or Poland. She was an affable, immensely competent person who could whip up anything from a snack to a banquet at a short notice and somehow managed to do not only the cooking and dishwashing but the serving as well."[61] That "girl" is reincarnated in the present day, later in the book: "The annoyances produced by the hired girl in the kitchen, who tosses your best china around with the utmost abandon while you are trying to be polite to your husband's boss after dinner, are too well known to require extended description."[62]

It must be admitted that Nelson and Wright devote an entire chapter, "The Work Center," to the kitchen. However, even here, the labor of the house is obscured by their persistent use of the passive voice. They describe the kitchen of "fifty years ago" as a work center on which they have modeled their contemporary ideas, but it is not clear who did the work in that original space: "Here, by the stove, children were bathed, food was canned, laundry was done, and meals were eaten." In contrast, we know who participated in recreation in that room: "In the evening people sat in rockers by the big, round table and read, sewed, studied, played games, and talked."[63] They conclude the chapter with a "Picture of a Work Center," but it is a list of appliances and construction details that contains no human presence: "It works beautifully for a large number of household tasks."[64] The authors' persistent use of the passive voice suggests that they feel distant from the people who perform the household labor, as if truly seeing that work and recognizing it as such is beneath them. This attitude is underscored in a completely separate passage, where they describe a recently constructed house "equipped with all sorts of storage units in addition to the usual closets." Although "originally it was believed three servants would be needed to keep the house in order," the authors triumphantly explain that because of the storage units, "it was found that two [servants] did the job very well."[65] In this passage, they equate living persons (servants) with inanimate containers and actually conclude that the servants are of lesser value.

While Nelson and Wright transform housework into distant, impersonal practice, they perform a curious rhetorical inversion elsewhere in their text, equating the house and its spaces with the human body in a way that reveals subconscious preoccupations about gendered identities. The most creative and forceful passages in the book appear in discussions of the kitchen—so closely, if obliquely, equated with the woman of the house—and the bathroom, where the body is rendered most vulnerable. In these passages, the house is conflated with the bodies it controls. The kitchen, for example, is cast as a producer of unpleasant sounds and smells, a room that should not be seen by guests and would ideally be blocked off from polite society: "The kitchen is a natural noise-producing center, and what sounds cannot be stopped at their source must be absorbed one way or another by the ceiling and walls and floors. There is also the problem of cooking odors, which are now free to move through the entire living area of the house."[66] They elaborate with a scientific description of the problem: "In fact laboratory analysis has disclosed that some of the fish mother fries on the kitchen stove is likely to condense on an upstairs windowpane within a matter of minutes. In the properly designed house this is not to be tolerated. Such a condition is dirty and it is wasteful."[67] Their vocabulary choices are suggestive: food could also be described as having an aroma, but bodies always have "odor" (especially, according to hygiene ads, female bodies), and the authors assert that the dispersion of such odors is "dirty." Thus the kitchen—the site of a woman's work—becomes a loud and dirty body that must be contained through Modern architectural design.

In a chapter on sound control, Nelson and Wright draw our attention to "the bathroom [, which] is the most annoying because it can be the most embarrassing. Everyone is familiar with the disagreeable interruption made by the noisy flushing of a toilet adjoining the main living space. And it is an unfortunate coincidence that the water closet, for functional reasons, is shaped almost like a trumpet. A trumpet, as one might well imagine, is no shape for suppressing noise at its source."[68] When they discuss the bathroom in greater detail, their vocabulary choices again suggest an elision between the space of the bathroom and the female body. "A shower thirty inches square is usable but not very pleasant," they advise. "If you can possibly do it, make it about four feet long by two and a half or three feet wide. This extra space will not make much difference in the size of the house, and it will turn a nasty little slot into a really luxurious place for bathing."[69] Their phrase "nasty little slot" elicits a sense of disgust and dirtiness, but it may resonate more specifically with the female body; not only is "slot" close to "slut," but a 1942 *American Thesaurus of Slang* listed "slot," along with "slit," as slang for female genitalia.[70] For Nelson and Wright, Modernist architecture is the ultimate controlling force: it can contain, and even erase, the physical embarrassments of the disgusting (female) body.

Brandt also employs the metaphor of the human body to underscore the importance of the decorating rules she introduces in her book. She advises, for example, that "formal balance gives a feeling of restfulness, stability and restraint," language that thoroughly wraps interior design into empathetic bodily response.[71] On the other hand, "when a room seems to be uncomfortable, you may be sure all the rules of scale, balance and proportion are 'violently violated.' "[72] In addition to the threat of bodily violence, she demonstrates her understanding of how to control the female body through social expectation and shame. In a lesson about scale, she deftly weaves together decorating choices and humiliating fashion choices to make her point:

> In order to select and arrange objects that look well together, you must develop a sense of scale. You should, for instance, know that a small-patterned tapestry is too small in scale for a large sofa, or that a "dinky" ashtray is too small for a sizable coffee table.... Keep in mind the same principles of scale that you use when choosing your clothes. If you are a short woman you aren't likely to buy a large wide hat and a huge handbag because they make you look shorter. If you are tall, you will avoid vertical stripes and cone-shaped hats that make you look even taller.[73]

If Brandt and Nelson and Henry Wright use the house and its furnishings to shame, constrain, and control the female body, Mary and Russel Wright exercise a slightly different logic. Their home, too, controls the body of the human inhabitant—most vividly, that of the housewife—but it does so through the relentless itinerary of manual labor that must be accomplished every day to keep it adequately maintained. Their account of the daily cleaning of the bedroom is particularly vivid because of the gendered immorality that it implicates in this scene of domestic destruction, with its expression of wanton, inappropriate feminine desire:

> To the housewife [the bedroom] is easily the biggest headache—more accurately backache—of all. As she stops in the doorway each morning, toting her dust cloth, carpet sweeper, and mop, consider the scene that confronts her:
>
> Gone is the sweet and charming picture of the night before: the draped and ruffled bed, the delicate night table, the sleek chests and bureaus, the skirted dressing table, all in the mellow glow of dainty, silk-shaded lamps. In the cold light of morning, where is the pretty illusion now? Bedcovers cascade to the floor, and lamp shades hang askew; the housewife must stumble over assorted shoes, slippers, and oddments of clothing that litter the carpet. Drawers and closets are open-mouthed, mute witness of the frantic hunt just made within their disordered depths. The elegant dressing table lewdly bares its skinny legs, and lint is a dingy film over everything.[74]

The hardworking housewives of America spend "millions of hours" to put these rooms back together again every day, their physical labor atoning for the bodily sins of the household. Elsewhere in the text, we find the routine of bodily and household maintenance suffocating every member of the house. In a description of the simple act of entering the house, the reader stumbles across this comprehensive list: "To do its job properly, [the front door and foyer area] should make it almost impossible for anyone to come in without wiping feet, putting down packages, and putting away coat, hat, scarf, umbrella, rubbers, galoshes, and the like, and conversely should make it easy for them to find their possessions on the way out. It must also be easy to clean and to keep in order."[75] Here, the house becomes an agent of enforcement, allowing no one inside who has not followed the proper rules for dress and comportment, and simultaneously ensuring that all members of the household are appropriately attired and represented to the world outside when they depart the boundaries of the house. The latter part of their text includes pages of lists of cleaning activities, which in themselves create a vivid form of corporeal control. The Wrights rely on the 1920s innovations of Christine Frederick and the booming academic field of home economics in their recommendations for minimizing unnecessary work, with the result that they legislate details such as how many times to walk around a bed as it is made (the answer: once) (fig. 28).[76] And as they delve into these details, the house and the housewife are inescapably

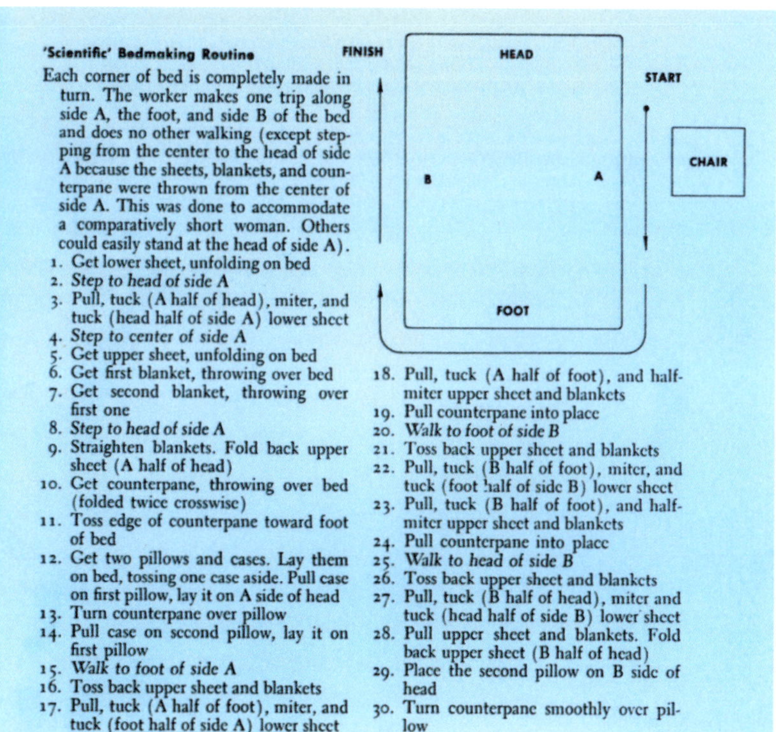

'Scientific' Bedmaking Routine

Each corner of bed is completely made in turn. The worker makes one trip along side A, the foot, and side B of the bed and does no other walking (except stepping from the center to the head of side A because the sheets, blankets, and counterpane were thrown from the center of side A. This was done to accommodate a comparatively short woman. Others could easily stand at the head of side A).

1. Get lower sheet, unfolding on bed
2. *Step to head of side A*
3. Pull, tuck (A half of head), miter, and tuck (head half of side A) lower sheet
4. *Step to center of side A*
5. Get upper sheet, unfolding on bed
6. Get first blanket, throwing over bed
7. Get second blanket, throwing over first one
8. *Step to head of side A*
9. Straighten blankets. Fold back upper sheet (A half of head)
10. Get counterpane, throwing over bed (folded twice crosswise)
11. Toss edge of counterpane toward foot of bed
12. Get two pillows and cases. Lay them on bed, tossing one case aside. Pull case on first pillow, lay it on A side of head
13. Turn counterpane over pillow
14. Pull case on second pillow, lay it on first pillow
15. *Walk to foot of side A*
16. Toss back upper sheet and blankets
17. Pull, tuck (A half of foot), miter, and tuck (foot half of side A) lower sheet
18. Pull, tuck (A half of foot), and half-miter upper sheet and blankets
19. Pull counterpane into place
20. *Walk to foot of side B*
21. Toss back upper sheet and blankets
22. Pull, tuck (B half of foot), miter, and tuck (foot half of side B) lower sheet
23. Pull, tuck (B half of foot), and half-miter upper sheet and blankets
24. Pull counterpane into place
25. *Walk to head of side B*
26. Toss back upper sheet and blankets
27. Pull, tuck (B half of head), miter and tuck (head half of side B) lower sheet
28. Pull upper sheet and blankets. Fold back upper sheet (B half of head)
29. Place the second pillow on B side of head
30. Turn counterpane smoothly over pillow

intertwined, with advice about personal grooming mixed with information about the necessary "Daily Grooming" of the living room.[77]

Finally, Williams discusses the Modern house as a place of bodily containment in the particular case of female inhabitants. In *New Homes for Today*, Williams describes a dual-function bedroom where the female body's private needs are literally masked—repressed—under the guise of a more socially acceptable public face. "The bedroom," he reports, "has become a combination sleeping, dressing, and sitting room with books, radio and lounging chairs instead of the traditional five piece bedroom suite." With specific attention to the vanity table, the site of confrontation between a woman and the social expectations for her appearance—the site, in many respects, of greatest vulnerability for the female body—he writes: "Another surprise will be a concealed dressing table in the wardrobe. When you open a pair of doors, mirrored on the inside, this dressing table will light up so that the toilet articles are visible only when the dressing table is in use. Such a bedroom can be transformed quickly into a sitting room or study, even the bed could be recessed in an alcove if desired."[78] His bedroom seeks to hide the evidence of a woman's grooming labor, of the hours she spends preparing herself to look elegant enough to then work in the Modernist kitchen.

Fig. 28. "'Scientific' Bedmaking Routine," *Guide to Easier Living* (1950), 151. From *Guide to Easier Living* by Mary and Russel Wright (1950), reprinted in 2003 by Gibbs Smith Publisher; by permission of the publisher.

Elsewhere in his publications, Williams is less specifically concerned with hiding the female body and instead presents the house as an agent that hides and, indeed, protects all human bodies. As he associates the Modern house with themes of control and the human body, his prose represents a moment of transition in my own text. While I have been describing how these varied authors invoke Modernism as a force of gendered control, in the following section I will argue that these writers also use Modernism as a proxy for their own investments in racialized social control. In *The Small Home of Tomorrow*, Williams lists a variety of futuristic household technologies. Any one of them, alone, would be empowering to the homeowner, but as he presents them in concert, the effect is that of a house that is impermeable to the atmospheric effects of the outside world: "An air-conditioning lamp which kills all bacteria; Another lamp which collects all dust and pollen in the room; Still another lamp which prevents mold in the refrigerator … All-weather window glass; Heating and air-conditioning units sending forced air through the house—cool air in summer, warm air in winter; Fluorescent lighting for economy of current and elimination of heat; Polarized glass to permit clear vision but yet eliminate the direct entrance of the sun's rays; Screens built on the principle of miniature venetian blinds."[79] A human ensconced in this house would be shielded from all manner of dangers, from the microscopic to the global. Offered without any gendered signifiers, Williams's text suggests a concern for corporeal safety and privacy that transcends female or male identity. He proposes that Modernism might defend homeowners from external dangers, both environmental and social. He insinuates, further, that those living in such new houses have reason to fear threats from the outside, and that they merit Modernism's protection. The question of who, precisely, is protected within the shell of Williams's Modern house might be better answered through examination of the role of racialized identities in his books and those of his peers.

Modernism and the Construction of Race

All of the books studied in this chapter use implicit and explicit racialized metaphors to explain the work of Modernism. Closer scrutiny of how the authors engage with racialized concepts helps us to see more clearly the biases that shaped the White-dominated discourse of Modernism in the immediate postwar period. One persistent trope in the literature studied here is an equation between Modernism and cleanliness. Philosopher Shannon Sullivan notes that "non-white people have long been associated with dirt, filth, and pollution by white people," and she argues that it is not simply that Whites see non-White skin "as dark because unwashed," but that "their alleged dirtiness is a sign of a more intangible—though perceived as no less real—uncleanliness."[80] I suggest that the pervasive association of Modernism with cleanliness was, in effect, a strategy for affirming Modernism's capacity to signify racial Whiteness.[81] Indeed, in the passages from Nelson and Wright's *Tomorrow's House*, cited above, the dirtiness associated with women's work and women's bodies can be additionally understood as implicating bodies of color and the need to contain and correct them. The conflation of women and the non-White other is a classic example of a strategy for maintaining White male (Western) superiority described in, among other places, the work of Homi K. Bhabha and Edward Said.[82]

A preoccupation with Modernism's cleanliness appears throughout these books. Brandt casually refers to "Modern clean colors" but also goes further by explaining that Modernism enables (and thus reinforces) a lifestyle of cleanliness.[83] She notes that with the growing popularity of Modern designs, "We are leaning to lighter, more graceful furniture, with tapering legs, clean, straight-forward surfaces and pieces that are generally much easier to handle and maintain," and argues that ultimately "Modernism represents a way of living. It appeals especially to those who like uncluttered living."[84] While she states that Modernism fosters household cleanliness and tidiness, she wields her authority with greater emotional effectiveness when she implies that only a self-selecting group—"*those who like* uncluttered living"—will be drawn to the style. Race is never stated—nor, likely, was it conscious in her mind or the minds of her readers—but to the extent that Whiteness must always be defined against an other, her text allows her readers to perform precisely that act of self-definition. They can become "those who like uncluttered living," in contrast to those living in a cluttered home, following what Sullivan describes as the "unconscious habits of connecting whiteness with cleanliness and blackness with impurity."[85] Brandt's readers, by choosing Modernism, begin to participate in an unstated model of White identity.

The entire premise of Mary and Russel Wright's book is that a "modern" approach to managing the home will result in greater cleanliness. Although they do not explicitly endorse one style of furniture over another, the renderings in their chapter on the bedroom are uniformly examples of Modern design (fig. 29). After an extensive account of the "millions of hours" it takes to put the messy bedrooms detailed above "in order again before each nightfall," they conclude with an explicit endorsement of Modernism that, like Brandt's text, calls upon the reader to self-differentiate: "The bedrooms illustrated in this chapter are devoid of traditional furnishings … yet they possess qualities of charm, dignity, and a serene kind of beauty that cannot be found in traditional rooms. Learn to enjoy them."[86]

Indeed, the deeper history of the development of the *Guide to Easier Living* is wrapped up in the interrelationship of Modernism, cleanliness, and race. The Wrights dedicate their book to "Dorcas Hollingsworth, who for years served our household with great artistry," and Russel's archives contain a typed manuscript titled "Life without Dorcas," which, based on its content and date, was likely the very first draft for the book.

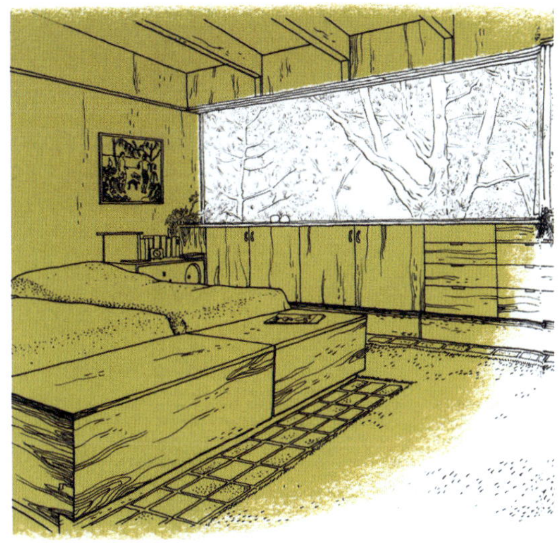

Fig. 29. James Kingsland, Bedroom designed by Richard Neutra, p. 66. From *Guide to Easier Living* by Mary and Russel Wright (1950), reprinted in 2003 by Gibbs Smith Publisher; by permission of the publisher.

In this manuscript, Russel and Mary, writing in the first person plural, set up the question of housekeeping and casual entertaining as a response to a crucial problem they encountered at the start of World War II: the loss of their household maid, Dorcas Hollingsworth. After an introductory chapter that narrates her work, they proceed to chapters that cover the bathroom, dining room, living room, entertaining, and the distribution of work—essentially the same topics that eventually appear in *Guide to Easier Living*. In the "Life without Dorcas" manuscript, however, all of their household management is cast in the shadow of losing the labor of Hollingsworth. The Wrights describe Hollingsworth herself in language that has overtones of patriarchal superiority and unacknowledged racism:

> We first saw Dorcas Hollingsworth one night in 1935 as she sat waiting at the end of the large living room of our penthouse apartment to be interviewed for the job of maid-of-all-work.
>
> Her exotic West-Indian beauty alone was enough to make us choose her quickly instead of 10 or 12 other applicants. And the tremble in her voice, the tears in her wonderful eyes, made us feel that we had done a good deed when she thanked us and told us how hard she had job-hunted for days.
>
> For the next six years Dorcas came in every day at 8 A.M., leaving at 8:30 P.M.—except on Thursdays and Sundays—when she left at a vague 2 o'clock.[87]

When they explain their distress after she left their employ, the Wrights invoke a comparison to Southern lifestyles: "For the next three years we became as the White Russian royalty,—or the old southern 'aristocracy.' And no Southerner or Russian ever came harder by his plight. Shoe horns and collar buttons accumulated—and three years of dust."[88] While they could have selected examples of aristocratic living from across the United States, it is notable that they compare themselves to the region known for its history of enslaved African Americans. The sentence displaces their Whiteness onto the "White Russian royalty," but the web of associations is clear. Hollingsworth's work in the house is understood in part through race: she is not merely of the servant class but is a servant of color working in a household owned by Whites. When the *Guide to Easier Living* is seen as a response to losing Hollingsworth's labor, the entire project of keeping the Modern house clean begins to look different from the text we thought we knew. It is not merely about simplifying household tasks—it is also about simplifying who is in the house. The *Guide to Easier Living* makes the house self-sufficient, not dependent on the labor of women of color, and as a consequence the book teaches its readers how to be racially White. The Modern house, in the Wrights' telling, is a domain where cleanliness and order are enforced in the front foyer, where Whiteness can be exercised exclusively.

Williams also invokes the association between Modernism and cleanliness, and its presence in books by an African American architect, who had already spent much of his career discussing the role of race in his professional identity, raises additional questions. He writes in 1946: "Many people say they would like a modern home if it did not have a flat roof, pointing out that a home should not resemble an office or factory, most of which have flat roofs. On the other hand, they like the features of the modern homes such as the large windows, simplicity of plan and sleek streamlined appearance."[89] His choice of adjectives—"sleek streamlined"—reflects his familiarity with a common discourse around Modernism; such terms, with their connotations of immaculate surfaces, had been popular for over a decade.[90] His language may also represent a nod, however subliminal, to the Whiteness of Modernism in a bid to make a connection with the portion of his audience that he assumed would be White. Williams had employed a comparable rhetorical strategy in a well-known autobiographical essay from 1937. Originally published in *American Magazine*, this complex and contradictory text powerfully describes the racism he has encountered as an African American professional, but also includes some statements clearly intended for its predominantly White readership. In one such passage, he writes, "White Americans have a reasonable basis for their prejudice against the Negro race, and if that prejudice is ever to be overcome it must be through the efforts of individual Negroes to rise above the average cultural level of their kind."[91]

Williams's *New Homes* text is notable, however, in that it largely avoids the call for the reader to self-differentiate. Unlike Brandt and the Wrights, all of whom were White, he does not ask his readers to consider themselves as distinct in any way—to "learn" or become "one who likes"—but rather addresses them as a unified mass market; they are the "many people" who like Modernism. Williams deploys the same rhetorical strategy in his 1945 book, where he also associates Modernism with cleanliness: "[Modern houses] can, as is demonstrated in this book, be attractive, smart houses, and through open space arrangement, large window areas and simplicity of interior, reflect a feeling of spaciousness and personality. … Its broad sunlight [*sic*] windows, its close proximity to the outdoors and uncluttered interiors give one a new sense of freedom.… This is the accepted floorplan of today, and is emphasized in the plans herein presented."[92] He maps cleanliness onto Modernism but presents it as a strategy for all, the "accepted floorplan of today." Sullivan notes the White inclination to "police the boundaries between the two [races] so as to maintain a strict separation," and if cleanliness is a proxy for Whiteness in Williams's text, he seems not particularly interested in policing its borders.[93] His books, which refer to a symbolic code of Whiteness but do not ask readers to identify as such, might thus have more effectively found an audience of diverse races.

Just as Williams is subtly different in his use of the Modernism/cleanliness trope, he is also pointedly different from his peers in how he values style. Nelson and Wright demand fealty to Modernism, but Williams, in both his 1945 and 1946 books, embraces a wide range of architectural styles. In fact, his architectural practice is, to this day, recognized for his confident deployment of multiple period styles.[94] In numerous interviews during his lifetime, Williams presented himself as an architect who responded first and foremost to his clients' wishes, and this accounted in large part for the stylistic diversity of his built work. A 1948 *Time* magazine profile noted: "Some architects have been known to sniff at Williams' work; esthetically it breaks no new ground. But Williams, who does not like the severity of modern designs, makes no bones about his ability to work over old ground. He gives a new look to Early American, Spanish, Cape Cod, and judges his work by one standard: 'If I build the kind of a house a client wants, I'm a good architect.' "[95] In his comprehensive study of Williams's career, architect Wesley Howard Henderson suggests that Williams was ultimately motivated, as a designer, by the needs of the floor plan; his responses to clients began with sketches of the rooms that they needed in their homes. Henderson offers the intriguing metaphor of the exterior of the house as a "skin" that Williams applies once the interior program has been determined.[96]

The metaphor of architectural style as a skin can be used to analyze the designs offered in the 1945 *Small Home of Tomorrow* in particular. In this book, several designs that, from the exterior, seem different in style are revealed, upon further scrutiny, to have almost identical floor plans. "The Monterey," a "California adaptation of colonial," features an off-center entrance and a second-floor balcony that spans the width of the house (fig. 30).[97] Ten pages later in the text, "The Devonshire," a "combination of the English cottage developed around a modern plan," seems, at first glance, quite different from the Monterey with its dormered second-floor windows and the stepped-down roofline at the left end of the house (fig. 31).[98] However, comparison of the two floor plans uncovers strong similarities: in both, the entrance on the first floor brings us into a hall with stairs and then leads left into a large living room; the living room faces an outdoor space to the back of the house and opens onto a dining area behind the stairs; the dining room itself then connects to a kitchen, which completes the first-floor circulation by returning to the hall. The second floors are likewise very similar, with the exception of the position of the closets. In another case, "The Suburban," a home inspired by "the simplicity of the Regency style," has a floor plan that almost mirrors "Contemporary Number Five," an example of "conservative" "modern domestic architecture" (figs. 32, 33).[99] Both offer entrances directly into one end of a large living room with a doorway to the dining room on axis with the front door; the kitchen is immediately behind both dining rooms, and an outdoor space is positioned at the junction of living and dining rooms. Each has the bedroom zone accessible from the dining room. Yet the exteriors of these two houses are stylistically quite different. "The Suburban" exudes traditional formality with its hip roof, symmetrical bay windows, and broken pediment over the front door. In contrast, "Contemporary Number Five" flaunts its asymmetry, with horizontal bands of windows wrapping around the corners of the living room and bedroom, a singular porthole window for the bathroom, and its low-pitched roof with deep eaves.

What to make of these houses, so different on their exteriors but so similar in their floor plans? To extend Henderson's metaphor, what to make of these houses that present different skins to the world but possess the same interior lives, with similar patterns of usage and habits of everyday living? Although it would be irresponsible to suggest that Williams himself thought of the disconnect between exterior design and interior program in racialized terms, the surprises of his designs echo the powerful point that he makes in the opening passage of his 1937 article, "I am a Negro." In a series of striking anecdotes, he describes the disconnect between, on the one hand, his own, internal sense of self and professional accomplishments and, on the other hand, the external limits imposed on him by the racism of a White-dominant society. "I am an architect," he begins.

> Today I sketched the preliminary plans for a large country house which will be erected in one of the most beautiful residential districts in the world, a district of roomy estates, entrancing vistas, and stately mansions. Sometimes I have dreamed of living there. I could afford such a home.
>
> But this evening, leaving my office, I returned to my own small, inexpensive home in an unrestricted, comparatively undesirable section of Los Angeles. Dreams cannot alter facts; I know that, for the preservation of my own happiness, I must always live in that

Fig. 30 (right). Paul R. Williams,
"The Monterey," Frank Jamison,
renderer, *The Small Home of
Tomorrow* (1945), p. 15.

Fig. 31 (below). Paul R. Williams,
"The Devonshire," Frank Jamison,
renderer, *The Small Home of
Tomorrow* (1945), p. 25.

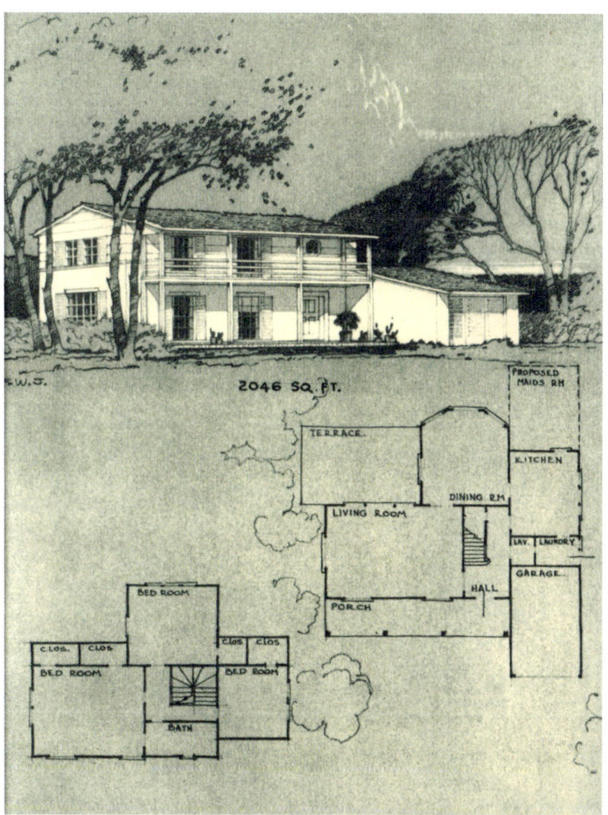

2046 SQ. FT.
PROPOSED MAIDS RM
TERRACE
KITCHEN
LIVING ROOM
DINING RM
LAV. LAUNDRY
GARAGE
PORCH
HALL
BED ROOM
CLOS. CLOS
CLOS CLOS
BED ROOM
BED ROOM
BATH

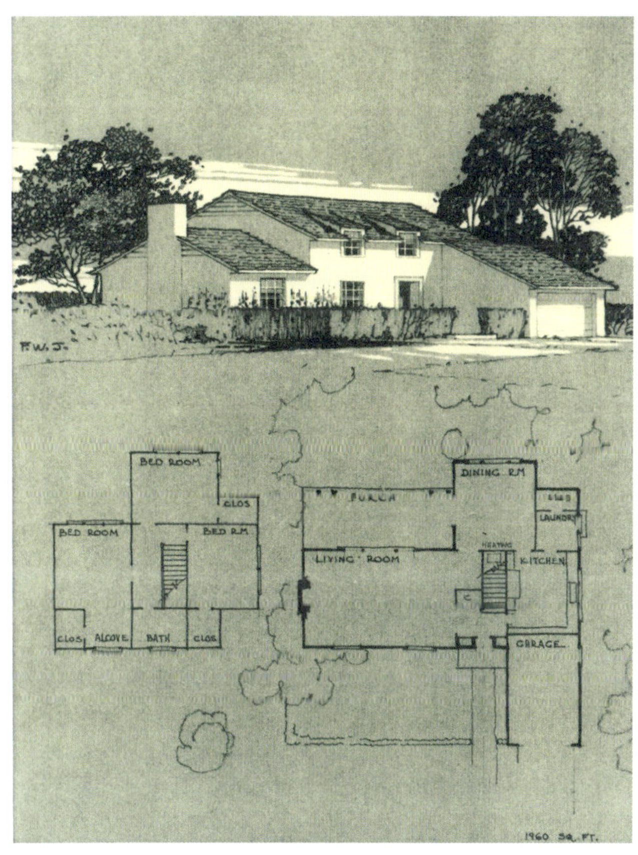

BED ROOM
CLOS
DINING RM
BED ROOM
BED RM
PORCH
LAUNDRY
LIVING ROOM
HEATING
KITCHEN
CLOS ALCOVE BATH CLOS
GARAGE
1960 SQ. FT.

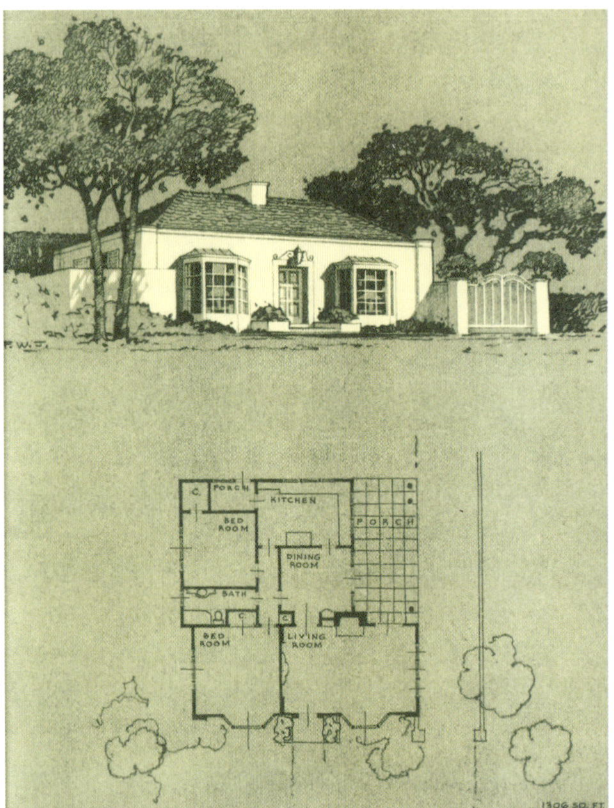

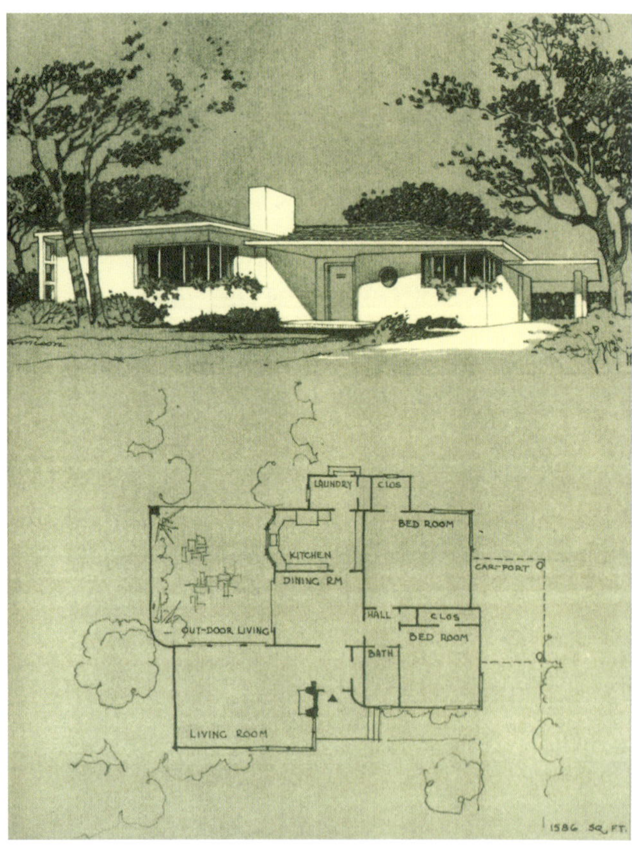

Fig. 32 (above). Paul R. Williams, "The Suburban," Frank Jamison, renderer, *The Small Home of Tomorrow* (1945), p. 35.

Fig. 33 (right). Paul R. Williams, "Contemporary Number Five," Frank Jamison, renderer, *The Small Home of Tomorrow* (1945), p. 45.

locality, or in another like it, because ...
I am a Negro.[100] (ellipses original)

In this essay written for a largely White readership, Williams's opening is a forceful description of the lived experience of racism: he encourages his readers to identify with his sense of self and professional self-sufficiency, then reminds them that although he is no different from them (and, in fact, is more accomplished than most), how society reads his skin color changes his passage through our world completely. The overriding message of Williams's essay is the importance of individual achievement as a means for surmounting racism: "I had noticed that most whites, especially those most bitterly prejudiced, seldom regard Negroes with enough attention to distinguish one from another. And while I felt the futility of any attempt to break down their aversion to my race, I believed that if I could shock, or startle, or in any way induce those white people to regard me, not as 'just a Negro,' but as Paul Williams, an *individual* Negro, I might then be able to sell my ability."[101] Just as he asks his White readers and White potential clients to see him as "an *individual* Negro," he might say that what is important in understanding a person is recognition and respect for the internal. So, too, what drives his house designs is the family life enabled by the specific interior design. The exterior style is not an afterthought, but it is fundamentally neutral in its relationship to the interior; it is another choice the client can make, but it does not bear on the qualities of the lived interior. In contrast to Nelson and Wright, who argue that Modernism is, in essence, the only ontologically correct style of the Modern era, Williams displays a radical pluralism in his approach to architectural style.[102]

Finally, racialized identities also circulate through these texts when the concept of "freedom" is invoked. "Freedom" is applied to different contexts, and frankly seems to mean different things, for Williams and for Nelson and Wright. Although I have already cited Williams on the topic of freedom and interiors, the passage in *Small Home of Tomorrow* bears more extended quotation: "[Modern design's] broad sunlight windows, its close proximity to the outdoors and uncluttered interior give one a new sense of freedom. Much of our living is now outdoors and we have moved to the rear of the house near the garden, the patio, or the terrace. The living room, dining room and sometimes a bedroom all fitted with large windows are grouped around this outside area."[103] His text evokes the experience of bodily freedom: the body freed from confined, cluttered living spaces, the body free to explore the outdoors, and, importantly, the body free to enjoy the outdoors in a private garden or backyard. This association appears elsewhere in Williams's books in his use of the word "rambling" to describe large living rooms in houses designed for the countryside ("a large rambling living room is the dream of many city dwellers") or for an independent bachelor ("large, informal, rambling, all-purpose living room with adjoining bar").[104] The term connotes unconstrained, leisurely walking in a natural environment, an experience that few Black Americans may have had in this period of resurgent racism and entrenched Jim Crow laws across the South.[105] Williams's houses provide the space for that freedom, even if they cannot rewrite the American landscape at large.

Nelson and Wright are also concerned about freedom, but they focus the term on a different object: freedom from social conformity. In the schematic political and cultural history of the twentieth century that they offer in their opening chapter, they propose that industrial growth after World War I brought the "average citizen" unprecedented economic freedom, "But for the most part he was like a chip tossed around in a strong current, and of this kind of freedom he was terrified." They warn: "When people become afraid of freedom, they try to give it up. They regiment themselves, because regimentation provides a comforting sense of security, of belonging to something. The comfort doesn't last, but people try anyway." With a quick gloss on contemporary politics, offered just as the Second World War has finally ended, they turn to their real concern:

> We know how regimentation worked in Germany and Italy. In our own country it is less blatant, because what we are destroying is cultural, not political, freedom. Every week tens of millions of people rush to the movies, where the usual film preaches that there is no need to worry—there is always a happy ending. … Over a million people belong to "clubs" which tell them what books to buy. … Modern man, put into a spot where he can't function on canned opinion, tends to get lost. He has no confidence in his taste or judgement. He is regimented.
> And so with our houses.[106]

Their concern is stridently expressed and passionate, and yet it also embodies the blindness of cultural Whiteness on the eve of the war's end. African Americans fought to defend the freedom of the American "lifestyle" in the military across Europe, only to return to a White-dominant society that did not grant them the same levels of freedom as those perceived to be racially White. Nelson and Wright did not intend any racialized meaning in their text, but their concern for freedom from social conformity, when so many Americans were not granted basic freedoms of access, education, and opportunity, reveals an unconscious position of White privilege. Put another way, it is the privilege of Nelson and Wright's presumed White readership to be lectured on the risks of willingly giving up freedoms at a time when many Americans of color were routinely denied those freedoms.

Scholarship on mid-century Modernism is strengthened if we can recognize the presence of this Whiteness and then see how it structures and limits the conversation. It appears again, later in Nelson and Wright's book, in veiled terms that become more legible to us when compared against Williams's text. Williams celebrates the backyard and the increased space of suburban lots not only for the "freedom" they allow; as he says, "there is also the matter of added privacy."[107] His texts suggest that privacy in the backyard or on the terrace might be linked to freedom—freedom from prying eyes or the judgment of White eyes, perhaps. Nelson and Wright, in contrast, rationalize the progressive reorientation of the house toward the backyard as a question of safety and defense against the dangers of the street: "A few decades ago the main rooms of a house were invariably placed on the street side. For this there were good reasons. Streets were relatively safe and quiet. Today the street can offer nothing more than noise, gasoline fumes, and danger, and there has been a steadily growing tendency, therefore, to reverse the old approach and put the living-rooms at the back where they could be tied in with the family's private garden."[108] Their rhetoric constructs a binary between dangerous and safe, smelly and natural, criminal and law-abiding, all of which terms also carry racialized associations: non-White and White. Indeed, Nelson and Wright's language describes a racialized understanding of space that has been theorized by sociologist George Lipsitz: "The white spatial imaginary idealizes 'pure' and homogeneous spaces, controlled environments, and predictable patterns of design and behavior."[109]

The ex-nominated Whiteness that shapes the Modernism of these White authors is not legible when we allow Whiteness to be the presumed standard, but it is thrown into some relief when we bring Williams into the conversation. Indeed, the model of Modernism that he sketches for his readers differs importantly from those of Nelson and Wright, the Wrights, and even Brandt. Williams presents Modernism as a style that is less invested in establishing boundaries against something and more committed to promoting the agency of those living within it, more willing to stand as one choice among many rather than the inevitably correct answer. Although the shifts in emphasis are subtle, it is possible that they point to a counter-discourse of Modernism. Williams himself cannot represent an entire counter-narrative, to be sure. However, to the extent that his books initiate conversations with readers and model a set of ideas for a broader audience, they may represent one building block that contributes to a larger counter-history of Modernism. Rather than a Modernism defined by distinctions and oppositions, it is a Modernism rooted in the contingency of everyday life that enables choice and action. This Modernism is neither categorically distinct from nor mutually exclusive of the Modernism presented by authors such as Nelson and Wright; the counter-narrative arises from the different values and focal points.

Conclusion: Interior Design as Control

Lest we be too bold in demarcating the distinctiveness of Williams's counter-discourse of Modernism, it is worth remembering that he, alongside the other authors studied in this chapter, understands Modernism as a force that governs gendered bodies and identities to some degree. Williams and Brandt, together, actually forge a fascinating dialogue on the subject of interior design and control. They are the only two authors, of those studied here, who provide clear rules for interior design and decoration, and who recommend one particular strategy for figuring out how to furnish living spaces: use graph paper to draw room plans and then, with "small cardboard cut-outs drawn to the scale of the furniture," suggests Williams, "try numerous arrangements on the floor plan of the room."[110] Brandt gives her readers step-by-step instructions so that they know what to expect: "most of your furniture will look like squares or rectangles. … These flat furniture drawings will give the effect of looking down on the furniture from the ceiling. From this position you would not see the legs or under parts of the furniture, only the tops" (fig. 34).[111] Once readers have been oriented, however, she quickly turns it into a game. "From then on the fun begins. It is a fascinating evening of entertainment to arrange the little black templates in one way or another on your floor plans."[112] The "game" of a room on graph paper with movable furniture cut to scale appears repeatedly in these years in a wide range of venues, including a 1940s home-decorating television show hosted by Paul MacAlister and advertisements for Herman Miller's interior-decorating services.[113] As a strategy for figuring out room designs, it gives the homemaker virtual omnipotence: she delineates her room on the inchoate, endless space of the graph paper, and then arranges and rearranges heavy furniture with the merest flick of a finger. As long as she can read the floor plan as a rendering of her own domestic space, she can evaluate multiple configurations through the eyes of her own needs, her friends' judgment, and her husband's and children's assessment. The mental work required to make the translation between plan and room is, again, knowledge that she creates as she "plays," and the insidious sum of this knowledge is that her home is always a site for appraisal by others. It might be more accurate to suggest that the floor-plan game gives the homemaker the illusion of omnipotence: it is, in fact, yet another tool through which social expectations are channeled, and another way that the design of the home becomes a vehicle of social control. Furniture is dropped onto the graph paper as the housewife attempts to forge an ideal "conversation group" or "work area" out of the extant ingredients of her home.

In a final merging of social and bodily control, both Brandt and Williams propose that graph paper can reveal a room's appropriateness to the passage of the human body. As Brandt notes, "Be sure there are traffic lanes that give easy access to closets and doorways," and offers a compelling (or shaming?) counterpoint sketch: a room so full of competing objects that visitors must follow a road sign to pass through it (fig. 35).[114] Williams concurs. "The furniture should always be plotted on the preliminary house plans," he advises. "Be sure passageway is left thru the room so that one

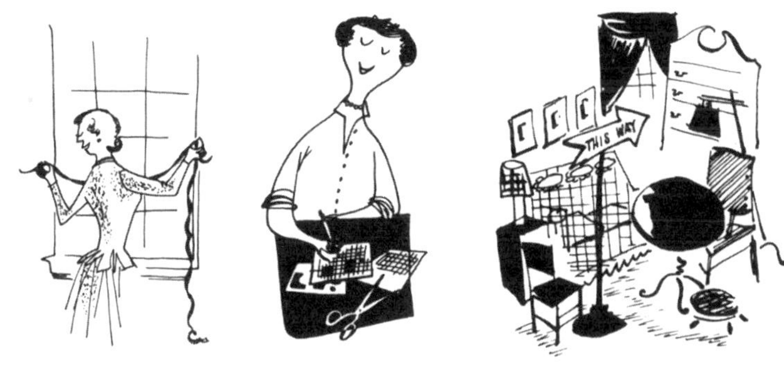

Fig. 34 (right). Marylin Hafner, decorative spot, p. 11. From *Decorate Your Home for Better Living* by Mary L. Brandt. Charles Scribner's Sons, 1950. Courtesy of the estate of Marylin Hafner.

Fig. 35 (far right). Marylin Hafner, decorative spot, p. 12. From *Decorate Your Home for Better Living* by Mary L. Brandt. Charles Scribner's Sons, 1950. Courtesy of the estate of Marylin Hafner.

may move freely from one room to another."[115] Yet once again, the points of emphasis made by each author are subtly different. Where Brandt tells us that the body must be directed along specific axes lest the room become a jumble of social faux pas, Williams reminds us that the goal of a good arrangement is bodily freedom. Neither author is specifically writing about Modernism in these passages, but their understanding of design and control is ultimately revealing. Both are concerned about meeting social expectations, but they implicate the embodied experience of those expectations differently: one—Brandt—uses it to restrict, whereas the other—Williams—uses it to preserve an arena in which to "move freely." Out of these differences, the strands of a counter-discourse of Modernism begin to come into focus.

Readers of these books in the postwar years may have opened their covers in order to learn about Modernism and to improve their houses and lifestyles, but as all six of these authors demonstrate, the authorial voice of advice literature and the authoritative control of Modernism were imbricated in a complex story about efficiency, freedom, and identity. Books were not the only place where consumers learned about Modernism in the home, however. Magazines were another major source of information, both through articles and editorial photographs and through the continually expanding world of consumer advertising. While magazines devoted to interior decorating thrived in the 1950s—titles such as *Better Homes and Gardens*, at thirty-five cents per month, or *House Beautiful* and *House and Garden* at fifty cents per month—Modern design arguably found a larger readership through the circulation of general-interest periodicals including *Life* and *Ebony*. What readers might have learned about Modernism from those two publications over the decade of the 1950s is the subject of the next chapter.

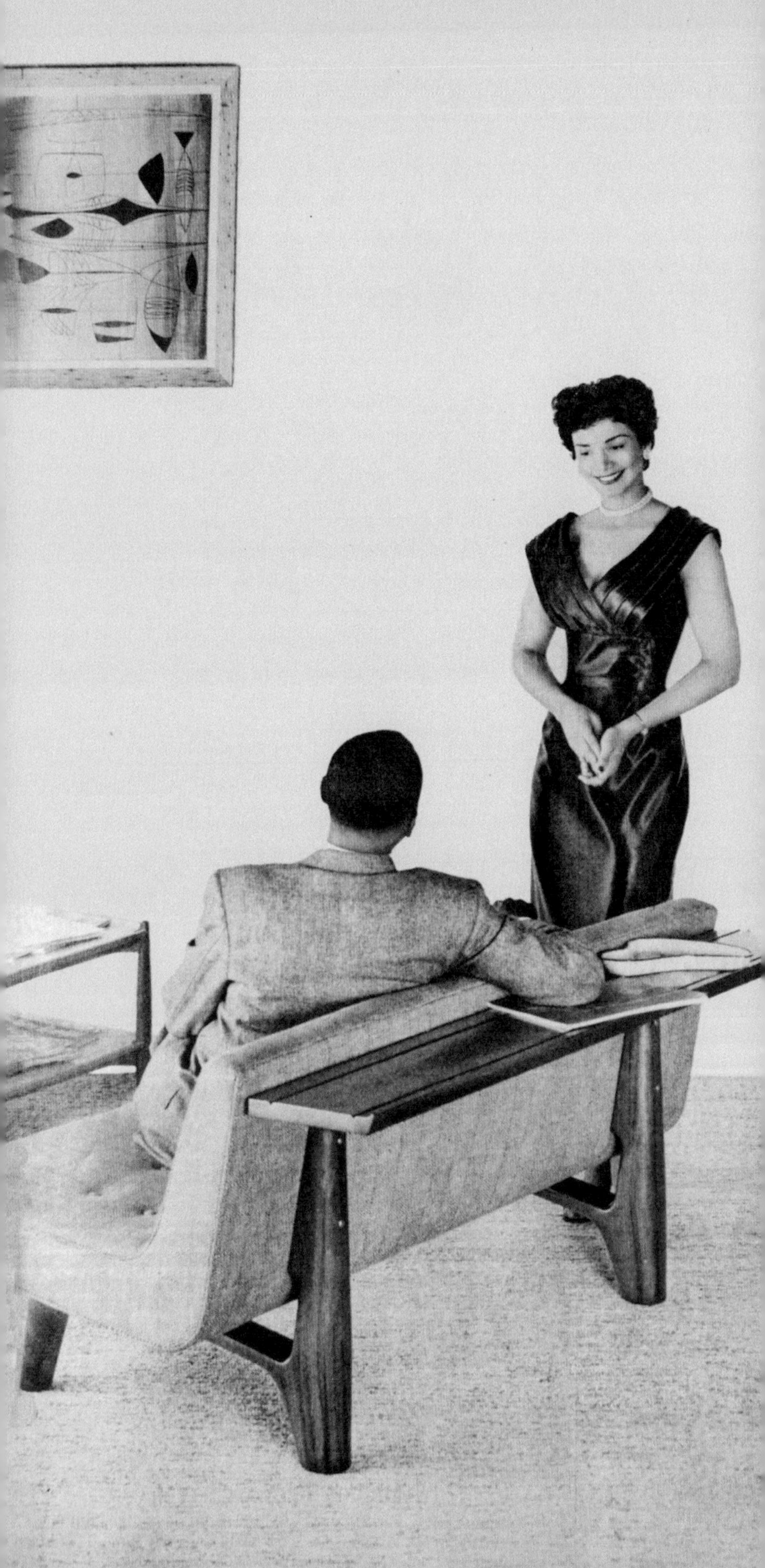

"Modern Design? You Bet!"
Ebony, *Life*, and Modernist Design, 1950–1959

In a 1954 advertisement for Chicago Metropolitan Mutual Assurance Company, the beaming couple are almost upstaged by the dramatic sofa on which the husband sits (fig. 36). The camera—and we, the viewers—approach the two in their home from behind the sofa. The upholstered seat and back are forged in a continuous, curved form, and are supported by a dramatically grained wood frame. The wood has been carved into two rounded, sculptural shapes that adhere to the back of the sofa, tapering as they rise and terminate, like two lily pad stems, in a trim shelf. The husband, his back to us, looks toward his fashionably dressed wife who, in her glimmering cocktail dress, pearl choker, and broad smile, quickly surpasses the sofa in our visual interest. The domestic space is further outfitted with a wood coffee table carved in gently biomorphic curves and a Miro-like work of abstract art on the wall.

Although the advertisement is for an insurance company, the photograph and its accompanying tagline—"Modern Design? You Bet!"—could easily be mistaken for a furniture promotion. The ad copy celebrates the "wonderful pride of ownership" that accompanies "the purchase of your first piece of furniture," and establishes material acquisition as the prerequisite for responsible adulthood. It further suggests that for a modern couple, Modern furniture and a modern insurance policy are necessary tools for executing a middle- or upper-class lifestyle. The Chicago Met advertisement is significant in the context of this study because of what it represents: an African American company speaking to the readership of the largest-circulation American magazine intended for a Black audience.[1] It is an example of image production made by and for the specific cultural experience of Black America, and it presents African American domesticity outfitted in Modern design.

Fig. 36. Advertisement for Chicago Metropolitan Mutual Assurance Company (detail), *Ebony*, December 1954, 89.

Is it possible that Modern design, when understood within the context of mid-century African American consumer culture, resonated with associations different from those it evoked within mid-century White American consumer culture?

This chapter examines the presence of Modern design in *Life* and *Ebony* magazines during the decade of the 1950s.[2] In both venues, Modernism was a symbol of the imagined "good life," and thus invested with optimism. However, the essential values and qualities of that fantasy lifestyle varied between the two groups. I argue that Modernism signified different priorities and ideals for the distinct consumer audiences of each magazine's readership: in *Life* Modernism was commonly associated with cleanliness, control, and affordability, whereas in *Ebony* Modernism resonated with sociability, bodily comfort, and elite class distinction. These differences are meaningful as indicators of the different lived experiences of White and Black Americans in the 1950s consumer world, where the Jim Crow system of segregation persisted throughout the South and cast long shadows in the North. These differences also suggest that Modernism, in each magazine, was a prop used to perform racial identity for the fantasy lives of its readers: readers encountered Modernism in *Life* as an accessory for an emerging identity of middle-class Whiteness, whereas in *Ebony* Modernism set the stage for the imagining of a particular African American upper- and upper-middle-class life.

As has been well documented, *Ebony* began publication in 1945 as a self-conscious copy of *Life*. It not only imitated the basic logo design and interior layout of the older magazine, but it also aimed to provide the same kind of reader experience: it relied heavily on photographic journalism, as did *Life*, and embraced a wide editorial range, including profiles of business leaders and entertainers, fashion, global politics, and art.[3] *Life* magazine had achieved one of the highest circulations of any periodical in the country by the later 1950s, according to a study conducted by Alfred Politz Research.[4] Almost one-quarter of the adult population in America read *Life*, and its demographic was disproportionately middle- and upper-middle-class educated Whites. *Ebony*'s readership in the 1950s was largely African American, and because it was sold primarily through newsstands rather than by subscription up until the middle of the decade, it had a large urban audience.[5] According to the magazine's own promotional material, its readership in the early 1950s was predominantly middle- and upper-middle-class African Americans, about one-quarter of whom had attended college and one-third of whom were homeowners; by 1959 it claimed that "an amazing 79 per cent of Negro households read EBONY magazine."[6] The audiences of *Life* and *Ebony* were thus roughly comparable, though by no means identical. Both publications were popular among professional, educated adults who were able to purchase automobiles and television sets, who owned (or aspired to own) their homes, and who self-identified as middle-class. It is important to recognize, however, that the material conditions of middle-class living differed significantly in the 1950s between White Americans and African Americans; census data, which do not break out African American households from a broader category of "nonwhite" households, list non-White household incomes as approximately 55 percent of White incomes.[7] Yet both magazines promoted a view of middle-class living anchored by homeownership and a community composed of fellow consumers.

This chapter investigates the symbolic resonance of Modernism in these two periodicals, through a study of both their editorial content and their commercial pages. As Sally Stein has persuasively argued, a reader's experience of a periodical is quite different from her experience of a book: the multiple voices and topics, the use of both text and image, and the mixture of editorial and commercial content in a periodical encourage an episodic, nonlinear encounter.[8] A reader may skip directly to an article of interest, thumb through the publication backward, or fail to discriminate between information provided by professional journalists and information provided to sell a product. I have endeavored to distinguish between editorial and advertising content in the narrative that follows. However, ultimately, the messages about lifestyle and Modernism that were conveyed by these publications were built out of the symbiotic cacophony of journalistic information and commercial address. Any scholarly assessment must acknowledge the different sources of material and yet respect the lived experience of a reader, for whom fact and fantasy intermingle.

While Modernism was an accessory of the good life—conjured forth in advertisements and articles—for readers of both *Life* and *Ebony*, its use as a signifier of racial identity was more complicated. A persistent set of codes that racialized Modern design as White appear in the editorial and advertising content of *Life*; these codes also appear in the advertisements that crossed the two publications. The racialized references are persuasive, if unstated, and they cultivate an idea of Whiteness as distinct from non-White races. In the editorial content and advertisements exclusive to *Ebony*, however, such racialized signs are largely absent. I contend that this lack itself signifies an alternative view of the good life. It suggests that for readers of *Ebony*, Modernism could be a tool used to forge a middle-class identity beyond respectable assimilation; one trope that recurs is the Modern home and community of color celebrated in and of itself, defined outside the axis of White/non-White, and potentially independent of the racial constraints of a White-dominant society. Such a reading is possible in the Chicago Met advertisement. The Modernist sofa sequesters the couple in their own home, establishing a physical space of freedom and agency. The sofa even takes on their joint identity: its right leg doubles as the woman's leg, while the man's suit blends into its upholstery. It thus embodies the strength of their married union and constructs an independent space to preserve it. We, the visitors, are perpetually on the outside of this domestic scene. The history of Modern design has, to date, privileged the White contexts in which it appeared, but through the lens of *Ebony* Modern design is revealed to have different contours. In concert with my argument in chapter 1, this chapter offers more than one narrative about Modernism, and proposes that in the popular culture of these magazines, we can see both a familiar discourse of Modernism and a counter-discourse of Modernism. If in *Life*, Modernism signifies control, discipline, and cleanliness—in short, the preservation of a newly articulated sphere of Whiteness—by contrast, in *Ebony*, Modernism is a sign of social confidence, economic success, and physical comfort. It is a tool to create an arena of empowerment for bodies of color.

Ebony and *Life*: Editorial Content
The Professional Modernists

Modernism coursed throughout the editorial pages of *Life* and *Ebony* in the form of feature articles on design, architecture, and art; accessories for fashion spreads; and in the interior settings of individuals profiled in the magazines. A comparison of several feature articles introduces key thematic differences between the Modernism that *Ebony* presented and the Modernism that *Life* offered. As a weekly, *Life* had more editorial inches than *Ebony* to devote to coverage of the arts and probably devoted a larger percentage of its editorial space to that subject than did *Ebony*. For example, *Life* published articles on major European Modern artists (including Raoul Dufy, Constantin Brancusi, and Georges Rouault), whereas *Ebony*'s coverage was largely focused on artists practicing in the United States. In addition, *Life* published articles on the history of art before the Modern era and ran several feature articles over the course of the decade about major art institutions (Philadelphia Museum of Art, Portland Art Museum, Metropolitan Museum of Art), two topics that *Ebony* did not cover.[9] However, *Ebony* regularly featured articles on established fine artists—among the individuals profiled during the 1950s were Jacob Lawrence, Richmond Barthé, and Marion Perkins—and it is accurate to state that it, like *Life*, considered the fine and applied arts an appropriate part of its journalistic mandate. Indeed, there are striking moments of coincident editorial projects. In 1951, both magazines published profiles of figurative sculptors who carved bulbous, abstracted bodies out of stone: Chaim Gross (*Life*, January 8, 1951) and Marion Perkins (*Ebony*, October 1951).[10] Both published articles in 1952 about artists whose artistic practice was essentially untutored, yet had resulted in professional recognition: *Life* profiled a retired dentist who made sculptural assemblages, while *Ebony* reported on a painter whose day job was as a janitor.[11]

In particular, two editorial subjects shared by these magazines in the 1950s illustrate how Modernism could be a tool of everyday, postwar middle-class living. Both publications reported on the careers of notable Modernist furniture designers, and both published articles that surveyed the up-and-coming generation of painters. In these articles, Modernism was presented as a profession, and the products created by these professional Modernists became objects that the middle- and upper-middle-class reader could own in literal and metaphorical ways. Literally, a reader might buy a table designed by profiled subjects Charles Eames or Add Bates. Metaphorically, a reader took possession of the field of Modern design or contemporary painting by learning about the objects; the paintings themselves might not enter a household, but their color reproductions in the pages of the magazines became part of the visual vocabulary of subscriber homes, arrayed on a coffee table or—as discussed in chapter 4—even hung on the walls. As readers contemplated acquiring such objects and paintings, the associations that attached themselves to Modernist practice in the 1950s became a part of the landscapes of their homes.

In the fall and winter of 1950–51, *Life* and *Ebony* both ran articles that profiled the work of an accomplished Modernist furniture designer: in September 1950, *Life* ran an article on the career and, more specifically, the recently constructed house, of Charles Eames, while in February 1951, *Ebony* published a piece on the career of furniture designer Add Bates.[12] The articles are remarkably similar in structure: both begin with a lead text and two photographs, then feature a few pages of photographs of the designer's work, and conclude with a final page of text that discusses the designer's broader career and philosophy. Yet despite the similar layout, the articles convey two very different views of Modern design. Indeed, while Eames's work is well known to design historians, when it is placed in dialogue with Bates's work, less recognized aspects of his aesthetic sensibility come to the fore.

The title page for each article includes both a photograph of the designer and a photograph of his work. In the Eames article, the larger photograph features his Los Angeles house, while a smaller photo, made by Peter Stackpole, captures the designer in his trademark bow tie, button-down shirt, and belted trousers (fig. 37).[13] In the Bates article, the larger photograph, made by Werner Wolff working for Black Star, depicts Bates in a T-shirt at work in his studio at a sanding machine, his brother, Leonard, at another worktable in the background (fig. 38); the second, smaller photograph is a view of his designs in situ in the New York apartment of "theatrical agent" William Morris, Jr. The *Life* spread emphasizes the designer's finished products, turning his physical body into an abstract design as he stands next to an air duct for his house, which has been painted with geometric patterns. His black shoes disappear into the dark floor, while his shoulders reach the height of one triangular pattern and his unsmiling face echoes the horizontal band of a second triangular design. With his hands in his pockets and hidden from view, he is not represented as a maker; he becomes simply part of the final design. In contrast, Wolff's photograph of Bates highlights his physical labor. The camera brings us right up to the edge of the massive piece of wood he is sanding, and his bare arms

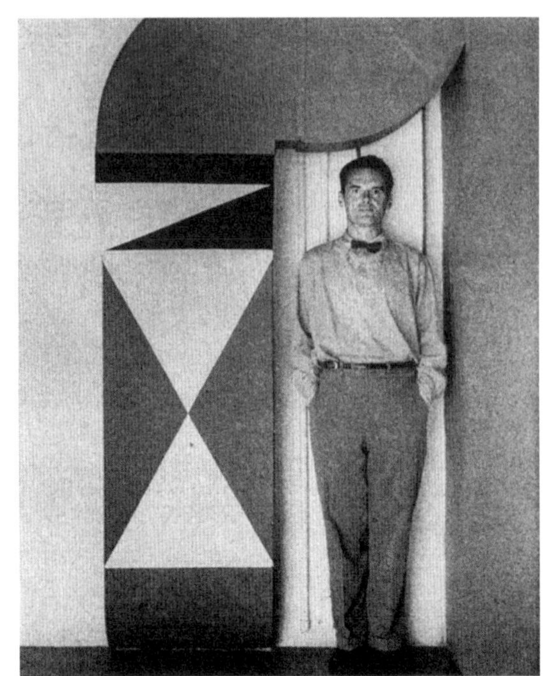

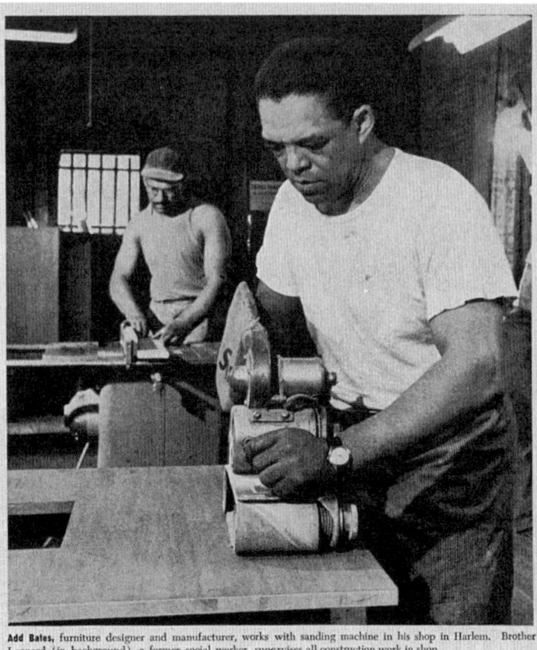

impress us with his capacity for work. Immediately behind the sander, we see Bates's brother engaged in a task at another worktable, fingers exposed in a position that connotes precision and fine skill. For the reader, the two men together dramatize the physical skill and strength that go into the fabrication of Bates's furniture.

At this moment in the early 1950s, the physicality of artistic labor was perhaps best represented in the iconic photographs of the painter Jackson Pollock at work; in the summer of 1949, before Hans Namuth made his well-known photographs, *Life* had published dramatic images of the artist painting in its notorious article "Jackson Pollock: Is He the Greatest Living Painter in the United States?" (fig. 39).[14] In the world of fine art, Pollock's physical work represented rebellion against polite artistry; it signified psychic exploration and, fundamentally, freedom. Translated to the article on Bates, the physicality of artistic production has additional meaning. Bates is not merely demonstrating artistic freedom, nor is he simply performing stereotypical masculine strength. He controls his own physical labor in an era when Jim Crow restrictions on the Black body endured. He and his brother are visually joined in the photograph, their poses almost twinned, and together they connote an artistic community. If the White artist exercises freedom in a vacuum—in a solo battle against the canvas—here the Black artist expresses his freedom through

Fig. 37 (above left). Charles Eames next to a heating duct, *Life*, September 11, 1950, 148. Peter Stackpole, photographer.

Fig. 38 (above right). Add Bates in his workshop, *Ebony*, February 1951, 70. Werner Wolff, photographer. Beinecke Rare Book and Manuscript Library. Yale University.

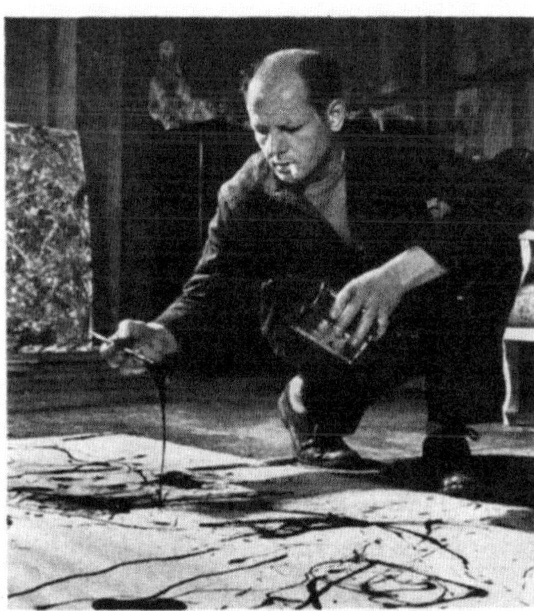

collaboration and shared labor. Indeed, the contrast between Bates's photographic representation and Eames's portrait could not be more stark. The Eames photograph removes the designer from his physical labor entirely, a point underscored by another photograph in the article that shows him not at work on a piece of furniture, but rather pinning delicate tumbleweed from the "Mojave desert" to a wall for inspiration.[15] The reader is meant to understand Eames as a cerebral artist: in his career, design products appear like Athena from the head of Zeus, arriving in the marketplace fully formed from his aesthetic vision with no messy construction that would disrupt the myth of their inevitability. In the pages of *Ebony*, artistic freedom is tightly tied to bodily expression, and Modern design does not simply appear, but rather is crafted from the hands and labor of a body.

The brief overview of Bates's career in the *Ebony* article underscores the theme of the uninhibited Black body. The final photograph shows Bates at his drafting table, the embodiment of his mental labor (fig. 40). The caption notes that he "began as an upholsterer in trade when 18 but was barred by AFL upholsterers union," and then during the 1930s "quit trade to become dancer and actor in WPA theater."[16] These few sentences trace the life story of a man who stepped away from his chosen career path when confronted with the racism of union labor and became immersed in a professional arena—dance and theater—where bodily expression was intimately tied to personal agency. Bates's career as a furniture designer has been little studied, and to date only tantalizing glimpses of information appear in the historical record. A well-known figure in Harlem social circles in the 1930s and 1940s, he received regular press coverage for his roles in dance and theater during the Great Depression.[17] As dance historian Susan Manning has noted, photographs of Bates in Edith Segal's *Black and White* were prominent symbols of racial integration for the leftist Depression-era Workers Dance League.[18] During the 1930s, Add and Leonard Bates had studios in the same building as painter Charles Alston and sculptor Henry "Mike" Bannarn at 306 West 141st Street; the building became an influential gathering place for artists and writers including Jacob Lawrence, Norman Lewis, Romare Bearden, Richard Wright, and Ralph Ellison, and was commonly known as "306."[19] Although few of Bates's individual commissions are currently known, Richard Wright claimed in a 1945 interview that he had collaborated with Bates on furniture for his own apartment.[20] Bearden later suggested that Jacob Lawrence, who was one of the youngest artists to hang around "306," ultimately became interested in depicting skilled labor in the immediate postwar years through watching Add and Leonard Bates in their shop.[21]

The articles on Eames and Bates, despite their radically different approaches to representing the work of design, espouse similar theories about Modernist design in general. Eames, whose works had previously been covered in *Life* (most recently, his prize-winning fiberglass chair designs), was described by the magazine as "a man whose chief concerns are simplicity, functionalism and economy" in design, and his already-famous plywood chairs "were based on Modernism's familiar premises of simple beauty and functional comfort."[22] Bates, on the other hand, had not appeared previously in *Ebony*, and the article's author quoted him extensively in an effort to explain the central tenets of Modern design to the magazine's readership. The design philosophy espoused by Bates shares many of the goals highlighted in the Eames article:

> Bates belongs to no particular school of designing, but like most modernists adheres to the cult of simplicity. He decries the "ornateness, fussiness and essential ugliness" of much of the traditional, Victorian-style furniture still being made today.
>
> He justifies the swift advance of modern furniture: "We are dealing with today's needs, not yesterday's. Designers are helping people to break with the past and throw off old ideas. More people today want furniture that is sensible and attractive, that is useful, comfortable, beautiful and easy to clean."[23]

While these two designers clearly shared a philosophical approach to Modern design, the designs depicted in their respective articles conveyed important aesthetic differences. Every photograph in the Eames article, while credited to Peter Stackpole, was likely the product of careful collaboration and artful construction between Stackpole, on the one hand, and the designer and his wife and partner, Ray, on the other.[24] The images

Fig. 40 (right). Add Bates at his drafting table, *Ebony*, February 1951, 73. Werner Wolff, photographer. Beinecke Rare Book and Manuscript Library. Yale University.

Fig. 41 (below). Cabinets by Add Bates, *Ebony*, February 1951, 70. Werner Wolff, photographer. Beinecke Rare Book and Manuscript Library. Yale University.

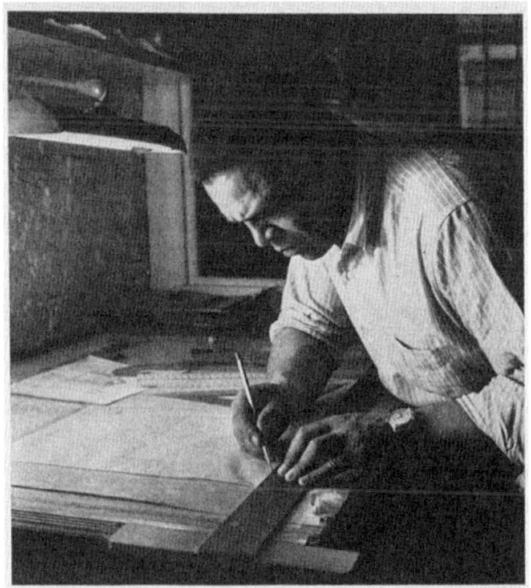

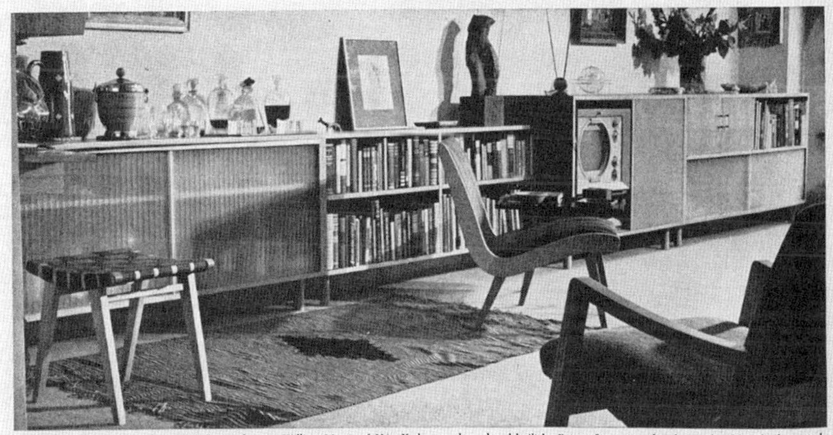

emphasize repeated geometric patterns in the house and in their designs, with no intrusion of ornament. Even on the wall of tumbleweed, a grid-like organization contains the tangles of whimsy, suggesting that their aesthetic vision incorporates non-Western wildness (from the "Mojave" desert) but is not defined by it. Bates's work, on the other hand, is surprisingly varied. The lead page features a photograph of a bank of living room cabinets that he designed and fabricated (fig. 41). This multifunctional grouping features minimalist rectilinear contours (similar to those in the Eames house) contrasted with short cylindrical legs and includes innovations such as frosted glass doors across a bar cabinet. Yet the article also includes examples of period-influenced breakfronts (one with latticework windows, another with crown molding and paneling) that Bates created for specific clients.

He states his preference for Modernist simplicity, but his work reveals the pressures of most furniture makers: his products must vary aesthetically in response to client demands.

Ultimately, it is the professional landscapes occupied by the two designers that differ, rather than their philosophies. Eames, the *Life* article explains, works with a team of designers in a workshop near his home, but he is "a vague businessman, [and] does not know how much money his chair has made for him."[25] Bates, in contrast, is presented as an active owner of his own growing business: "In three years his firm has grown from a one-room workshop operating deep in the red, to a $40,000-a-year business occupying two floors of a building in East Harlem."[26] Indeed, Bates's business appears to be anchored by relationships with individual clients, who "usually lean heavily on him for ideas in design," and who are pictured in the article and referenced in multiple captions.[27] The premise of the *Life* article is the broad affordability of Eames designs, and, consequently, the fact that he does not rely on individual commissions for his business. While *Life* notes that Eames would like to lower the prices of his designs further ("the modest retail price of his newest chair ($32.50) bothers him"),[28] *Ebony* emphasizes the expense of Bates's custom design and quotes him: "Custom-made furniture is more expensive than the factory-produced kind … but there are so many advantages to justify the price differential. … A human being has individual needs in everything, furniture included. That's where a custom maker comes in. The idea is to find out the tastes and needs of a person and build furniture to suit them."[29] It would seem that *Ebony* anchors the concept of Modern design not just in the physical labor of the designer, but equally in the physical comfort of the consumer. One photograph captures a woman sitting on a couch with her legs crossed on a Bates-designed Modernist cocktail table (fig. 42). This pose is not a misuse of the design, and the caption informs us that Bates designed the table to include four removable pads "on which persons can rest their feet while watching television programs." Between body and abstraction, expense and affordability, and the process and product of Modern design, *Ebony* and *Life* each emphasized different values that gave their readers profoundly dissimilar messages about the role of Modernism in their lives.

Life and *Ebony* also documented the younger generation of professional Modernist painters in a pair of articles printed at either end of the decade: in March 1950, *Life* published an article on nineteen young American artists,[30] and eight years later, *Ebony* magazine ran a similar article on young artists of import.[31] *Life* featured painter Edward John Stevens, Jr., on its cover (fig. 43), and Barbara Chase (now Barbara Chase-Riboud) appeared on the cover of *Ebony*, perched just above a street in Rome (fig. 44). As these two images suggest, there are points of overlap between the two articles. With their cover copy—"Nineteen Young American Artists" and "Leading Young Artists"—they seem to be selling a similar idea: these artists are cool people and readers will be cool, too, if they know about

Fig. 42 (right). Coffee table with removable cushions for resting feet by Add Bates, *Ebony*, February 1951, 72. Werner Wolff, photographer. Beinecke Rare Book and Manuscript Library. Yale University.

Fig. 43 (below left). Edward John Stevens holding a canvas, *Life*, March 20, 1950, cover. Arnold Newman, photographer.

Fig. 44 (below right). Barbara Chase in Rome, *Ebony*, April 1958, cover. Ettore Naldoni, photographer. Courtesy of the estate of Ettore Naldoni.

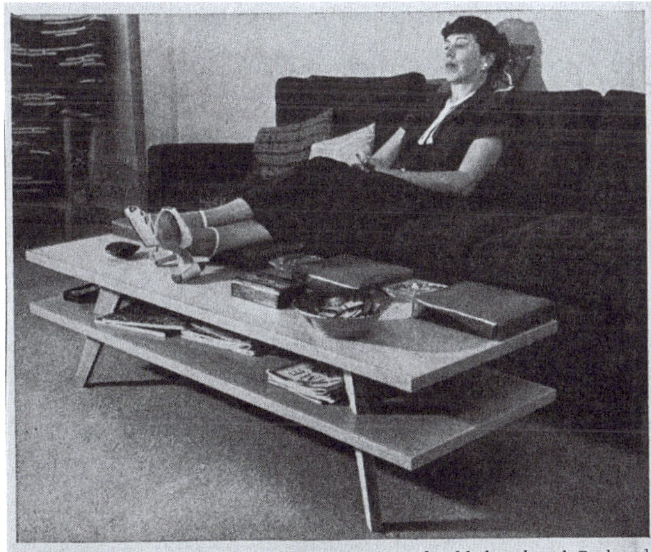
Low cocktail table designed for William Morris is made of light oak with Realwood Micarta top. The table has four rubberized hair-stuffed pads on which persons can rest their feet while watching television programs. Price: $185.

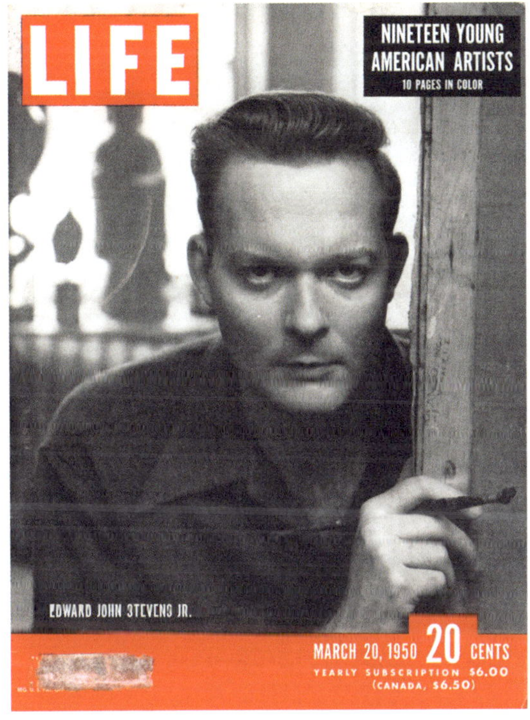

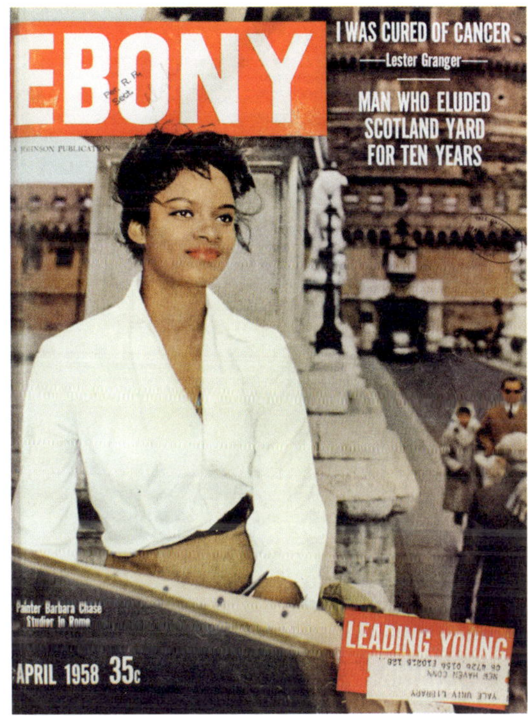

them. Yet there are also important differences between the two covers. In Arnold Newman's photograph of Stevens, the painter leans toward the camera, a quintessential tortured artist. In the background, we see the contours of several possibly non-Western sculptures creating a totem-like procession on a window sill. Stevens's head, directly in line with them, becomes yet another fetish object. In Ettore Naldoni's portrait, Chase is lit as if in a fashion shoot, framed so that we look up to her, seeing her entire torso, arms, and face; her white blouse and belted khaki skirt recall Audrey Hepburn's *Roman Holiday* costume. The photograph itself is hard to parse: she may be standing above the edge of a canvas, on which she may be working (is she holding a paintbrush in her hand?), but she is also clearly looking out onto the city of Rome. We see passersby on the street below, and they see Chase.

On the one hand, these two photographs reinforce the kind of analysis offered by art historian Ann Gibson. Stevens borrows the allegedly raw energy of the non-Western artifacts that decorate his studio—much as Eames borrowed tumbleweed from a Native American landscape—and he himself can even turn into one, without fundamentally risking his identity as a White, male member of Western society. As Gibson argues about mid-century Abstract Expressionism: "What distinguished the use of signs of ethnicities and sexualities that were *not* Caucasian and *not* heterosexual and male was precisely the binary it established between their 'modern' abstraction and that of other cultures and genders, and the position of control in which it placed the modern. To incorporate what was not-self was to master it and at the same time to claim its attributes."[32] Chase cannot afford to be limited by the associations to irrationality and primitivism that her race carries in the United States, and thus positions herself in the heart of the White, Western canon: ancient and Renaissance Rome. On the other hand, while such a reading is plausible, it may deter additional lines of analysis that allow us to further complicate this comparison. Why has Stevens been turned into an object in this photograph, while Chase is framed so that we—and the other figures in the photograph—are beneath her? She is visible, active, and in a position of relative power, higher than us. The Stevens cover does emphasize his interiority, while the Chase cover broadcasts her exteriority, her place as an object of the male gaze (perhaps ours, perhaps that of the man in sunglasses on the sidewalk). And yet, even as she is prevented from returning our gaze, her pose suggests self-confidence: she has a right to see the world, and, indeed, to be seen by the world—to be recognized as a professional.

The articles themselves share several themes. Both present their contemporary art in the context of a historical trajectory: *Ebony* argues that the current generation has broken free of the racial restrictions that shaped the careers of painters of the Harlem Renaissance, while *Life* suggests that the current generation of American painters has broken free of the tyranny of European artistic superiority that reigned "before the war."[33] Both

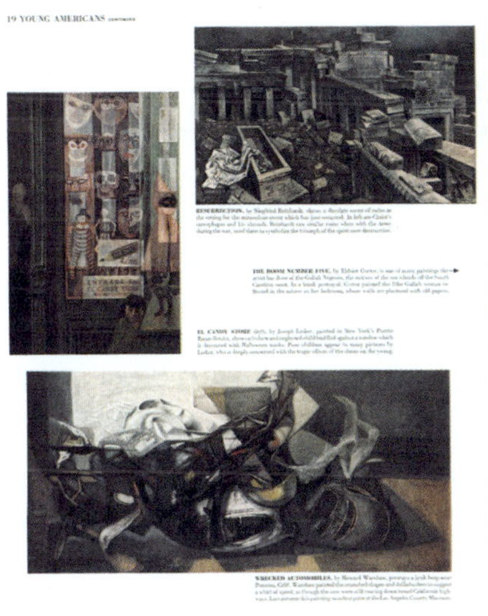

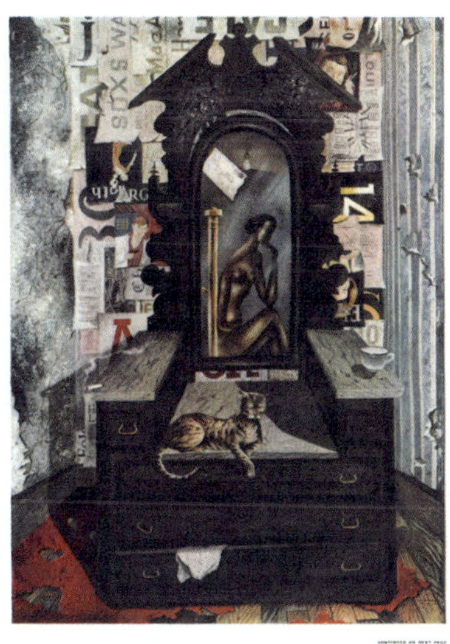

Fig. 45. "Nineteen Young American Artists," with paintings by Siegfried Reinhardt, Joseph Lasker, Howard Warshaw, and Eldzier Cortor. *Life*, March 20, 1950, 84–85.

feature a broad stylistic range of work, including expressive abstraction (Edwin E. Lewis and Barbara Chase in *Ebony*, and Theodoros Stamos and Hedda Sterne in *Life*), landscape paintings (Hughie Lee-Smith and Norma Morgan in *Ebony* and Aleta Cornelius and Hubert Raczka in *Life*), and the human figure. *Life* dedicates two spreads to examples of figurative paintings, and one includes the sole African American artist of the nineteen, Eldzier Cortor (fig. 45). Cortor's presence in the article, and the fact that he receives a full-page reproduction for *Room No. V* (1948), might reflect an inclusive editorial vision, but it also puts on display for *Life*'s largely White readership a nude female African American body, which the accompanying caption identifies as such: "*The Room Number Five* … is one of many paintings the artist has done of the Gullah Negroes, the natives of the sea islands off the South Carolina coast. In a frank portrayal, Cortor painted the lithe Gullah woman reflected in the mirror in her bedroom."[34] The selection of Cortor's figurative oeuvre, and its description, suggest that for White editors, curators, and readers, African American artists are expected to depict African American lives and are expected to speak for their race, first and foremost.

The two articles are notably different, however, in their journalistic tone. The *Life* article professes a considerable amount of skepticism about the overall value of the art. On its opening page, it summarizes its goals as such: "Seen as a whole, the[se] paintings raise many provocative questions concerning the future of U.S. art. Do they show serious attempts to evolve original and compelling styles—or are they still cluttered with stereotyped mannerisms? … In short, are they the signs of a new flowering of American art?"[35] With this tone, the article solicits populist buy-in from the reader: it willingly puts the art up for scrutiny, rather than adopting a professorial posture informing the reader that experts have already decreed the value of the work depicted.

In contrast to *Life*, *Ebony*'s rhetoric is unabashedly celebratory. The article announces, "The artists whose paintings are shown [here] … were chosen by EBONY as representative of a gifted group of Negroes who are making notable contributions to the nation's art."[36] This tone is, in general, in keeping with the publication as a whole. Moreover, its treatment of the artists' racial themes is notable: the article asserts, for example, that "while their styles differ … [these] artists share in common a noticeable degree of emancipation from purely racial subject matter."[37] It describes how Black artists in the 1920s and 1930s fought "hard to break clear of racial labels and to be regarded as individual painters who only incidentally happened to be Negroes," and says this about the current art scene: "Only a small number of today's younger Negro artists deal exclusively with Negro subject matter, and this group is rapidly thinning out."[38] On the one hand, the article offers trenchant resistance to the view in the White-dominant art world that an artist of color can speak only to experiences of color; it makes the claim that African American artists can speak to broadly human concerns: "Negro painters, like others in the profession, seek their subjects in the great wide world around them and use their individual skills and style to communicate their feelings."[39]

On the other hand, *Ebony*'s article does not seem to actually reflect the artistic goals of many of its artists, who avowed the importance of their race as a central part of their projects. The Opportunity Fellowship Program of the John Hay Whitney Foundation—many of the featured artists had been Opportunity fellows—was designed to provide educational support specifically to racial and ethnic minorities from underprivileged backgrounds in the United States. Many of these artists' applications pointedly discussed the importance of their racial heritage in their proposed art projects. Barbara Chase planned to travel to the "Negro Republics" of West Africa during her fellowship in order to study "Negro Art." Paul Keene, Jr., wanted to study form and space in "African primitive arts." Charles White planned to use his fellowship to create a series of prints that expressed "the meaning behind the spirituals, secular work and blues songs of the Negro people."[40] Merton Simpson, featured in the article but not a fellowship winner, became known in the later 1950s and 1960s as an influential dealer of African art.[41] It would seem that the article's claim that these artists transcend race in their work is more the agenda of *Ebony* and less so that of the artists themselves, and is in keeping with publisher John H. Johnson's editorial philosophy. Throughout the 1950s, the magazine defined Black success as individuals transcending race and achieving success on their own terms, in a self-referential bubble like that of the couple ensconced in their Modernist living room in the Chicago Met ad (see fig. 36).[42]

The two articles also differ in the way they use illustrational materials. In the *Life* article, readers encounter ten pages of color reproductions of works of art before they see any of the artists, who are collected together on the final page in a series of headshots that reduce them to so many cogs in an art-world wheel (fig. 46). In *Ebony*, every photograph includes the artist with his or her work. Sometimes the artist is posed next to the work, as in J. Edward Bailey's portrait of painter Paul Keene (fig. 47). Sometimes the artists are actually working on a painting or are holding their physical creations; photographer Howard Morehead captures Charles White leaning on a painting, paintbrush in hand (fig. 48).[43] In all cases, they are thoroughly immersed in their art. These photographs share with the Bates images what might be described as a person-centered approach to documenting art: they emphasize the physical work behind the work of art, the process rather than the isolated artistic product. *Ebony*'s photographs of Modernist painters and designers, when taken together, assert the value of everyday professional and personal actions, regardless of location or status. These artist and designer portraits exemplify the magazine's persistent promotion of individual agency in Black lives and Black professional success.[44]

But in the context of mid-twentieth-century fine art, these portraits also have a specific political resonance. As we see African American artists working on their art, lifting their art, posed in undeniable positions of owning their own creative accomplishments, we see them in action, and these images become, in a very basic way, an instantiation of action painting. Abstract Expressionism was an allegedly transcendent art idiom: according to the critical industry of the day, it spoke to universal truths of human experience and was inherently apolitical. An action painter like Pollock did not merely create art as an expression of the psyche but rather made universal statements through art.[45] When Black artists became action artists, however, something happened to transcendent apolitical posturing. In a decade when racial segregation was still the law in many states, these photographs reveal not just the politics of everyday life, but the politics of Black agency. Apolitical action painting becomes highly political painting in the hands of these artists. For readers of *Ebony*, Modernism was not merely a backdrop for everyday life or a point of academic debate, but rather was an expressive tool that invested a user with power. The photographs that make up the *Ebony* article argue that Black artists have the right to create and to be seen in the act of creating.

Professional Modernism appears elsewhere in the pages of *Ebony* and *Life*, in a context that is—at the outset—less profound than the articles just discussed: it surfaces repeatedly in a long-running advertising campaign by Lord Calvert Whiskey. The "Men of Distinction" campaign ran throughout the first half of the decade and offered testimonials by various men who had "distinguished" themselves professionally, usually in the worlds of business or art. *Life* ran ads featuring, among others, Modernist architect Wyatt C. Hedrick, designer James Harley Nash, novelist Erskine Caldwell, and Caleb Hammond of the Hammond Map Company.[46] *Ebony*'s

Fig. 46 (right). "Nineteen Young American Artists," *Life*, March 20, 1950, 93.

Fig. 47 (below left). Paul Keene, Jr., next to his painting *Atlantic City*, *Ebony*, April 1958, 34. J. Edward Bailey, photographer.

Fig. 48 (below right). Charles W. White painting, *Ebony*, April 1958, 34. Howard Morehead, photographer.

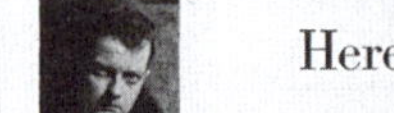

YOUNG AMERICANS CONTINUED

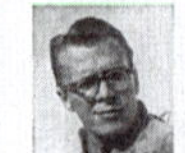

Franklin Boggs, 35

Born in Indiana, Boggs went to school in Philadelphia, was a war artist and is a resident artist at Beloit College, Wis.

Aleta Cornelius, 28

Miss Cornelius, married to ex-ski trooper, has young daughter, is teaching at a YWCA in Pittsburgh, her home town.

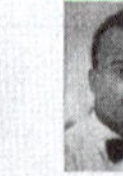

Eldzier Cortor, 34

A native of Richmond, Va., Cortor studied in Chicago and won a Guggenheim Fellowship to paint in West Indies.

Frank Duncan Jr., 34

Born in Chicago, Ill., Duncan went to Yale art school, was a war artist and has since won several Guggenheim awards.

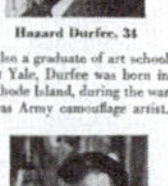

Hazard Durfee, 34

Also a graduate of art school at Yale, Durfee was born in Rhode Island, during the war was Army camouflage artist.

Dean Ellis, 28

Born in Detroit, Ellis began exhibiting at 18, was an infantryman in the Pacific. He has won several regional prizes.

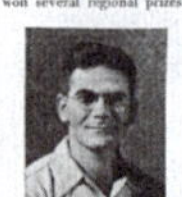

Joseph Lasker, 30

A New Yorker, Lasker works full time for a TV service company, has just won the Prix de Rome fellowship for 1950.

Here are the 19 artists

At some time during their lives these 19 young people, whose paintings LIFE has shown, gave up the American dream of making a fortune and decided to paint pictures. To keep themselves going while they painted, they made frames, taught school, took jobs as welders, shoeshine boys, glass grinders and advertising agents, won scholarships to study both here and abroad. What do they have to show for their efforts so far?

Plainly they have learned their trade well. All skilled technicians, they have assimilated both the technical innovations of the European moderns and the traditional American methods of factual reporting. The results, though derivative in some cases, are not slavish imitations. In many of their paintings, however, the techniques seem almost too perfect, as the emotions of the artist fail to rise above the mechanics of production. Though the feelings are unmistakably there, they often lack the deep convictions of maturity. The painter, a little overconscious of himself and his medium, has tried too hard and too seriously to deliver his message.

Despite their self-consciousness and immaturity, it is an encouraging sign that these young painters do have something to say about the world around them—the romance of a city in the moonlight, the bustle of an oil field, the forlornness of the slums, the treachery of the enemies of liberty. As it stands now, the work of the young Americans is vigorous, exciting and rich in variety and experimentation. What remains for them is to achieve the balance between technique and emotion that lifts a painting to the stature of greatness.

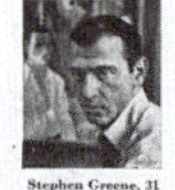

Stephen Greene, 31

Winner of the Prix de Rome fellowship last year, Greene grew up and studied in New York, has taught in Midwest.

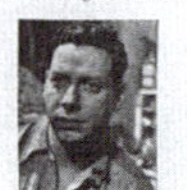
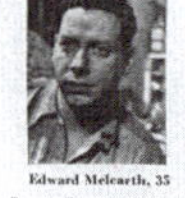

Edward Melcarth, 35

Born in Kentucky, Melcarth grew up in Europe. From there he went to Harvard and is now teaching in New York.

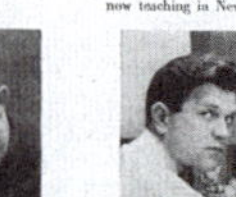

Kenneth Nack, 27

Nack, a Chicagoan, was artist for Air Force during war. He has done industrial murals in Midwest, now lives near Paris.

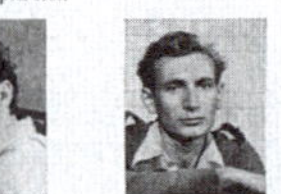

Bernard Perlin, 31

A Southerner, Perlin studied in New York, painted in Poland on a scholarship, was an artist-reporter in Near East.

Alton Pickens, 33

Born in Seattle, Pickens has won scholarships on the West Coast, has exhibited in New York, now teaches in Indiana.

Hubert Raczka, 25

A native of Buffalo, Raczka has painted there all his life except for four years of service in the Pacific with the Marines.

Siegfried Reinhardt, 24

Born in East Prussia, Reinhardt moved to St. Louis in 1928. Self-taught, he studied art by copying Old Masters.

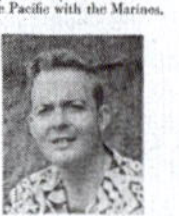
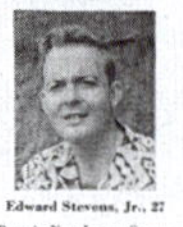

Honoré Sharrer, 29

Born in West Point, N.Y., she was taught how to draw by her mother, went on to art school at Yale, married a professor.

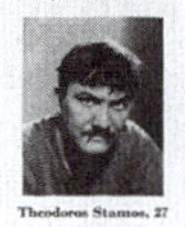
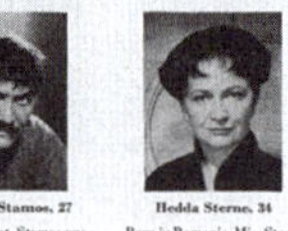

Theodoros Stamos, 27

Of Greek descent, Stamos was brought up in New York. To pay for art school, he worked as a florist and a hat blocker.

Hedda Sterne, 34

Born in Romania, Miss Sterne studied art in Paris. She came to New York in 1941, married a cartoonist, Saul Steinberg.

Edward Stevens, Jr., 27

Born in New Jersey, Stevens (cover) started exhibiting at 20, teaches in Newark, N.J., spent last summer in Africa.

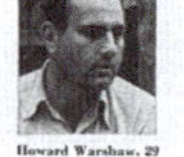
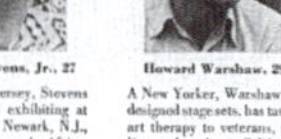

Howard Warshaw, 29

A New Yorker, Warshaw has designed stage sets, has taught art therapy to veterans, now lives and teaches in California.

93

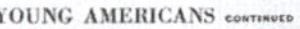

Paul Keene Jr., an Opportunity Fellowship winner, is abstract stylist, teaches at Philadelphia Museum School Of Art. Painting, "Atlantic City," is valued at $700. Keene studied in U. S., Paris, Haiti.

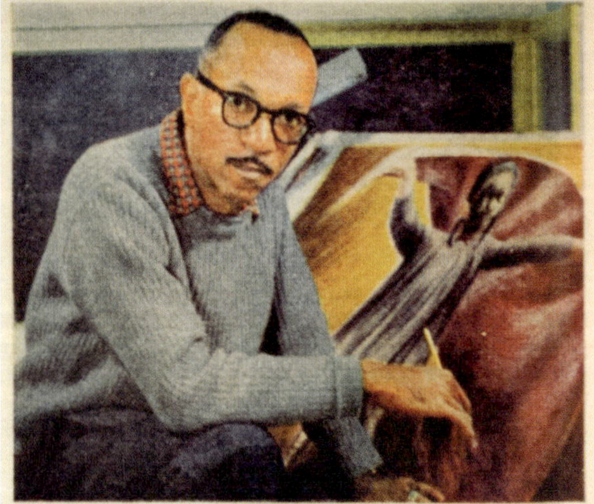

ads included Modernist architect Hilyard Robinson, graphic designer Georg Olden, actor James Edward, and publicist W. Beverly Carter.[47] In the advertisements that are published in *Life*, the men usually appear in a single portrait photograph, invariably alone, in a room that signifies their professional and financial success: in a typical example, architect Hedrick perches, one knee up in a posture of ownership, on the edge of a table next to a model of a massive office building (fig. 49).[48] In *Ebony*, by contrast, the men are always represented twice: architect Hilyard Robinson, for example, is shown first in a professional setting, meeting with a colleague over a drafting table, and secondarily as a host in his own home, gathering with two men around a cocktail table to enjoy a drink of whiskey (fig. 50). In the *Life* advertisements, the graphic design always prioritizes the tagline "For men of distinction … ," with the individual subject's name in small print. In *Ebony*, the most prominent copy incorporates the subject's name and is tailored to the testimonial — "Mr. Hilyard R. Robinson, Successful Architect … Successful Host" — while the tagline is relegated to a smaller, inset box. The Lord Calvert advertisements in *Life* promote a story of professional success as one of solitary pursuit and individual satisfaction, whereas *Ebony*'s ads tell a story of professional success that involves recognition and respect from one's colleagues and peers.[49] In fact, because the photographic rhetoric of the Lord Calvert advertisements in *Ebony* so closely mirrors its dominant journalistic mode, where protagonists are represented at work and engaged with others, they look deceptively similar to editorial content elsewhere in the magazine. This effect is further enhanced by the sequestered Lord Calvert logo and tagline. Casual readers might reasonably assume these men are subjects of short feature articles rather than spokesmen for a commercial product.[50]

Modern design can be seen in several of the Lord Calvert advertisements in *Ebony*, particularly in the homes of men who have built successful careers in the arts. Robinson is photographed wearing an elegant dark smoking robe and standing with one hand on his television, toasting two friends who are seated in a pair of Jens Risom–like webbed lounge chairs, the ice bucket and Lord Calvert bottle arranged on an amoeba-shaped plywood table between them. The caption notes that "Robinson's tastefully decorated home in Washington, D.C., reflects his success," and that he is "a charming and considerate host." In another ad, the photographer captures designer Georg Olden sprawled in a Saarinen Womb Chair, chatting with a friend happily reclined in a Risom chair, a wall of books balanced among bricks and planks of wood behind him (fig. 51). The ad describes Olden's home as "beautifully furnished," but also calls out the eccentricity of his design sensibility: "Here [at home in St. Albans, Long Island], Mr. Olden entertains friends, who are always delighted by his imaginative interior decoration."[51] Indeed, Olden may have adopted his bookshelf from the Wrights' *Guide to Easier Living*, where they suggest an "inexpensive, home-made storage wall" made of "wooden shelves placed

Fig. 49 (right). Advertisement for Lord Calvert Whiskey, *Life*, March 13, 1950, 138.

Fig. 50 (below left). Advertisement for Lord Calvert Whiskey, *Ebony*, February 1952, 47. Beinecke Rare Book and Manuscript Library. Yale University.

Fig. 51 (below right). Advertisement for Lord Calvert Whiskey, *Ebony*, October 1951, 43.

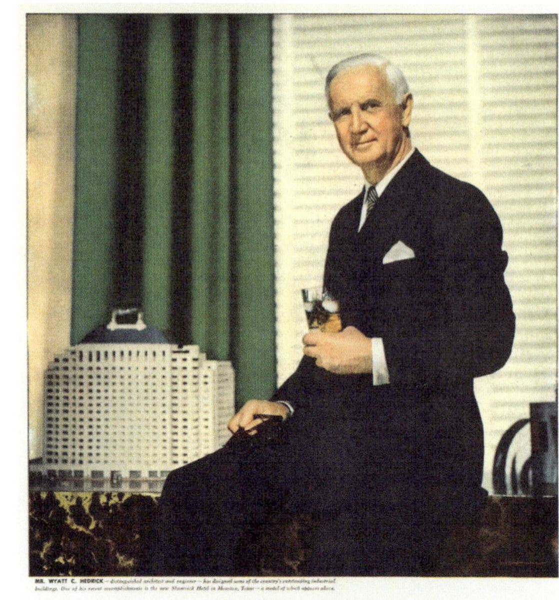

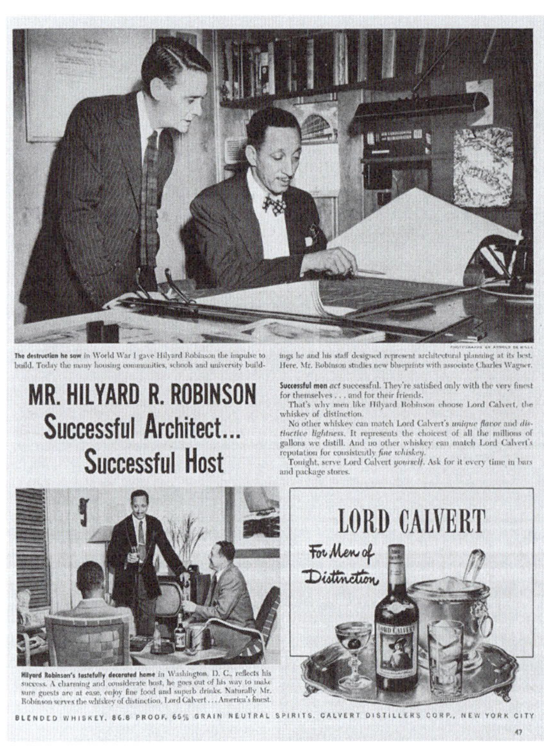

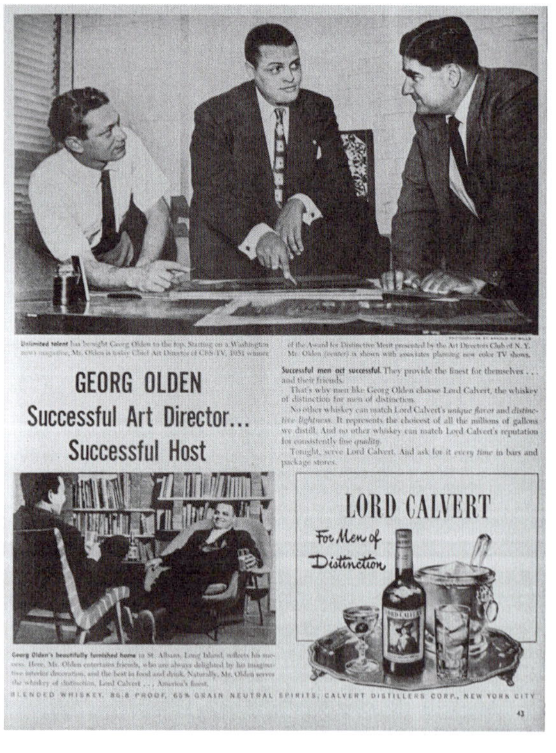

on bricks or cinder blocks."[52] *Ebony*'s Lord Calvert ads suggest a strong connection between Modern design and the lifestyles of Black professional Modernists: those engaged with visual Modernism in their professional lives carry that sensibility into their homes. Modernism is a tool of professional agency, and in the home becomes a symbol of professional success as well as a vehicle of Black bodily comfort and confident sociability.

Photographic Rhetoric: People, Spaces, and Silhouettes

While Modernism—and Modern design especially—can be seen in feature articles that address the topic, it permeates both *Ebony* and *Life* in a more diffused, broad-reaching way over the course of the 1950s. It is helpful to analyze its presence through the frameworks of three photographic styles used in editorial photography: the person-centric photograph, the interior-space photograph, and the silhouette. Each of these photographic idioms contributes to the expressive message of the magazine and helps to frame the meaning of Modernism for its readers.

The Lord Calvert photographs, despite their commercial genesis, exemplify the first photographic style: the person-centric photograph.[53] In fact, they demonstrate very effectively the challenges of reading Modernist design in the editorial pages of *Ebony* and, to a lesser degree, *Life*. The photographs of Robinson and Olden in their homes appear on the pages of *Ebony* in black-and-white reproductions that are approximately five inches wide and three inches high. They are small photographs, and the details are difficult to read. They prioritize the men and their social interactions, with the furnished setting as a largely secondary point of interest. To a more extreme degree, this kind of photographic language permeates *Ebony*'s monthly profiles of successful individuals who represent a wide variety of professional achievement: as Johnson himself explained, the magazine's mission was to celebrate the careers of "lawyers and farmers, school teachers and chorus girls, ministers and bellboys, scientists and bootblacks."[54] A profile article typically includes numerous photographs of the subject, over several pages, engaged in their work. The photographic illustrations are not merely journalistic—"journalistic" denoting that they are intended to capture newsworthy events—but rather possess a distinctive rhetorical lens that I call person-centric: the camera is positioned crouching at the hip of the subject looking up, and inevitably concentrates closely on the face and, perhaps, the upper torso and hands engaged in work; the frame might capture the subject in conversation with another person, collaborating together on a professional task, but little else is included within the boundaries of the printed image. Without fail, every article ends with a photograph of the subject at home, frequently with a spouse or family but occasionally alone, reading or listening to music. These "at home" images focus on the faces, bodies, and relationships of the sitters, and it is only at the very edge of the image (again, reproduced very small) that a reader can sometimes discern the interior setting. All of these photographs encourage the viewer to identify with the personhood of the subject, with qualities such as her fortitude, his confidence, her professional authority, or the closeness of his family. By offering positive images of African Americans to which the reader can relate, frequently made by African American photojournalists, these photographs exemplify what Deborah Willis has repeatedly described as the empowering work of photography: the power of an image to "convey a sense of worth and self-worth" in the face of a racist society.[55]

Moreover, in positioning us, the viewer, in intimate proximity with the subject, they invite us into the story and do not expect us to be taking notes on secondary issues such as the decorative context. In one typical example, the magazine profiled dancer and anthropologist Pearl Primus. Several photographs in the article highlighted her choreographic innovations and her travel and research in multiple African countries, but the final photograph, made by Dennis Stock, features her at home with her parents, her head on her mother's knee (fig. 52). As printed, this image is so tightly cropped that the edge of a chair on which her father sits and a partial view of the window treatments are the only information available about the interior setting. The photograph's logic presumes that readers want to know about Primus's relationship to her parents, who brought her to the United States at age two from Trinidad, and are less interested in how her home is decorated. A similar logic governs Jean Launois's photograph of a railroad redcap, Harold Washington, sitting at home with his wife and sons in a 1952 article profiling his career and his extraordinary linguistic skills (fig. 53). While the squared edge and nubbly fabric of the couch on which he sits, combined with the geometric pattern on the window curtains behind his sons, suggests a Modernist interior, the photograph ultimately gives the reader too little information, at too small a scale, to actually represent Modern design.[56] Instead, we are more intrigued by Washington's sons' animated energy.

The person-centric photographic language occurs in *Life* as well, although with some subtle differences. The magazine does, for example, occasionally publish photographs of a profile subject "at home," but those images tend to include more contextual information—more evidence of home-decorating style and possessions—than the ones in *Ebony*. A profile of Rudolph Bing, the recently appointed chief executive of the Metropolitan Opera, concludes with a photograph, by Eileen Darby, of Bing and his wife in their living room (fig. 54).[57] The two gaze at each other from two lounge chairs across a room sparsely furnished with eighteenth-century-styled chairs and pier table. Indeed, although the ostensible subjects of the photograph are Bing and his wife, the image conveys more about the space they inhabit than about the people themselves. If *Life* magazine tends to contextualize its profile subjects within a decorative milieu, *Ebony* resolutely emphasizes embodied experience and embodied power in its photographs. Ultimately, the prevalence of the

Fig. 52 (right). Pearl Primus with her parents at home, New York, *Ebony*, January 1951, 58. Dennis Stock, photographer.

Fig. 53 (below left). Harold Washington with wife and sons at home, Los Angeles, *Ebony*, March 1952, 72. Jean Launois, photographer. Beinecke Rare Book and Manuscript Library. Yale University. Courtesy Jean Launois/ Black Star.

Fig. 54 (below right). Rudolph Bing and wife at home, New York, *Life*, February 12, 1951, 89. Eileen Darby, photographer.

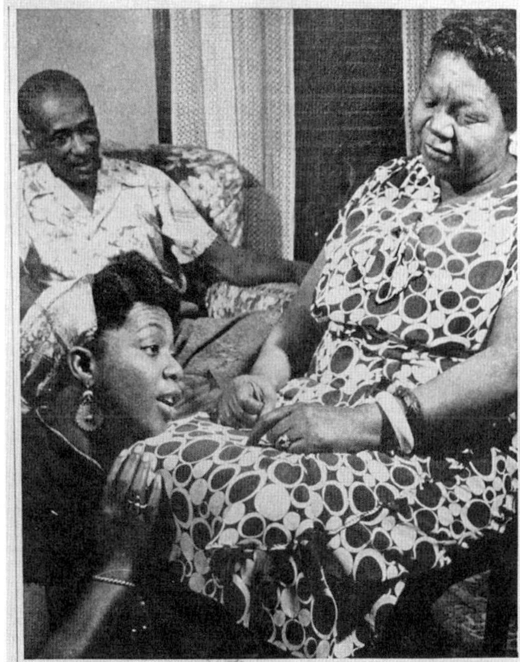

Only daughter in family of five, Pearl is deeply devoted to her parents who come from Trinidad. Pearl is a naturalized U. S. citizen. She hopes to weave African dances into a dance revue to be titled *Black Symphony*.

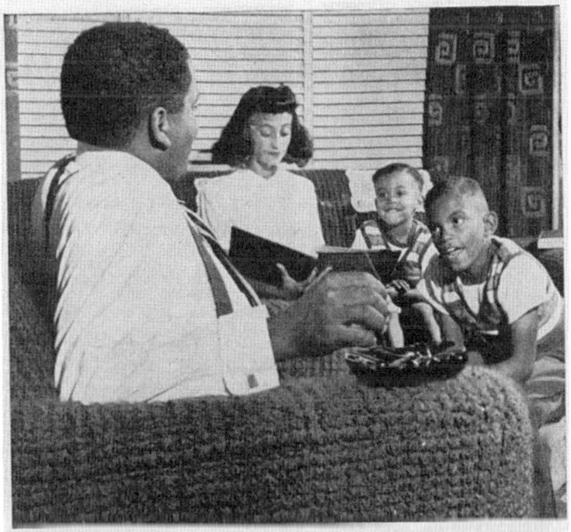

At home, Harold Washington relaxes with wife and sons, Michael Cazeau, five, and Harold, Jr., seven. Mrs. Washington is reading bedtime stories, but youngsters are more eager to hear Dad tell of his DP experience at the depot.

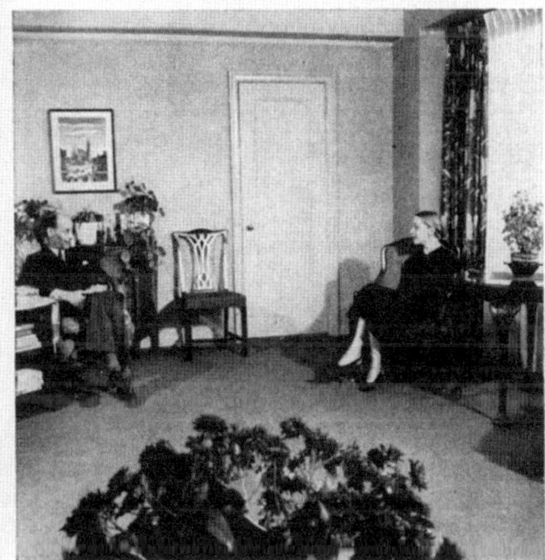

AT HOME, a three-room apartment in New York's Essex House, Rudolph Bing and wife Nina live simply and quietly in surroundings of modest elegance

person-centric photographic rhetoric makes it difficult in many instances to read Modernism in the lives represented in *Ebony*.

The *Life* photograph of Bing and his wife at home claims to be a person-centric photograph, but its rhetoric operates more in the vein of another popular photographic language: the interior-space image. As discussed in chapter 1, this type of photograph was commonly used to represent Modernist design, appearing with great frequency in shelter magazines such as *Better Homes and Gardens* or *House Beautiful*. Its logic celebrates the spaciousness of an interior setting and is characterized by a higher viewpoint than that of the person-centric photograph: in these images, the camera stands at adult height looking slightly down into a room, conveying a sense of mastery and ownership.[58] The photograph usually emphasizes an expanse of uncluttered floor and, in Modern homes, large picture-plate windows, against which the furniture is dramatically set. The furniture objects themselves become actors in the theatrical arena of the room. Although this photographic style could be used to document any type of interior, it was particularly effective for Modernist interiors, where photographers could arrange the simple contours of the Modernist furniture with contrasting, bold textures into dynamic compositions. *Better Homes and Gardens* perfected the rhetoric of the interior-space photograph in its images of Modernist homes in the early 1950s. In one typical example from 1952, a coffee table casually strewn with magazines welcomes us into a living room (fig. 55); the furniture is carefully positioned to exaggerate the openness of the carpeted floor and to highlight—and help us identify—the unusual leg design in the bench (by George Nelson), coffee table (by Isamu Noguchi), and couch (by Nelson).

As did photographers for *Better Homes and Gardens*, those working for *Life* and *Ebony* used the rhetoric of the interior-space photograph to illustrate Modernist interiors. However, ultimately this common visual language was used differently in the two publications to make contrasting statements about Modernism and class. In *Life*, the spacious rooms outfitted with Modernist furniture tend to represent middle-class affordability, whereas in *Ebony*, the photograph usually celebrates Modernism as a marker of elite living. These broad trends are by no means monolithic: examples can be found in *Life* that promote the high status of Modernism, and middle-class Modernist homes are occasionally seen in *Ebony*. However, the strongest message offered by the editorial team at *Life* is clearly in favor of Modernism's affordability, and at *Ebony*, the elitism of Modernism.

Life uses the rhetoric of interior-space photography to present Modern design in homes marked as broadly affordable in articles throughout the decade. In 1953, it introduces Herman Miller's designs as wise choices for cost-conscious readers.[59] In its January 5 issue, the magazine publishes what it claims are the results of an unprecedented collaboration among trade builders: a model home for a second generation of postwar home buyers that is "engineered for quick, cost-saving construction." These prospective homeowners are no longer willing "to take anything they can get"; the magazine suggests that "now what most home-seekers want is a reasonably priced house combining features that come only in houses they have not been able to afford."[60] In a large color photograph of the model living room for this affordable home, a sofa, side chairs, and bench by George Nelson for Herman Miller are arranged around Herman Miller's coffee table designed by Isamu Noguchi (fig. 56). The photograph, which uses a wide-angle lens to look slightly down into the room, emphasizes the open "sweep" of floor and legibility of individual objects.[61] Although in reality it must have been rigged from a vantage point on the wall above the fireplace, where no one would plausibly stand, the image invites the viewer in with its expansive foreground, each piece of furniture occupying a clearly demarcated space, and creates a pleasing fiction of ever-expanding space through additional zones of living beyond the sofa and the wall of glass. *Life* conveys a similar message five years later, in a 1958 article on the need for "more livable homes." Part of a series on the housing crisis, this article features "small houses that are pleasant to live in and inexpensive to buy" designed by "mass builders" and intended for middle-income families.[62] A photograph of a Seattle-area house uses the hallmarks of the interior-space photographic rhetoric — open expanse of floor, wall of windows suggesting a world beyond the room, carefully positioned Modernist furniture — to represent the concept (fig. 57). At the center of the sparsely furnished living room stands the Herman Miller bench by Nelson, its distinctive slatted top and modest legs creating a bold pattern against the bare floor. In the context of an article about large-scale suburban housing developments, this image proposes that Modern design is an accessible tool for achieving commonly held desires for "a larger living room," "flexibility of … floor plan," and "charm."[63]

In *Ebony*, readers repeatedly encounter the rhetoric of interior-space photographs in feature articles, but rather than depicting middle-income Modern houses, these photographs are of expensive Modern homes (several homes by architect Paul R. Williams appear throughout the decade). Thus, in *Ebony*'s interior-space photographs, rather than representing broad access as it did in *Life*, Modernism becomes a symbol of elite living. A 1954 article takes readers inside the "ultra-modern home" of Dr. Howard H. McNeill, a Bloomfield Hills physician.[64] The $200,000 house on a twenty-nine-acre estate is hardly a home most readers can imagine acquiring, but its broad expanses of windows, extensive built-in cabinets, and high-tech systems mark it as indubitably Modern. The dramatic image of the living room by photographer Mike Shea follows the interior-space rhetoric: the high, wide angle view emphasizes the expanse of the room, framed by walls of windows, flush wood paneling, and a cantilevered fireplace (fig. 58). The huge "free-form couch" is almost the sole piece of furniture in the room, floating on the vast sea of the wall-to-wall carpet.[65] Its

Fig. 55 (right). Interior view of a living room, Brookings, South Dakota, *Better Homes and Gardens*, March 1952, 60. Photography, Inc., photographer.

Fig. 56 (below). Interior view of a model living room, *Life*, January 5, 1953, 12. Arnold Newman, photographer.

Fig. 57 (bottom). Interior view of a living room, Seattle, Washington, *Life*, September 15, 1958, 71. Julius Shulman, photographer.

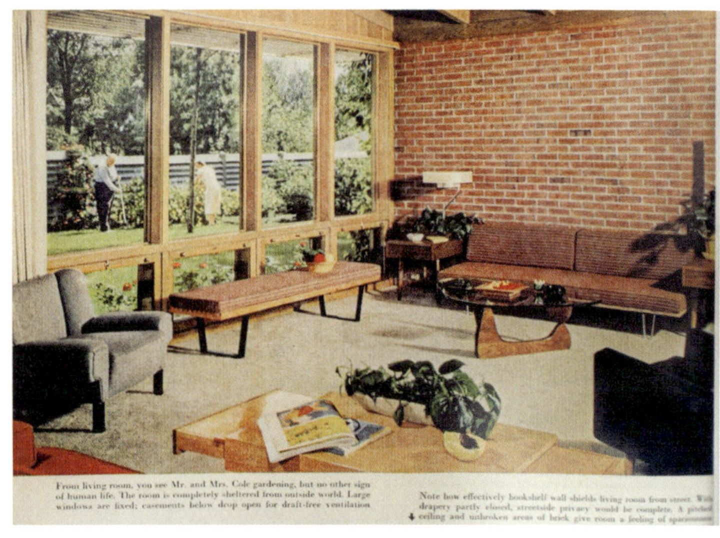

From living room, you see Mr. and Mrs. Cole gardening, but no other sign of human life. The room is completely sheltered from outside world. Large windows are fixed; casements below deep open for draft-free ventilation.

Note how effectively bookshelf wall shields living room from street. With drapery partly closed, streetside privacy would be complete. A pitched ceiling and unbroken areas of brick give room a feeling of spaciousness.

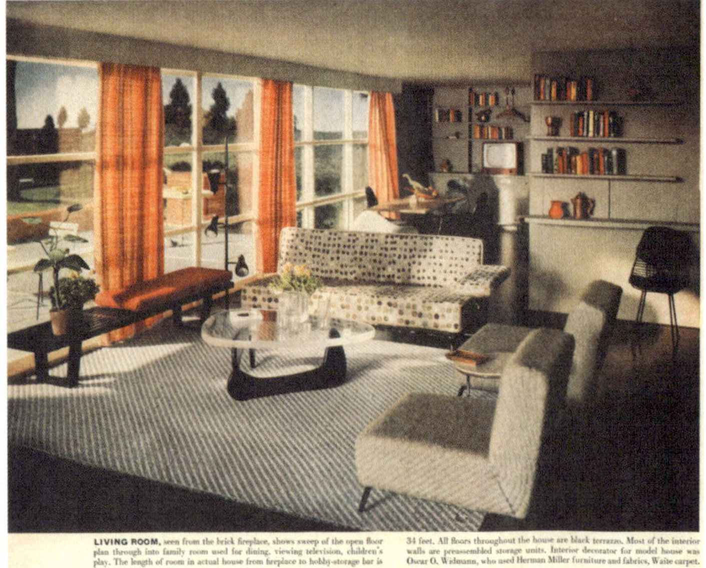

LIVING ROOM, seen from the brick fireplace, shows sweep of the open floor plan through into family room used for dining, viewing television, children's play. The length of room in actual house from fireplace to hobby-storage bar is 34 feet. All floors throughout the house are black terrazzo. Most of the interior walls are preassembled storage units. Interior decorator for model house was Oscar O. Widmann, who used Herman Miller furniture and fabrics, Waite carpet.

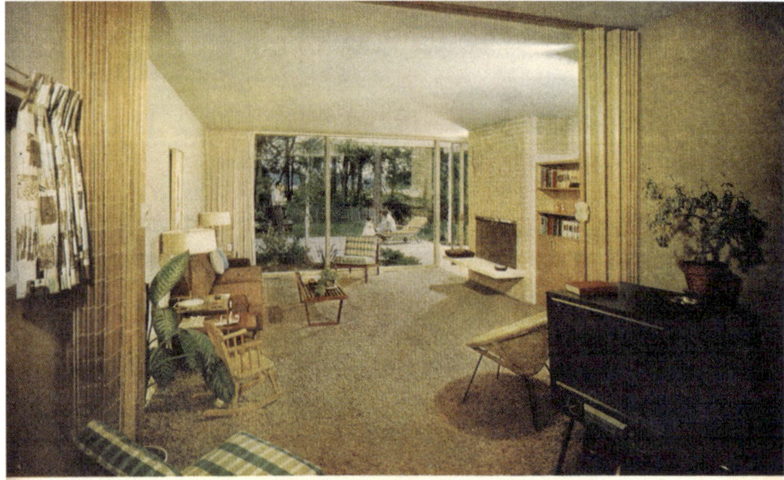

SENSE OF SPACE is achieved with a wide-open plan which can convert to privacy. The glass wall at south end, without overhang, keeps heating bills low. Kitchen and dining areas behind the fireplace also open to patio. The bamboo curtain (*foreground*) closes to make the study-bedroom a separate private area.

composition of interlocking arcs and gridded tufting give it a pronounced Modernist sensibility that resonates with the architecture. Five years later, another extravagant house offers an even more emphatic Modernist statement (fig. 59). This "luxurious $250,000 home" of the cosmetics executive S. B. Fuller, in Robbins, Illinois, features circular interior spaces and curved exterior walls. The lead photograph of the living room, made by a local studio—again, following the appropriate rhetorical style—presents readers with a wide, uncluttered floor, punctuated with objects seemingly selected to make a graphically powerful statement: a blue Saarinen Womb Chair rhymes with a blue Womb Settee, while a low, wide pedestal table set for coffee echoes a slim side pedestal table beyond it; the entire vignette is framed by a massive arced couch.

The high viewpoint in both of these *Ebony* photographs—as in the *Life* photographs—gives the viewer a sense of possession and control: we look down into the room, imagine that our bodies can enter the space because of the openness of the floor, and are invited to sit in the strategically placed seating furniture. But what does it mean that Modernism facilitates an affordable home in *Life*, while it defines an elite home in *Ebony*? In *Ebony*, through these photographs, Modernism remains a thing apart—a distinctive style that the magazine connects to wealth or professional work in the arts. The fact that *Life* emphasizes the affordability of Modernism may reveal the unstated desires of its readers who are striving to identify themselves as White in the immediate postwar decade: they want access to an identity of Whiteness that is always shifting, and expect choices in their home designs that will allow them to perform that racial position.[66] By contrast, the connection between Modernism and elite living in *Ebony* limits Modernism to the realm of African American fantasy. It reflects the limits of Johnson's vision for racial equality through individual achievement and consumption, and also suggests that complete financial access and a full range of choices are not yet, in the 1950s, entirely on the table for Black middle-class consumers.

Modern design appears in the editorial imagery of *Ebony* and *Life* magazines in one final photographic trope: the silhouette. In the silhouette, a photograph is edited so that the background is deleted, leaving the subject to appear to float, its two-dimensional contour emphasized, against a field of white or another solid color. This photographic rhetoric deprives subjects of narrative context, and they seem to hover in a single plane, arrayed before the viewer with no purpose except to be gazed upon. The silhouette is frequently used in women's fashion features and in articles and advertisements for Modern design, and occasionally readers find silhouetted images that bring women and Modernism together. An early example of the silhouette view of Modern design appears in a 1951 article on Herman Miller furniture in *Life* magazine with photographs by Bernard Hoffman.[67] Over four pages, designs by George Nelson and Charles and Ray Eames float against a field of white. Although some objects could be

Fig. 58 (right). Interior view of a living room, Bloomfield Hills, Michigan, *Ebony*, November 1954, 43. Mike Shea, photographer.

Fig. 59 (below). Interior view of a living room, Robbins, Illinois, *Ebony*, February 1959, 36. Herrlin Studios, photographer.

Fig. 60 (bottom). Herman Miller bedroom furniture, *Life*, May 14, 1951, 90–91. Bernard Hoffman, photographer.

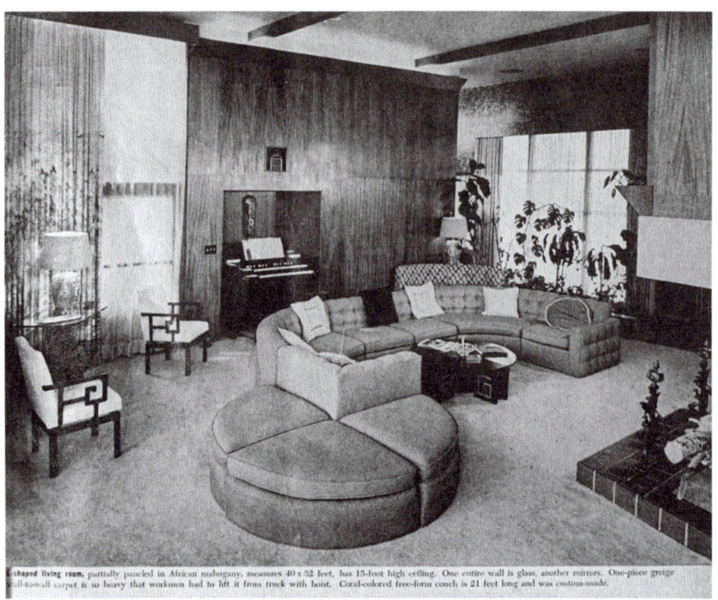

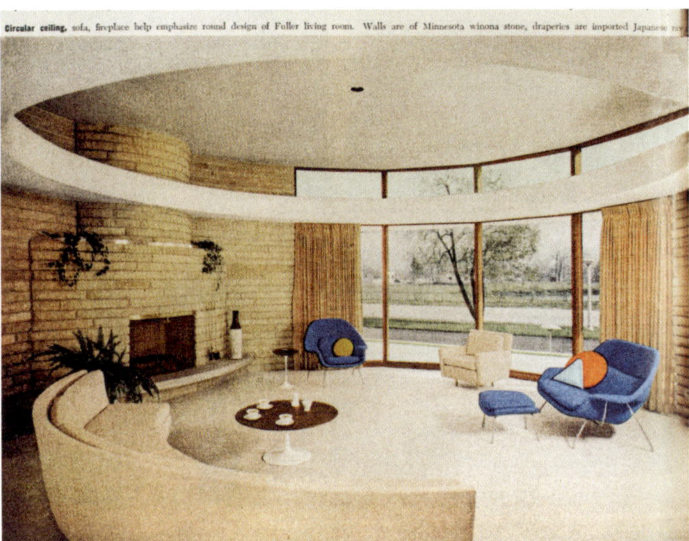

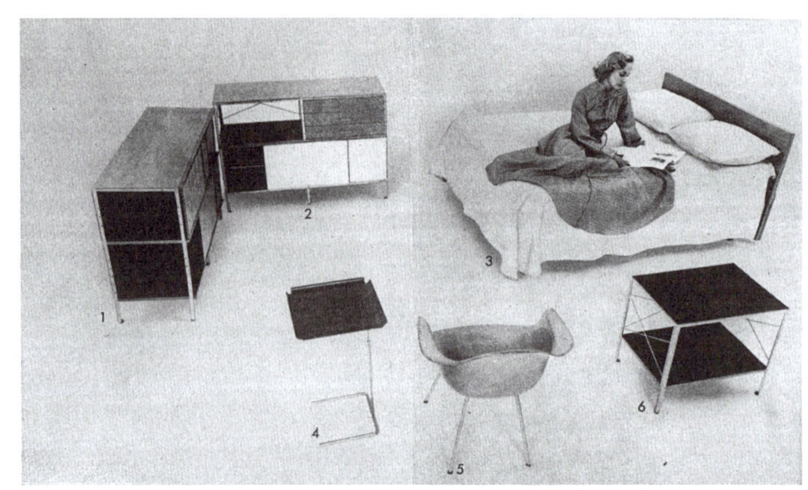

interpreted as in dialogue with others—creating a suspended vignette of sorts—many are isolated in terms of scale and perspective, and the silhouette rhetoric draws our attention to the contours, angles, and composition of the objects as abstract works of art rather than functional objects. On each page, a member of the ideal White, suburban nuclear family is depicted, isolated on a floating piece of furniture: a dog perches on a chair on the first page; a man reclines and reads the newspaper on the second; a woman curls up on a bed on the third, her dress spread around her like an inkblot on the white page of the bedspread (fig. 60); and a young boy leaps from a cushion on the fourth. The prevalent use of the silhouette rhetoric for both women's bodies and the bodies of Modern furniture is distilled in a series of ads for Nemo Girdles that ran in *Life* in the spring of 1950 (fig. 61). The model's body, seductively revealed while her face is obscured, is shaped into a set of ideal, gentle curves through the power of the foundation garment. She is draped diagonally across Eero Saarinen's Model 72 side chair, whose own gentle curves both echo and embrace her. The abstract design of the chair sets the standard for the abstract design of her body, and both are flattened into a graceful two-dimensional pattern by the silhouette eye of the camera.

Hardoy's Butterfly Chair was the frequent favorite for *Ebony's* photographers, perhaps for its graphic appeal in silhouette form, and it was used as a prop in numerous fashion features over the course of the decade.[68] In two notable images, made by *Ebony's* fashion photographer Christa, the canvas seat has been removed and the female model stands inside the empty frame: Dorothy Dandridge, in one of her many publicity profiles, is shown in 1952, and an unnamed model in 1953 (figs. 62, 63).[69] While Christa's photographs take advantage of the bold two-dimensional pattern of the chair's frame, they also bring to the surface the associations that swirled around all of these images of women posed in Modern designs in both *Life* and *Ebony*. In figs. 62 and 63, the popular chair is stripped bare so that we can see the model. Her clothing remains intact, but we are encouraged to visualize her body also freed from the fabrics that cover it. Indeed, Dandridge's eccentric, strapless outfit already seems to be in the process of deconstruction. Just as the female body is presumed to be the appropriate object of a consuming male gaze, so, too, Modern design—with its sensuous organic curves and unusual profiles—is presented as the delectable treat for a hungry eye. In November 1953, *Ebony* published a fashion column on raincoats that had been photographed at the newly opened Abby Aldrich Rockefeller Sculpture Garden at the Museum of Modern Art in New York. The distinctive wall and patio stonework reveal the location, and the gray masonry serves as a ready made backdrop for the silhouette approach to the models' bodies. The silhouette photographic eye captures the contours of a Modern sculpture, and it also captures the contours of a model in a Modern raincoat (fig. 64).

Fig. 61 (right). Advertisement for Nemo Girdles, *Life*, April 3, 1950, 56.

Fig. 62 (far right). Fashion Fair: Portrait of Dorothy Dandridge, *Ebony*, March 1952, 75. Christa, photographer. Beinecke Rare Book and Manuscript Library. Yale University.

Fig. 63 (below left). Fashion Fair, *Ebony*, August 1953, 85. Christa, photographer.

Fig. 64 (below right). Fashion Fair, *Ebony*, November 1953, 101. Herbert Loebel, photographer.

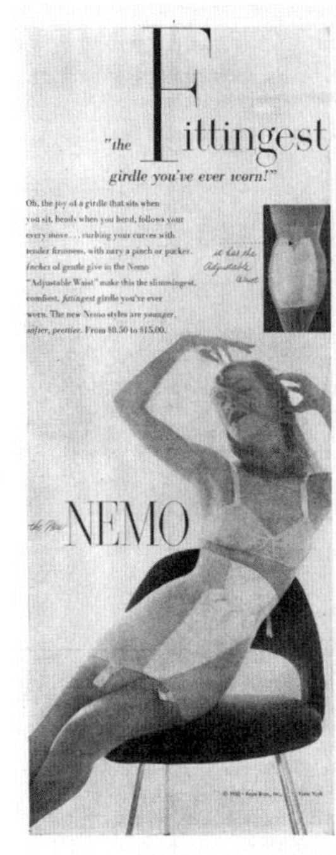

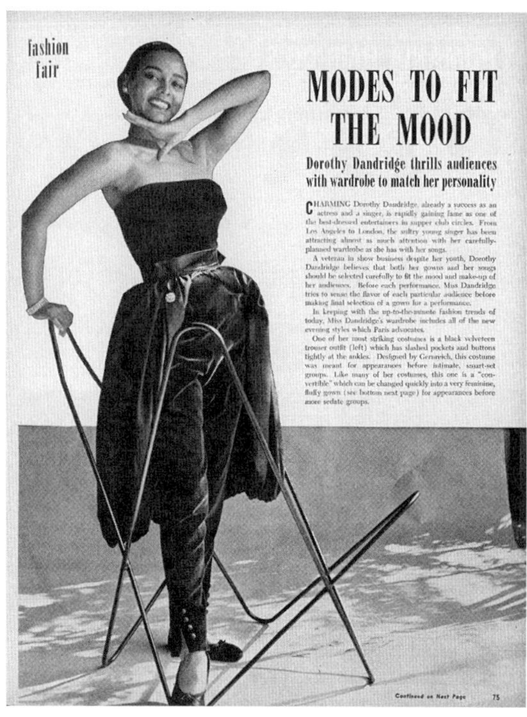

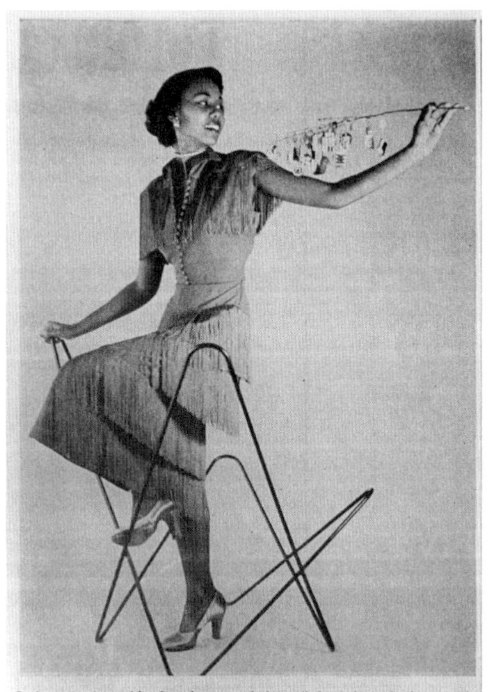

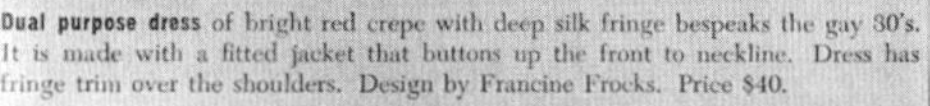
Dual purpose dress of bright red crepe with deep silk fringe bespeaks the gay 30's. It is made with a fitted jacket that buttons up the front to neckline. Dress has fringe trim over the shoulders. Design by Francine Frocks. Price $40.

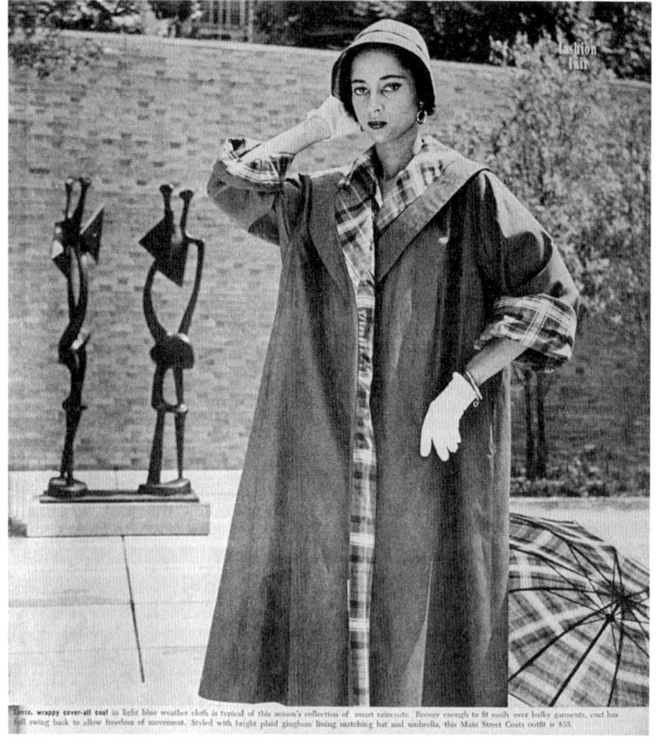

The silhouette rhetoric, in flattening out bodies and objects, emphasizes their pleasing, curving contours. It simultaneously dehumanizes the human and makes sensuous the inanimate object. While it fetishizes shape, it also renders physical heft and form elusive. Women and Modern design become satisfying optical patterns for the possessing male eye. Whereas Modernism appears in *Ebony* and *Life* over the course of the 1950s with pointedly different symbolic resonances—the empowered body on the one hand, rather than the abstracted intellectual concept on the other; the tool of artistic professional identity, sociability, and elite living on the one hand, rather than of the common family on the other—both publications persist in connecting Modernism to women, and then forging associations among women, Modernism, and consumption. It is no wonder that the silhouette became one of the most prevalent tropes in printed advertisements over the course of the decade, appearing in promotions for everything from soap to televisions. Yet a closer look at the way advertisements narrated everyday life for readers of *Ebony* and *Life* during the 1950s will open more doors for interpretation: if Modernism is a tool for elite fantasy in *Ebony*, then what are the narratives that fill out that fantasy life? If Modernism is a tool for modest suburban living in *Life*, does it provide access to all members of the middle class, regardless of race?

Ebony and *Life*: Commercial Content

In the commercial pages of *Life* and *Ebony*, Modernism repeatedly alludes to race in multiple, sometimes overlapping and sometimes contradictory, narratives. A wide variety of advertisements use Modernist interior settings to promote their products, and in many of these ads—appearing in both *Life* and *Ebony*—Modernism is coded as racially White. And yet the story is not as simple as that, because the same advertisement that appeared one month in *Life*, and then a month later in *Ebony*, may have resonated with different meanings for its readers, depending on the context. In this section, I will explore the presence of Modernism in various advertisements from *Ebony* and *Life*, and argue for ultimately a multivalent mid-century Modernism: one story emphasizes Modernist design as a tool of cleanliness, social control, and isolation; another story emphasizes Modernist design as a tool that empowers the user by promoting bodily comfort and forging community. The first narrative is written largely through *Life*'s White corporate culture and that of many national advertisers, and is familiar—although perhaps not quite in these terms—because of the White biases of the field of design history. The second narrative appears within advertisements intended for audiences of color and has been largely overlooked by historians. In the first narrative, Modernism is wrapped up in a larger project to establish and define the boundaries of Whiteness. In the second narrative, Modernism enables users of color, and while it is not racially marked as such, its effectiveness at generating community makes it visible as a tool for demarcating an African American upper-middle- and upper-class identity. When viewed in tandem with the messages about Modernism that Paul R. Williams offers in his architectural books (discussed in chapter 1), this second narrative contributes to a deeper understanding of a possible "counter-discourse" of Modernism in mid-century America. Here, as elsewhere in this book, I model the term "counter-discourse" on the critical media scholarship of John Fiske, and the practice of critical race theorists such as Derrick A. Bell, Jr., and Richard Delgado: "By exploring the power dynamics in society and by looking at the ways that the dominant discourses and narratives are constructed, 'effective' counter-histories and counter-knowledges challenge the dominant point of view."[70]

It is possible, of course, that the racialized identities that coursed through advertisements in this decade are a consequence of the structure of the advertising industry itself. *Life* and *Ebony* both relied heavily on advertising sales to support their publication. In the years immediately following World War II, as the advertising industry grew, national corporations developed advertising campaigns either through in-house marketing divisions or, with increasing frequency, contracted advertising agencies. As *Ebony*'s publisher John Johnson recalled, in the late 1940s, when his marketing team tried to convince these agencies of the value of buying advertising space in their publication, they were largely rebuffed. Agencies argued that African Americans read *Life* and thus did not need to see the same advertisements in *Ebony*.[71] Johnson then took the unusual step of appealing directly to the corporate executives of individual companies and, according to publishing company lore, signed Zenith and Elgin watches as a result of these one-on-one meetings.[72]

White corporate America began to appreciate the possibilities of an African American consumer market by the early 1950s, and, as historians Jason Chambers, Robert Weems, and Brenna Wynn Greer have chronicled, a career in "special market" positions slowly opened to a generation of Black pioneers.[73] In 1948, Ebony profiled the emerging careers of men it called "Brown Hucksters," and in 1953 these professionals founded the National Association of Market Developers (NAMD), which provided marketing training and professional networking.[74] Their rank-and-file members came from advertising agencies and corporations, where Blacks had been hired as envoys to the African American market. As the "Negro Market" gained visibility, corporations and advertisers employed several different approaches to reach it. Johnson—who, by virtue of his position as publisher of a highly successful magazine, became the most prominent spokesperson for this market—initially argued that companies would reach Black consumers simply by appearing in a venue such as *Ebony*.[75] However, in the early 1950s, this strategy was deemed insufficient, and the special market professionals frequently suggested that companies run ads with African American models.[76] A 1955 *Advertising Age* article on *Ebony* claimed that

Johnson did not ask for advertisements that catered to African American identity, "but gets it anyway. Nearly all of the large-space national advertising in which models are used employs Negro models."[77] While some companies merely replaced White models with African American models in their ads, others did develop distinct advertisements for this different market context. As Johnson himself commented in *Advertising Age*, "It's a funny thing, but when a man becomes sold on the Negro market he thinks everything should be Negro."[78] While the exclusivity of an "everything Negro" market may sound colonialist to twenty-first-century ears, to borrow Jason Chambers's terminology, it reflects an attitude that was pervasive in the period: it was assumed that Whites knew little of Black culture and needed to learn about it from African Americans.[79] "We don't oppose it," Johnson added, "since it gives Negroes more jobs."[80]

In the discussion that follows, I examine a variety of advertisements that appeared in both *Life* and *Ebony*, and trace the presence of Modernist interior design as it courses through this historical tapestry. From the many competing images and voices, certain themes can be discerned. When Modernism appears in the context of a predominantly White consumer culture—in the pages of *Life*, or in an advertisement with White models in *Ebony*—it is frequently accompanied by language and references that reinforce an idea of Whiteness. Whiteness is not called out as such, however; as Fiske notes, "a key strategy of whiteness is to avoid definition and explicit presence."[81] Instead, it is invoked through normalizing, positive images and by contrasts drawn against racialized and disempowered others. However, when Modernism appears in the arena of Black consumer culture—with Black models, in the pages of *Ebony*—it rarely carries these connotations. The absence of White racializing rhetoric around Modernist design in these situations is significant. *Ebony*—as well as, more personally, Johnson himself—was criticized for proposing that Black middle-class culture in mid-century America might simply be a copy of White culture.[82] The absence of signifiers of Whiteness in these Modernist advertisements opens up the possibility that the magazine's picture of mid-century African American culture was more nuanced than critics gave it credit for. If, in some advertisements, Black culture seems to merely mimic White culture, in other advertisements we see an effort to establish a Black American upper-middle-class lifestyle and class identity on its own terms, outside the polarizing landscape of racial identity. In this latter group of ads, Modernism is not glossed with Whiteness, and instead symbolizes empowered consumers who have the agency to generate and define their own communities of like-minded African Americans. This message of cultural distinctiveness is not uniform within the magazine—Modernist advertisements with White models appear alongside Modernist advertisements with African American models, creating a cacophony of address in any given issue—but it slowly emerges throughout the decade. Johnson wrote of the possibility that buying power could be a "demonstration of racial equality"—at least in the consumer realm—in a well-known 1949 editorial. Equality is different from outright imitation, and in the editorial he bluntly argued for the value of "driving the finest car, wearing the finest clothes, living in the finest home. It is a worthy symbol of [the Negro's] aspiration to be a genuinely first class American."[83] In advertisements that feature African Americans in Modernist settings, we see images that construct African Americans as fully equal, "normalized" consumers—to use a term invoked by historian Greer—acting out the American dream of material acquisition according to images and standards set by their own community.[84] Modernist design, in this context, acquires a counter-narrative of symbolic meaning.

Modern Design and Whiteness

In *Life*, Modernist interiors very frequently appeared in advertisements for cleaning supplies, paints, and floorings. All three of these product categories share an agenda of cleanliness: if a housewife was not actually using a product to clean her house, then by painting her walls or covering her floors, she was creating an unblemished foundational level. As Dianne Harris has argued, in postwar American culture cleanliness in the home was a particularly loaded topic, associated with order and peacefulness after the horrors of war. As the ideal of a suburban home became increasingly popular, cleanliness could be implicitly contrasted against the dirtiness and congestion of cities; and, as suburban development was overwhelmingly engineered to prevent racial integration, the cleanliness of a suburban home thus became associated with a concept of racial Whiteness.[85] While Modern design might seem a clever choice in cleanliness advertisements—the simple furniture forms, often elevated with slender legs, helpfully reveal open expanses of clean floors—its dominant presence suggests a deeper logic, some of which has already been explored in the work of the authors discussed in chapter 1.

Two advertisements from *Life* further illuminate the connections between Modernism and cleanliness. In a 1953 ad for General Electric vacuum cleaners, a housewife extends the cleaner throughout the entirety of her Modernist living room (fig. 65): the nozzle cleans the rectangular ottoman by the sliding glass doors, the Modernist still-life painting above the fireplace, and beneath the pair of armless lounge chairs. Indeed, while the housewife is herself rendered as racially White, wearing a pink dress, her multiple cleaning ghosts are utter Whiteness—blank forms populating the illustrated room. In an ad for Bissell rug shampoo from 1958, the White housewife (this time in a blue dress) stands in the newly cleaned path on her rug, framed from the back by a Modernist gridded window and sideboard and a sculpted wooden armchair in the foreground (fig. 66). In both, there are dynamics of exposure and defense. The GE housewife scurries around the room, protecting it from contaminants at all vantage points. The Bissell wife balances carefully in the path of cleanliness,

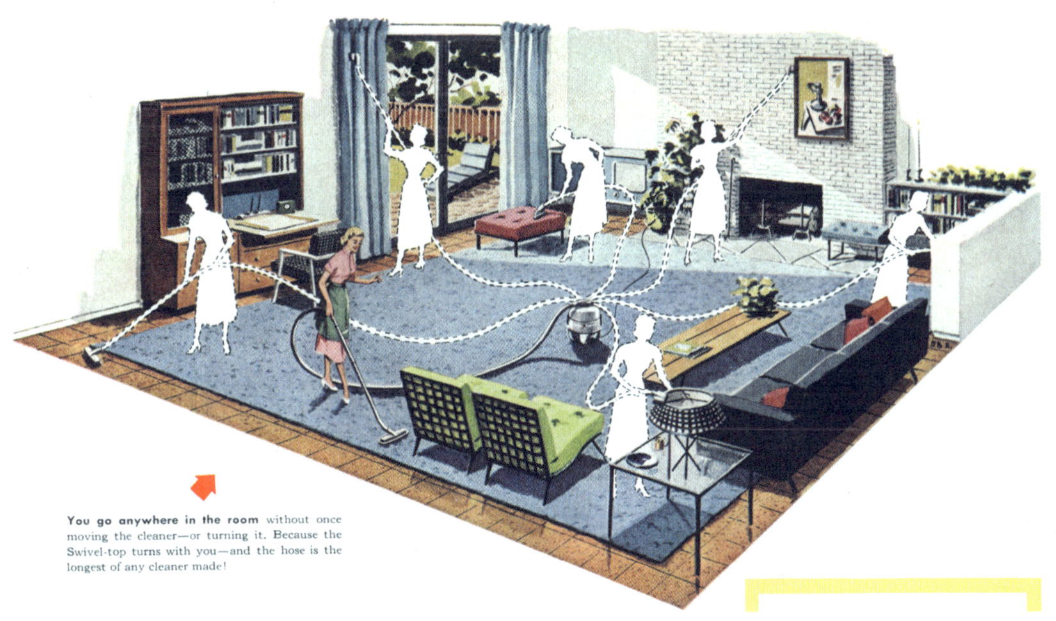

Fig. 65 (above). Advertisement for General Electric Vacuum Cleaner (detail), *Life*, October 5, 1953, 81.

Fig. 66 (right). Advertisement for Bissell Rug Shampoo (detail), *Life*, April 7, 1958, 49.

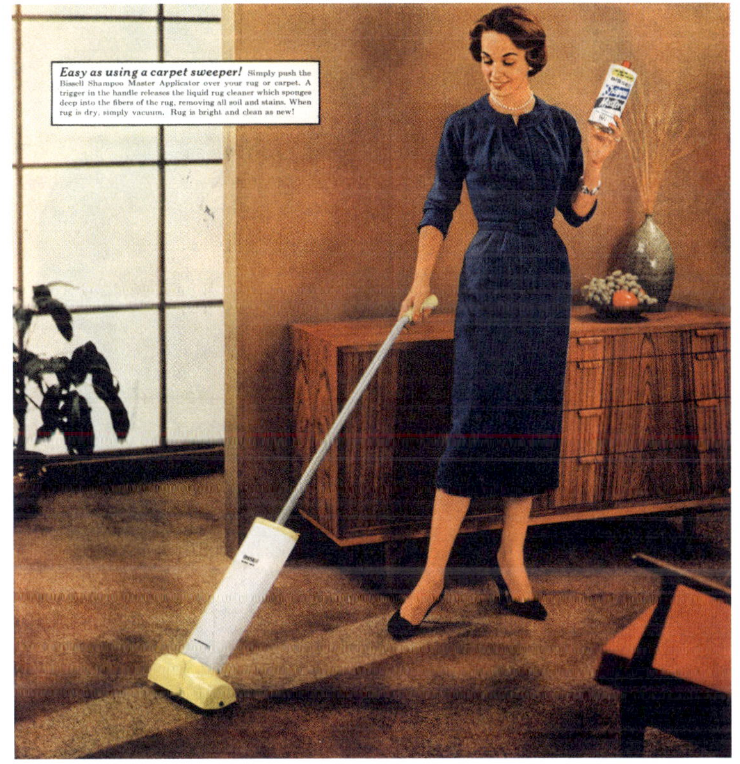

surrounded by a presumably dirty, brown rug and practically cornered by her Modernist sideboard; that object will be revealed when the rug is clean and she moves out from in front of it, suggesting that Modernism sets high standards of cleanliness to which the housewife must submit. These Modernist homes—and women—defend against dirt as well as outsiders, implied by the clear window in the GE ad and the frosted glass in the Bissell ad. The underlying references to purity could readily be associated with the Whiteness of both models as well, although their racialized identities are so deeply subsumed within the normal imagery of suburbia as to be almost unnoticeable, or invisible to the casual reader. Harris has described how White privilege circulates in postwar culture without being recognized as such: the "apparent ineffability of white privilege in its myriad forms."[86] This privilege of Whiteness, which could be described as Whiteness ex-nominated (using Roland Barthes's term), has made itself so powerful and so pervasive that it does not need to be seen—and, indeed, should not be called out as such.[87] These advertisements forge a connection between cleanliness and Whiteness, however ex-nominated, and also establish an association between Modernism and cleanliness. Through associative logic, then, Modernism is linked with racialized Whiteness.

Cleanliness and Modernism are connected in other types of advertisements in *Life* as well. Automobile ads, for example, routinely depict a vehicle next to a Modern house with Modernist furniture, and boast in the copy that the car has "clean lines" or embodies a "clean, crisp new fashion."[88] Modern design even shows up in an ad for Gleem toothpaste: a White family with bright, white toothy smiles eats together in a Modernist kitchen with a George Nelson ball clock on the wall.[89] Interestingly, a few ads are published in *Ebony* that follow the rhetorical logic of cleanliness and Modernism; and, because almost all of these ads include White models, I argue that they also promote the logic of Modernism and Whiteness. In a 1952 ad for Bruce floor wax, a White housewife stands on her polished parquet floor pushing a mop; the glimmering floor recedes behind her underneath a squared Modern side table and pair of low, Modern side chairs.[90] An ad for Modess feminine napkins depicts a White teenage girl seated at a George Nelson–like desk, talking on the telephone as she confidently schedules a date (fig. 67).[91] Given the predominance of White models in these Modernist-cleanliness ads, it would appear that the companies made no particular effort to provide a point of identification for the Black readership of *Ebony*. They may have assumed that African American middle-class culture was simply willing to mimic the styles and standards of White American middle-class culture (or they may not have even noticed the Whiteness of their models). However, in the context of the pages of *Ebony* magazine, these ads also foreground an idea of racial difference—the White teenager is different from an African American teenager—and, in so doing, suggest difference around the style of Modernism: Modernism is a style for the White teenager, which is different from the

Fig. 67 (right). Advertisement for Modess Sanitary Napkins (detail), *Ebony*, May 1950, 11.

Fig. 68 (below). Interior view of a bedroom, living room, and kitchen in a model row house for *Life* magazine, 1958. Julius Shulman, photographer, Job 2642. Getty Research Institute, Los Angeles (2004.R.10).

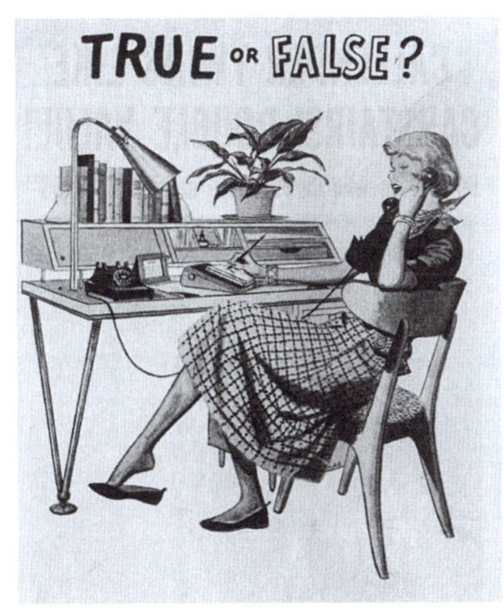

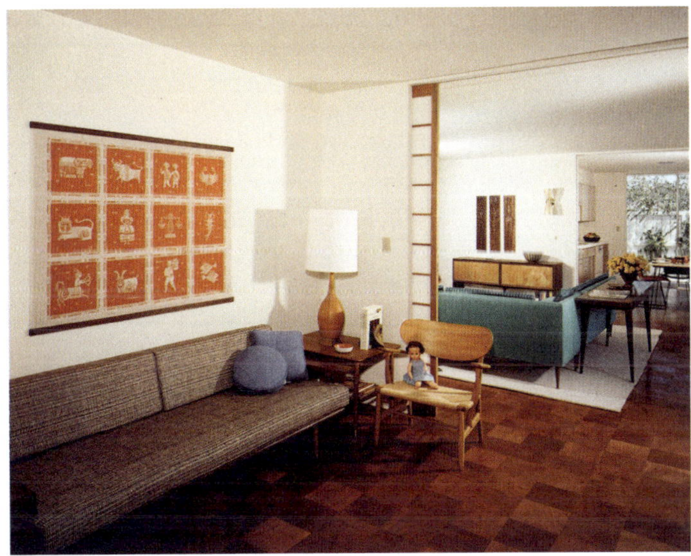

style for an African American teenager. Of course, what is an appropriate style for Black consumers, the presumed viewers of an ad in *Ebony*, is left unanswered in this rhetoric; all that is stated is the connection between Modernism and White consumers.

The web of semiotic references that connects Modernism, cleanliness, and Whiteness occasionally spirals beyond the commercial column inches and erupts in the editorial content of *Life*. In the aforementioned 1958 article series on housing, one issue focuses on affordable housing models, and specifically proposes row houses as a cost-efficient architectural form that maximizes internal spaciousness and capitalizes on shared outdoor space.[92] Architect Edward Durell Stone provides illustrations of a model Modernist townhouse, outfitted with Harry Bertoia chairs in the kitchen and Modernist storage furniture in the hallway (fig. 68). In his explanatory text, he introduces a set of associations that deserve further discussion. "Our row houses, while small, have a certain elegance," he writes. "A gracious home shapes the family. I think that a householder living in one of these houses would wear a jacket for dinner and his wife would light the table with candles. The children would acquire good manners, they would sit up straight and not sprawl about on the furniture. Charming surroundings do, I believe, influence people. I have tried to incorporate in my small houses an atmosphere that would encourage disciplined, gracious living."[93]

Stone's language suggests that Modern design might assist in class elevation, but it goes beyond that. His references to "discipline," "good manners," and sitting up straight imply that the inhabitants of the house need both bodily and moral correction. The opposite of good posture and manners could be sloth and rudeness, characteristics that can have class connotations. Yet in his emphasis on discipline and correction, he insinuates racial difference as well: if poverty is commonly connected to non-White communities in the United States, then his language references a history of physical correction exerted by Whites on non-Whites, African Americans in particular. Ultimately, in Stone's account, the row house, along with its furniture, is given a position of authority over its inhabitants and could even be said to exercise that authority through physical discipline. Richard Dyer points out that "will is literally mapped on to the world in terms of those who have it and those who don't, the ruler and the ruled, the coloniser and the colonised."[94] In Stone's design, Modernism is a colonizing force, disciplining a non-White body into wearing a dinner jacket, sitting up straight. Underscoring this is an assumption that Modernism is fundamentally a style of Whiteness.

Swapping Race In and Out

Several companies created parallel advertisements for publication in *Life* and *Ebony*: the layout and copy were almost identical across the two magazines, but White models posed in the *Life* version and African American models were featured in *Ebony*. These ads raise important issues: If the White and Black versions are essentially identical, can either one claim to be the standard that the other copies? They offer a visual representation of Johnson's claim that buying reputable brands can allow anyone—regardless of race—to become a "genuinely first class American," and hold out the possibility of an equal, not imitative, upper-middle-class consumer lifestyle.[95] Chronologically, these pairs of ads were published at the same time as some of the White-populated advertisements discussed above. This should remind us that the messages about racialized identity in *Ebony* are multiple, overlapping, and occasionally contradictory: some views of *Ebony* suggest a Black middle-class culture that largely copies White middle-class culture, while other views offer a distinctive culture of equality.

In early 1951, Schlitz Brewing Company published a series of hand-drawn advertisements in *Life* and *Ebony*. In several cases, the advertisements were almost identical, save for slight alterations in the figures: in *Life* the models had slight modifications to face, hair, and skin to assert their White identity, while in *Ebony* changes in face, skin tone, and hair texture established the models' Black identity. One pair of ads, which ran concurrently, showed a husband and wife sitting on a Modernist sofa, the beer perched on a marble-top Modernist end table, the husband's arms trapped in a skein of yarn while his wife wraps it into a ball (figs. 69, 70).[96] The self-contained world of resolutely normative, married life depicted in each seems to present a vision of interchangeable equality: both Black and White husbands put up with their knitting wives, furnish their homes in geometric, unornamented Modernist objects, and long for a sip of Schlitz beer. The fact that the ads ran simultaneously further suggests that one does not have to be the model that the other imitated. Indeed, the only evidence suggesting that Schlitz took the White version to be the "original" and *Ebony*'s the "copy" is the presence in the former of the artist's signature, which has been erased in the latter. Despite this intriguing moment of consumer equality, by later 1951 and early 1952 Schlitz changed strategies and began sending *Ebony* ads with White models that it had previously published in *Life*. One 1952 ad that appeared first in *Life*, and then two months later in *Ebony*, showed a White couple in a gallery of Modern art, suggesting once again that Modernism was a prop used to define White lifestyles, not Black.[97]

RCA Victor also sponsored a series of ads in *Life* and *Ebony* that were essentially identical in layout and copy, with models of different races used for each publication. When compared side by side, two 1953 advertisements suggest a Modernist world of consumer equality (figs. 71, 72): a wife sits on a low, armless, Dunbar-like chair with large upholstered foam cushions, her knitting (again!) held in her right hand, her legs propped on an accompanying ottoman; her husband perches on the ottoman, looking back at her to smile as he tunes the television.[98] In both, the face on the television screen is a White woman, and this creates subtly different dynamics in the two images. In the *Life* advertisement, the wife tilts her head as though she sees the woman on the screen as her reflection—they are both milk-white-skinned with blond hair, although in different styles—a joke to which the husband seems to be responding as he looks back at her. In *Ebony*, the mirror-joke disappears, and the husband and wife seem to share a conversation, she in mid-comment, that is separate from the content of the television program. Their separateness could well be a metaphor for a segregated society. While the television with its White world is the possession of the *Ebony* couple, as they sit comfortably in their Modern living room, in *Life* the White woman actually sees herself in the television, and her ownership over this culture is at once more profound and more effortless than that of the African American couple. Combined

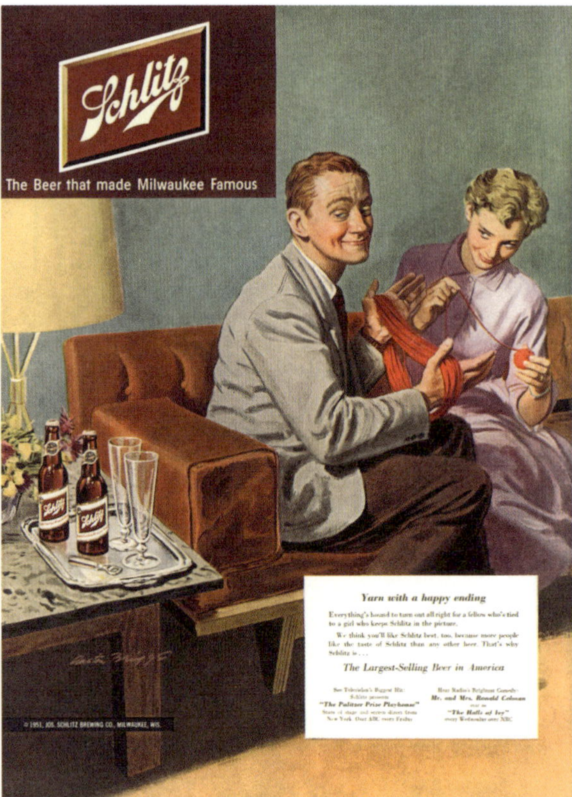

Fig. 69 (above). Advertisement for Schlitz Beer, *Life*, February 5, 1951, 36.

Fig. 70 (right). Advertisement for Schlitz Beer, *Ebony*, February 1951, 14.

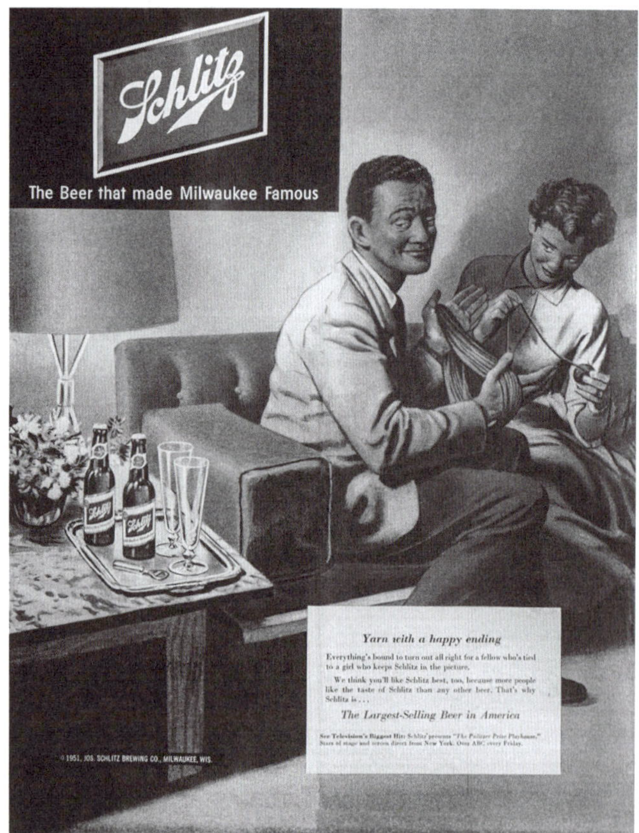

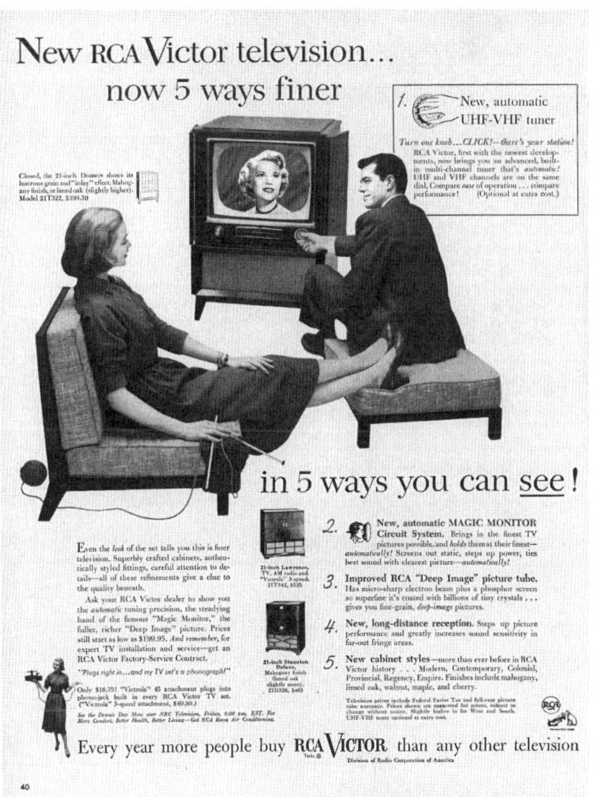

Fig. 71 (above). Advertisement for RCA Victor Television, *Life*, May 4, 1953, 40.

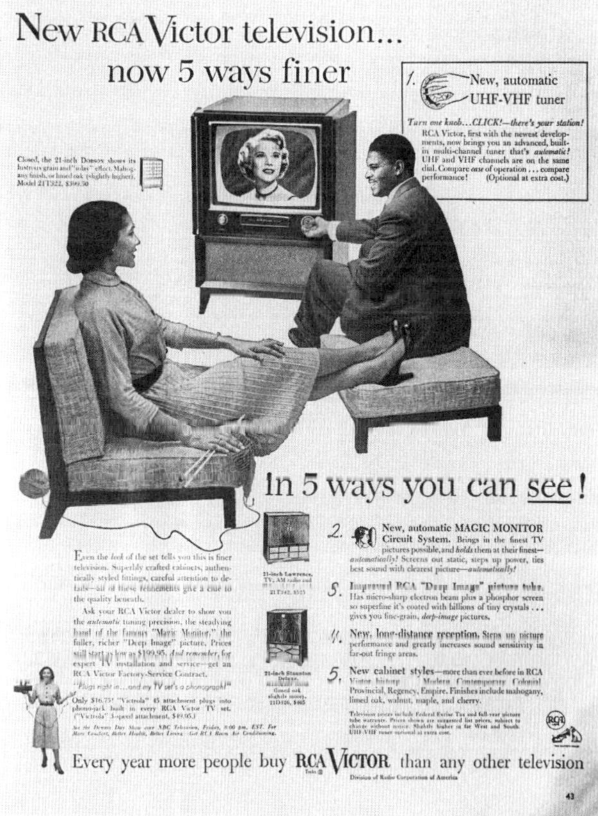

Fig. 72 (right). Advertisement for RCA Victor Television, *Life*, July 1953, 43.

with the fact that the *Life* ad ran two months before the *Ebony* ad, they suggest that White consumer culture and Modernist furniture constitute a model that Black consumer culture could copy but not entirely own.

RCA Victor continued to run similar ads in *Life* and *Ebony* throughout the first half of the decade. By the middle 1950s, the company had adopted the silhouette rhetoric and presented advertisements in which multiple television consoles were photographed against a field of white, occasionally with a female model or children interspersed. A pair of ads from 1954 included an array of consoles on a field of white, framed with a Modernist daybed, striped throw pillows, and a side table at the top of the image and a single glamorous model—White in *Life*, Black in *Ebony*—demonstrating the swivel function on one unit.[99] The televisions, Modern furniture, and women—regardless of race—were all celebrated for their pleasing visual contours. Yet by the later 1950s, RCA was, like Schlitz, placing ads with White models in both *Life* and *Ebony*. The company ran an advertisement in both magazines in the summer of 1957 that featured a White model in an elegant white evening gown, standing in a white room, next to a television console with a Modernist design; her face appeared on the television screen as the ad announced "a new kind of TV—lean, clean, and mirror-sharp!"[100] The White model, Modernist aesthetic, and claim to cleanliness again connected Modernism to a performance of Whiteness.

One final example of a parallel advertising campaign complicates further the narrative of Modernism and race. A pair of 1952 ads for Motorola television present identical scenes: in both, a large image at the top of the page shows a chaotic birthday party tamed by the television, to which the group of children is glued (including at least one boy lying on the floor, head propped in his hands) while two mothers in aprons stand in a doorway at the left edge of the image trading exasperated glances, one with her hand to her forehead (figs. 73, 74).[101] Not only are the lead images similar, but so too are the layout and remaining images in the ad. Yet there are key differences between the two top images: in *Life*, it is a hand-drawn illustration, and the birthday room is full of large upholstered chairs and sofas, with wainscoting on the walls; in *Ebony*, it is a photograph, and the birthday room is furnished with two skeletal Eames chairs and a low bookcase. The *Ebony* birthday party carries more signifiers of Modernism than does the *Life* party; it boasts identifiable chair designs, has a much broader expanse of undisturbed, open floor, and has large picture windows (covered by blinds). The *Life* party does appear to have Modernist art hanging on its walls, but the overall effect of the room is a much more traditional decorative scheme.

How should we interpret the substitutions made between the April ad in *Life* and the May ad in *Ebony*? Did Motorola remove White models, only to reinsert their presence with Modernist furniture? This hypothesis strikes me as implausible because it presumes that the equation between

Whiteness and Modernist design was consciously recognized by White consumers and advertisers. On the contrary, the numerous, recurrent associations I have noted between Whiteness and Modern design likely operated at the level of preconscious recognition because of the invisibility of racial Whiteness for White Americans. Modernism was simply a "natural" style for middle-class audiences who wanted to see themselves as White rather than a style employed to explicitly bolster White racial identity. However, it is possible that when the advertising artists (whether White or Black) created the set for the *Ebony* ad, they sought to deploy props that would readily mark the scene as suburban middle-class, reflecting the presumed setting in the *Life* ad. They therefore chose the "celebrated" plywood chairs known simply as "the Eames chair" (according to *Life*'s 1950 article on the Eames house), which were filling suburban homes at a rate of three thousand per month, and added architectural elements that suggest suburbia.[102] The artists behind the *Ebony* Motorola ad may have used middle-class suburbia (usually glossed as White) as their mental model, but in its finished form it suggests something far more independent. A reader who came across this ad in *Ebony* would be unlikely to know its counterpart in *Life*, and would instead read it at its face value. What she would see is an African American community—eight children vying for the best view of the television, two mothers sharing the misery of hosting the party   gathered together in a home. Moreover, this community possesses history in the form of art on the walls and books on the shelves, but is protected from the assaulting gazes of the outside world by blinds and curtains. Home is a sanctuary, albeit one strewn with ribbons and torn wrapping paper, filled with nothing more than the everyday strains of domestic order. Indeed, the domestic banality of the scene is itself a productive counterimage to stereotypes of dysfunctional African American families or African American women reduced solely to sexual objects.[103] If the advertisement began as a copy of a White model, the dialectical relationship between Black and White does not simply end there. The achievement of Black middle-class Modernist suburbia embodied in this advertisement exists as a statement of equality in purchasing power and the potential assertion of social autonomy. This African American community operates according to its own frames of reference—including, importantly, the husband watching a Black actress on TV in the illustration in the lower left corner of the advertisement—and is free of the racial confines of mainstream American culture. A few months before this advertisement appeared, *Ebony* published an article on Negro dolls that engaged with this vital concept of an independently asserted Black identity. The article celebrated the arrival of "realistic" Negro dolls to the toy market, in contrast to the "grotesque" stereotyped models that had dominated in previous decades, most commonly "a ridiculous, calico-garmented, handkerchief-headed servant."[104] Just as the Motorola ad offered a vision of "realistic" Black domestic life to readers, these new dolls were praised

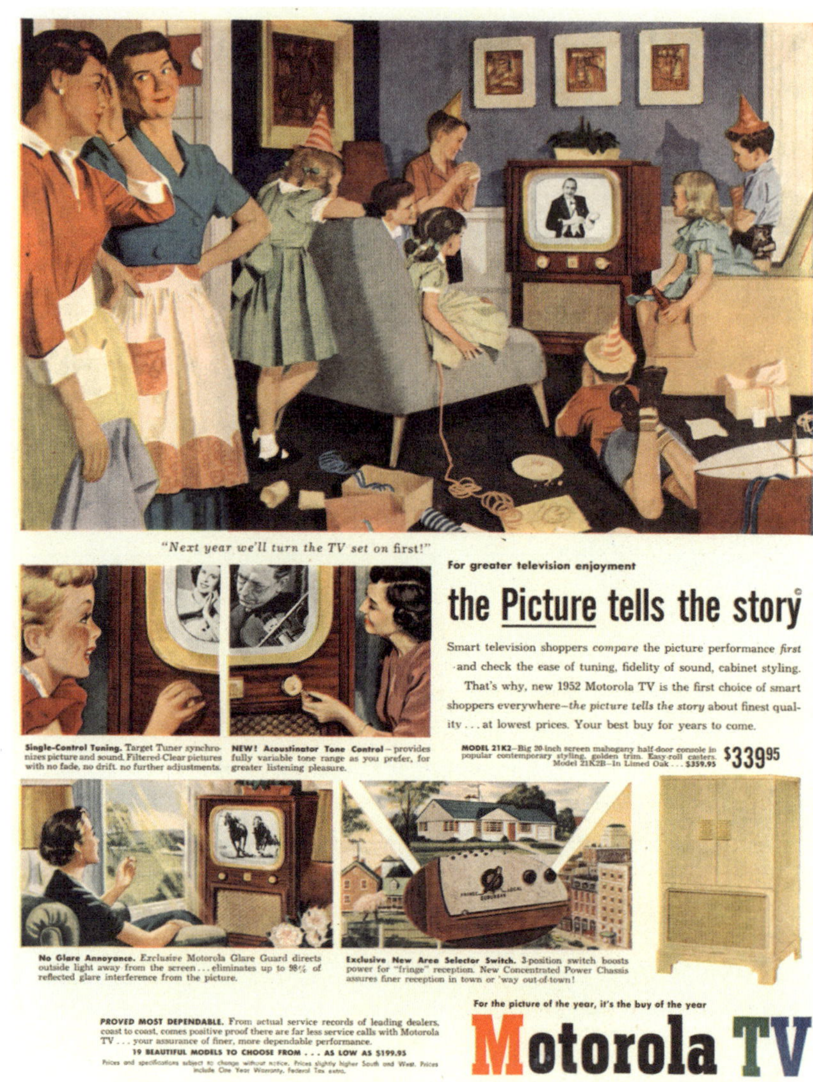

Fig. 73. Advertisement for Motorola Television, *Life*, April 14, 1952, 111.

for their skin tones, "rang[ing] from deep brown to a golden honey," and their "delicate features … and modish clothes," which could enrich "the world of childhood fantasy."[105] The advertisement offers a vision of a Black middle-class community that enjoys its design savvy, financial strength, and freedoms on its own terms, much like the dolls, who embodied an "understanding of us as we are."[106]

Modern Design and the Black Consumer

There was, finally, a very small group of advertisements that featured Modernist furniture in *Ebony* for which no corollary existed in *Life*. These advertisements suggest a different approach, on the part of companies

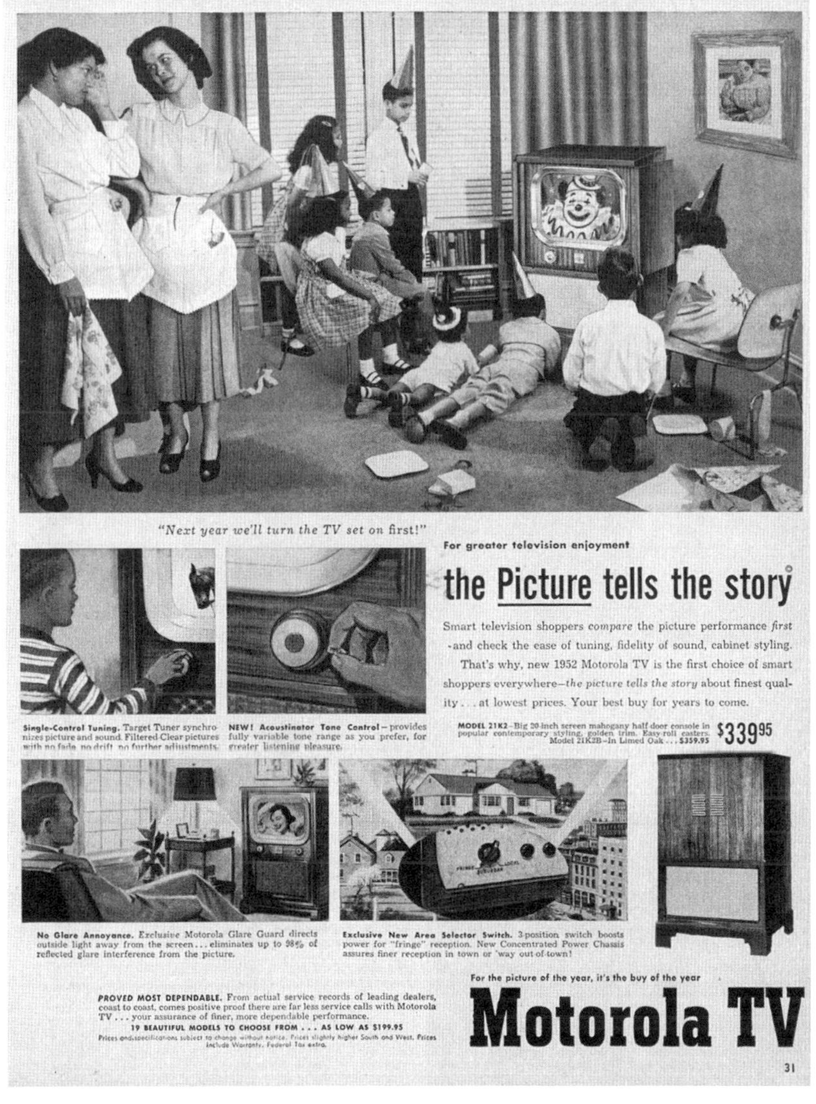

and their advertising agents, from the advertisements discussed above. They continue to demonstrate the unevenness and complexity of cultural identity as forged in the pages of *Ebony*. As historian Chambers has documented, many of the Black advertising professionals who entered the field in the late 1940s and early 1950s found that "mainstream agencies approached black consumers as if they wanted to be white."[107] The two advertisements discussed in this section, rather than simply replicating for Black audiences what had been created for Whites, demonstrate an attempt to craft an address that targets the Black consumer world specifically. In these advertisements for a Black audience that depict Black consumers enjoying Modernist

Fig. 74. Advertisement for Motorola Television, *Ebony*, May 1952, 31. Beinecke Rare Book and Manuscript Library. Yale University.

designs, Modernism is connected semiotically to class, specifically middle- and upper-class lifestyles. Class is defined in three parts, each of which is wrapped up in Modernist props: one part is material acquisition and status display; one part is the power of bodily autonomy and confidence that comes with material wealth; one part is the power to be represented as a community. Modernist design in these advertisements is a class status symbol, but is also the tool that allows the models to relax and the infrastructure that helps to forge a community of color.

One notable instance of Modernism in advertising appears in a 1954 Ballantine Beer ad from *Ebony*: in the photograph, an African American woman sits in a Butterfly Chair, next to a light-wood amoeba-shaped table and a bottle of beer; her male counterpart stands behind her, pouring his own glass of beer, the two of them and their furniture silhouetted against a blank white backdrop (fig. 75). Unlike the people portrayed in many other ads discussed in this chapter, the two look into the camera lens, engaging the viewer in a direct address. In the ad's most intriguing device, she holds up a copy of *Ebony* magazine (its cover logo just visible) folded back to show the very ad in which she sits; that smaller ad shows her holding up the magazine again, which contains yet another ad with her holding the magazine, and the image recedes in infinite recursion to the tiniest printer's dot. It is worth noting that no comparable advertisements appear in *Life* in the decade of the 1950s. Ballantine Beer published a series of boldly colored, line-drawn illustrated ads in *Life* that ran concurrently with the *Ebony* ad, but the aesthetic is demonstrably different, featuring gatherings of families and guests in fully rendered homes. In the *Life* advertisements, the copy highlights the "something special" quality of the "American-type brew" and suggests that readers serve it to their guests as a gesture of hospitality.[108] In the *Ebony* ad, the copy also emphasizes the flavor of the beer and refers to its appropriateness as "good company straight through an evening of sociability." However, it addresses the reader as the hostess of the evening and flatters her with a sense of financial superiority, describing how she should shop for her guests: "Next time … every time … ask the man for Ballantine Beer." With their setting whited out, these two could be anywhere—their own home, a friend's home—but as they look at the reader and hold up the magazine, they seem to be forging a specific community. They create a circle of engagement between us, holding *Ebony*, and themselves, holding *Ebony*, and the implied code is a social circle of like-minded African Americans. In contrast to the Motorola birthday party gathering, who close the blinds against the outside world, and even in contrast to the RCA Victor couple, who talk about the television but do not see themselves in it, the Ballantine couple have social agency, and they act outward from the page, building relationships to infinite degrees of connection among all *Ebony* readers.

In the context of *Ebony*'s pages, moreover, this advertisement resonates in several key ways. As the woman sits in the distinctively Modernist

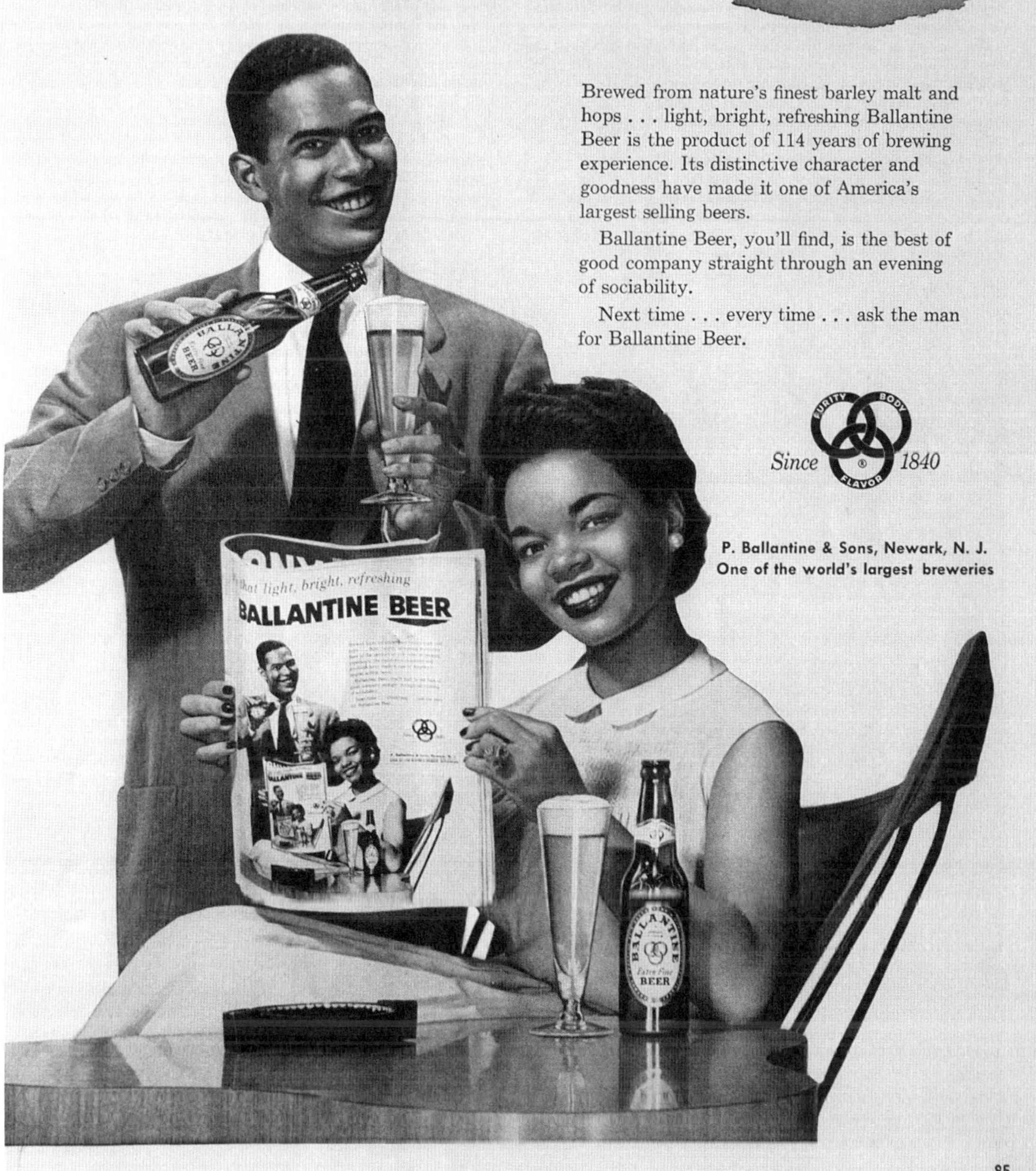

Fig. 75. Advertisement for Ballantine Beer, *Ebony*, November 1954, 85.

chair, and rests her drink on an unusual Modernist table, it cements a connection between Modernism and femininity that readers find elsewhere in the magazine. By implying that this couple has the respect and clout to tell "the man" what they want, the advertisement offers an association between upper-class financial strength and Modernist possessions, much like the home of S. B. Fuller. Indeed, the Modernist table is the prop that brings us, the readers, into cocktail chatter with the couple: the glossy finish of the abstract tabletop extends to the lower edge of the photograph, stopping, metaphorically, at our lap as we pull up a chair to join them. Finally, although the woman is leaning forward to show us her copy of our copy of *Ebony*, we imagine that shortly she will lean back in her Modernist chair, assuming a reclined position of casual confidence. She is nice enough to have welcomed us, but the Modernist furniture ensures that we know she is the social superior.

A final example of the embrace of Modernist design within a distinctly African American context is the advertisement that opened this chapter: the 1954 Chicago Metropolitan Mutual Assurance Company ad (see fig. 36). Our attention is divided between the female model and the large Modernist sofa; while her dress and jewelry are signs of the couple's financial wealth, so, too, is the complex, sculptural form of the sofa. In a heteronormative era when the husband is meant to be the breadwinner and the wife his symbol of success, the Modern sofa becomes the irreducible signifier of both feminine glamour and financial health. Indeed, as the husband sprawls across the sofa, he exercises ownership over the object and claims its expanse as his rightful domain. The Chicago Met couple, pointedly, do not engage the viewer. We approach the sofa, and the husband, from behind, as if we are intruding; the wife is perhaps just about to walk around the sofa and greet us, but for the moment she and her husband are caught in a private connection that excludes us. The intimacy of their shared glance implies confidence and self-satisfaction that does not need external approbation, and we are encouraged to read their choice of Modernist furniture the same way: selected in the marketplace for meanings that resonate for them—glamour, wealth, bodily confidence—rather than for a White consumer.

Conclusion

The view of Modernist design that *Life* magazine presented in the 1950s is largely the one that has dominated design history: after several decades of attempting to develop affordable designs that would be accessible to middle-class consumers, Modernist designers in the postwar period finally had the technological expertise to realize their democratic goals. Yet in dialogue with the Modernism on the pages of *Ebony* magazine, *Life*'s Modernism clearly was also invested in excluding non-White audiences.

The rhetoric of democratic appeal is revealed to have strong filters that segregated by racial color.

At the same time, the story of Modernism that *Ebony* tells is far from simple. While in some places it seems to copy White consumer culture, in others it is possible to discern a distinctive approach and set of associations. Modernism in *Ebony* is often elite and is tightly tied to embodied experience, both of its creators—painters and craftsmen—and of its empowered users who recline, put their legs up, and rest their drinks on Modernist surfaces. The typical politics of most history-of-design narratives champion those designs that are mass-produced and broadly affordable; under that rubric, *Ebony*'s Modernism might be written off as less radical and more bourgeois. Yet in its resolute focus on the empowered, embodied actor in the deeply segregated decade of the 1950s, the Modernism we see in *Ebony* has a distinctly political edge. Modernism in *Ebony* enables the human body—specifically, the body of color—and creates arenas in which the user has agency and self-possession; rather than appearing as a tool of discipline and segregation, it promotes strength and forges community. While the Modernisms of *Life* and of *Ebony* are not mutually exclusive, they have key different points of emphasis, which help to bring into focus the possibility of multiple narratives of Modernism. Not only does this line of inquiry suggest that the forms of Modernist design might have resonated differently in different contexts—and that there might, therefore, be multiple counter histories of Modernist design—but it raises the question of how historians assign value to designs to begin with. The dominant canon of Modernist design as taught in the United States has venerated the idea of broad economic access and has placed less value on qualities such as physical comfort.

The designs of the Herman Miller Furniture Company appeared in many of the images featured in *Life*, especially, and the next chapter investigates those designs in greater depth. How do race and gender appear in these objects when we investigate them as retail items and abstract form? How do these objects engage with the concept of comfort?

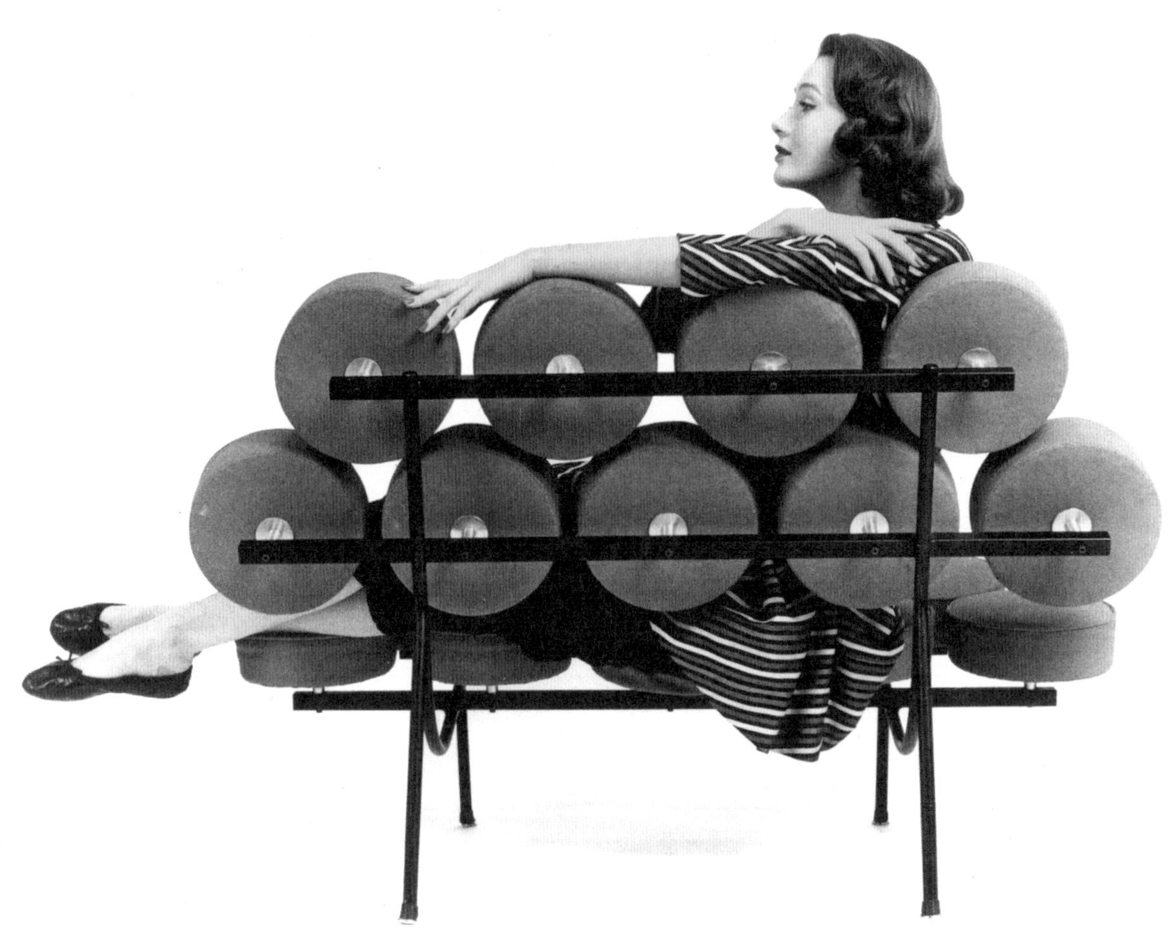

Like a "Girl in a Bikini Suit" and Other Stories
Narrating Race and Gender at Herman Miller

A photograph of Hilda Longinotti, executive secretary at George Nelson Associates, posed on the Marshmallow Sofa has become a popular image of this well-known object manufactured by the Herman Miller Furniture Company (fig. 76). She reclines on the sofa, her face in profile, while we are given a clear view of the geometric structure of the sofa. The black steel frame creates a grid of three horizontal and two vertical lines, from which protrude disk-like cushions; the nine that are suspended in two rows forming the sofa's back create a symmetrical pattern which is thrown into disarray by Longinotti's asymmetrical pose. The sofa's form is so unusual that its function is not readily apparent. Is a sitter meant to squeeze onto a single disk? Alternatively, how might one sit across multiple cushions? The photograph of Longinotti's body draped across the object serves two functions simultaneously: it provides evidence that the sofa can be sat upon, perhaps even comfortably, and it documents the abstract geometries around which the sofa is designed. It both celebrates the Platonic form of the object and seems to humanize it with the presence of a beautiful White woman.

This chapter investigates how race and gender were inscribed into objects manufactured by the Herman Miller Furniture Company between the late 1940s and the late 1950s, of which the Marshmallow Sofa is but one example. In these years, George Nelson, coauthor of *Tomorrow's House* (discussed in chapter 1), served as design director for the company.[1] Nelson's many responsibilities included designing new furniture pieces, consulting on the business practice, generating a market identity through advertising and publicity, and, in all, being a steward for the company's aesthetic reputation. Within three years of his hiring in 1945, Nelson had brought several new designers to the company, including Charles and Ray Eames, Paul Laszlo,

Fig. 76. Hilda Longinotti, of the George Nelson Office, posing on a Marshmallow Sofa, c. 1956. Courtesy of Herman Miller Archives.

and Isamu Noguchi. He had also established his own design firm, called George Nelson Associates, based in New York City. As recent scholarship has revealed, few of the famous designs that came out of the Nelson office were created by Nelson himself; most began with the pencil of one of the many talented designers who worked in the office, and then were developed in conversation with Nelson and others.[2] Similarly, the furniture designs that originated in the Eames studio were not solely authored by Charles or Ray Eames. Numerous scholars and former colleagues have described the design process in the Eames studio as deeply collaborative, and most designs were subjected to a lengthy development process.[3] All of the designs coming out of these offices were then framed through the corporate marketing lenses of Herman Miller, and disseminated to the public through advertisements, catalogues, and strategically placed editorial reviews. Thus assigning authorship for specific designs is a complex task. It perhaps makes the most sense to understand these designs as the product of individual creativity that was nurtured within the larger milieu of the aesthetic and intellectual interests of the office (Nelson's or the Eameses'), which was then positioned by the company for public consumption.

In this chapter, I move away from the broader print culture that introduced Modernism to the mid-century consumer public, and instead focus on some of the specific products offered to that public. In particular, I analyze two different types of objects sold by Herman Miller and designed by the Nelson and Eames offices: storage furniture (including case pieces and wall storage systems) and seating furniture (including lounge chairs, side chairs, and sofas). In addition to tables and desks, these items made up a significant portion of the Herman Miller product line offered to individual consumers in the immediate postwar years (Herman Miller's identity as a manufacturer primarily of corporate office furniture emerged over the course of the latter 1950s). My analysis follows several methodological routes, which I use to build a composite argument about race and gender in these mid-century Herman Miller products. I argue that the Herman Miller Furniture Company largely imagined a White, heteronormative consumer audience for its designs, and that these designs functioned in the symbolic landscape of the postwar years to unconsciously affirm White superiority and gender normativity. My first methodological framework is formal: I examine the objects as works that engage us visually. Nelson, Eames, and the many artists and designers in their offices were steeped in avant-garde artistic practice, and their decisions about shape, contour, composition, color, and material merit close attention. It is not an accident that the photograph of Longinotti allows us to enjoy the unimpeded parade of circular cushions even as we struggle to make out her entire body. I suggest that these furniture pieces are best understood as exemplars of abstract design, related to the move toward abstraction in European and US painting in the first half of the twentieth century.

Yet design objects are not merely things of visual delight; they are functional as well. My second avenue of methodological inquiry bridges the formal and the functional through the lens of empathy. An empathetic object could be defined as that which anticipates the bodily needs of the user and provides a harmonious—or empathetic—experience. A user finds empathy in an object typically through two sensory routes. First, an object may present a form that looks accommodating to the user. This could be described as *visual empathy*, or the way that certain forms present themselves to our visual senses and, through our imaginative response to them, invite the prospect of comfortable interaction. Second, an object may be, in fact, physically satisfying to interact with. This might be referred to as *physical empathy*. Visual and physical empathy are not always mutually reinforcing; indeed, one can readily exist without the other. Empathy is not merely an academic lens through which to analyze design objects, however. In both its visual presentation (visual empathy) and the embodied experience it fosters in a user (physical empathy), a design object participates in a dynamic of power: an object can ingratiate itself with a user; dominate, restrict, or confine a user; or, simply, surprise a user. In what follows, I examine the empathetic qualities of these designs and read their engagement with the human body through mid-century constructions of identity and power.

Finally, a third methodological approach situates these objects within the larger commercial context of the postwar period through the study of Herman Miller's promotional materials and George Nelson's own writings. An analysis of this archival material reveals the narratives that suggested who should buy an object like the Marshmallow Sofa and how it might be used. They tell stories not just about function, but more deeply about mid-century performances of identity: who owns this furniture, who uses it, and in what ways.

As this chapter interrogates the products of the Herman Miller Furniture Company from multiple angles, it also poses a larger, fundamental question: How do we study the power dynamics of race and gender in the history of design? In each of the methodological routes that I follow, I explore the implications of these axes of identity. Can we ascribe racialized or gendered identities in an object based on how we understand the historical identity of its designer? Is there room for creative reuse of an object in the hands of a consumer? If so, would this constitute a counter-discourse of its Modernist power? What is the role of advertising and marketing? Ultimately, is it possible to claim that race or gender—which are performed under continually shifting circumstances—inhere intrinsically in a series of abstract forms that are industrially manufactured? What is race in a modular storage cabinet, anyway? What is gender in a lounge chair? Each methodological route laid out in this chapter gives us different tools for finding purchase on these artifacts, and together they allow us to build a multipart narrative of Herman Miller's participation in—and construction of—racialized and gendered economies of power in the postwar period. I argue that abstraction itself was laced with ex-nominated White, male power in the 1940s and 1950s, and that we might therefore be able to interpret the abstract forms of these designs as complicit in maintaining a White, heterosexist status quo. Moreover, the empathetic qualities of these designs are not straightforward: some objects that express visual empathy do not, in fact, possess physical empathy. While they may look comfortable, they actually exert strict control over the user's body, metaphorically recalling the limitations on the Black American body during this period of persistent Jim Crow culture. Finally, the images and words that framed Herman Miller designs in their original historical moment clearly invested their forms with a variety of racialized and gendered connotations. These promotional materials participated in an unconscious discourse that taught consumers how to think of themselves, and classify others, in racialized and gendered ways. As Longinotti poses on the Marshmallow Sofa, we are encouraged to gaze upon the abstract beauty of the sofa much as we gaze upon her beauty—a male gaze that consumes her bare ankles and wrists alongside the gleaming steel brackets that hold the cushions in place. The photograph asks us to fetishize the sofa as a glamorous movie star and in so doing sets in motion a variety of complicated dynamics of power that reveal the biases of postwar White American consumer culture.

Herman Miller, Modern Design, and Postwar Status

How can we understand Herman Miller's furniture from the perspective of the culture in which it was first created? Postwar America experienced a booming consumer culture, fueled in part by the dramatic growth of segregated suburban housing developments and a marked increase in the birthrate that were documented in periodicals such as *Ebony* and *Life*, discussed in chapter 2.[4] Moreover, as I described in the introduction, the phenomenon of suburbia spawned countless sociological studies, academic and popular, purporting to describe the new formations of social status that the suburbs enabled. Within this consumer world—fueled by images of consumption and questions of status—how did a manufacturer of Modernist furniture position itself? What class of consumer bought Modernist furniture in general, and Herman Miller products in particular?

One approach to this question would be to consider the retail prices of Herman Miller objects in this period. With the exception of the Eames plywood and plastic chairs, the prices listed for Herman Miller products tend to put them in the middle and upper levels, but not luxury levels, of furniture items.[5] Indeed, internal correspondence at the company reveals some tension over the price and attendant identity of its products for consumers. As early as 1947, as he refined the designs of his first set of case pieces, Nelson reminded company president D. J. DePree

that the furniture they were creating was expensive: "We make a line of
furniture which is high in price and is equally high in quality," he asserted
to DePree. "Everything the company does therefore, in its relations with
possible buyers, has to conform with this situation."[6] From Nelson's perspective, Herman Miller would be most successful if it cultivated an aura
of elitism and distinction in its publicity that would justify the higher retail
cost of its objects made of expensive materials and embodying refined
craftsmanship. However, by the mid-1950s, DePree was openly expressing ambivalence about Herman Miller's higher prices against some of its
competitors and its strategy for cultivating associations of expense and
exclusivity. In a 1956 report, he insisted that "we must constantly be trying
to get our product to the users at a lower price," and then posed a question about the company's future market position: "Will [Herman Miller] be
a household word by 1961? or will it be a well known name in the 'class'
market?"[7] DePree implies that he would prefer Herman Miller products to
be broadly accessible — perhaps conforming to the image of furnishing
mass suburbia promoted in 1953 by *Life* magazine (see fig. 56 in chapter
2). At the same time, the ambivalence of his final two questions suggests
that he recognizes the difficulties in achieving that status: he knows that
the company's identity has been invested in the "class" market, and that it
may not be possible to change profoundly both the means of manufacturing (allowing them to produce designs at a lower cost) and the upper-level
market identity of the brand.[8]

Yet while actual 1950s prices are an important piece of data, they
can also be deceiving. As William H. Whyte explored in *The Organization
Man*, 1950s suburban consumers took on increasing amounts of debt, turning to payment plans to acquire many desired household goods that were
beyond their immediate household budgets; as he describes, "In a continually expanding economy, they [young, suburban homeowners] reason,
future prosperity will retroactively pay for today, and there is, accordingly,
no good sense to self-denial."[9] Moreover, Whyte noted, group pressure
affected consumers' perceptions about which products were necessary
and which were luxuries: as more households acquired a "luxury" item,
that item, without diminishment of price, became a necessity.[10] Ultimately,
decisions about what constituted "affordable" for durable goods such as a
dining table or sofa could be highly individual. Perhaps the trenchant question is not what class of consumer bought Modern furniture, but rather this:
When a consumer bought a Modernist piece of furniture in the 1950s, what
class identity did she hope to project? With the increasingly complex construction of social status, class identity was not defined merely in economic
terms, but also through subtler demographic criteria, such as urban, suburban, or rural situation; level of education; race; and type of work (white-
collar, blue-collar).

The many social commentators and pop sociologists of the
period offer clues about the status associations for Modernist furnishings.

As I argued in chapter 2 in my reading of *Ebony* magazine, for African American consumers Modernism may have connoted upper-class or, at the least, upper-middle-class success. E. Franklin Frazier, the highest-profile sociologist writing about mid-century African American culture, has very little to say about particular consumer tastes, however. In his 1957 study *Black Bourgeoisie*, he complains that "the décor of [wealthy Negro homes] reveals the most atrocious and childish tastes," but he provides no analysis of popular styles—Modernist or period-revival.[11] By contrast, several White authors write about class identity and decorating taste in the postwar world, but they tend to assume—according to the ex-nominated Whiteness of the dominant culture—that all consumers are White. Vance Packard, in his best seller *The Status Seekers*, defines class differences by income and education, and insists that class manifests itself in taste. In his interpretation, the "lower classes" in American society prefer "frills on everything," and he elaborates by describing a recent sociological study: "The lower-class people preferred a sofa with tassels hanging from the arms and fringe around the bottom. The high-status people preferred a sofa with simple, severe, right-angled lines."[12] Although he does not use the specific term "Modern," his description of "simple" furniture with geometric contours could well be Modernist; moreover, the term "severe" was often used in association with Modernism, perhaps to describe its lack of ornament, but perhaps also implying some kind of disciplinary bodily relationship. This latter point I will return to later in the chapter. Packard's discussion also includes a variety of "ethnic-class groupings," all of which are White; the implicit message is that Black Americans exist outside of such ethnic and class distinctions. Mid-century critic Russell Lynes is more specific in his assessment of class differences. In *The Tastemakers*, he notes that the highest-level corporate executives furnish their suburban houses with "everything from Chippendale and Sheraton to Empire, but not much later; there is nothing modern."[13] However, among "younger executives Modern furniture is acceptable and originality in its use is admired."[14] From these two authors, it appears that Modern furniture, with its simple forms, tended to evoke the lifestyles of the suburban, White, college-educated, white-collar upper-middle class, or upper class. To the extent that it might have been more popular among younger consumers, Modern furniture signaled upward status ambitions.

This analysis differs somewhat from the image of Modernism presented in *Life*, where, as discussed in chapter 2, the style was regularly presented as broadly affordable. However, rather than understanding Packard and Lynes to be in contradiction with *Life*, it is perhaps more accurate to see all of them as constituting a more complex fantasy whole: for consumers who thought of themselves as White, Modernism was presented both as broadly affordable and as the style of successful young professionals on an upward trajectory. The sooner one could buy this furniture, the sooner one could claim to be on an upward path; thus affordability was not associated with cheapness or mass taste, but rather the strategic first rung on a ladder of social mobility. Whether this logic is airtight is beside the point, and indeed its imprecision is the logic of many large-scale marketing campaigns that call on the consumer to buy products to simultaneously distinguish herself and fit in with the crowd.[15]

The association between class improvement and Modernism is reinforced in other texts from the period. In *The Organization Man*, Whyte described a shift over time in the consumption patterns of residents of Levittown, Pennsylvania: after living in suburbia for a few years, residents felt more financially empowered and consequently expressed "a strong demand for higher-priced brand lines and better 'taste.' In furniture, for example, 25 per cent of Levittowners had mixed-style furniture—i.e., otherwise indescribable—but only about 2 per cent said they would buy this kind again; 67 per cent wanted modern."[16] John Keats, in his muckraking pseudo-novel *The Crack in the Picture Window*, invokes the seductive optimism that Modernist furniture represents when he describes a scene in which prospective home buyers examine a model suburban house: "In a dream they inspected the tiny building, stared at the strange, yet somehow uncomfortable-looking modernistic furniture, at the picture window which seemed to make the living room so much larger."[17] The fictional protagonists in Keats's book ultimately sell their older furniture—"another generation's chattels"—and buy the "popular new furniture," which is Modernist.[18]

Herman Miller's own marketing in the period reflects this set of shared assumptions about the status and appeal of Modernism among White writers and their assumed White audiences. After embracing editorial publicity in publications such as *Life* in the early 1950s, which promoted its products as affordable and even "bargain-priced," by the mid-1950s the company was advertising in only one general-interest magazine, the *New Yorker*, which its marketing office pointedly described as an "upper income audience publication."[19] The internal tensions that DePree expressed—about whether the company should be known as a "household name" or only in the "class" market—are reflected in these periodicals, where Herman Miller products oscillate between being, on the one hand, an entry ticket into a more elevated class and, on the other, a marker of distinction. These apparent contradictions are present in another discussion of company objectives from c. 1956, where DePree noted that one primary goal was "to supply a number of living needs for the people of good taste in the $5000 to $7500 a year income brackets."[20] Whyte identified five thousand dollars in 1956 as the income line "beneath which middle-class life is impossible."[21] Thus Herman Miller's stated range, which adds 50 percent to that bottom line, clearly identifies both emerging middle-class families and those firmly in the upper middle class. Indeed, by 1959, a marketing memo described the ideal consumer: "The principal market for Herman Miller home furniture exists among younger families of intelligent people of increasingly good income."[22] Herman Miller ultimately wanted to promote itself as a symbol of a life on a quick route toward the top of the social and financial hierarchy of the White suburbs: simultaneously affordable and a mark of achievement.

Russell Lynes's contributions to this discourse merit further discussion, because of his nuanced attention to the relationship between taste and class. Lynes's *Tastemakers* grew out of a much-read article, entitled "Highbrow, Lowbrow, Middlebrow," where he proposed a distinction between tastes (or "brows") and classes. The article, which originally appeared in *Harper's Magazine* in 1949, was graphically distilled into a humorous chart, illustrated by Tom Funk, that appeared in *Life* (fig. 77).[23] In this chart, Modern furniture, represented by an Eames plywood chair, is located at the very top, firmly ensconced in the "highbrow" realm. However, the point of the chart (and the article) is that high*brow* and high*class*, while closely related, are not necessarily interchangeable. In his text, Lynes argues that the highest-class executives are attracted to old furniture, which stands as a symbol of family longevity and establishment membership. Highest brow, on the other hand, gravitates toward the new, the transgressive, and the Modern. Judging from the other commodities and pastimes represented in the chart, Lynes's formulation of highbrow has some similarities to the avant-garde: intellectual and independent (at least theoretically), and willing to resist social niceties.[24] While highbrow taste could possibly be found among the high-class, Lynes believed that certain impulses in that class—such as allegiance to establishment—ultimately conflicted with the tenor of independence in the highbrow.

Although high-class and highbrow were not synonymous in Lynes's analysis, part of the appeal of Herman Miller's products may have been their ability to speak to both identities. With its higher price point and the general cultural association of Modernism with upward wealth ambitions, Herman Miller furniture had higher-class connotations. In an oral history interview from the 1990s, one woman recalled her life in the 1950s: "[Our] house had a large backyard, the largest plot on the block, and it had a swimming pool. ... We did a lot of backyard entertaining—big brunches, swimming parties, barbecues. You were trying to live out this ideal of life in the suburbs, in a way, that you saw in *Life* magazine. But you always considered yourself just a little above it. You know, you had the Eames chair."[25] At the same time, the furniture claimed highbrow status. *House Beautiful* described Nelson's first design for Herman Miller, the Slat Bench, as "the bench with the high I.Q.," essentially branding it as intellectual furniture.[26] In 1947, *Interiors* magazine noted that Nelson's new line of furniture for the company had "the self-selling, naturally good looks of things designed without condescension—with the idea that the ultimate user has good taste, too, and a spine that can take only so much stooping, squatting, and hard knocks at the end."[27] This language simultaneously evoked a physical spine—the comfort of the furniture—and a moral spine: a

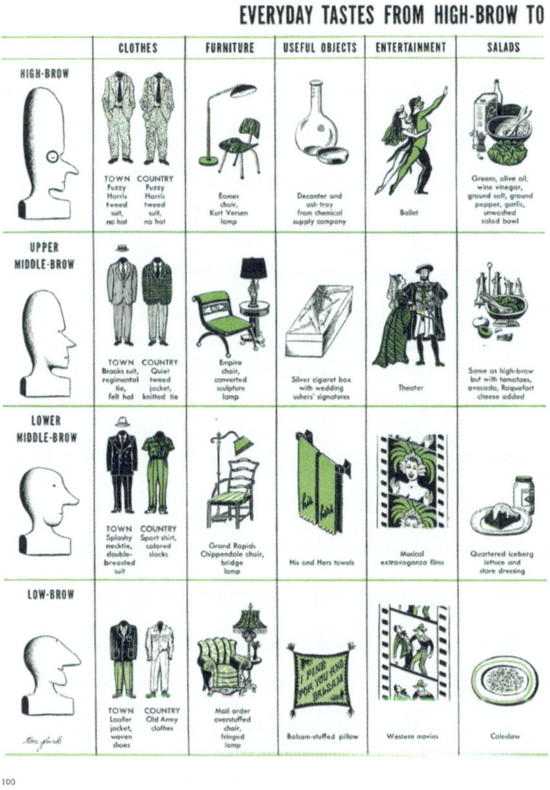

Fig. 77. Tom Funk, "Everyday Tastes from High-Brow to Low-Brow Are Classified on Chart" (detail), *Life*, April 11, 1949, 100.

willingness to stand up for one's taste and not accept the dictates of conventional furniture trends.

If, ultimately, Herman Miller managed to forge a combination of both high-class and highbrow associations to its products, then this may give us a useful purchase on how the furniture constructed identity for its consumers. As highbrow emblems, for example, one might expect Herman Miller's Modern furniture to express some avant-gardist, critical views about American culture, and to embody those views for consumers. As symbols of high-class living, on the other hand, one might expect the furniture to reinforce certain establishment biases. A closer look at the designs as well as the way the company's publicity materials manipulated race and gender reveals a fairly conservative approach to these axes of identity, suggesting that Herman Miller was perhaps ultimately more high-class than highbrow.

Furniture Form: Abstraction In Design

In the following sections of this chapter, I pursue different methodological approaches in my examination of Herman Miller's 1940s and 1950s furniture. In this section, I examine furniture form from a perspective that might be labeled pure aesthetics or pure design: color, shape, materials, textures. In the next section I will continue to examine form, but from the perspective of the human body that interacts with it.

When we give our sustained visual attention to the storage items, chairs, and sofas manufactured by Herman Miller in the immediate postwar years, we discover that geometric forms dominate; they are arranged in bold compositions, and use contrasting materials and colors to create vibrant patterns. In the aesthetic language of twentieth-century art, many of these designs could be described as abstract. Their use of regular, large shapes, blocks of color, and overall pattern echoes the painterly abstraction of contemporaneous New York artists such as Mark Rothko and Jackson Pollock, and even artists of the preceding generation in Europe, including Piet Mondrian and Wassily Kandinsky. However, the term "abstract" is slippery in the field of decorative arts. In the fine arts, the poles of abstract and representational seem relatively straightforward: representation is defined against the experience of a preexisting visual world, and a painting (or sculpture) is understood to either represent the figurative world or not. Would we therefore consider a chair to be representational if it includes carved floral ornament or a ball-and-claw foot? Such a definition seems overly strict. Instead I propose the following: "representation" in design is a reference to preexisting historical types and languages of ornament. Thus a chair in a historical revivalist style could be understood as representational; like representational painting, a revivalist design uses form to reference something specific that lies beyond the object. In contrast, a fully abstract design eschews historical reference through its form, composition, and ornament (or lack thereof). It refers to its materials and its immediate function, but does not point to a referent outside of its physical being.

According to this definition of abstraction, which relies on its resistance to external references, Herman Miller's mid-century products can be understood as fundamentally abstract. Among the Nelson office's earliest designs were the Slat Bench and a variety of case pieces intended to be combined in different configurations. The bench is multifunctional (figs. 78, 79). It provides seating but is also designed as the foundation for a set of smaller cabinets. The slatted wood seating surface creates a geometric pattern that early advertisements celebrate (fig. 80): interlocking shadows of parallel lines emphasize repetition and order, the composition evoking Russian constructivism. Even the short sides of the bench create an abstract pattern as the end grain of the slats alternates rhythmically with the band of wood along the edge. For the larger cabinets, Nelson established a standard height, and intended that their variable widths could be combined and recombined to meet any consumer's specific space limitations and functional needs (fig. 81). They contain varying arrangements of drawers, drop desk surface, shelves, even hi-fi storage and a mesh cover for a speaker. The cabinets themselves are standard rectangles with precisely milled edges, impeccably mitered corners, and drawer and door fronts that

Fig. 78 (right). Slat Bench, introduced 1945, George Nelson, designer. Herman Miller Furniture Company, manufacturer. Maple and ebonized wood, 14 × 18 ½ in., width variable (35.6 × 47 cm). Photograph published in *Herman Miller Collection* (product catalogue, 1956), A4. Courtesy of Herman Miller Archives.

Fig. 79 (below). Slat Bench and basic cabinet series, introduced 1946, George Nelson and Ernest Farmer (George Nelson Associates), designers. Herman Miller Furniture Company, manufacturer. Veneered hardwood, maple, ebonized wood, chrome-plated pulls, 38 × 92 × 18½ in. (96.5 × 233.7 × 47 cm). Photograph published in *Herman Miller Collection* (product catalogue, 1952), 73. Courtesy of Herman Miller Archives.

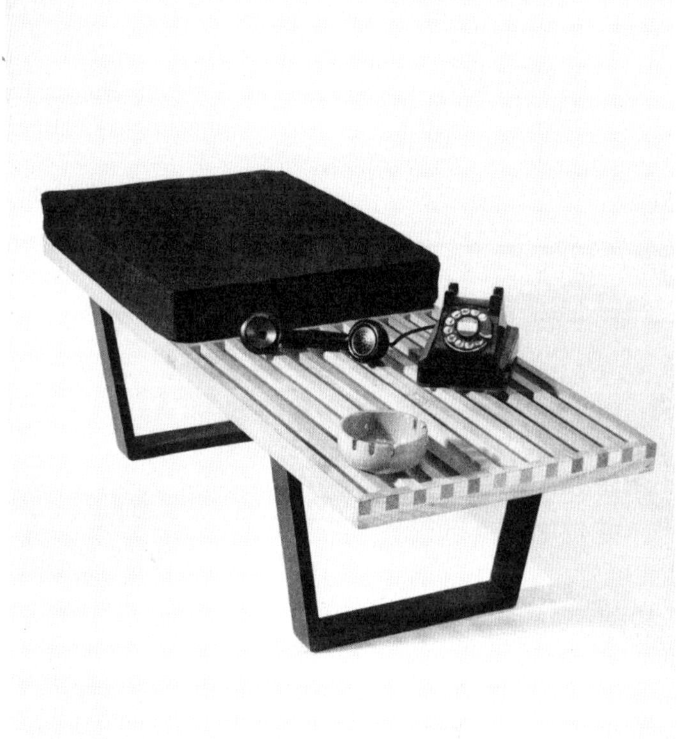

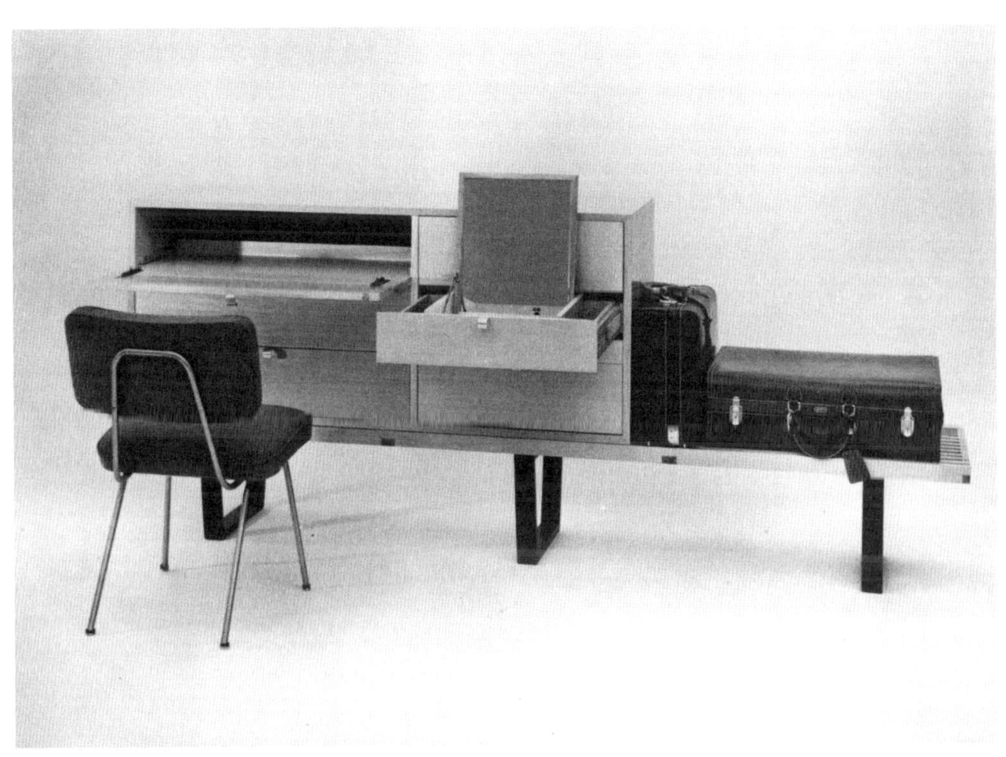

Fig. 80 (right). Advertisement for Nelson Slat Bench. Herman Miller Furniture Company, c. 1956. Courtesy of Herman Miller Archives.

Fig. 81 (below). Basic cabinet series, introduced 1946, Ernest Farmer (George Nelson Associates), designer. Herman Miller Furniture Company, manufacturer. Veneered hardwood, chrome-plated pulls and legs, 39½ × 120 × 18½ in. (100.3 × 304.8 × 47 cm). Photograph published in *Herman Miller Collection* (product catalogue, 1952), 73. Courtesy of Herman Miller Archives.

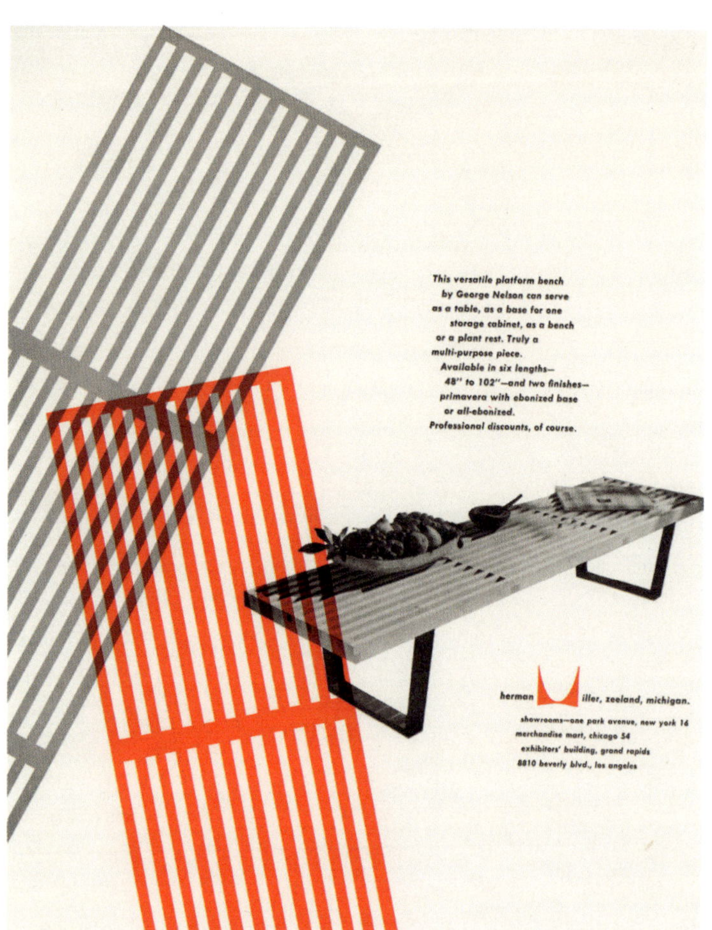

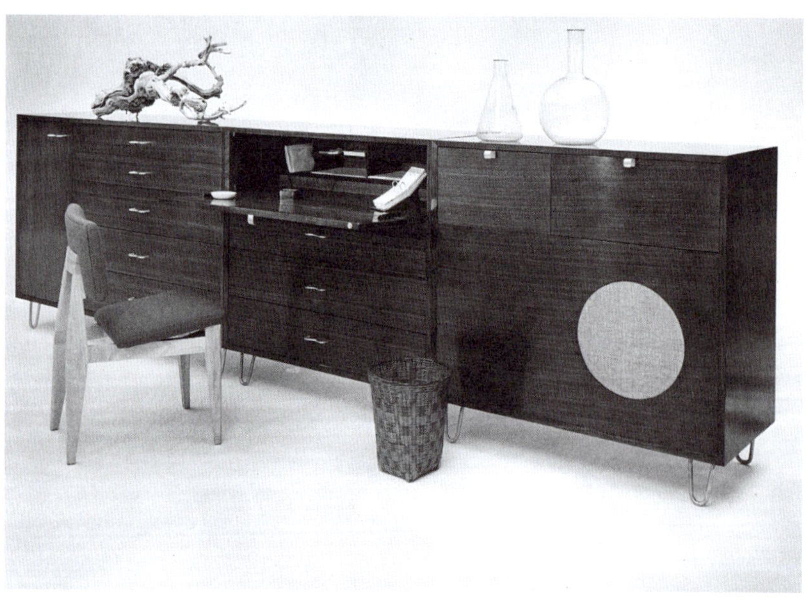

lie flush with the outer plane of the rectangle. Indeed, they are boxes that can be perfectly lined up against other boxes, and when we see a bank of them, they become a flat plane of interlocking geometric shapes: rectangles, squares, circles. The drawer pulls, which are in essence a series of repeating geometric shapes, punctuate the plane of the box. They draw attention to the geometric order of the wood and create a syncopated, secondary pattern on the surface. The 1951 Herman Miller product catalogue emphasizes the rationality and scientific efficiency of this line. With a minimum of waste or visual distraction, the text explains, these pieces are eminently practical for the smaller homes of the postwar landscape. They precisely meet the storage needs of an individual consumer, and create a "custom-designed, built-in effect … carefully planned to 'go together' in various groupings to suit the architecture of the room and the requirements of practical living."[28] But, through the lens of metaphor, one might ask: Does it meet the requirements of practical living, or does it enforce a relentlessly practical living space? Nelson's rational system is designed to contain all of the random, miscellaneous detritus of everyday life; an interior outfitted with these pieces is an interior in which anything irregular has been hidden away, safely compartmentalized and transformed into a clean, neutral front. As *House Beautiful* notes, a storage unit door "conceals [the] less decorative objects" of domestic living.[29]

The Eames studio also designed storage furniture in the postwar period.[30] Their "Eames Storage Units"—also known as ESUs—have more color and variety than Nelson's immaculate storage containers (fig. 82).[31] Individual plywood panels in plastic-coated primary colors, interspersed with perforated metal grills or simple metal cross braces, are arranged and contained within a single, all-encompassing steel skeleton. While the panels have some variety, the symmetry and regularity of the steel skeleton is ultimately the dominant feature of the ESU. In the Herman Miller product catalogues of the 1950s, where a parade of more than sixty ESU options are presented to readers, the panels are quickly reduced to small-scale variations within a larger, highly uniform system (fig. 83) If Nelson's storage units evoke a late Kandinsky composition with their varied geometries punctuated by small, bold drawer pulls—just as Kandinsky overlaid his colored geometric abstractions with black calligraphic accents—the Eames units recall Mondrian's neoplastic abstraction. The steel grid of the ESU expands beyond any single object, as do Mondrian's orthogonal black lines, which always point to a larger grid beyond the frame of the painting. The ESU even takes over the page of the catalogue—which is divided into black-lined boxes, like the units in the storage device—demonstrating that it contains the material and color variety as well as language and item specifications.

To be sure, some of the Nelson and Eames designs veer far from voracious, all-encompassing case pieces. Nelson's office designed several notably exuberant chairs. Whereas the case pieces are buttoned-up

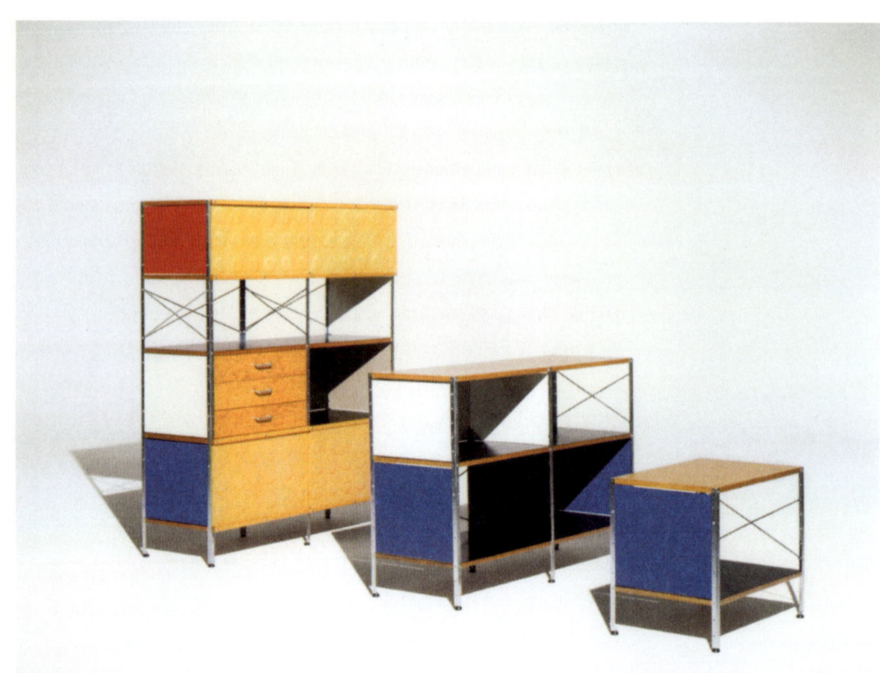

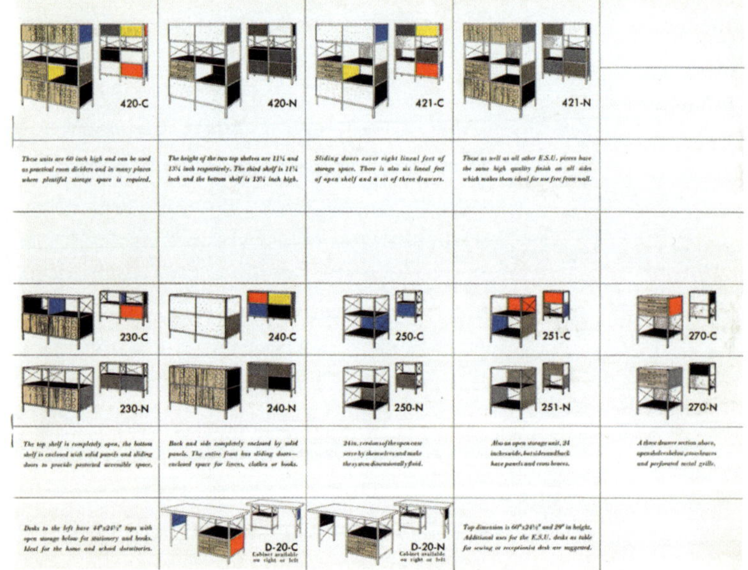

Fig. 82 (above). Eames Storage Units (ESUs), introduced 1950, Charles and Ray Eames, designers. Herman Miller Furniture Company, manufacturer. Steel, laminated plywood, sizes variable. Courtesy of Herman Miller Archives.

Fig. 83 (right). Varied configurations of the Eames Storage Units in *Herman Miller Collection* (product catalogue, 1952), 105. Courtesy of Herman Miller Archives.

and restrained to a geometric grid, the chairs refuse to be contained: they stand out and insist on being seen from all sides. One example is the Coconut Chair, designed by George Mulhauser in 1955 (fig. 84). It might once have been an equilateral triangle, lying flat in a plane, but then its center was pulled out to a point in the third dimension. The object hovers uncertainly in its extruded state, its edges subtly curved under the pressure and always appearing just about ready to snap back into two-dimensionality. It has a plastic shell and a foam cushion molded to the shell; the unpiped upholstery underscores the fundamental flatness of the design. Although the chair predates Sputnik by two years, as art historian Michael Darling has noted, it evokes an alien ship in its form.[32] Its three slender legs jut out of the plastic shell, mimicking the imaginary telescoping landing gear of a UFO, lightly touching down in the living room. The tripod configuration of steel legs and struts references contemporary scientific instruments, which used three legs for maximal, efficient stability; and yet, for a chair, having only three legs carries an inherent risk of instability.[33]

The Marshmallow Sofa, designed primarily by longtime Nelson Associate Irving Harper, is a similarly irrepressible object that commands attention (fig. 85). If the Coconut Chair is a triangle under pressure, then the Marshmallow Sofa is folded graph paper inscribed with rows of identical circles; its skeletal metal frame was intended to hold eighteen disk-like upholstered cushions, nine for the seat and nine for the back. According to office lore, an inventor had presented the cushions as the product of a new technology that would allow for foam extrusion and upholstery as a single, cost-effective mechanical process.[34] Harper originally envisioned the sofa as a dramatic incarnation of the possibilities of mass production:[35] if the cushions could be fabricated in large quantities, then customers could choose the colors to install on the frame, creating infinitely customizable, affordable sofas. In actual fact, the means to upholster the cushions did not lend itself to large-scale replication, and they ultimately had to be hand-sewn. The sofa was, consequently, so expensive that very few were sold, and the piece inadvertently became a true marker of distinction.[36] Some design critics have referred to this object as "pop" design, because it seems to allude to Roy Lichtenstein's use of benday dots. However, the design predates Lichtenstein's paintings by about five years. When it first appeared in the Herman Miller catalogue in 1956, it more likely read as pure abstraction: circles pinned against an underlying grid of squares, with no reference to any historical precedent of a sofa.

The Eames studio also created chair designs in these years that resisted the grid-like uniformity of their storage furniture. The plywood chairs, plastic chairs, and leather lounge chair are deeply entrenched in American visual culture and thus, to twenty-first-century eyes, may appear less flamboyant and overtly attention-getting than the Nelson office chair designs. However, a focused examination of these familiar objects reminds us of the abstract, almost uncanny qualities in their design. Each plywood

Fig. 84 (right). Coconut Chair, introduced 1955, George Mulhauser (George Nelson Associates), designer. Herman Miller Furniture Company, manufacturer. Plastic, foam, steel, upholstery variable, 33 × 40 × 32¾ in. (83.8 × 101.6 × 83.2 cm). Courtesy of Herman Miller Archives.

Fig. 85 (below). Marshmallow Sofa, introduced 1956, Irving Harper (George Nelson Associates), designer. Herman Miller Furniture Company, manufacturer. Steel, foam, upholstery variable, 31 × 52 × 29 in. (78.7 × 132.1 × 73.7 cm). Courtesy of Herman Miller Archives.

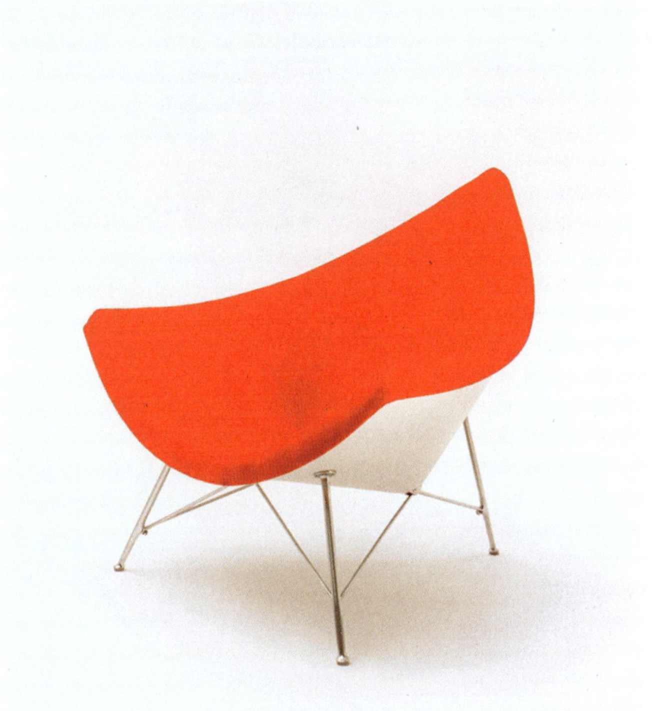

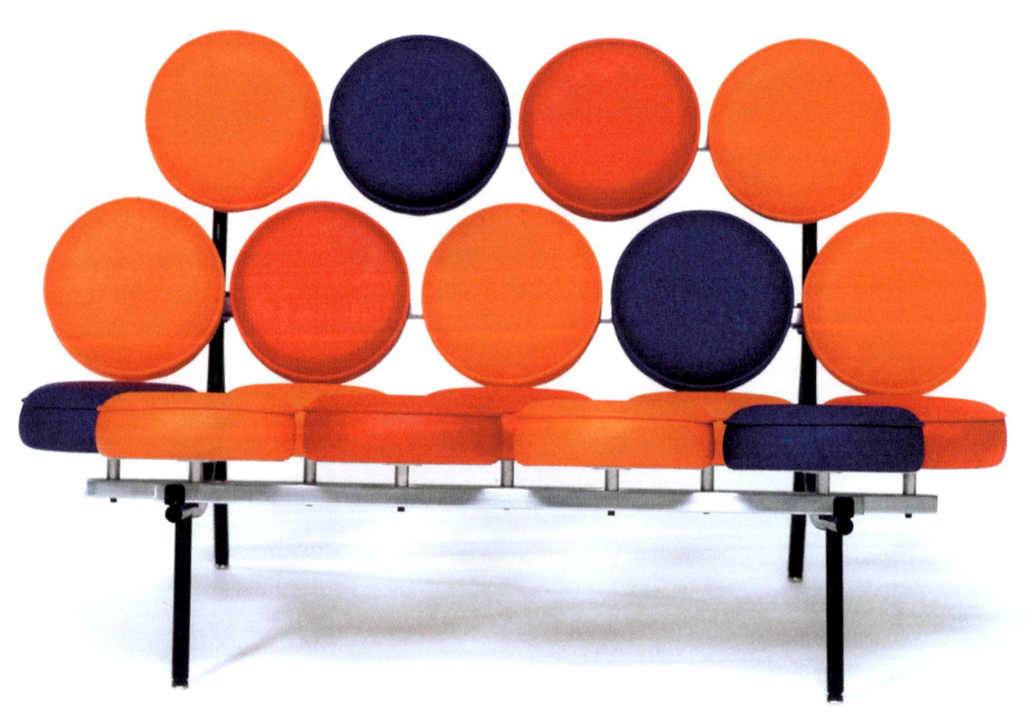

and plastic chair, for example, is a composition of delicate, compound curves that undulate across multiple axes (figs. 86, 87). The designs are at once static—clearly anchored by the principle of bilateral symmetry—and in a state of continuous development, as each plane of a seat or back follows an inexorable curve, morphing imperceptibly into another plane with no clearly demarcated corners. In all of the chair designs, there is a clear distinction between the legs, which tend to be minimal and angular, and the rounded sculptural forms of the back and seat.

The design of the Eames Lounge Chair is more emphatically regular than either the plywood or plastic chair collections (fig. 88): its plywood shell curves in only two planes, not the subtle three of the plywood-only designs, and each cushion is a rounded, symmetrical shape that can be visually organized as a sequence of pairs (the top two form an identical pair; the seat cushion appears almost identical to the ottoman cushion; and the two armrests mirror each other). Not only is the design more obviously indebted than the plywood or plastic chairs to an underlying system of order, but it is the most historically charged of all the Eames office designs. The tufting and piping on the cushions recall upholstered club chairs from the nineteenth century, as does the leather of the cushions. Just as not all paintings are definitively either abstract or representational, this object has strong abstract features that are nonetheless permeated with representation.

The abstraction of Herman Miller's postwar products—largely ahistorical, nonreferential—has resonance with how abstraction was understood in the contemporaneous art world. In the years around World War II and immediately thereafter, the artists of the so-called New York School explored abstraction in painting with increasing intensity. For many of these artists, abstraction allowed one to strip away the specific contingencies of everyday life that appeared in representational art, and made possible the goal of capturing deeper, universalizing truths in human experience. Comments by Jackson Pollock or Mark Rothko, two of the best-known artists of the New York School, attest to this idea. Pollock famously said, "The modern artist, it seems to me, is working and expressing an inner world—in other words—expressing the energy, the motion, and other inner forces."[37] Mark Rothko, collaborating with Adolph Gottlieb, wrote in his well-known manifesto to the *New York Times*, "We favor the simple expression of the complex thought. … We are for flat forms because they destroy illusion and reveal truth."[38] Against the larger historical tableau of the contemporaneous art world, the geometric forms of Herman Miller furniture that so profoundly resist any historical references might have been understood as abstract, and therefore acquired overtones of universality and transcendence.

In addition, the Nelson and Eames office designs have a persistent engagement with the concept of flatness, which likewise became increasingly important for Modernist painters over the course of the 1950s. In

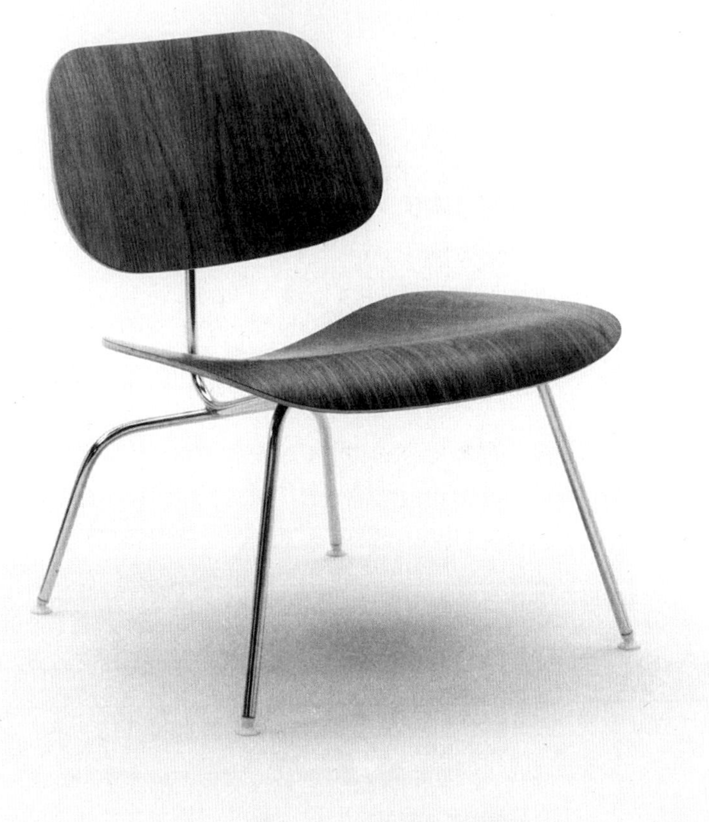

Fig. 86 (above). Molded Plywood Dining Chair with Metal Legs (DCM), introduced 1946, Charles and Ray Eames, designers. Herman Miller Furniture Company, manufacturer after 1948. Molded plywood, steel, 29½ × 20½ × 20½ in. (74.9 × 52.1 × 52.1 cm). Courtesy of Herman Miller Archives.

Fig. 87 (right). Detail of Herman Miller advertisement featuring a Molded Plastic Low Armchair (LAR), 1951, Charles and Ray Eames, designers. Herman Miller Furniture Company, manufacturer. Molded fiberglass-reinforced plastic, steel, 24¼ × 24 × 24½ in. (61.6 × 63 × 62.2 cm). Courtesy of Herman Miller Archives.

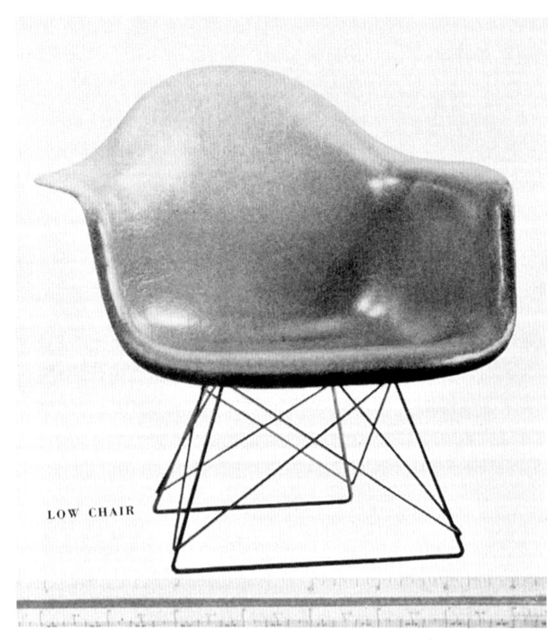

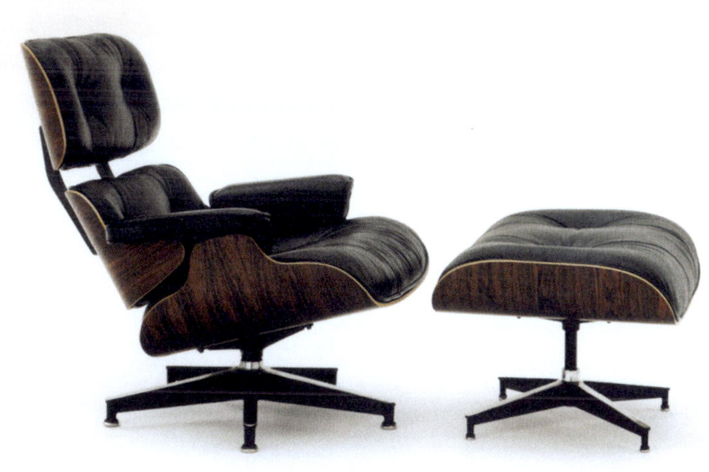

Fig. 88. Lounge Chair and Ottoman, introduced 1956, Charles and Ray Eames, Don Albinson (Eames Studio), designers. Herman Miller Furniture Company, manufacturer. Leather, foam, molded plywood (veneer variable), steel; chair: 31½ × 33½ × 35 in. (80 × 85 × 88.9 cm); ottoman: 17¼ × 26 × 20¾ in. (43.8 × 66 × 52.7 cm). Courtesy of Herman Miller Archives.

each of the designs just described, the three-dimensional object readily refers back to an imagined state of origination: a two-dimensional drawing, nothing more than pencil lines on a piece of paper lying on a drafting table. The case furniture is a composition of two-dimensional squares and rectangles; the Coconut Chair seems to be a temporarily extruded triangle, while the Marshmallow Sofa is a folded piece of graph paper; and the plywood and fiberglass chairs hover in their curved state, as if ready to return to a flat, rounded blob shape at the slightest poke of a finger. This flatness, in itself, resonates with associations to truth in the postwar period. It is not merely that we might interpret a designer's sketch as the true essence of a design—form, structure, proportions, and mechanics stripped of temporal distractions such as color or texture. More broadly, in an art world dominated by the formalist criticism of Clement Greenberg, the two-dimensionality of the painter's canvas—or the designer's drafting paper—becomes a stand-in for truth: as Greenberg wrote in a 1954 essay, if art before the twentieth century was a time "when the painter was obliged to create an illusion of the same kind of space as that in which our bodies move," by the mid-twentieth century, painters had achieved a new level of truth, creating works that embrace the flat "curtain" of the canvas across the "proscenium stage" of Old Master paintings:

> The spectator can no longer escape into it [the painting] from the space in which he himself stands. If it deceives his eye at all, it is by optical rather than pictorial means: by relations of color and shape largely divorced from descriptive connotations, and often by manipulations in which top and bottom, as well as foreground and

background, become interchangeable. Not only does the abstract picture seem to offer a narrower, more physical and less imaginative kind of experience than the illusionist picture, but it appears to do without the nouns and transitive verbs, as it were, of the language of painting.[39]

Greenberg celebrates the distilled truthfulness—the lack of deceit—of the abstract painting that points to its physical flatness. The Nelson and Eames office designs, too, continually remind us of their origin in flat drawings and two-dimensional shapes, and in so doing perhaps claim a similar truth value. Ultimately, when Herman Miller's postwar designs are placed in dialogue with contemporaneous American abstract art, it is possible to read the former as expressing transcendent truths about postwar human living.

Yet as scholars such as Ann Eden Gibson, Michael Leja, and David Craven have demonstrated, when we look more closely at these claims to universality and truth in abstract painting, the actual lessons of history tell us something slightly different.[40] Artists like Lee Krasner, a White woman, or Norman Lewis, an African American man, whose paintings demonstrate a fully formed, aesthetically sophisticated embrace of abstraction, had neither the critical exposure nor the commercial success of their White male counterparts. Indeed, women artists and African American artists, as discussed in chapter 2, were often weighed down by expectations that their art must address—voluntarily or involuntarily—the life experiences of a specifically gendered or raced existence. What becomes clear in this scholarship is the fact that Abstract Expressionism's universal language was universal only for White men. Women or artists of color may have attempted to use their art to speak of transcendental truths, but they were less successful in harnessing that specific language of abstraction because society perceived their selfhood as limited by race and/or gender and thus not a voice for universal experiences. As Gibson argues, "even in the most abstract art, personal identity counted in both production and critical interpretation."[41] If the presumed subjective position for a New York School artist was a White male, which marked as other any identity of femininity or racialized color, then we could say the White male position in the mid-twentieth-century US art world was ex-nominated, to borrow Roland Barthes's terminology. The ex-nominated position has the power to "spread over everything and in so doing lose its name without risk."[42] In the case of race, Whiteness is never questioned because it is never named, and it becomes an implied standard; only races of color are named and thus identified, and remain as exceptions to the rule. A similar act of marking happens with gender: the male position is presumed and left unstated, while the female position is clearly identified as different.

If abstraction—with its attendant claims to truth and universality—is actually a language of White masculinity in mid-twentieth-century America, then it might provide us the tools to deepen and refine how we read the abstract forms of Herman Miller furniture. Following this line of reasoning, the refusal of reference in these triangles, squares, curved forms, and grids could be interpreted as an implicit statement about a canon of power defined by the Western patriarchal tradition. In their persistent invocation of Platonic or near-Platonic forms, perhaps we can understand these objects as privileging an ideal at the expense of the specific, a philosophical approach to furniture at the expense of the needs of everyday living. Yet this argument, as intriguing as it might be, needs to be supported through additional lines of analysis and methodological approaches. To propose that abstraction in design is necessarily equivalent to abstraction in painting may be overly reductive, and while it opens the door to suggestive interpretive possibilities, it cannot be a point of conclusion. Indeed, the very concept of abstraction in design merits further consideration, which I undertake in the following section.

Empathy in Design:
Visual Form and the Imagined Body

Thus far, my discussion of abstraction in design has been limited to visual form: triangles, circles, grids, ornament, and historical reference. Yet this line of analysis neglects entirely how the human body interacts with these objects, something we might call empathetic form. How do we imagine, when we look at these objects, that the human body interacts with them? How is the human figure invited to use these designs? Do these designs anticipate a user? In this section, I continue my examination of form in Herman Miller's mid-century designs, but I take on the question of how these forms engage with the human body. In fact, the terms "abstraction" and "figuration" that guided the discussion in the previous section are relevant here, too, although now I propose that we refract the abstraction/figuration dichotomy along a different axis: some objects look as though they welcome a human user, and could be said to be more "figurative," while other objects do not appear to anticipate a human—indeed they seem to exist despite the user—and could be understood as fundamentally "abstract." In this schema, a "figurative" design is one that possesses visual empathy, that suggests through visual appearance that the object is pleasant to use. Alternatively, an "abstract" design does not possess visual empathy; its form does not visually invite the user to engage with it.

Within this adjusted abstract/figurative dichotomy, the Nelson office designs for Herman Miller can still be understood as abstract, not figurative. These designs are visually motivated by pure geometric forms and appear to arise directly from intellectual manipulations on a piece of drafting paper, with scant attention to the needs or desires of the human user. As their geometries dominate their appearance—a viewer sees squares before she sees a cabinet, or a triangle before a chair—they look fairly unaccommodating to the human body. Nelson explained years later, perhaps tongue in cheek, that his design for the Slat Bench was motivated in part by a desire to create an unaccommodating seat for clients: "The reason slats were used rather than a solid plank was partly to save lumber, but mostly to create a seating surface sufficiently uncomfortable to induce visitors to leave in twenty minutes or less."[43] The drawer pulls on the basic cabinet series are shallow and thin, and are most easily grasped by the tips of one's fingers (see fig. 81; figs. 89, 90). They force the user to be delicate with the object, rather than accommodating the full strength and torque of a hand, wrist, and arm motion. The Coconut Chair's deep, reclining seat, lack of armrests, and three legs present a challenge for the potential sitter: one must rely on one's own sense of balance to sit down into the seat, because there is nothing to lean on. Nelson himself warned users, "This chair needs practice and agility to sit in comfortably."[44] Indeed, if the tripod was the standard for establishing a level field for scientific instruments, then its use in a chair suggests that Nelson might have equated the human body with a scientific specimen to be measured. It is perhaps revealing that among the early publicity images for the chair was a series of photographs with no human beings but with Nelson's dog sitting in the chair (fig. 91).[45] Finally, the Marshmallow Sofa poses additional challenges to the human user. The individual cushions, each ten inches in diameter, are too small to accommodate adult hips and backsides, leaving sitters to uncomfortably straddle two disks. Moreover, if one sits too far to one side of the sofa, with no counterweight to anchor the piece, the skeletal steel frame is at risk of flipping over.[46]

As visually empathetic forms, the Eames office designs are substantively different from the Nelson designs. The plywood chairs may be abstract in the sense that they do not refer to any historical forms and have no ornament. However, their shapes are less rigidly geometric and have sinuous contours that appear to be biomorphic because they recall the human figure. In the Dining Chair with Metal Legs (DCM), one imagines that the sheets of plywood were wet, a person sat down on them and leaned back, and the plywood gently melded to her body (see fig. 86). When we look at this chair, we see not just a landscape of curves, but the ghost of the person who occupied it before us. The plastic chair has a similar fluidity, apparently molded around a seated figure (see fig. 87). The lounge chair also recalls a human body (see fig. 88). Its tilted head cushion and dual-button tufting evoke eyes in a human head; its splayed-open arms and its casually placed "feet" (ottoman) all mimic the actions of a user's body. Indeed, its leather-covered cushions, which soften and wrinkle with age, tangibly create an embodied form.[47] While the plywood and fiberglass chairs call forth a body through negative space, the leather lounge chair actually doubles as the body that will ultimately sit on it. The Eames chairs may not be flamboyant like the Nelson chairs, but they are arresting in their blatant sensuousness, in their visual evocation of a body that touches them and is touched by them.

Fig. 89 (right). Basic cabinet series, introduced 1946, Ernest Farmer (George Nelson Associates), designer. Herman Miller Furniture Company, manufacturer. Veneered hardwood, ebonized wood, chrome-plated pulls, 39½ × 120 × 18½ in. (100.3 × 304.8 × 47 cm). Photograph c. 1947. Courtesy of Herman Miller Archives.

Fig. 90 (below). Drawer Pulls, introduced 1946, George Nelson Associates, designers. Herman Miller Furniture Company, manufacturer. Chrome-plated metal. Photograph by Ezra Stoller, published in *Herman Miller Collection* (product catalogue, 1952), 11.

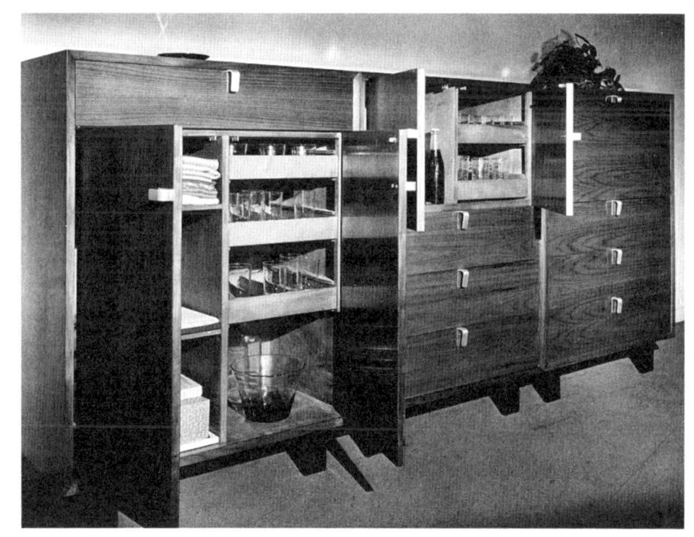

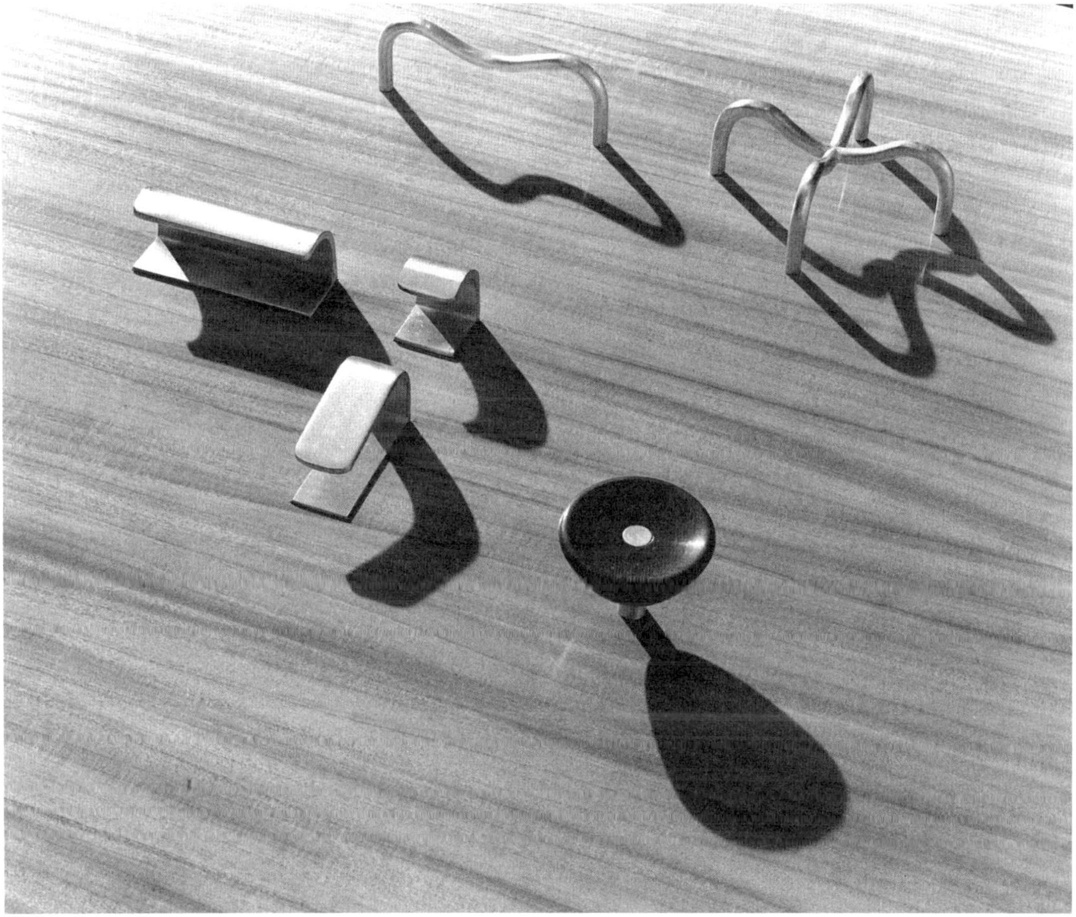

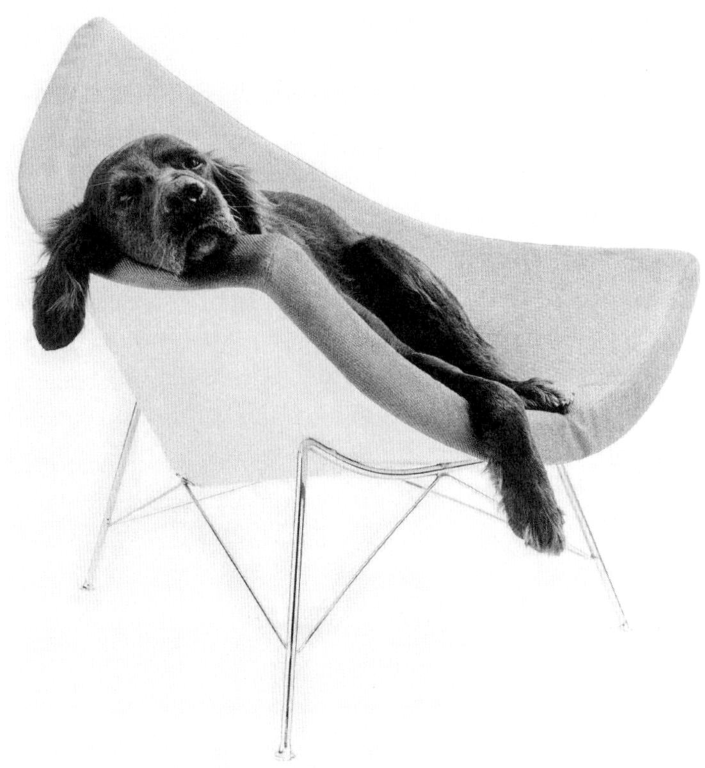

Fig. 91. George Nelson's dog in the Coconut Chair, c. 1956. Vitra Design Museum, Estate of George Nelson.

What is the meaning of the difference between the Eames designs, which visually welcome the body, and the Nelson designs, which seem to deny a body? The Eames designs might be read, through their visual form, as inviting the specificity of an individual human body, and can be described as possessing visual empathy. The art historian Amy Lyford has written about Isamu Noguchi's use of abstraction in sculpture in the postwar years—the years when his coffee table became a best seller for Herman Miller—and she argues that for Noguchi abstraction was a vehicle for transcending racial specificity, demonstrating the possibility of "becoming a body in the world."[48] Abstraction and the figure are not opposed in her history, and an analogous set of propositions can be made about the Eames office designs. Those designs offer visual empathy through their form, and thus suggest the possibility that an abstract form—if we circle back to my previous discussion and posit abstraction as lack of historical references and use of geometric forms—can cradle a human body, that an abstract form can also be figurative. Nelson's designs, in contrast, deny the individual body. They speak to a universal concept of the body—a body that opens drawers, a body that sits down to rest—but their generality reveals a philosophical place of privilege. It is not just that Nelson's designs are fundamentally alienating or bodily uncomfortable. In their abstraction—in their lack of visual empathy, their lack of figuration—they presume a level of authority over the lives of those who use them. They do not have to cater to the body, because the place of White privilege assumes that it knows all bodies. Ultimately, the deep abstraction of Nelson's designs can be read as a sign of their assumed supremacy, of their racial Whiteness.

Yet the evocation of an individual body through visual form is not the only way to understand empathy in design. The *visual empathy* of the Eames objects—their visual expression of bodily comfort—allows us, as viewers, to imaginatively project our bodies into contact with them. This type of response to an object has been the subject of numerous philosophers and may originate in the late nineteenth-century writings of Robert Vischer, who theorized about the psychology of human responses to physical and visual stimuli. In an essay from 1873, he noted that "we thus have the wonderful ability to project and incorporate our own physical form into an objective form," and even suggested a human impulse to animate the inanimate form: "Where there is no life—precisely there do I miss it.... Thus I project my own life into the lifeless form, just as I quite justifiably do with another living person."[49] The mid-twentieth-century American psychologist James J. Gibson, who studied the embodied experience of vision, coined the term "affordance" to explain how a human looks at an object and visually perceives its physical use. He argued that the concept of affordance allowed a connection between a person and her environment—"it is both physical and psychical, yet neither"—and went so far as to assert that "what we perceive when we look at objects are their affordances, not their qualities."[50] Likewise, I suggest that what is initially visually arresting about the Eames plywood and plastic chairs is the void where a body should sit, and the engineering of the curves and materials of the legs are of secondary concern.

In the field of design, however, this sight-based empathetic response is only one modality for understanding empathy. Another must be the actual, physical interaction that the object allows, or the *physical empathy* of its design. A physically empathetic object creates a satisfying bodily interaction with itself. In the case of domestic designs—such as the Herman Miller seating and storage objects currently under discussion—physical empathy can be understood as allowing for the embodied experience of comfort. If we expand our discussion of figuration and empathy in the Eames chairs to the arena of physical empathy, additional questions arise. As the Eames designs visually and imaginatively evoke a specific body, is it possible that they also, in fact, physically limit the user's body by prescribing an ideal body? Charles and Ray Eames's initial experiments with compound curves and bent plywood were conducted

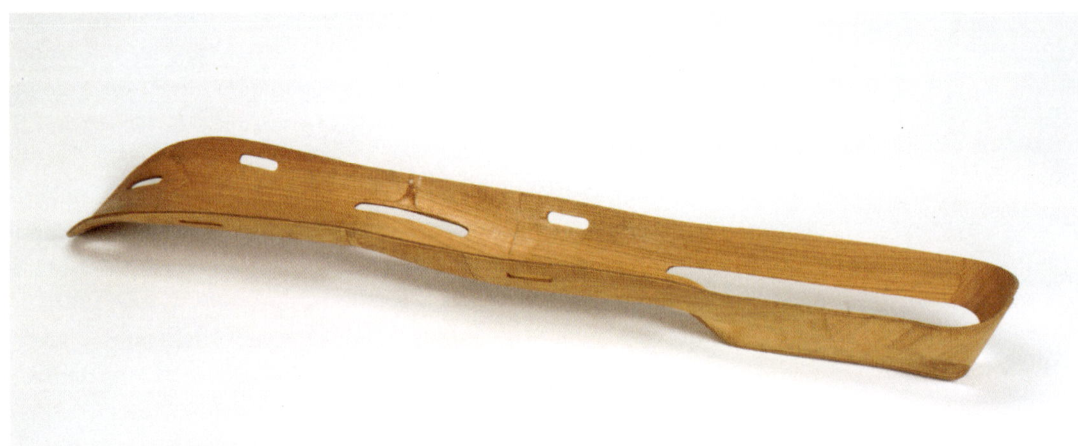

Fig. 92 (above). Leg splint, 1943–45, Charles and Ray Eames, designers. Evans Products Co., manufacturer. Molded plywood, 42 × 7 in. (106.7 × 18.7 cm). RISD Museum, Providence, R.I. Gift of Dr. and Mrs. Armand Versaci. Image courtesy of the RISD Museum.

Fig. 93 (right). Eames leg splint at use in the field, c. 1945. Courtesy of the Eames Office.

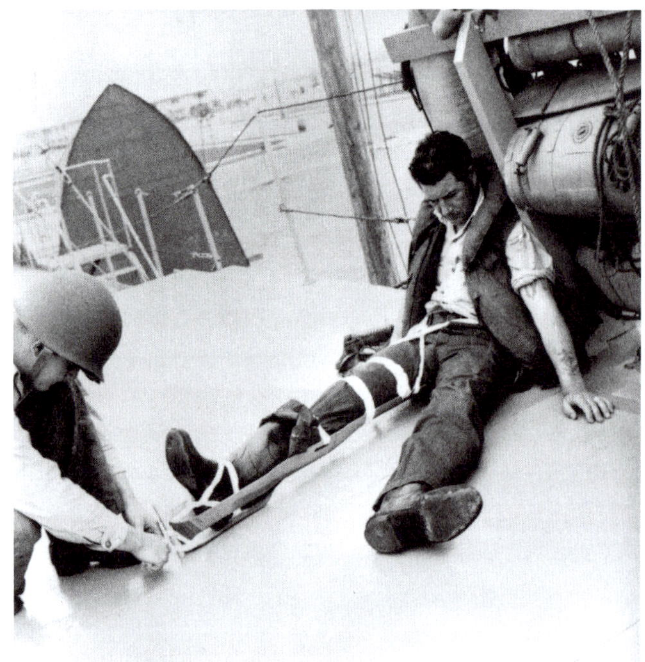

during World War II, when the designers developed leg splints used in the battlefield for medical evacuations (fig. 92). A leg splint is a prescriptive form: it offers a template of ideal health against which the injured body is anchored, and provides the guideline for able-bodied recovery (fig. 93).[51] Using the same technology, the postwar Eames chairs provide a template for an ideal body. They make visible the healthy body through our imagined reading of the ghost of the chair's previous sitter reclining against the compound curves, and they make invisible any disabled body, such as the disabled body of the veteran.[52] As the splint controls the wounded leg, the curves in these chairs physically discipline the bodies that sit in them.

This analysis is indebted to a critique of ergonomics, which design historian Elizabeth Guffey describes as the "standards … [that] measure and quantify the human body."[53] The proposed body for these chairs becomes one way that the designer exercises control, or, as Guffey writes, "how design contributes to a socially designed misfit."[54] Indeed, the Eames-designed body may not have gender or race identifiably imprinted upon it, but an ideal size is.[55] There are bodies that are demonstrably too small or too large to be comfortable in these inviting designs: hips that slide around, unmoored against the relentless, continuous curves, or thighs that spill out, pushing against the inflexible edges of the arced contours. Moreover, the angles of the chairs prescribe certain postures and, with their specific curves, disallow alternative uses (or, at least, comfortable alternative uses). Evidence of the discipline these chairs might exert over users is demonstrated in the Motorola television advertisements discussed in chapter 2 (see figs. 73, 74). While the White children in the *Life* image pile onto the upholstered furniture in their living room with relative comfort, the Eames chairs that populate the living room of the *Ebony* ad are less forgiving to the Black children. Two children uncomfortably squeeze onto the chair on the left, each with a leg falling off the side and the girl apparently holding onto the edge of the chair to keep her balance (fig. 94). The girl in the chair on the right leans far forward, her head over her lap as she strains toward the television, as if she is trying to resist the chair's insistence that she recline (fig. 95). The prescriptive form of the ghost-like body in the Eames chair is not simply a specific size, but it also holds a particular, unmoving pose: it insists on stillness, which these children gamely try to resist. (This feature may explain why so many generations of elementary school furniture are modeled on the Eames plywood and plastic designs.) Indeed, for all of its lack of comfort, Nelson's Marshmallow Sofa is more available for alternative uses and movement by the sitter's body than any of the Eames chairs: Longinotti's photograph (see fig. 76) demonstrates but one example of a model sitting on the sofa in an unorthodox pose, and others from the Nelson archive, such as fig. 96, suggest that he wanted to promote its flexibility, if not comfort. It is a sofa that inspires movement, rather than enforces stillness, to counter its lack of visual and physical empathy.

While the Eames designs might have greater visual empathy than the Nelson designs, ultimately their physical empathy is lacking: rather than providing comfort, they demonstrate a presumed position of authority over the body of the user. The strategies of the Nelson designs and the Eames designs differ, but they both result in a message of control over the body that uses them. Nelson disregards the individual in the pursuit of Platonic purity, and assumes that the bodies of all users will submit to his abstract reasoning, while Eames offers specificity and thus locks the user into a prescribed body form.[56] In a historical period dominated by racial segregation and prohibitions on the movements and actions of the Black body, the

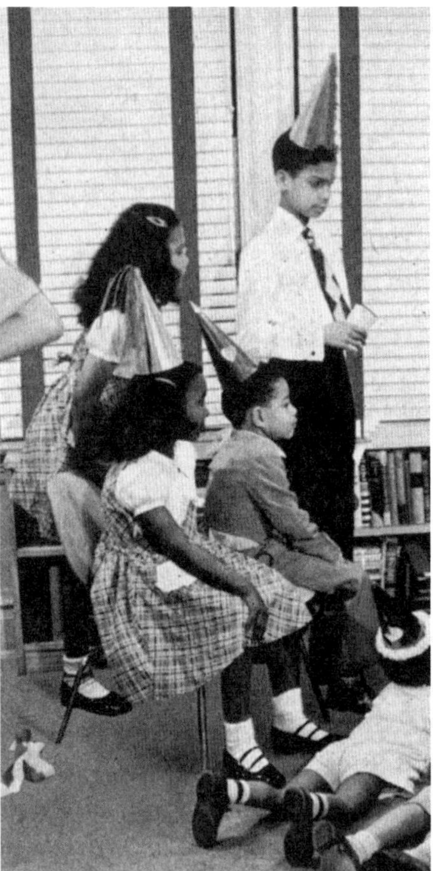

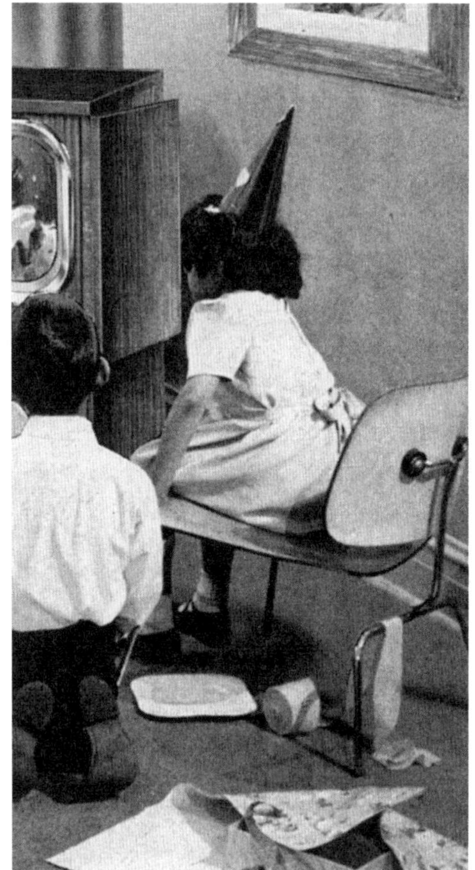

Fig. 94 (above). Detail of Advertisement for Motorola Television, *Ebony*, May 1952, 31. Beinecke Rare Book and Manuscript Library. Yale University.

Fig. 95 (above right). Detail of Advertisement for Motorola Television, *Ebony*, May 1952, 31. Beinecke Rare Book and Manuscript Library. Yale University.

Fig. 96 (right). Model on the Marshmallow Sofa, c. 1956. Vitra Design Museum, Estate of George Nelson.

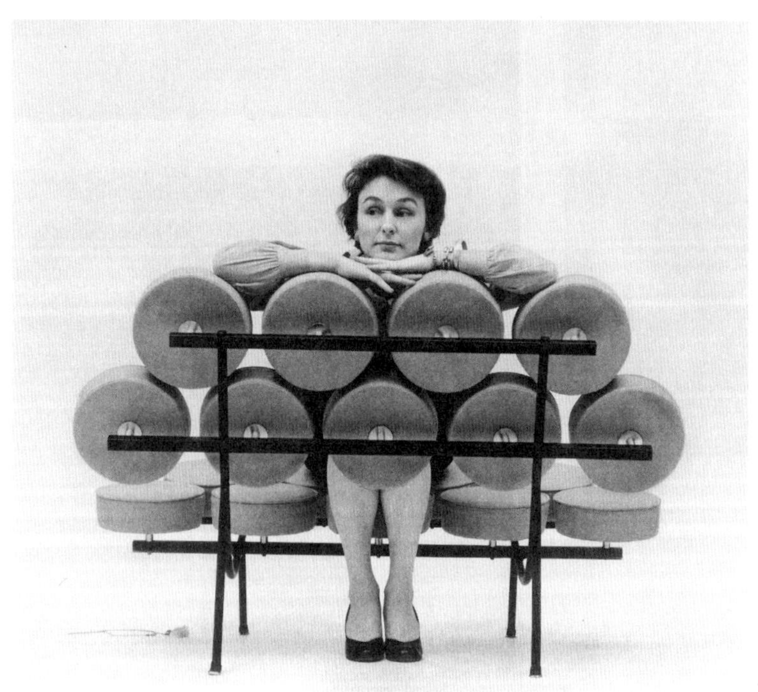

authority exercised by these designs can be understood as an expression of racial Whiteness, a way of defining and maintaining racial privilege. The racial identity of the designers—all of whom were White—is undoubtedly important here, but my analysis is not intended to ascribe conscious racializing agendas to the designers. Rather, we should recognize that these objects strategically control bodies and legislate physical behaviors through their visual and physical forms, and I argue that we should contextualize this control within the larger historic moment. In an era when White bodies could control bodies of color, and did so in order to define superiority and establish racial identity, to design objects that discipline bodies into specific comportment is an act of White privilege.

Accessories and the Construction of Whiteness at Herman Miller

A close reading of the forms of Herman Miller's mid-century designs suggests some avenues for understanding how they may have participated in the construction of racialized identities for consumers. However, the formal analyses of these objects that I have conducted over the previous two sections must be accompanied by an additional methodological approach that contextualizes them in their historical period. A study of Herman Miller's own publicity materials and the magazines in which these objects appeared allows us to explore how the designs were framed for the consuming public. By situating the objects within the photographs, articles, and advertisements where consumers would have encountered them, we can develop a more nuanced view of the role of racialized identity in Herman Miller products at mid-century.

As I have discussed elsewhere in this book, Dianne Harris has studied the architectural experience of racial Whiteness in postwar suburbia. She argues that postwar suburban architecture, much of which seems unremarkable to historians, actually constructed and enforced an idea of ex-nominated Whiteness.[57] She studies various aspects of postwar suburban design, including architectural plans, commercial architectural renderings, and representations of suburban homes in magazines, and uses a twofold method to analyze the construction of Whiteness. She examines how Whiteness was defined both positively (Whites "deciding what they are") and negatively (Whites identifying "what they are not").[58] In arguing that Herman Miller's Modernist designs carried associations to racialized Whiteness, I follow Harris's model of both positive and negative definitions: I examine both how these designs promote Whiteness positively and how they construct it negatively, through contrast with racialized others. To the extent that the designs are based on flatness, abstraction, and control of the human body in their forms, as I have argued in the two preceding sections, Whiteness is positively fashioned in them. In this section,

I demonstrate how Whiteness was constructed for these objects positively—depicted White users—and also negatively, through absence or implied contrast, in Herman Miller's publicity materials.

Herman Miller products appeared in a wide range of magazines during the 1950s beyond *Life*, including shelter magazines such as *Better Homes and Gardens*, *House Beautiful*, and *House and Garden*, and women's general interest magazines such as *Woman's Home Companion* and *Woman's Day*. (While Modern design appears regularly in *Ebony*, as discussed in chapter 2, there are very few instances of recognizable Herman Miller furniture included in editorial or advertising imagery; the Motorola advertisement discussed above is one of the very few examples.)[59] In the shelter and women's magazines, whether the furniture was part of a featured home article or served as props in a fashion photograph, the people depicted interacting with the furniture were always White.[60] Moreover, some of the terms used in these publications to describe Modernist furniture generally imply racialized readings. Modern furniture, for example, was repeatedly praised for its ability to facilitate a clean, tidy, and spacious home, qualities that might have insinuated racial Whiteness, a rhetorical strategy I have analyzed in chapters 1 and 2. For example, a 1954 advertisement for Masonite Presdwood in *House and Garden* featured a "brilliant, beautiful … clean-lined, functional chest" made by Herman Miller.[61] As philosopher Shannon Sullivan has suggested, "unconscious habits of connecting whiteness with cleanliness and blackness with impurity" pervade American culture, and Richard Dyer traces this stereotype even further back in history, connecting Whiteness with purity in the Christian church; he argues that "to be white is to have expunged all dirt, faecal or otherwise, from oneself: to look white is to look clean."[62] One particularly animated editorial in *Better Homes and Gardens* noted that many Modernist interior decorators seemed to want "no truck with the past," and were determined to "make a clean sweep" of older furnishings. The author described the resulting atmosphere: "They would have no ancestral residues. No nostalgia. Their new houses are really designed for a race of very young orphans of unknown parentage. With amnesia, if possible."[63] The implied fantasy was of inhabitants with no history and no ethnicity, either. Modernism's blank slate became White through the erasure of any signs of otherness. Herman Miller, as an exemplar of Modernist design for these publications, epitomized this ex-nominating Whiteness.

In its own publicity materials, Herman Miller staged racial identity through a rhetoric of binary identities in which Whiteness was contrasted against, and defined by its difference from, a variety of racial others. This rhetoric appears in a series of photographs staged by Herman Miller in the late 1940s and 1950s that illustrate the product catalogues; some of these were created specifically for the publications, while others were taken from the showroom floors.[64] Nelson's office oversaw much of the

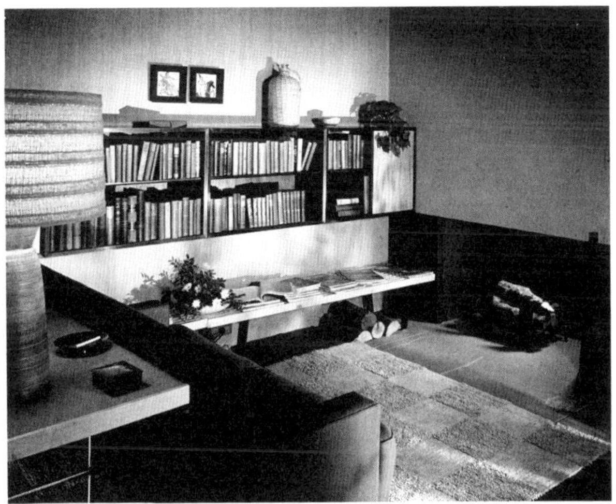

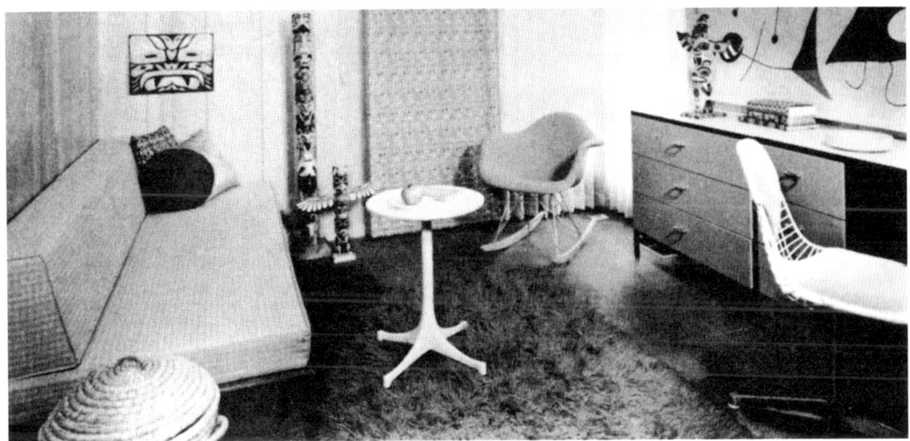

staging of the showrooms, staging of the catalogue photographs, and the design of the catalogues, and can be considered artistic authors of these images.[65] The Eames studio was responsible for images of its own products (and designed the installation of the Los Angeles showroom for Herman Miller).[66] Race begins to appear in these images in the props used to accessorize the rooms. The props, not all identical, merit our attention. In various photographs, the props include the following: driftwood, a woven basket with an abstract pattern, and laboratory flasks (see fig. 81);[67] a loaf of bread cut open, cheese, and a rustic, earthenware-type pitcher,[68] and a hand thrown ceramic dish with a folk-inspired snake decoration.[69] In a model room whose photograph appeared in catalogues from 1948 through 1952, plants, a glass jug covered in wicker weaving, and books and magazines accessorize the space (fig. 97);[70] a 1961 catalogue showed an assortment of miniature Northwest Native American totem poles in a model room "for the young student" (fig. 98).[71] In an image of the Eames ESUs from the 1952 catalogue, probably staged by the Eameses, woven baskets and bowls from Native American nations are interspersed with the cabinets (fig. 99).[72] In a picture of Nelson's Comprehensive Storage System (CSS), Oaxacan folk figurines and a trio of Nayarit horn players park on different shelves (fig. 100).[73]

In all of these images, the props were distinct from the furniture because they were not for sale.[74] Thus within each photograph the viewers found a binary relationship between product and nonproduct. Despite the many differences among these props, the recurring binary relationship of product/nonproduct encouraged the viewer to associate all of the products together on one side (available for purchase) and all of the accessories on the other side (not for sale, and thus inconsequential). Out of these two broad opposing categories, additional characteristics begin to emerge. The props are one of a kind, as opposed to the mechanical multiples that are the Modern designs. They are nature as opposed to industry, and hand as opposed to machine. They are decoration and exuberance, as opposed to austerity and restraint. (Indeed, the outliers in this pool of examples are the laboratory flasks in fig. 81. Despite their industrial pedigree, their presence in a domestic setting is emphatically whimsical.)[75] They offer a depicted body, as opposed to the implied body of the abstract furniture. They are primitive as opposed to cultured. They are, finally, racially colored—black, brown, tan, red—as opposed to white. The "other" represented by the props in these photographs is quite heterogeneous, but because it is always positioned against the industrial, rational, White self of the products, the images encourage the conflation of variety into a single binary difference: all colors, all bodies, all props are simplified into the opposite of White identity.

The Whiteness that these images forge is characterized by financial power—the ability to purchase—and control over others. Owning the furniture and the props in a fictional tableau, apartment, or house would imply possession of other cultures, the ability to appropriate as needed, and ultimately the power to contain and exercise intellectual control over their existence. These rooms admit to the enormity of a postwar global self-awareness, but they do so through the privileged, powerful eyes of a White, Western collector: the others in the world are firmly kept in a place subordinate to the rational, Modern Western world, displayed on shelves divorced from any context like objects isolated in a museum display. To the extent that some of these objects appear to be examples of tourist art made available to White travelers by indigenous craftspeople, they are doubly filtered: they represent what a craftsperson knows a White outsider wants to see of her heritage. As Sullivan notes, "Whiteness as possession describes not just the act of owning, but also the obsessive psychosomatic state of white owners. Commodifying non-white peoples and cultures, unconscious habits of white privilege tend to transform them into objects for white appropriation and use. The benefits accrued to white people through this process include not merely economic gain, but also increased

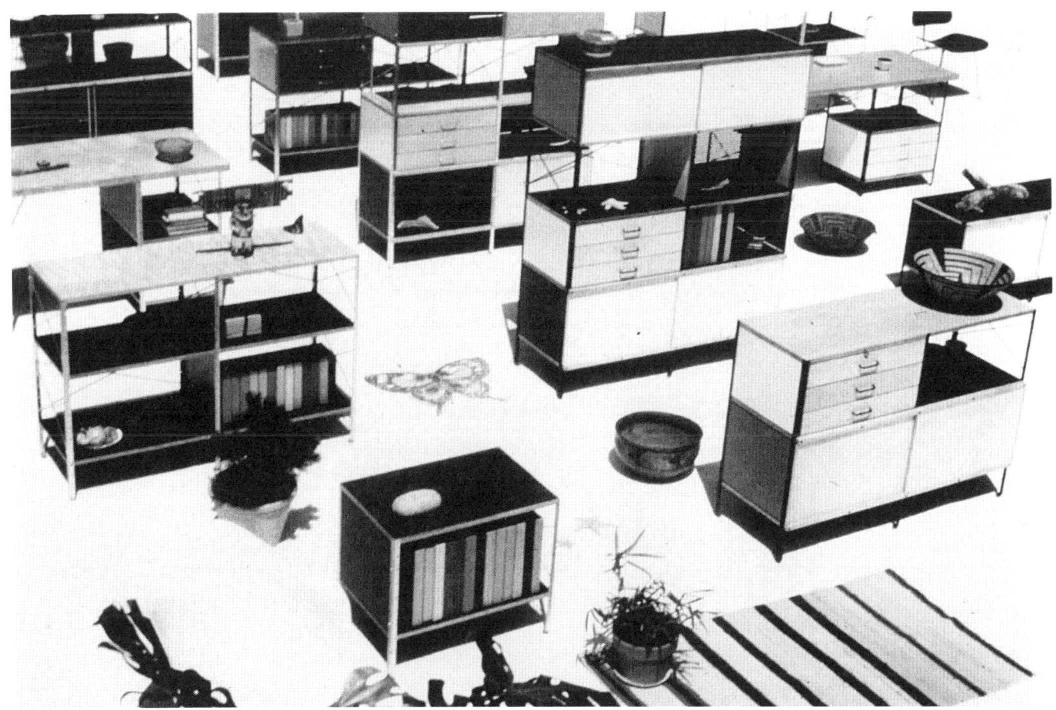

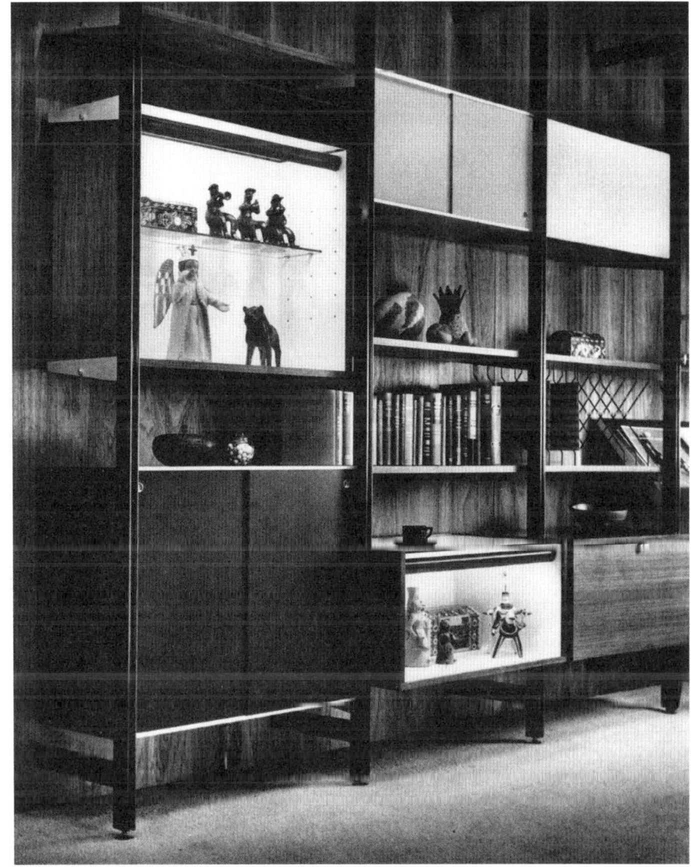

Fig. 99 (above). Display of Eames Storage Units. Photograph published in *Herman Miller Collection* (product catalogue, 1952), 103. Courtesy of Herman Miller Archives.

Fig. 100 (right). Comprehensive Storage System, introduced 1959, George Nelson Associates, designers. Herman Miller Furniture Company, manufacturer. Steel, veneered and laminated plywood, sizes variable. Photograph published in Herman Miller product catalogue, c. 1961. Courtesy of Herman Miller Archives.

ontological security and satisfaction of unconscious desires."[76] The storage units convey this dynamic with particular effectiveness. If the grid of storage devices represents the rational, White Western world, then among the ESUs the Native American vessels struggle and assimilate uneasily (see fig. 99): they expand beyond the boundaries of the grid, challenging its effectiveness, and are occasionally banished to the floor beside it. The CSS seems more confident in its ability to contain and systematize all of the variegated otherness of the global marketplace: its grid firmly colonizes many competing artifacts, holding each in its proper, predetermined place (see fig. 100). Indeed, in another photograph in the 1960–62 catalogue, a different CSS configuration is accessorized with a collection of books; prominently visible on the spine of one is the title *The Conquest of Peru*.[77]

At this juncture, it bears noting that the Eameses had popularized a decorating aesthetic of dense accumulation that provided, in the words of Peter and Alison Smithson, "extra-cultural surprise."[78] In their house, first made known to the world in 1950 through photographs in *Arts and Architecture* magazine (and subsequently *Life*), they arranged countless objects of varied geographical origins; Pat Kirkham's astute analysis of this "functional decoration" draws attention to both the relentless precision with which the varied objects were placed in the house as well as the pervasive Romantic sensibility that seemed to govern the Eameses' curating.[79] The photographs used in Herman Miller's publications demonstrate a related, but markedly different, approach. While the Eameses delighted in accumulation, often hiding their Modernist furniture entirely underneath layers of Native American textiles or carefully arrayed folk figurines from many different cultures, the metaphorical balance of power in the Herman Miller photographs is different. In the commercial photographs, the Modern designs are highly visible and legible, while the accessories are few, firmly presented as the items that stand out for their difference: they are not for sale. Moreover, the use of non-Western artifacts in these commercial photographs differs from how some other Modernists of the postwar period engaged with non-Western objects. Josef and Anni Albers offer a single contrasting example. These two Modern artists—Josef, a painter, and Anni, a textile artist—traveled to Latin America numerous times in the middle decades of the twentieth century. Both were inspired by the art that they saw on their travels, and called upon it in their work; they also eventually built a collection of more than one thousand objects.[80] Their appreciation of this aesthetic tradition distinct from their own was shaped by years of study and a deep understanding of its history and culture, and they celebrated these objects not as exotic curios but as complex works of art in a tradition different from their own.

The tendency to position Herman Miller's Modernist design through racializing lenses is found in other contemporaneous documents. A 1956 Herman Miller advertisement features a vibrantly colored mask from Bali suspended against a field of white in its upper left corner (fig. 101).[81] Like

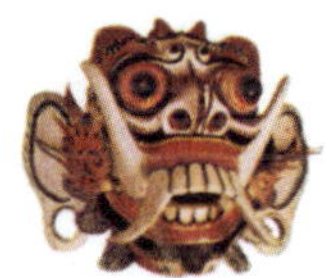
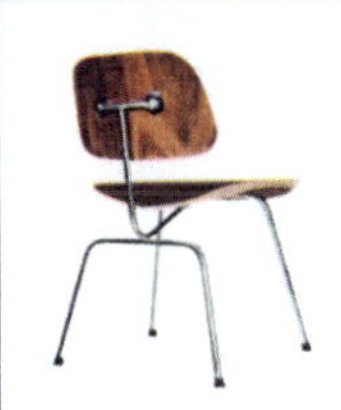
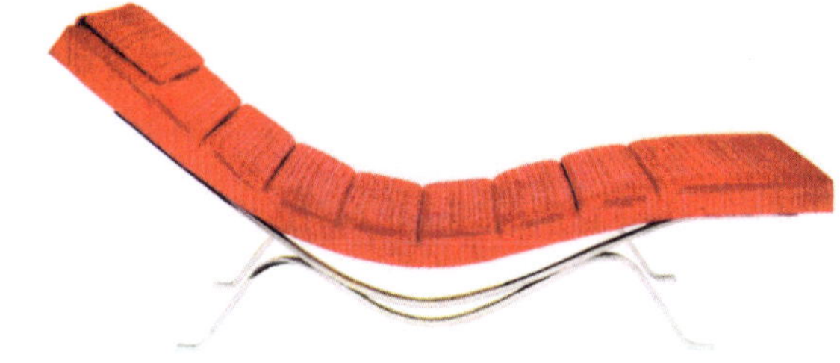
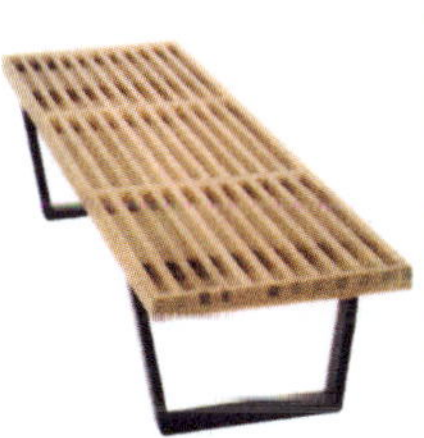
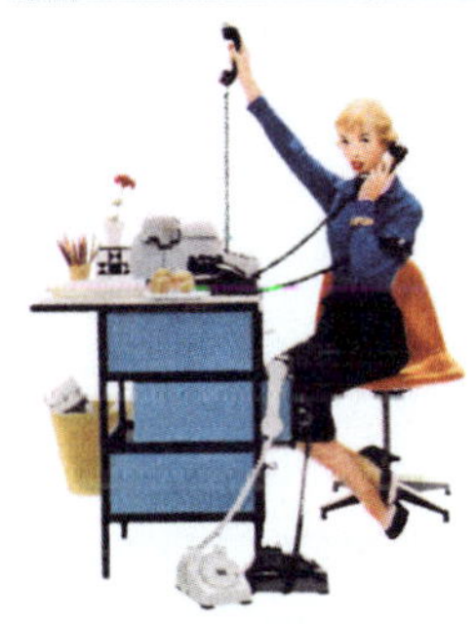
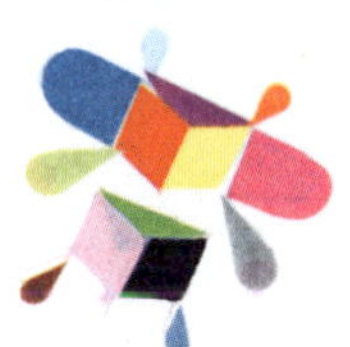
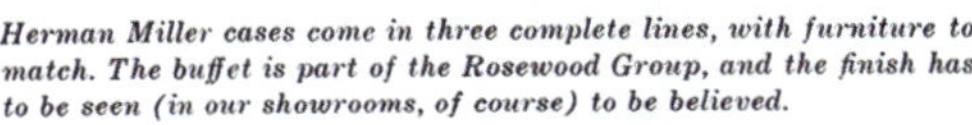
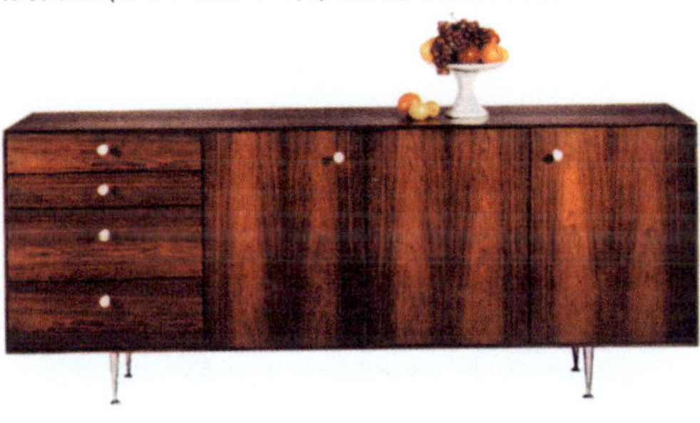
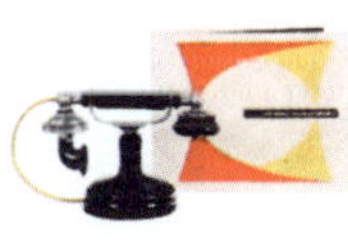

Fig. 101. Advertisement for Herman Miller, *New Yorker*, May 12, 1956, 29. Courtesy of Herman Miller Archives.

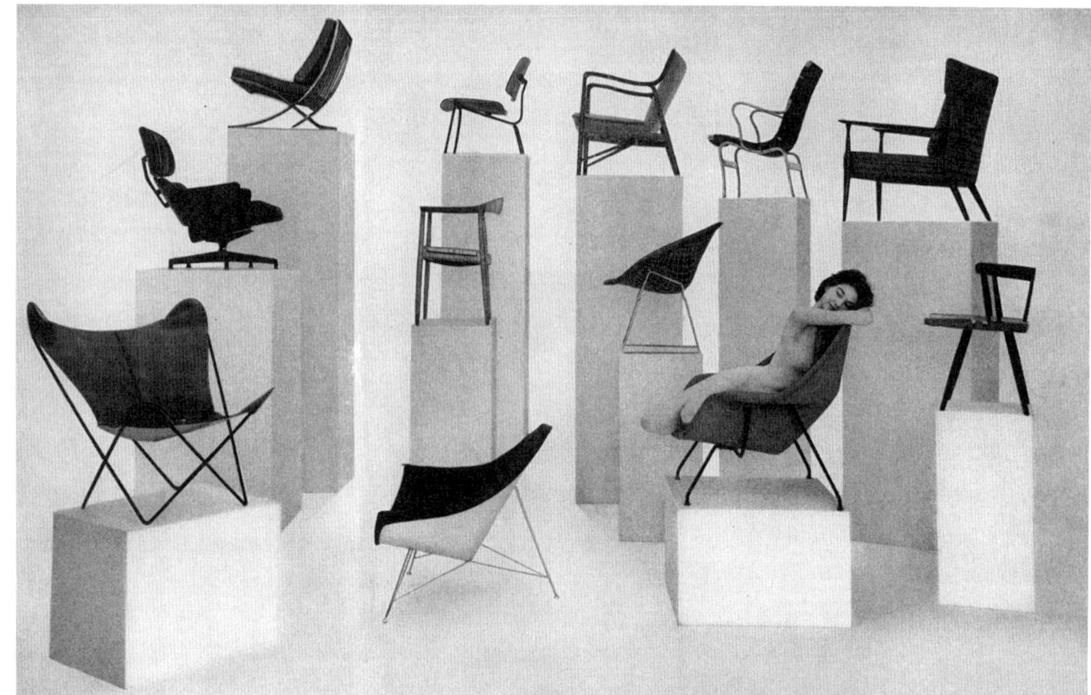

Fig. 102. John Rawlings, untitled photograph accompanying the article "Chairs," by George Nelson, *Holiday*, November 1957, 140–41. Courtesy Private Collection, California.

the accessories that persistently appeared in the Nelson-staged catalogue photographs, its presence in the advertisement seems to function as a rhetorical point of contrast to the Herman Miller products, floating elsewhere in the ad against the same white background. "Herman Miller's designers, Nelson, Eames and Girard, are a many sided lot," explains the ad copy that accompanied the mask. "George Nelson, whose office designed most of the pieces on this page, is also a fanatical photographer of curiosities. Sample: the Javanese mask." The text links the mask to Nelson and seems to provide two levels of meaning to the products displayed elsewhere in the ad. First, the mask is evidence of Nelson's creativity (as he loses himself in "fanatical" photography of such objects), and the complex scope (or "many sides") of his artistic genius. Second, the mask is trivialized as a "curiosity," another "side" to Nelson that is clearly less important than his side as a designer. His ability to appreciate the irrational other is, ultimately, a sign of his power over it: he may photograph the masks (and be casually inaccurate about their geographical origin), but he can appropriate the aesthetic lessons he needs from them without letting them consume him.[82] In this, his gesture recalls the position of the White male Abstract Expressionist who, as Ann Gibson argues, can absorb the properties of the irrational, primitive other without losing his social position of mastery.[83] A contemporaneous account of the use of accessories in the Herman Miller showrooms, "such as Indian artifacts," describes their function as "lend[ing] character to the settings," which firmly places them in a subordinate position, one that enhances the products without ever overshadowing them.[84]

Indeed, the following year, in the high-end glossy magazine *Holiday*, Nelson wrote an article about chairs in which he invoked race. He notes that not all cultures use chairs for sitting: "The Watussi, Bedouins, Eskimos and New Irelanders do not [use chairs when they feel like sitting down], and neither do the Okinawans, Hottentots or Outer Mongolians." While he is quick to remind his readers that, "historically, the presence or absence of chairs has not been an entirely reliable indication of the level of a culture," citing "the emperors and nobles of Japan [who] have squatted with monumental grace and dignity for centuries," his examples effectively set up a racial binary: non-White peoples do not use chairs, while White cultures do.[85] The implied conclusion is that the Modernist chairs featured in the article are evolutionarily appropriate for its White readers, exemplified in the White nude model shown in the accompanying photograph made by fashion photographer John Rawlings (fig. 102).

Gender in Herman Miller Designs

Not only does Rawlings's photograph for *Holiday* suggest that Modernism be read as White, but it also introduces questions about the role of gender in mid-century design. The narrative of this chapter has thus far investigated how we might read race into Herman Miller's products, and as I shift to a discussion of gender, it is vital to reflect on points of contrast and overlap in these lines of analysis. Race is one avenue for talking about how power is modeled in this furniture, and just as racial relationships are about identity and power, so too are gendered relationships. It is therefore unsurprising to discover recurrent gendered tropes in the marketing literature and imagery around Herman Miller. Postcolonial theorists have reminded us that the racialized other is often feminized in the eyes of Western patriarchal power, and we miss a key part of the story about Herman Miller furniture and the construction of power if we neglect to investigate how these objects participated in the construction of gendered identities as they engaged with race.[86]

In 1953, as George Nelson's office was fully immersed in designs for Herman Miller, Nelson himself published a compendium of Modern seating designs, titled, simply, *Chairs*. In his introduction to the volume, he describes the distinction (traced above in my introductory discussion) between case furniture that creates a uniform, background grid, and chairs that stand out, literally and figuratively. Referring to the open floor plans of suburban ranch houses, he writes, "When the walls disappear, the only place left for furniture is out in the open. Hence silhouette becomes important, and most traditional designs for seating become unusable." He

Fig. 103. Photographer unknown, Frontispiece, *Chairs*, Whitney Publications, New York, 1953.

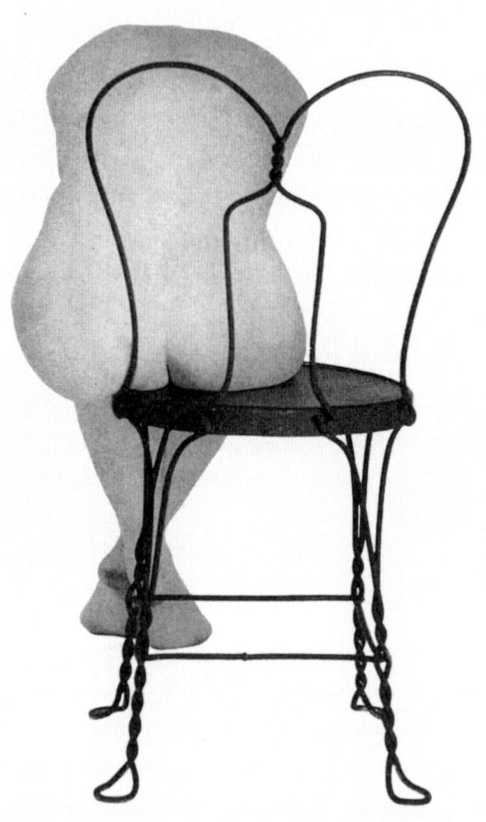

continues: "In this … landscape the chair remains as one of the unassimila-
ble objects and in consequence it becomes very conspicuous. It becomes
as much a piece of sculpture as an object of utility. One might now compare it to a girl in a Bikini suit, who has to pay more attention to her figure
than the ladies in the bathing costumes of the Mack Sennett era."[87] The
image that serves as the frontispiece for the introduction is a striking photograph of a nude female figure seated on a twisted steel-rod ice-cream-
parlor chair (fig. 103). This photograph is clearly indebted to surrealism: the
woman's body becomes an abstract form, her waist echoing the contours
of the chair back and her crossed legs mimicking the chair legs, the pads
of her feet the same shape as the feet of the chair. Moreover, there is a pal-
pable uneasiness in how her left buttock, misaligned with the chair, presses
into the edge of the seat. Yet the photograph is also indebted to some
very mainstream chauvinism, even misogyny: her head has literally been

cut off. The tired metaphor of woman as object is given new life as we consider every chair in a living room as a possible stage for a diva-like self-presentation, every chair as the object of the male gaze.

In 1957, in his *Holiday* magazine article, Nelson again returned to the topic of chairs and again invoked the idea of the chair as a woman. In the Rawlings photograph that accompanies the text, we experience a scopic delight in discovering the nude figure as our eyes explore the contours of each chair presented in silhouette (see fig. 102). Nelson's text reinforces that delight in a few rhetorically powerful passages. He describes, first, the experience of watching a woman sit in Hardoy's Butterfly Chair:

> The Hardoy in the traditional sense is not really a chair at all, for you cannot sit on it. You drop into it and are enfolded, much like a ball in a catcher's mitt, or a glass float in a fishnet. This in itself is revealing, for it indicates that our society is somewhat less formal in its habits than others. [A time-traveler visiting the world of 1957] would have to conclude that either the usual attitudes about modesty had been junked, or that women wore slacks. A dress, in this contraption, usually travels upward rapidly to a point somewhere between knee and hip, which is why it is customarily photographed with a child, a large dog or a nude.[88]

Later, Nelson turns to a discussion of his own office's Coconut Chair, admitting that the design requires "practice and agility" from the person sitting in it. However, he qualifies the chair's functional limitations by anthropomorphizing it and appealing to the visual pleasure it provides: "We continue, however, to admire its elegance while making no mention of the fact that to enjoy the view one naturally sits in something more comfortable."[89] His language raises the question: Which view—that of the chair, or the nude in the chair? Indeed, a similar message was insinuated in the 1956 Herman Miller advertisement that featured the mask from Bali; the copy, likely written by Nelson, describes the 5490 slat steel chaise (see fig. 101): "Probably the most spectacular piece in the Herman Miller line—expensive too—is the chaise. … Properly filled (we are referring to you, Madam) it is guaranteed to put a new glint into the most tired husband's eye."[90]

The attention-getting Marshmallow Sofa was, appropriately, photographed with a White woman sitting on it, and the image of Hilda Longinotti reclining on the sofa became one of the best-known representations of the design (see fig. 76).[91] The photograph reveals many of the gendered power dynamics that are at play in Nelson's other discussions of chairs. We, the viewers, look at Longinotti from behind the sofa: the photograph dramatizes the fact that however she sits on this object, no matter where she is viewed from, her body is always on display. Indeed, the sofa possesses neither physical nor visual empathy; rather, it functions as a stage setting for the voyeuristic consumption of the female figure. With her sculpted curls and striped dress, she becomes an extension of the abstractions of the sofa. The round cushion at her bust playfully alludes to the shape of her imagined figure and seems to admit to some self-awareness of the gender politics of the image. But the premise of the image is the tantalizing glimpses we are given of her, and the expectation that our gaze desires to see more. The pleasure comes in the work of our imagination: we see her bare wrists, bare ankles, the drape of her skirt falling away from her legs, and our curiosity is seduced. Is she on a bubble sofa or in a bubble bath? The photograph reinforces the point that it is a sofa to look at—or to look at someone sitting on—but is not for sitting one's own body on.

If Nelson's chairs are women to be gazed at, then it is possible to understand the Eames chairs as complicit with the same political vision. Formally, they are objects composed of unusual curves that are visually pleasing to look at. Functionally, their curves promise to caress the human body, providing physical delight to the fatigued sitter. Certainly, there is a frequently discussed trend in advertisements from the later 1950s and 1960s that depict men sitting in the lounge chair; it provides comfort to them in the domestic sanctuary of the suburban home after a day in the tiring work world (figs. 104, 105).[92] While this might seem to contradict the claim of the chair as the object of the male gaze, an alternative interpretation foregrounds the profoundly intimate physical interaction between the sitter and the chair in these advertisements. In each, the man reclines deeply into the chair, completely relaxed (or occasionally asleep), his body fully embraced. In a society where heterosexual relations were considered normative, the intimate embrace of the chair would have to be that of a woman. Indeed, a 1959 advertisement produced by Herman Miller for the lounge chair seems to give viewers the idealized, heteronormative nuclear family of the suburbs: father cradles baby, both of them asleep, cradled by the mother/chair (see fig. 105).

If women are frequently equated with the racialized other, then it is important to recall that in its first three decades of production, the Eames Lounge Chair was made with rosewood veneer, a wood sourced from tropical rainforests.[93] This markedly "exotic" material perhaps turns the chair more fully into a servant: the chair is entirely identified as nurturing and non-Western—perhaps recalling a figure such as the Wrights' servant Dorcas Hollingsworth from chapter 1—and it exists solely to make the man of the house comfortable. From a broader perspective, it is worth considering how these images associated with Herman Miller products—either generated by the company or using their products—depict people interacting with the furniture. White men sit comfortably, in full possession of the objects. White women sit, perhaps comfortably, but always on view for the White men in the house: they and the furniture are objects of the possessing male gaze. African American children sit awkwardly and uncomfortably, rarely allowed to take ownership of the ghost-like body that precedes them as a model in the chair.

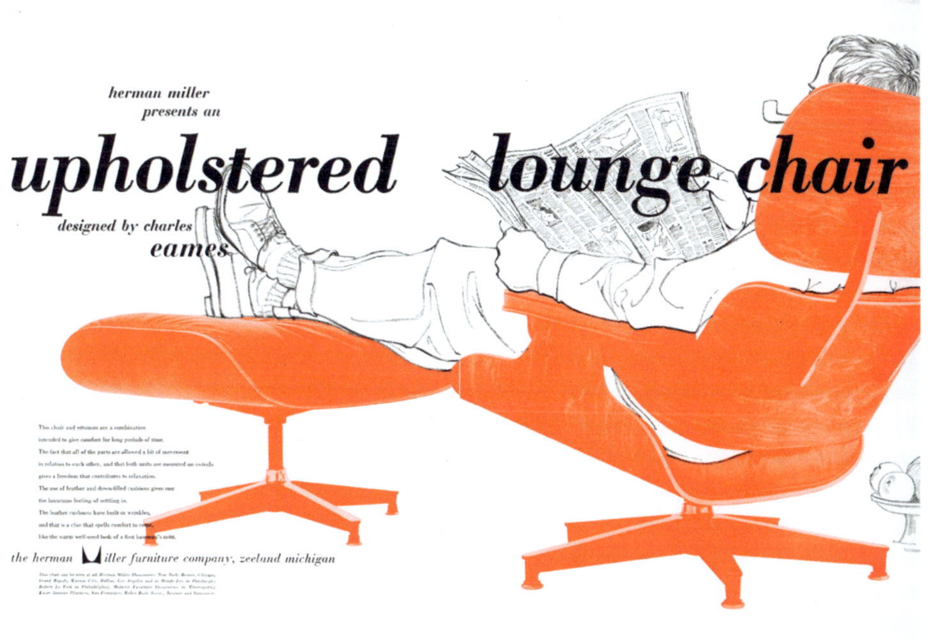

Fig. 104 (above). Advertisement for the Eames Lounge Chair. Herman Miller Furniture Company, c. 1956. Courtesy of Herman Miller Archives.

Fig. 105 (right). Advertisement for the Eames Lounge Chair. Herman Miller Furniture Company, 1959. Courtesy of Herman Miller Archives.

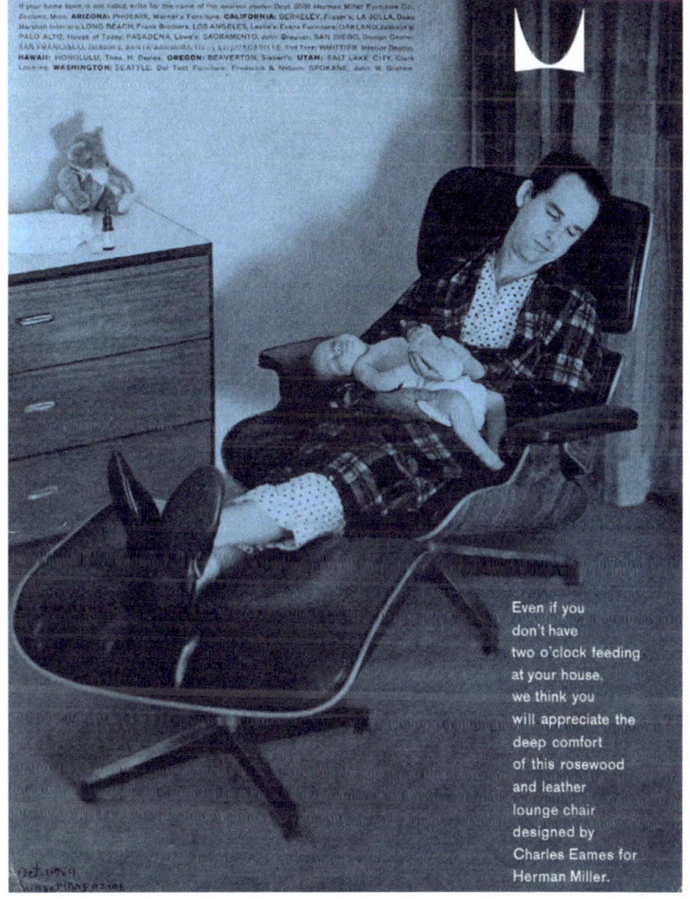

Conclusion

In 1960, Nelson raised hackles among the residents of the new suburban development in Park Forest, Illinois, when he reportedly quipped, in a press conference, that "housing developments like Park Forest are more fit for 'lima beans than human beings.'"[94] His alleged critique—in keeping with the general tenor of his published writings—positions him as an outsider who is critical of the conforming culture of the mid-century suburbs. Like Herman Miller's designs that flattered consumers for having a "high IQ" and a "spine" that resisted current popular period-revival decorating trends, he may have considered himself "highbrow." And, indeed, White suburban consumers may have considered themselves to be "highbrow" in buying this furniture—individualistic, resisting the conformity of the landscape that surrounded them.

Yet within the ideology of the suburbs, conformity and individuality are no more than two poles in the same discourse. As theorist Slavoj Žižek argues, "the very notion of an access to reality unbiased by any discursive devices or conjunctions with power is ideological," and we must be aware "of how the very gesture of stepping out of ideology pulls us back into it."[95] The call to be an individual is, in the end, no less ideological than the conformity it means to resist. In providing commodities that advertised their owners' independence of mind and body, Nelson, Eames, and Herman Miller merely staked out another neighborhood in the ideology of postwar suburbia. Ultimately this assessment is reinforced by the consistent manipulation of gendered and racial signifiers for consumers in the publicity photographs, advertisements, and writings relating to Herman Miller's products in the postwar decades. Far from mounting a critique of existing power structures, these images and designs ultimately reinforced a traditionally gendered, White worldview. As such, the designs may have been high-class, but they were not nearly the critical avant-garde of the highbrow. White women were understood as objects of beauty, properly celebrated on a pedestal for male gazes; people of color were included to the extent that they provided accent and variety against the dominant rational, "clean-lined" Modernism. Moreover, the abstract transcendence of the furniture's geometries and bold patterns—which could be read as a language of White patriarchal power—was ultimately invested in exerting physical control over its users. Models of color and White women had fewer reasons to feel ownership—and may, in fact, have physically felt less comfortable—sitting in these designs than the White men who were the presumed standard of suburban American society (and which should recall Norman Rockwell's patriarch portrayed in fig. 1). While there may be no essentially "White" form or "feminine" line in these objects, their invest-ment in the politics of race and gender emerges in the narratives spun around them and in the ways they were deployed for use in the postwar world. This chapter has not pursued the particular counter-narrative of

Modernism in African American lives as suggested in Williams's writings and in *Ebony* magazine. However, by focusing on how Herman Miller's products engaged constructions of racial and gendered identity, it illuminates a counter-interpretation of these canonical forms of American Modernist design from the mid-century decades.

The accessories that populated mid-century homes are important for understanding Herman Miller's designs, and they merit further examination. The use, collecting, and display of these varied objects are the subjects of the final chapter.

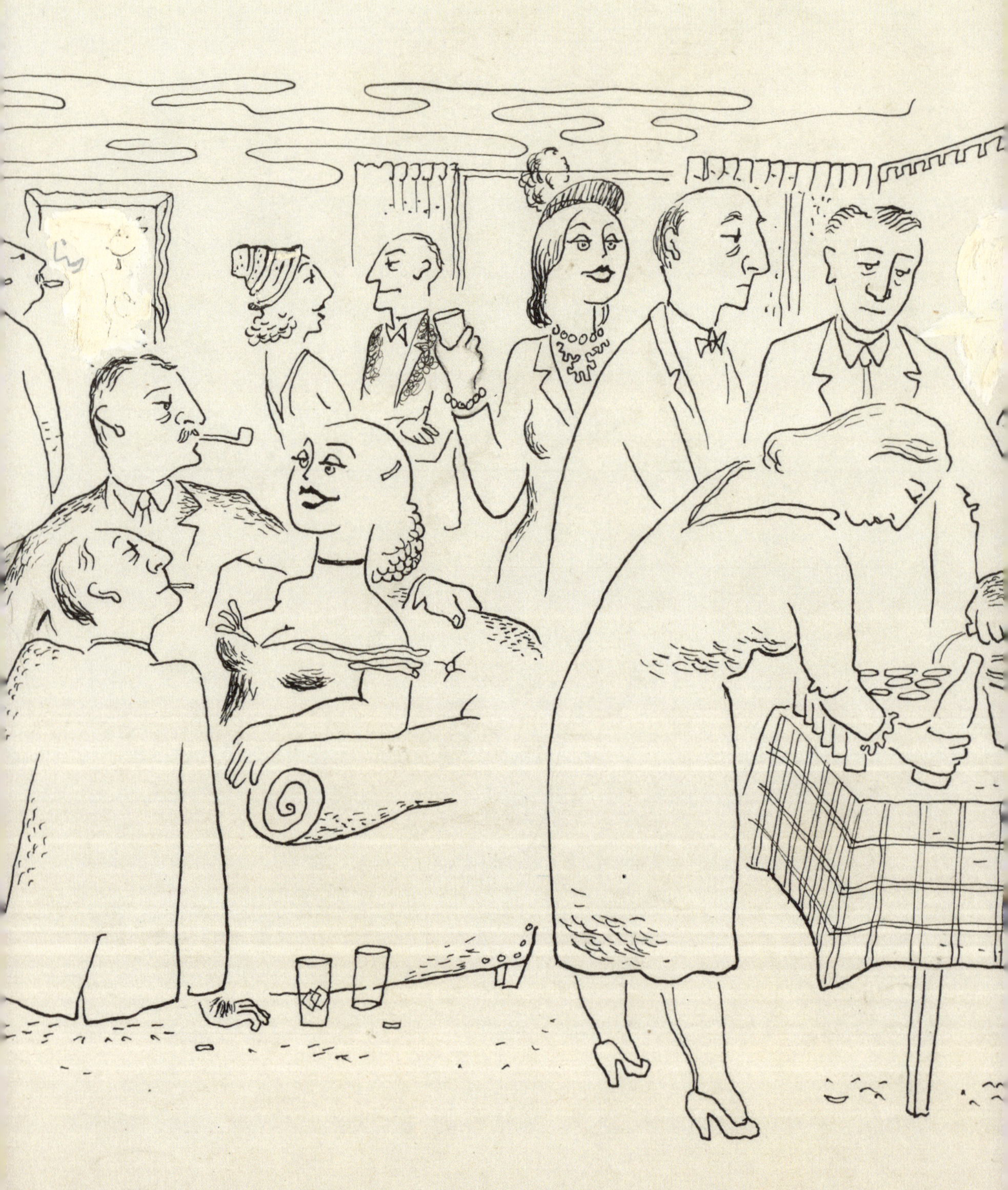

"The Quick Appraising Glance"
Decorative Accessories and the Staged Self

Russel Wright built his design career on the small-scale decorative accessories that filled suburban homes. Best known for the plates, dishes, and tabletop serving items in the American Modern line,[1] Wright also coauthored *Guide to Easier Living* (discussed in chapter 1) with his wife Mary, and designed glassware, ashtrays, serving platters, candy dishes, vases, cocktail shakers, and bookends. In a 1948 column for the *New York Times*, he persuasively describes the power of these deceptively small objects: "In any room the accessories assume greater visual prominence than furniture or background, simply because of their greater proximity to the eye and the hand. It is by the accessories that the guest is most apt to judge the taste of the owner."[2]

Wright's statement quickly exposes a pervasive truism of postwar suburban culture: the tendency to judge one's neighbors. But while judgment can be rendered on innumerable fronts—how one's children behave, how one's front lawn is kept, how loud one plays music—Wright points to the small objects that decorate living and dining spaces as a particular site of assessment. According to the advice of decorators, designers, and advertisers, these are the pieces that stand out against the "stark nakedness" of the furniture, in the words of one author, "personalize a room," and "supply an opportunity for artistic expression in their collection and composition."[3] Mary L. Brandt, whose book *Decorate Your Home for Better Living* was also discussed in chapter 1, weighs in on the transformative value of accessories, reminding her readers that "they give warmth, personality and the lived-in look to a room. You could furnish two rooms exactly alike, and yet they will seem to be entirely different merely because of the difference in accessories."[4] Freighted with the power of self-expression, these objects become far more meaningful than their diminutive size might suggest. They acquire the authority to represent one's sense of self and identity before the evaluating eyes of visitors to the home. As one 1956 sociological study of suburbia notes, the adult homeowner "automatically watches for the quick appraising glance which will tell him that the recently acquired property item is acceptable and desirable."[5]

Through his reference to "the eye and hand," Wright's comments actually point to something beyond mere neighborly judgment. Many of these accessories cater directly to the body: they are the small objects that are picked up, held in the hands of hostess and guest alike. As such, they become material proxies for the owner: they serve the body of the guest—providing snacks, liquids, a repository for cigarette ashes—at the direction of the hostess. These objects tend to be tools for socializing, and so they are not merely a locus of judgment for their symbolic value but are a means of assessing how well a homeowner tends to the physical comfort of her guests. In short, they represent her capacity for hospitality.

This chapter has three sections that examine different types of decorative accessories marketed for the postwar suburban home. In each, I consider how these objects—through form and through marketing narratives—claimed to provide homeowners with symbols that marked their taste, identity, and self-perception as social agents through racialized and gendered lenses. In the first two sections, I examine the designs in terms of form, decoration, and functional engagement with the body of the user. First, in "The Playful Self," I explore the design of cocktail glasses, focusing on objects designed by Russel Wright and Freda Diamond. These frequently irreverent designs belie the unrealistic pressure put on middle-class housewives of diverse races to achieve a perfectly casual hospitality—a "festive and relaxing" atmosphere, in the words of one expert—through the correct deployment of an endless assortment of specialized glassware.[6] Moreover, the popularity of applied decorations designed by Diamond and sold through the mass-production Libbey Glass Company must be examined for their narratives that defined Whiteness as a condition of property ownership. Second, "The Artful Self" examines decorative ceramic accessories such as ashtrays, cigarette boxes, and pitchers manufactured by the Associated American Artists. These intentionally sloppy pieces were intended to express the informal nonchalance of the hostess, who could casually meet the needs of her guests with these modest objects. They failed as commercial products in part, however, because of their ambiguous commitment to racialized and gendered identities. Finally, "The Ordered Self" moves away from functional accessories to interrogate how homeowners were advised to hang art on the walls. Ranging from Audubon prints to authentic and fake African masks and figurines, the selection and arrangement of objects on the walls of the home was a tool to order one's identity for social consumption. Using pictorial evidence from *Ebony* and *Life* magazines, I argue that non-Western artifacts were treated differently in the two magazines, and suggest that by tracing the path of these accessories, we may uncover another facet in a counter-history of Modernism.

The Playful Self

Cocktail parties, and the drinking glasses that are the tools of their success, were a central motif in the myth of the postwar suburbs. Up until the end of World War II, only 35 percent of liquor in the United States was consumed at home, according to a survey conducted by a trade association for licensed beverages, while 65 percent was consumed in bars and restaurants. However, by 1951 the home had clearly become the preferred location for alcoholic consumption, with 70 percent of liquor sales destined for the home and only 30 percent "bought and drunk on the outside."[7] *House and Garden* further attested to the centrality of cocktail drinking at home when, in 1954, the editors suggested a variety of bridal shower themes and included (alongside "linen" and "kitchen") a "Bar shower."[8] Mary and Russel Wright promote cocktail parties in *Guide to Easier Living* as "the easiest way of entertaining large groups with refreshments," and the vivid illustration that accompanies their text reveals much about how such parties were imagined (fig. 106).[9] Illustrator James Kingsland's drawing features two rooms full of animated guests, gesturing, laughing, and posing for one another. People cluster in groups of twos and threes, with a few women strategically placed as sexually audacious, bombshell figures to arrest the guests' (and viewers') eyes (at the end of the food table on the left side and on a couch in the right half). The bar itself is merely a table adorned with multiple bottles, glasses, and accessories at the far right of the illustration. While it attracts the viewer's eye because of the density of its plaid tablecloth pattern and the checked jacket of the man holding a cocktail shaker behind it, its power is subtle, if not subversive: it is the source of the energy that drives the rest of the scene, but it is not the center of the scene. As originally published, Kingsland's illustration crosses the gutter of the book, encompassing the entire expanse of the page spread from far left margin to far right; it becomes a surrogate for the party, which, it seems, should ideally expand to fill the rooms of one's house with convivial energy.

If cocktail parties are a paragon of suburban casual living, they are also—as Kingsland's drawing intimates—the site where suburban politeness seems to disintegrate. Not only does the glamorous woman in the illustrated living room, wearing a low-cut dress and choker necklace, attract the attention of two men (and their phallic surrogates, a cigarette and a pipe), but something risqué seems about to happen on the far left, where a man's hand reaches perilously close to a woman's backside, as she sits on the dining table. Indeed, one of the men at the bar is no less than a priest. In a satirical denunciation of suburban mores, *The Crack in the Picture Window*, author John Keats notes that in upper-middle-class suburban developments, "no one dared throw the kind of bring-your-own-bottle party. ... Instead, they relentlessly poisoned one another with Martinis—the cheapest and most virulent man-bane known to

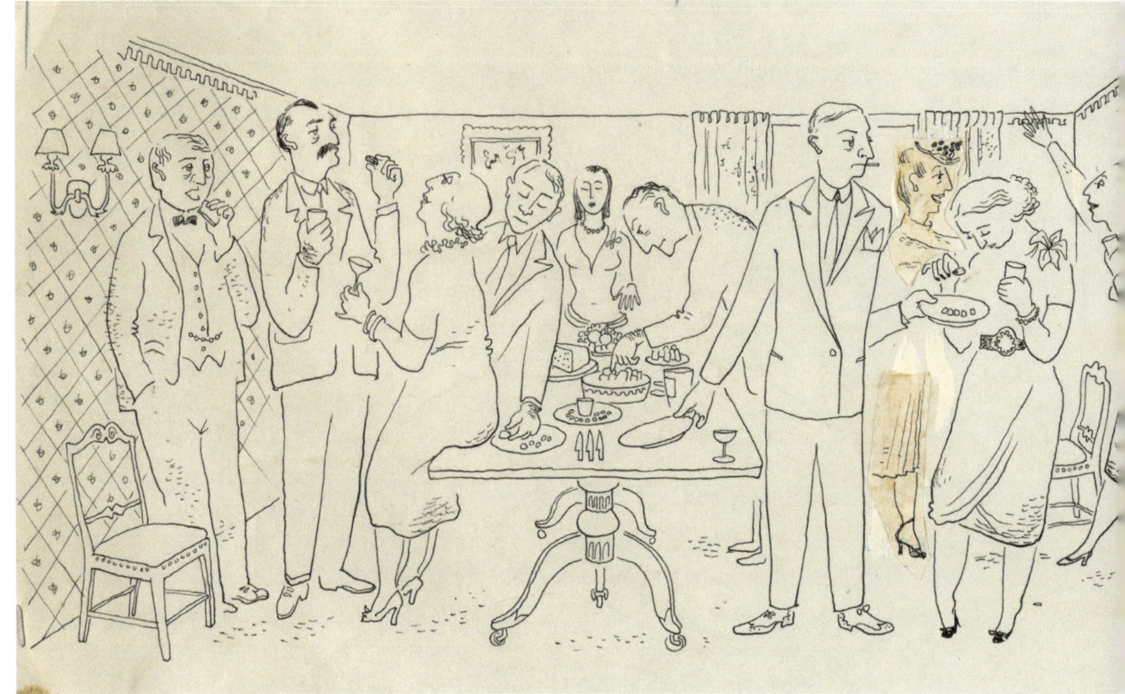

toxicology."[10] The behavior at such cocktail parties was filled with "coarse" jokes, "obvious" innuendos, and "prurient games" that left some inhabitants "slightly seasick."[11]

The playfulness of the cocktail party—teetering on the edge of complete social chaos—is invoked in numerous cocktail glass designs from the period. Wright's extremely popular American Modern dinnerware had been introduced in 1937 and might be understood as the designer's first successful attempt to make tools that would facilitate his ideal, more casual lifestyle (fig. 107). By 1949, he was actively developing a line of glass- and barware, manufactured by Morgantown Glass Works, that complemented the dinnerware (fig. 108). Marketed as the American Modern line, these glasses encourage a Modern, Wright-ian style of living that was ultimately codified in the *Guide*. The glasses share with the dinnerware an overall aesthetic of simple, biomorphic curves—the contour from the base through the stem and up into the cup is a seamless line—and there is no ornament to detract from the perception of the object as an organic whole unto itself. Such radically simplified, curved forms were called "coupe" in the trade, referring to the compact, streamlined, sporty car type (and distinguished from shapes such as "square" or "traditional" with a plain or decorated edge).[12] The designation "coupe" itself indicates that such forms were perceived as casual, and these glasses

Fig. 106. James Kingsland, "Cocktail parties can be the easiest way of entertaining," pp. 184–85. From *Guide to Easier Living* by Mary and Russel Wright (1950). Russel Wright Papers, Special Collections Research Center, Syracuse University Libraries.

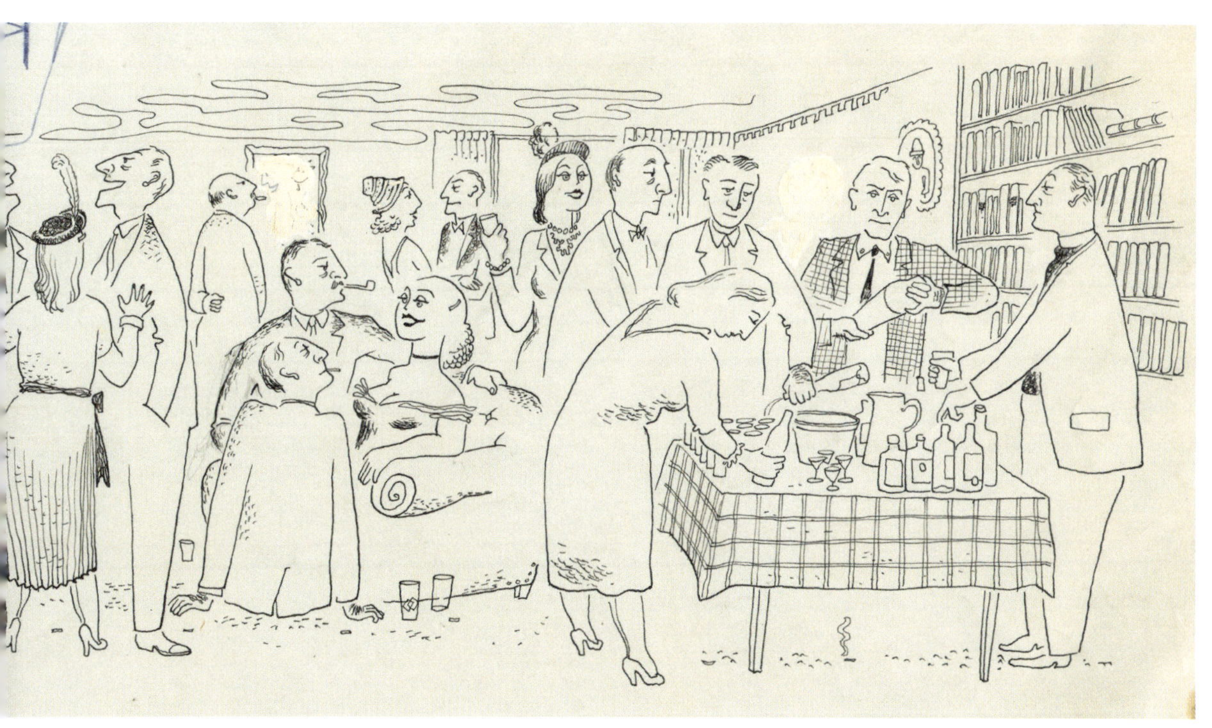

ably embody casual living: the lack of ornament frees them from historical reference, and the rounded forms have a playful air, seemingly alluding to balloons or balls. American Modern glassware was initially offered in four colors—coral, sea foam, chartreuse (a color referred to in the archives as "curry"), and gray—in addition to clear crystal.[13] The colors were intended to be mixed and to harmonize with the dinnerware palette, and in this the glasses further demonstrate casual living. Rather than dictating a table replete with identical matched items, the Wrights encouraged variety: with their tables set in several contrasting colors, they transformed an aesthetic that might once have been considered yard-sale jumble into the epitome of cool, self-confident casual entertaining.

Wright's designs for Morgantown were ultimately not as durable as he wanted, and therefore not as commercially successful as the company needed; manufacturing evidence suggests that the line was discontinued after 1951.[14] In the later 1950s, when the glasswares industry was dominated by fewer, larger companies that mass-produced fewer designs, Wright entered into a contract with Bartlett-Collins. For that company, he proposed a wide range of applied decorations that were intended to appear on various stock forms. The design that Bartlett-Collins ultimately produced was marketed under the name "Eclipse," and features gold and colored circles floating in an irregular pattern (fig. 109). The Eclipse design lacks the organic unity of the American Modern design—the circle pattern is merely placed on an existing body—but, like American Modern, it has

Fig. 107 (right). American Modern tableware, introduced 1937, Russel Wright, designer. Steubenville, manufacturer. Glazed earthenware, dimensions variable. RISD Museum, Providence, R.I. Gift of Mr. Robert Mehlman; Gift of Judith Tannenbaum in honor of Gertrude D. T. Schimmel; Gift of Mr. Glenn Gissler; Gift of Mr. James Brayton Hall. Image courtesy RISD Museum.

Fig. 108 (below). American Modern glassware, introduced 1950, Russel Wright, designer. Morgantown Glass Works, manufacturer. Glass, dimensions variable. RISD Museum, Providence, R.I. Gift of James Brayton Hall and Mark Hambleton Stevens in honor of Ellen Fitzgibbon Hall, RISD 1945. Image courtesy RISD Museum.

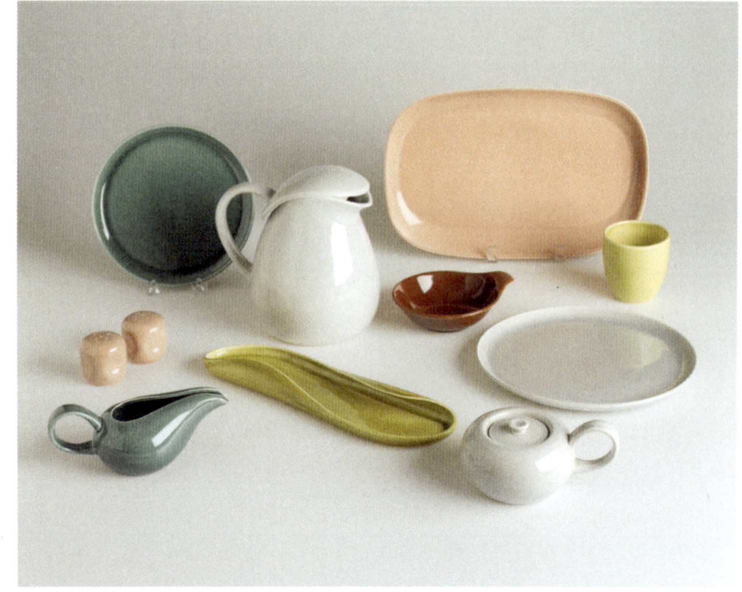

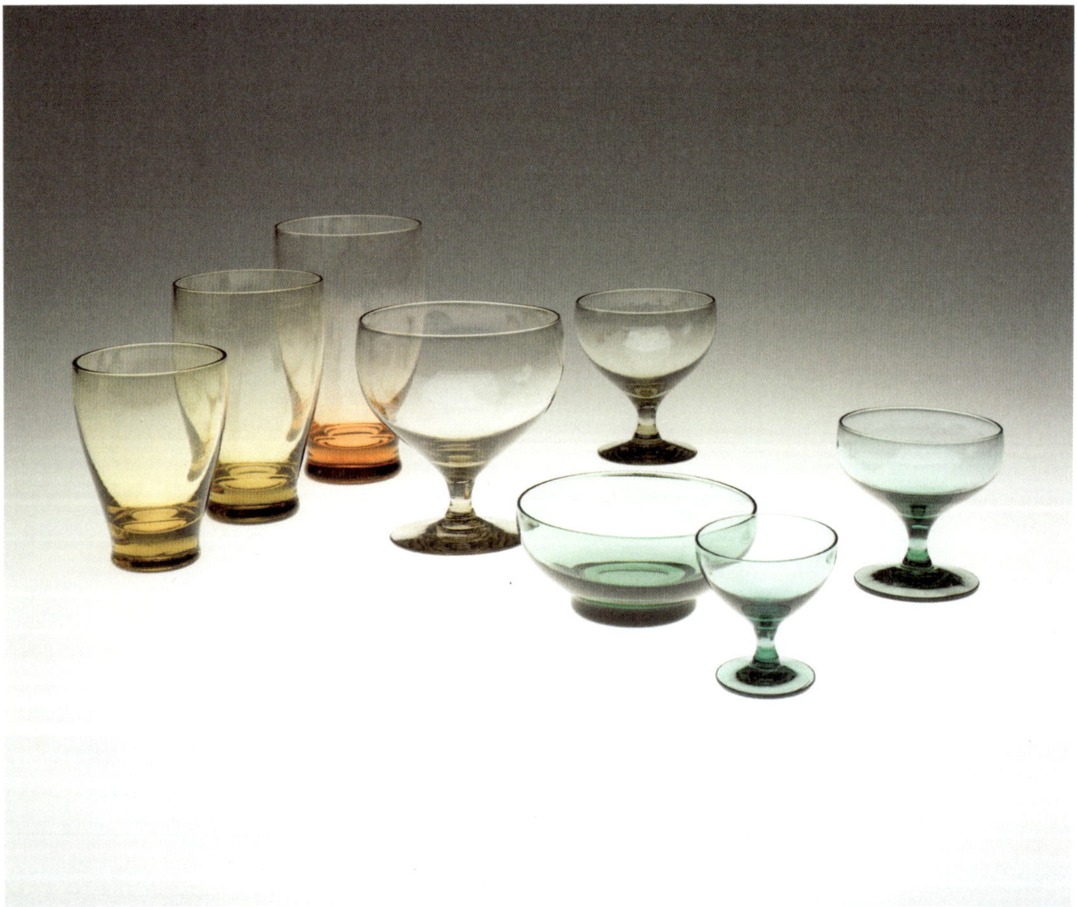

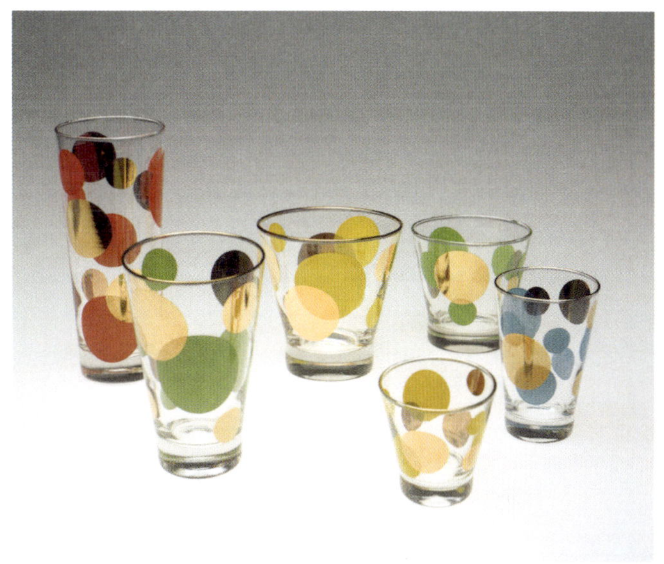

a playful, casual quality. As the circles hover on the transparent glass, they evoke balls tossed in the air or helium balloons slowly floating away. While these glasses were marketed for serving both nonalcoholic and alcoholic drinks (a smaller size was regularly advertised as "juice or cocktail"), their overt playfulness is admittedly incongruous in the context of drinking alcohol: Why should consuming a cocktail remind one of childhood pastimes? On the other hand, their explicitly positive tone is noteworthy. Neither Eclipse nor American Modern alludes to the underside of a "coarse" cocktail party that might leave one "seasick." Instead, they offer the ideal of joyful conviviality, uncontaminated by extramarital sexual conquests. They might be the perfect solution to the Wrights' own admonition, found in the *Guide*, to avoid barware with "gag appeal, or you'll end up with a mess of pornographic bottoms-up glasses."[15] However, several of Wright's unsuccessful proposed designs for Bartlett-Collins flirt with precisely that realm of "gag appeal." In multiple sketches, he presented designs that labeled the drinks contained therein "poison," "TNT," or "Keep Out of Reach of Children" (figs. 110, 111, 112). While the archival record around the reception of these designs is silent, their tongue in cheek tenor is evident (and they were presumably not intended to double as "juice" glasses). Wright likely made these proposals as examples of self-deprecating, jokey barware that occupied a persistent market niche throughout the period, and that reflected the duality of the cocktail party—at once the fabric that joined the community together and the means by which it could, figuratively, unravel.

Freda Diamond, like Wright, was a popular figure in lifestyle and accessory design in the postwar years, not least because her name appeared in countless advertisements for Libbey Glass Company, her

Fig. 110 (right). Russel Wright, Designs for Bartlett-Collins, c. 1956. Russel Wright Papers, Special Collections Research Center, Syracuse University Libraries.

Fig. 111 (below right). Russel Wright, Designs for Bartlett-Collins, c. 1956. Russel Wright Papers, Special Collections Research Center, Syracuse University Libraries.

Fig. 112 (bottom). Russel Wright, Designs for Bartlett-Collins, c. 1956. Russel Wright Papers, Special Collections Research Center, Syracuse University Libraries.

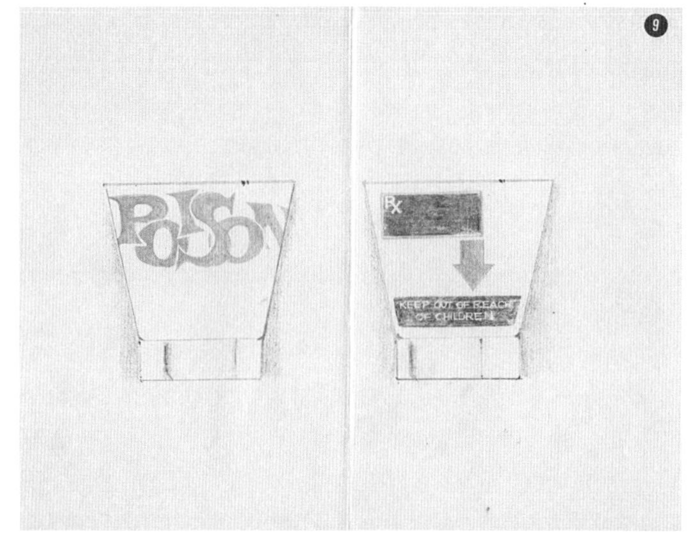

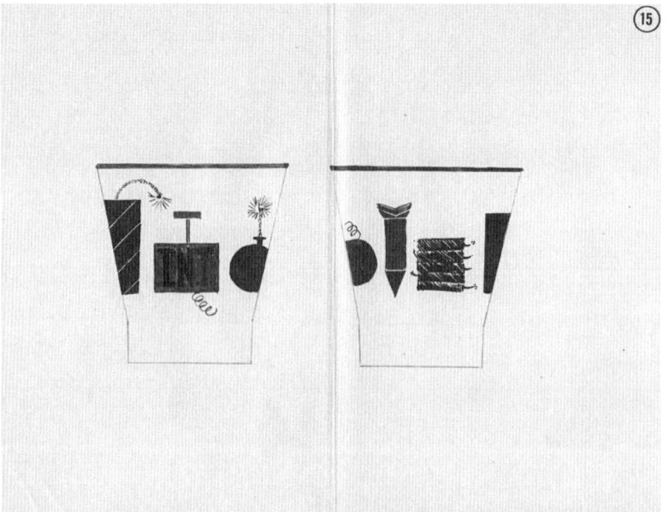

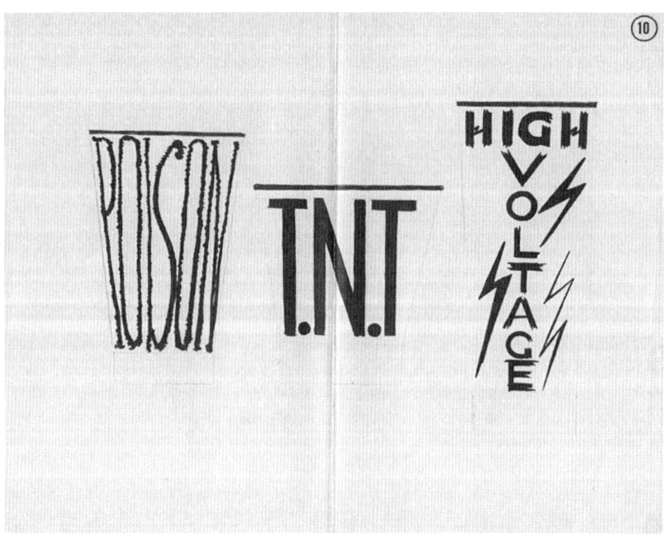

biggest client, throughout the 1950s. Famously described in 1951 as the designer who "today probably exerts more influence on the taste of the average home furnishings consumer than any other individual in the United States," Diamond had an illustrious career with furniture makers such as Herman Miller prior to her high-visibility work with Libbey after World War II.[16] Her mother, a Russian Jewish immigrant, was a close friend of Emma Goldman, the anarchist and feminist activist, when Diamond was young.[17] When Diamond worked with Libbey, unlike Wright in his work at Bartlett-Collins, she was responsible for designing the stock forms that were mass-produced by the company, as well as countless product lines with distinctive applied decorations to the glasses themselves. The radical politics of her childhood home may provide context for her career-long commitment to designing for "the great mass of American consumers."[18] Indeed, even her decorative work could be understood as an attempt to enliven daily experiences for the masses: as she commented in 1951, "by making everything alike, [you] reduce it all to a convenient but deadly monotony."[19] However, anarchist sympathies have no thematic presence in her illustrational motifs for Libbey. The overall conservative nature of these decorations is perhaps a consequence of the powerful commercial imperative exercised by the company, one of the most successful in the glass industry at mid-century. Yet Diamond alone is credited in publicity materials as the "one and only" designer for the various glassware lines, and photographs showing her at work in her studio, sketching directly onto glass forms, reinforced her authorship of the decorative motifs.[20] Typical of Diamond's applied designs of the early 1950s was the 1952 "Circus" line, inspired by the Oscar-winning film *The Greatest Show on Earth* and featuring varied acts and performers marching around the circumference of different-sized glasses (taller glasses were variously referred to as "beverage" or "double old-fashioned" sizes, whereas the shorter glasses were "juice" or "cocktail") (fig. 113). Her compositions included leaping lions, juggling clowns, and the acrobatic flips of trapeze artists flying across the clear glass; the overt, playful references to wholesome family entertainment were only modestly undercut by the calligraphic loop of a ring master's whip in these "colorful, chip-defying, thinly-blown party glasses." Slightly more subversive is Diamond's 1955 Aqua Ripple design, in which the circles of ripples create an optical effect of undulating glass (fig. 114).[21] The external contours of the tumblers are completely straight, and thus to see and to hold these glasses is to experience two contradictory sensations: one holds a smooth, coherent glass in one's hand but looks at a distorted, irregular, rippling view of that same hand through the glass. As one contemplates the split between the haptic and the optic, one is forced to question which senses can be trusted. The collapsing sense of bodily coherency might be a metaphor for the fragmenting social order of a cocktail party.

As implied by the short-fuse bomb in Wright's design or the surreal confusion that momentarily overtakes the Aqua Ripple glass user, the arena

Fig. 113 (right). Advertisement for Libbey Glass "Circus" line, Freda Diamond, designer. *Life*, April 28, 1952, 128.

Fig. 114 (below). Advertisement for Libbey Glass "Aqua Ripple" line, Freda Diamond, designer. *Better Homes and Gardens*, May 1955, 240.

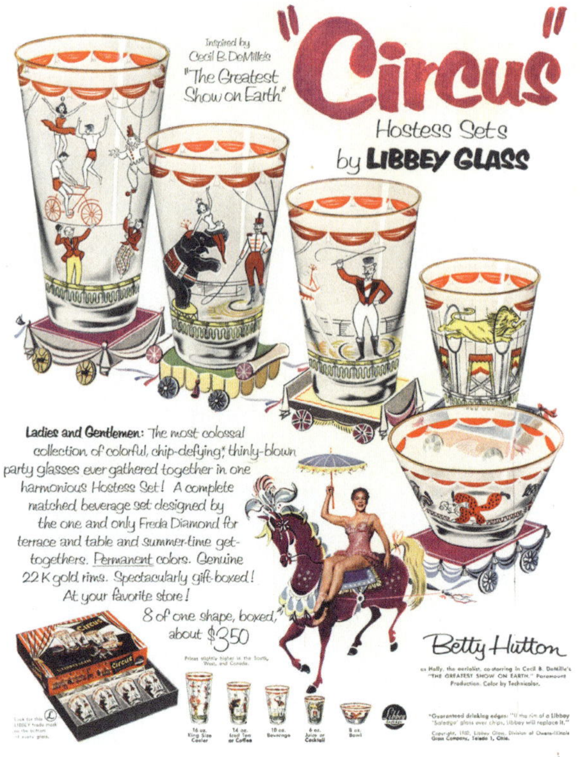

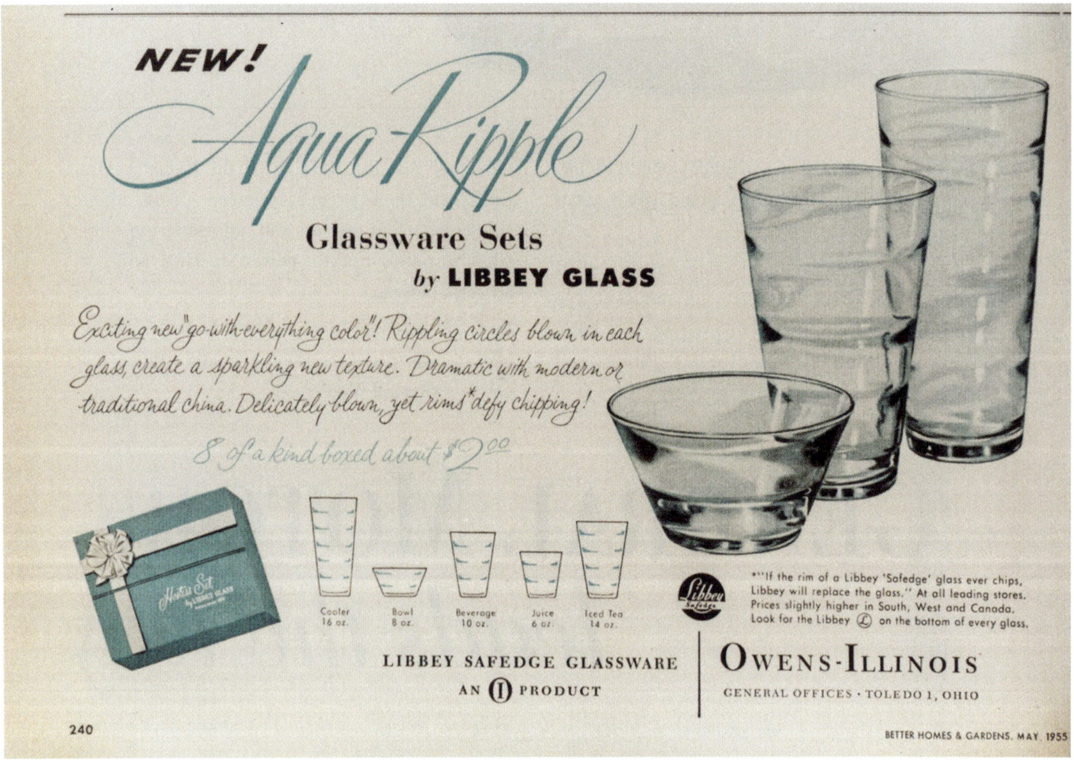

of the suburban cocktail party had a persistent dark edge. The potential for behavior that might undermine the heteronormative units of suburban society is implied in the period references to "pornographic" and "coarse" jokiness, and begs for more critical attention to the gendered responsibilities and entitlements around the cocktail party. Women might present themselves as sexual idols in the landscape of the cocktail party, like the two emphatically curvaceous figures in Kingsland's illustration (see fig. 106), but they are always limited to being objects of male attention. It is the men—their cigarettes and pipes pointed—who have the agency to act and to disrupt the status quo. Indeed, in *The Crack in the Picture Window*, the initial suggestion of sexual infidelity begins with an overture by one male resident of the fictional suburban community, Henry Amiable, toward the protagonist, Mary Drone: under the bridge table, "Mary became aware of the insistent pressure of Henry's knee. She edged away, but Henry's knee followed."[22]

If alcohol-infused parties turn women into objects of masculine attention, such gatherings also turn women into domestic objects who must perform specific hostessing skills effectively and appropriately. Time and again in the literature of the period, the cocktail party is the arena of social expectation and peer pressure, and would seem to be almost the inverse of the informal lifestyle it purports to exemplify. *House and Garden* advises that young married couples be aware that hosting alcoholic parties is an obligation—"Not only must they give parties, they must be armed against unexpected guests"—and offers suggestions for how to stock a "cupboard cellar" "from the point of taste, budget, space, mixing, and serving."[23] The article singles out the responsibilities of the housewife as follows: "Obviously, no one expects to walk into a young household and call for the kind of drink that would stump the Ritz barman. On the other hand, people do have pronounced preferences; and it's fun for the hostess to be able to offer her own drink specialties." The very next month, as *House and Garden*'s editors provided guidance on how to host summer cocktail parties, they noted, "Summer weekends (and summer weekenders) are invariably thirsty, and the summer hostess must be equipped to keep a small Niagara of cold drinks flowing."[24]

The glassware itself contributes to the air of enforced etiquette standards through its multiple forms. Throughout the 1950s and 1960s, glassware manufacturers promoted multiple specialized forms that were allegedly correct for different kinds of drinks: old-fashioneds, highballs, and cocktails were just a few of the more than fifteen specialized types commonly found in the marketplace. (In one "Guide to Glassware Usage," the Glassware Institute of America specified nineteen "of the most popular shapes and sizes in glass tableware.")[25] *House and Garden* professed that such proliferation was "nonsense" and reassured readers that they could survive with only six different glass types to offer to guests.[26]

Wright, for all of his exhortations to embrace more relaxed etiquette standards in *Guide to Easier Living*, readily participated in this

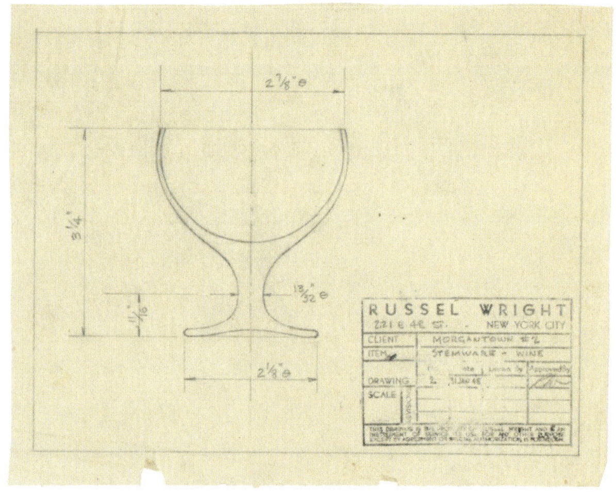

Fig. 115. Russel Wright, Wineglass design for Morgantown Glass Works, 1949. Russel Wright Papers, Special Collections Research Center, Syracuse University Libraries.

multiplicity of drinking forms. Indeed, the operative philosophy behind the *Guide* seems to be fundamentally at odds with the goal of a product designer: the book encourages streamlined, pared-down living, whereas a product designer builds her career by continually convincing consumers of new needs in the home and then designing new objects to meet those needs. The contradictions in Wright's glassware designs seem to go even deeper, however. The singular, sinuous contour created by his Morgantown designs is a bold assertion of simplicity: these objects morph, as if in a single breath, from bowl to stem to foot (fig. 115, see fig. 108). They appear to be the product of one line, flowing in a continuous, subtly shifting arc, and as such they seem to embody one of the canonical precepts of Modernism: a modest, unified form arises from the rigorous study of function. Yet if he has truly examined functional needs, then Wright might do well to explain what distinguishes the requirements of a glass to hold water and a glass to hold wine, or a glass to hold a martini. Instead of allowing a powerful, simplified design to actually do the work of holding multiple distinct beverages, he created at least nine different forms for the American Modern line. By designing such specialized objects as a "highball," "wine goblet," and "pilsner," he revealed himself as complicit with commerce over Modernism.[27] Moreover, his multiple glasses reinforce a basic structure of control over the human body: how much of what kinds of beverages humans should consume. His designs reinforce the work of manufacturers who have determined that a wineglass should be smaller than a water glass because humans should drink a smaller volume of wine than of water, and a smaller volume still of gin in a martini (or juice in the morning). Rather than challenge this authority that governs without consent or, perhaps, even recognition, Wright's designs perpetuate control over bodily consumption.

Moreover, if Wright had achieved a Modernist, unified glass design, he might have removed from domestic duty the chore of distinguishing

between correct and incorrect glassware. Instead of liberating the housewife with a single glass that could be used for all purposes, his glasswares
simply reinforce traditional etiquette and reinscribe a woman's role in maintaining it. Cynically, in a series of article drafts written in the mid-1950s,
Wright reveals a previously guarded disdain for women's loyalty to tradition.
In a set of notes for a proposed article for *Women's Home Companion*, he
ruminates on his own (clearly superior) tendency to organize tasks through
lists, a mark of Modern efficiency in contrast to "housewives [who] just hate
lists and for that reason I believe that they waste a great deal of time." His
allegiance to functional process over etiquette propriety reaches a more
judgmental tone when he writes, "I think that the hostess today who says,
no, don't bother, I'd rather do it myself, is a ridiculous martyr, or it may be
that she has such a poor sense of organization that she can't stand having
other people in the kitchen."[28] Also in 1954, Wright drafted a short set of
notes titled "What I Don't Like About American Women." Although these
brief notes may be little more than a shorthand rehearsal of larger ideas,
some of their mean-spirited complaints are surprising, given Wright's public face as the efficient husband-helper in *Guide to Easier Living*. Among
the items in his list of complaints: "[Hostesses who] hate housework, they
'bitch' about it; they get themselves and their families into a terrible state
about it; and yet they over-decorate their homes with all types of 'foo-foo'
femininities and fashionable elegances that make for a lot more housekeeping than is necessary."[29] Wright's American Modern glassware has
no applied decoration and, in its austere contours, might be considered
the opposite of "foo-foo femininities." On the other hand, its numerous
forms create congestion and overload in a glass cabinet and the glassware
enforces complex codes of correct entertaining: woe betide the housewife
who serves wine in a pilsner glass. These glasses do little to actually help
women become more efficient.

There are few traces in Wright's own archives that allow us to
reconstruct Wright's development of the American Modern glassware line.
The earliest drawings associated with the line are dated 1948, and the
latest are 1951. A series of photographs documenting table displays at
B. Altman's from 1949 are probably the first public presentation of the
glassware: it was conceived and introduced to the public as a complement
to the American Modern ceramic line (fig. 116). During its brief existence,
Wright's publicist, Virginia Burdick, distributed a series of press photographs of the American Modern glassware and tablewares. These promotional images are intended to inspire specific narratives. Some photos
depict an after-dinner coffee gathering, while others promote a new
"children's set" (that includes the breakage-prone American Modern
glassware) and specifically conjure up a "birthday party table setting."[30]
Yet others spin stories that are purposefully racialized. Accompanying one
photograph, showing American Modern plates set with cut-glass goblets
(instead of American Modern glassware), the caption reads: "So basic is

Fig. 116 (right). Table setting featuring American Modern tableware, glassware, and tablecloth at B. Altmans, New York, 1949. Worsinger Photo. Russel Wright Papers, Special Collections Research Center, Syracuse University Libraries.

Fig. 117 (below right). "Traditional table setting" featuring American Modern tableware, publicity photograph by Virginia Burdick Public Relations, c. 1951. Russel Wright Papers, Special Collections Research Center, Syracuse University Libraries.

Fig. 118 (bottom). "A Chinese meal" featuring American Modern tableware, publicity photograph by Virginia Burdick Public Relations, c. 1951. Russel Wright Papers, Special Collections Research Center, Syracuse University Libraries.

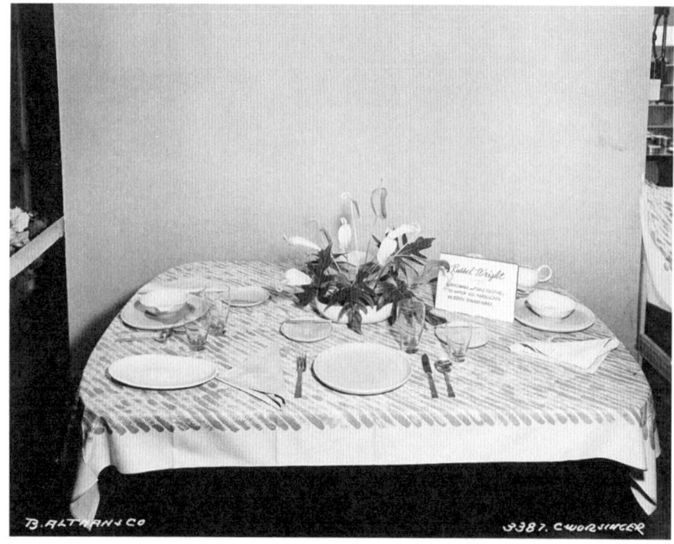

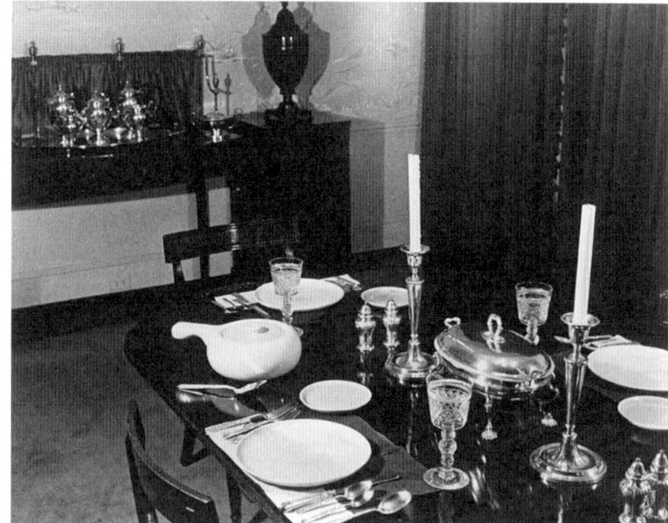

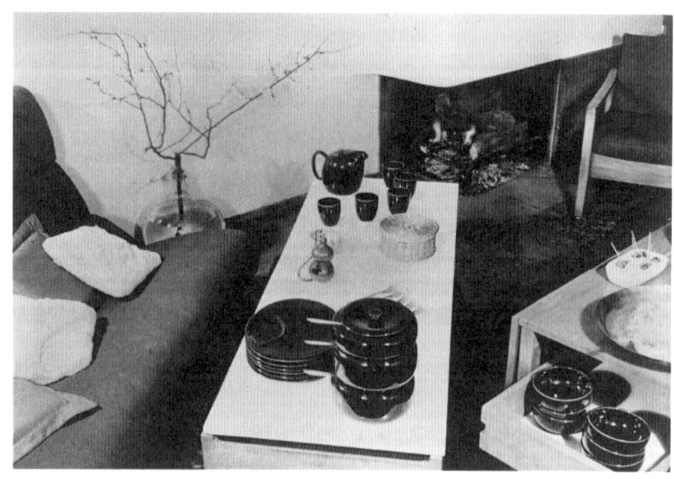

this dinnerware with its simple design forms and softly mottled glaze with a handcrafted look that it can be combined beautifully with glassware and silver of the English tradition" (fig. 117).[31] In another, depicting an "informal buffet service," we see "hostess party set plates, triple stack server, teapot, water mugs and soup bowls. Note wicker basket and small bottle for soy sauce. This can be a Chinese meal" (fig. 118).[32] While neither of these latter two vignettes used the American Modern glassware, it is worth pausing to consider the expansive neutrality of the American Modern line suggested by this publicity campaign. The message is that Wright's American Modern designs persist and endure through a wide range of domestic scenarios and racialized encounters. These plates and glasses can cater to adults and children, and can accommodate both the "traditional" Anglo-White and the racialized other. Notably, Wright's designs do not disappear into non-Western influences—their forms, shapes, and colors continue to be recognizable in the "Chinese meal"—but they mingle with varied accessories and (literally) take on the flavor of another culture. They are thus expanded in their relevance. American Modern is almost a stand-in, here, for White Western culture that travels abroad and borrows other cultures in order to reshape them for consumption at home, similar to the White Modern artist of chapter 2 or the White Western traveler in chapter 3.

The racialized Whiteness of the American Modern line became more overt in an advertising campaign that ran in 1952 in shelter magazines such as *House Beautiful* and *House and Garden*. By this time, the glassware had been discontinued, and the advertising focus was on the ceramic tablewares; Wright apparently had a plan to expand the line throughout the decade with additional serving items.[33] The series of ads ran almost every month with the tagline "Enduring American Originals," and featured a group of three or four American Modern objects silhouetted against a white backdrop and paired with an object representing the history of American creativity. In some cases, the reference is textual—a picture of the title page of *Moby Dick*, accompanied by copy that reads, "True beauty is timeless—in dinnerware as in literature"—while in other examples the advertisement makes comparisons between American Modern and visual art (Audubon's birds), architecture (Independence Hall in Philadelphia), craft (early American furniture), music ("Oh Susanna" and "St. Louis Blues," in two different ads), and technology (Edison's phonograph).[34] In all cases, the examples embody creative expression and innovation achieved in the past. They skew toward popular art and folk expression, which is intended to imbue American Modern with an air of broad, classless appeal (fig. 119). The dinnerware becomes just the most recent addition to a canon of universal, even democratic American expression, or as one ad puts it, "Early American furniture   American Modern dinnerware—both distinguished by the enduring simplicity, the timeless quality, of great design!"[35]

The folk tradition that is invoked in these ads, however, is persistently White. References to the Revolutionary War and Thanksgiving allude to a historical narrative of the United States dominated by White protagonists, and every artist or author cited, with the exception of W. C. Handy, who wrote "Saint Louis Blues," is White. Indeed, the presence of Handy's song—represented as sheet music in the advertisement, with no specific reference to the composer—is an exception that helps to prove the rule (fig. 120). A work of art created by an acknowledged master of the blues, itself an African American music form expressive of the Black experience in the United States and made famous by Black performers, is taken out of its original context and, in this advertisement, simply recast as an object of generic achievement; when it becomes generic, within the context of the White readership of shelter magazines such as *House and Garden*, the default coding of its racial identity becomes White. Wright's American Modern specifically allies itself with exemplars of White American culture and strategically appropriates Black culture to establish a broad White ownership over the history of American creativity.[36] It is important to note that Russel Wright himself was not responsible for creating the marketing campaigns for his tablewares in the 1950s. A restructuring of his business allowed him to focus primarily on design and leave the marketing and contract negotiations to others. Thus it is not possible to directly attribute the White racializing agenda of the 1952 American Modern campaign to Wright himself. However, in light of the history behind the development of the *Guide to Easier Living* manuscript (see chapter 1), it is possible that he carried with him many of the White prejudices—so ingrained they were hardly recognizable to their protagonists—common in this period.

Freda Diamond's designs should also be interrogated for how they engage with the construction of gendered and racialized identities in the 1950s. Like Wright, she can be faulted for complicity with the industrial imperative to create more specialized products so that consumers have more items to purchase. Libbey credited her with the invention, in 1942, of an immensely successful marketing device, the "Hostess Set," which forced a consumer to buy an attractively boxed set of six or eight glasses of a single size (perhaps as a gift, or a gift to oneself), rather than purchasing the glasses open stock.[37] All of her designs for Libbey Glass Company consist of multiple forms and sizes that complement one another to create a set but allow for distinct beverage uses. Indeed, in the years around 1950, when she produced numerous decorations for stock glass shapes for the company, advertisements reminded consumers that the decorations could be used to identify the different shapes: "Here are merry-making glasses of enormous distinction in a *matched service* ... on each shape a *different* scene! Now you know you have the proper glass for every drink: highball, cocktail, an old-fashioned, wine, pilsner, sour, or cordial. There are even *matching jiggers*."[38] Yet at the same time as she was producing eight or

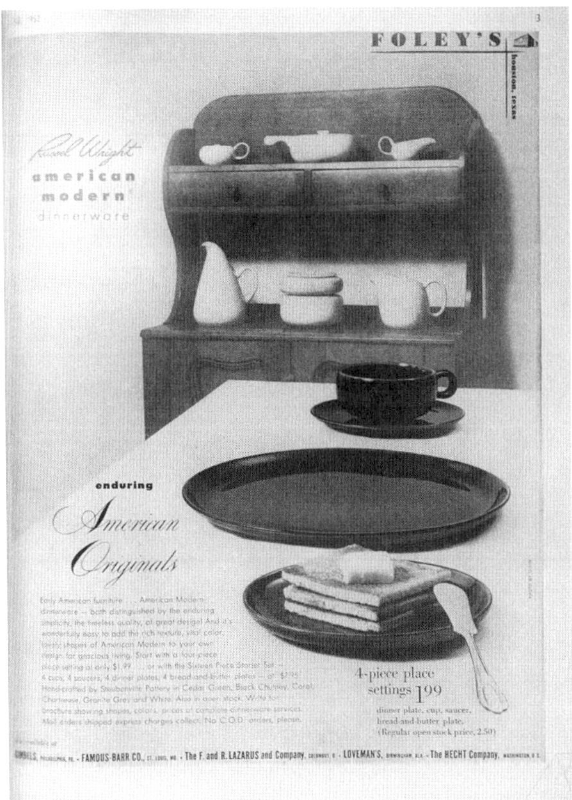

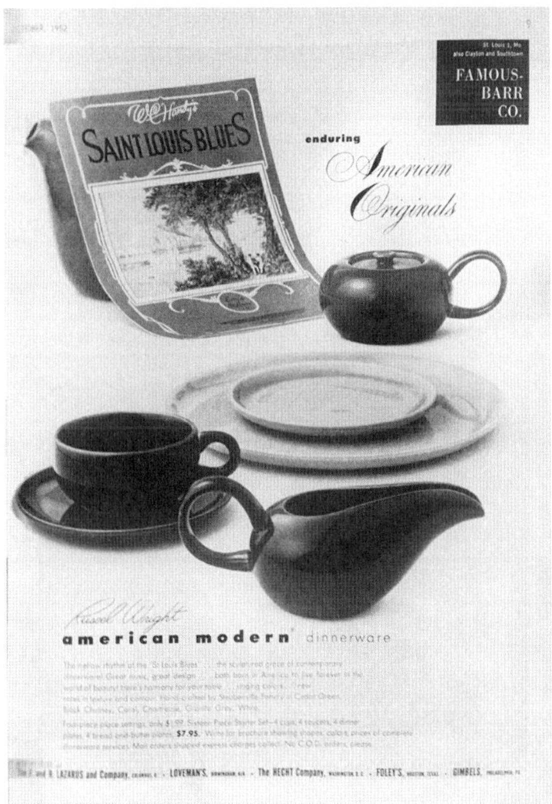

nine specialized designs for a given line, Diamond also dispensed advice that encouraged housewives to resist the dictates of the etiquette and glassware industry. In interviews published in newspapers across the country, she reminded consumers that various glass forms could be used for many different purposes—in essence, encouraging them to lower the requirements for appropriate housekeeping and simplify their housework:

Fig. 119 (above left). Advertisement for American Modern Dinnerware, Russel Wright, designer. *House and Garden*, June 1952, 3.

Fig. 120 (above right). Advertisement for American Modern Dinnerware, Russel Wright, designer. *House and Garden*, October 1952, 9.

With our summer brides in mind, we asked Miss Diamond what are the "starting" basic items in glassware for the new homemaker. Here is her experienced answer:

"Four generous-sized tumblers. These can be used for milk, iced tea, iced coffee, lemonade or high-balls. Four water goblets (stemware). Four fruit-juice glasses (stemware or tumbler) for juices or whiskey sours. Four sherbets (stemware) for desserts, puddings, champagne. Four cocktail glasses (stemware) for cocktails or wine."[39]

In contrast to the fifteen (or nineteen, or six) specialized shapes recommended in the literature quoted above, Diamond has reduced it to a minimum of five different glasses.

While Whiteness circulates around Russel Wright's designs largely through the narratives proposed by his marketing materials, Diamond's applied decorations engage questions of race directly through their representations. Throughout the 1950s, she developed numerous decorative lines for Libbey Glass Company that feature human figures. These illustrations are overwhelmingly White, not just in terms of how the human figure is rendered, but also in terms of their context and associations. One popular design introduced in 1953, for example, was called "Highlanders" (fig. 121). "Certain to win the hearts of plaid-conscious Americans," the publicity specifically called out pride in an ethnic White heritage.[40] Customers could buy glasses in specialized shapes—from Hi-Ball to Old Fashioned or Cocktail—featuring a Scottish man wearing the appropriate tartan kilt of eight different Highland clans, rendered "correct in every detail."[41] Other designs included a line inspired by the "famous prints" of Currier and Ives, meant to invoke "old-fashioned hospitality" and featuring White Americans in sentimental turn-of-the-century settings such as in a horse-drawn sleigh, riding a bicycle, or summer haying beneath trees in full leaf (fig. 122), or the "Curio" line, which consisted of representations of "collectors' curios" out of a western European tradition, such as "old musical instruments," "old ships," and "old carriages."[42] A set of tumblers decorated with images of Christopher Columbus's *Santa Maria* (1951) offered a more concrete connection between evocative images of past technologies and White European colonialism. It is notable that Diamond's figurative decorations depict White protagonists and engage with a historical view that is predominantly white and Westernized, and she rarely depicts non-Whites; in one rare example, a dark-skinned woman with a large basket of fruit on her head appears in the Caribbean Cruise line of 1960, offering an exoticized view of a non-White.[43] Overall, a White perspective is presumed, to the complete exclusion of anyone else in society. To buy her glasswares and hold them in one's hand at a cocktail party is to tacitly—perhaps even blindly—identify with the idea of total White ownership of cultural production. As I have discussed elsewhere in this book, Whiteness becomes an ex-nominated quality for her consumers.[44] Even the book Diamond published in 1953, *The Story of Glass*, weaves a narrative that is entirely focused on Western history and pointedly ignores any references to glassmaking elsewhere in the world; it begins with ancient Rome, continues with medieval stained glass, and concludes with the Industrial Revolution in western Europe. While Heisey Glass Company advertised in *Ebony* magazine in the 1950s and *Ebony* used Heisey products in their test kitchen, Libbey Glass did not advertise in the magazine during that decade.[45] In the years when *Life*'s readers regularly encountered advertisements for the Circus line, Treasure Island line, Santa Maria line, and many others, *Ebony*'s readers did not.

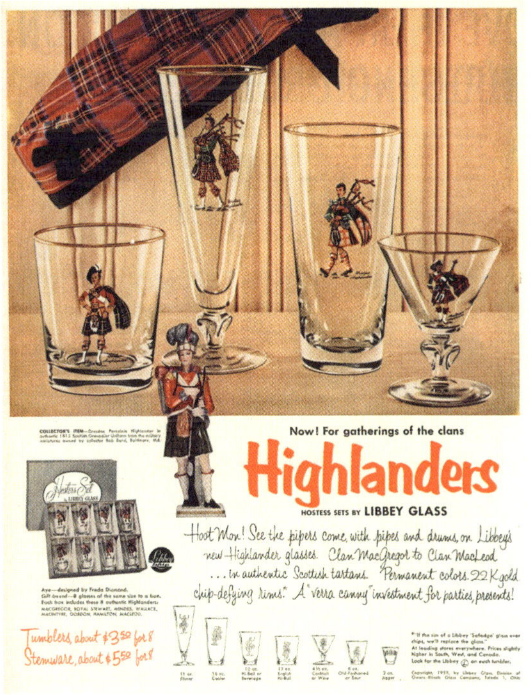

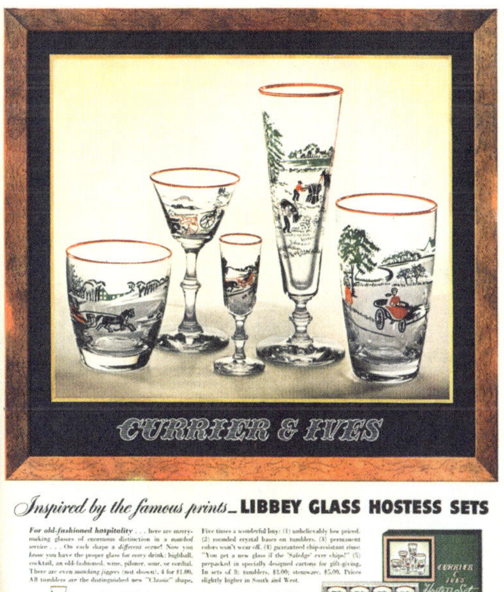

If cocktail parties were the epitome of casual entertaining and the informal lifestyle of the suburbs, the forms of cocktail glasses reveal a complex, darker side to this playful ritual. The multiplicity of forms served to remind women of any race that strict etiquette expectations persisted, despite the radically simplified contours in both Wright's and Diamond's designs. And the marketing campaigns and figurative messages associated with these Modernist forms insistently invoked a tradition of White ownership and White superiority. The playful cocktail party was, in fact, riddled with strict guidelines for White consumers and left little room for improvisation.

Fig. 121 (above left). Advertisement for Libbey Glass "Highlander" line, Freda Diamond, designer. *Life*, November 2, 1953, 70.

Fig. 122 (above right). Advertisement for Libbey Glass "Currier and Ives" line, Freda Diamond, designer. *Life*, November 14, 1949, 147.

The Artful Self

The decorative knickknacks that accessorize a living space—the vase on a mantel, the ashtray on a coffee table, or a candy dish on a side table—are perhaps less freighted with expectations of casual behavior than cocktail glasses. Like cocktail glasses, ashtrays or candy dishes are vehicles for serving a body that consumes, and are props in the ritual of entertainment: a candy dish proffers treats, whereas an ashtray is a receptacle for the waste generated by human consumption. These objects demonstrate the owner's generosity in tending to the needs of her guests and affirm that the owner is a part of a community that enjoys her hospitality. Yet they have the potential to represent something more permanent than a cocktail glass: if they are placed on a mantelpiece or table, they become part of the tableau of a room, the scene that greets the houseguest, the self-presentation of the homeowner. As a writer for *Ladies' Home Journal* noted in 1954, "A colorful fruit bowl, a copper dish, a china horse, or an inlaid box are not essential to our living, but such things can provide true joy and give personality to our surroundings which the most carefully selected furniture, fine fabrics, and an excellent color scheme will never provide."[46]

This section examines the ceramic decorative accessories produced by Associated American Artists in the early 1950s. These objects were marketed as artful additions to the home and as such should be understood to occupy a transitional place: they are simultaneously works of art—hence formal emblems of an establishment—and casual knick-knacks that provide "personality" and forge human connections between hostess and guest. Associated American Artists (AAA) is best known, today, as the publisher of affordable prints that were sold through a mail-order system beginning in the 1930s and continuing through 2000.[47] AAA made its first foray into tablewares in the 1940s, through brief collaborations with Steuben crystal (1940) and Castleton China (1949). In the summer of 1950, the business announced a new product line, "Original Creations from the Ceramic Collection."[48] This collection of decorative and functional ceramics, designed and decorated by AAA artists and manufactured in kilns run by AAA, was soon given the name "Stonelain." "Stonelain" was itself a manufactured word, designed for marketing; as AAA's publicity materials and hundreds of advertisements and publicity pieces explained throughout 1950 and 1951, the name was meant to evoke both "stoneware's durability and porcelain's texture." (Its pronunciation was, however, somewhat less intuitive: "*Stone-lin*," directed the company's publicity manual.)[49] Yet by 1954, weak sales caused AAA to phase out Stonelain entirely. Over the course of its brief history, Stonelain uneasily occupied that transitional status between artful object and tchotchke, which may explain in part its lack of commercial success.

AAA promoted, over the course of its sixty-six-year existence, affordable prints by "famous American artists" as an opportunity to own an elite art object. The implication was that the purchaser, as a consequence of finances or background, was a novice in the world of the fine art market, but yet appreciated the aesthetics and values associated with fine art; through the prices offered by AAA, the patron was empowered to join the elite status group of fine art collectors. Likewise, AAA marketed Stonelain with numerous, overt associations to the elite institutions of the fine art world. One early advertisement boasts of "a rare opportunity to own limited 'first editions' of Stonelain," evoking the upper echelons of print and rare book collecting. It assures consumers that the "rare beauty" of a single Stonelain object will "lend a wealth of interest" to the home, and will "become a treasured heirloom as its usefulness and great originality is admired from generation to generation."[50] Another ad presents the new line as the heir to "that ancient art of ceramics" and explains that the "ox-blood red" glaze has been "unknown since the early Chinese." Such historical references foster associations to the acknowledged masterpieces found in museums. The advertisement concludes by informing the consumer that each Stonelain product "carries a thought-provoking title and an identifying booklet with the artist's biography," which further references the establishment classifications presented on museum labels.[51] Advertisements like these, placed in local newspapers by individual department stores, usually borrow their language directly from AAA's own publicity materials. The Stonelain product catalogues themselves feature even more imaginative immersions into this elite art-world fantasy:

> Have you ever stood before a protected case of ceramic objects in a museum and marveled at their beautiful shapes and deep, brilliant glazes? You knew instinctively that these were priceless objects that museums and connoisseurs scoured the world for, and that each cost a small fortune. Yet, these pieces too were created originally as simple utilitarian or decorative objects to serve in the home. They cost little at the time of their creation—but today, they are priceless treasures.
>
> What if we were to say to you: we believe that the talented members of the Associated American Artists have created a number of ceramic pieces in the mode of our day that are every bit as magnificent in their own way as the ancient pieces that now take our breath? And, what if we added that you can own these collector's items at prices ranging from $3.50 to $50.00?[52]

For all of the references to traditional ceramics in the marketing verbiage, the Stonelain objects themselves did not readily evoke historical associations. Instead, they seemed to explicitly engage several trends in Modernist art practice. In the initial collection of 1950, many objects were decorated with expressive vignettes that showcased the painterly skill of the artist or with surrealist figures and pictograms. William Gropper's large *Equestrienne* vase exemplifies a painterly approach to decoration: with fluid, sketchy brushwork, the artist captures a dancer, arms held aloft, balancing precariously on a galloping horse (fig. 123). The horse, with its head tucked down and hooves gathered inward, is a bundle of potential energy that anchors the bottom of the vase, while the flamboyant gesture of the dancer's arms and right leg echoes the object's upward expanding contour. Indeed, Gropper manages to convey the disorienting blur of a heated, chaotic circus ring that seems fully at odds with the massive solidity of the tall

Fig. 123 (right). *Equestrienne* (vase), 1950, William Gropper, designer. Stonelain, Associated American Artists, manufacturer. Glazed stoneware, 13 × 10 in. diam. (33 × 25.4 cm diam.). Collection of Patricia Shaw.

Fig. 124 (below right). *River Patterns* (platter), 1950, Julio de Diego, designer. Stonelain, Associated American Artists, manufacturer. Glazed stoneware, 2¼ × 19¼ × 12¼ in. (5.7 × 48.9 × 31.1 cm). Collection of Patricia Shaw.

Fig. 125 (bottom). *Repose* (cigarette box), 1949, Robert Cronbach, designer. Stonelain, Associated American Artists, manufacturer. Glazed stoneware, 3 × 7 × 4½ in. (7.6 × 17.8 × 11.4 cm). Collection of Patricia Shaw.

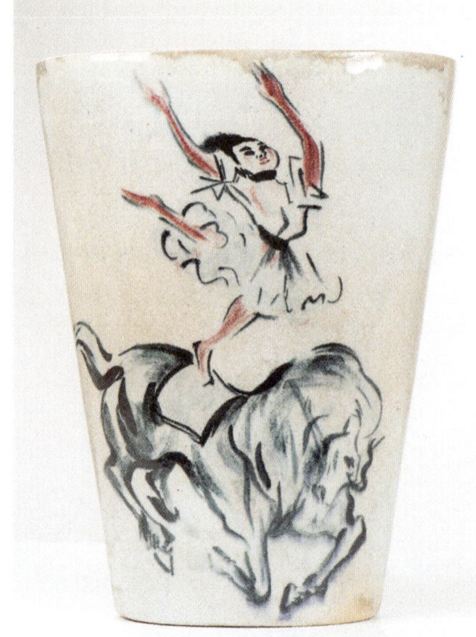

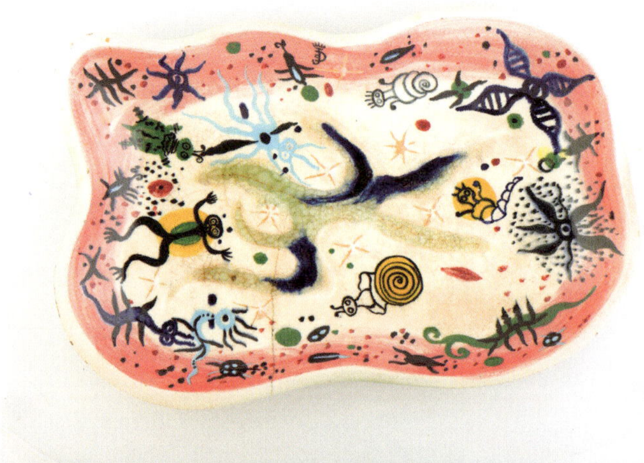

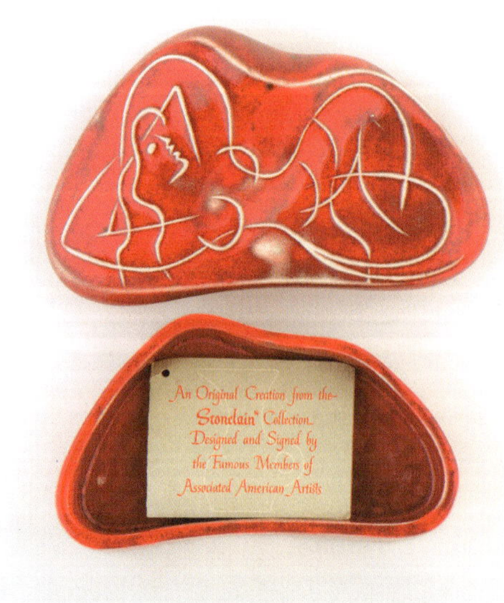

ceramic form. A more surrealist decorative approach is evident in Julio de Diego's monumental platter, *River Patterns* (fig. 124). Its organic, irregular form is enhanced by the assortment of playful, squiggle-like water creatures sprinkled across its broad bowl that recall the whimsical two-dimensionality of a painting by Joan Miró. The top, clear glaze was added last, and allowed to crack and rupture in firing, furthering the effect of watching the constantly shifting, occasionally inscrutable environs of a riverbed or tidal pool.[53]

Additional objects in the 1950 Stonelain collection reference still other trends in Modern art. Robert Cronbach's *Repose* cigarette box features a voluptuous, reclining nude, rendered in calligraphic, interlocking arcs (fig. 125). The simple profile of her face and the strong lines of her figure—instead of touching her body, we touch the contours of the box as we lift its top—recall the erotic simplicity that infuses Picasso's drawings of nudes from the 1920s onward. Nathaniel Kaz created a sculptural figurine of Johnny Appleseed as part of a small group of American folklore characters (fig. 126). The attenuated angles of his head, torso, and limbs transform the figure into a type of three-dimensional cartoon, simplified and distorted into a pattern of angular exaggerations reminiscent of Gropper's cartoonish AAA lithograph *Paul Bunyan* of 1939 (fig. 127). Nura Woodson Ulreich contributed a pitcher, the bold geometric design of which seems indebted to Bauhausian abstractions: a tall, wide cylindrical body is covered with a graphic pattern in which rectangular forms alternate with loose, painterly curlicues (fig. 128). All of these diverse objects share not only the bright colors of Stonelain's proprietary glazes, but also a lighthearted and almost playful air. The animated brushwork is clear evidence of the artist's presence—well understood in this age of action painting—but for the most part that presence seems buoyant, casual, and carefree, rather than pensive or brooding, as in the practice of a Willem de Kooning or Jackson Pollock. At times, indeed, the carefree quality is almost careless, as imprecise gestures and loose washes of color veer toward messiness.

In 1951, several new kinds of objects were introduced to the Stonelain line, and the character of the collection began to change. Whereas the first year featured a variety of plates and small, low bowls that could be either snack dishes or ashtrays, the new additions tended to be taller and more sculptural. The greater variety of forms may have been offered as a result of market research, which AAA claimed to have done in preparing the 1951 line.[54] Arvi Tynys contributed multiple items, and it was largely in response to his bold, sculptural, "amusing" forms that the *New York Times* described the entire line as possessing "touches of whimsy."[55] A small pitcher, entitled *Baby Tusk*, makes a powerful statement through its three-dimensional form and was offered in four monochrome glazes (fig. 129). The body of the pitcher forms a continuous arc through the spout; its bold, concave line is balanced by the sharp angle of the handle protruding off the opposite side. The object seems to possess a vibrant potential

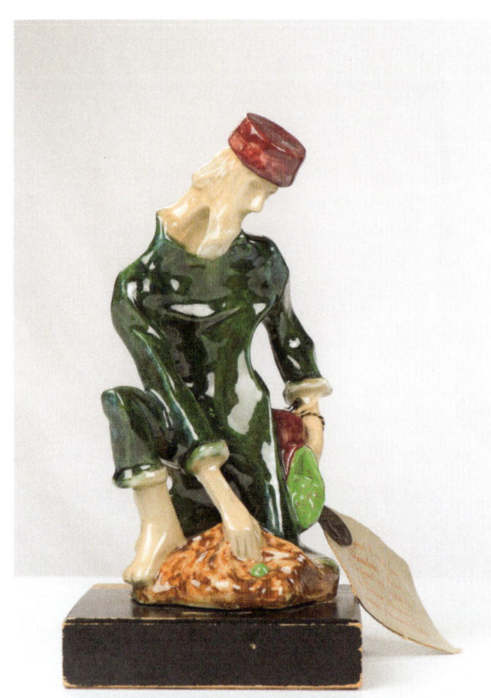

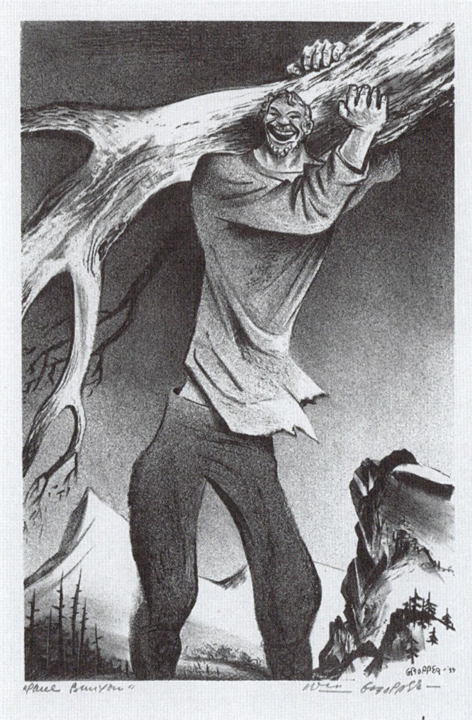

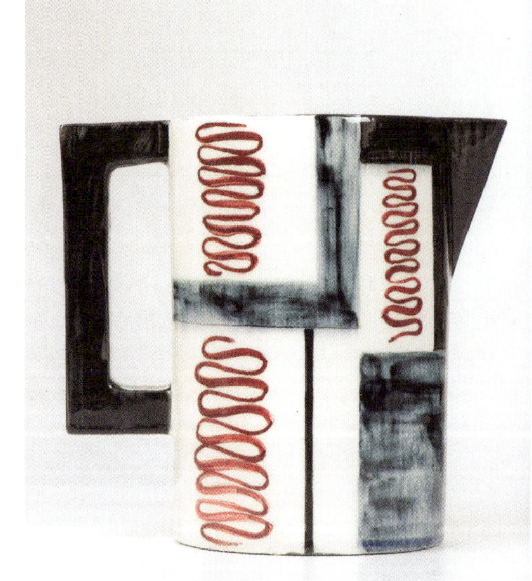

Fig. 126 (above). *Johnny Appleseed*, 1950, Nathaniel Kaz, designer. Stonelain, Associated American Artists, manufacturer. Glazed stoneware, 9¾ × 5 × 5¼ in. (24.8 × 12.7 × 13.3 cm). Collection of Patricia Shaw.

Fig. 127 (above right). William Gropper, *Paul Bunyan*, 1939. Lithograph, 13½ × 8 in. (34.3 × 22.5 cm), Associated American Artists. Ackland Art Museum, University of North Carolina at Chapel Hill, Gift of W. P. Jacocks, 58.2.150.

Fig. 128 (right). *Seven Seas* (pitcher), 1949, Nura Woodson Ulreich, designer. Stonelain, Associated American Artists, manufacturer. Glazed stoneware, 9 × 9 × 6 in. (23.8 × 25.1 × 15.6 cm).

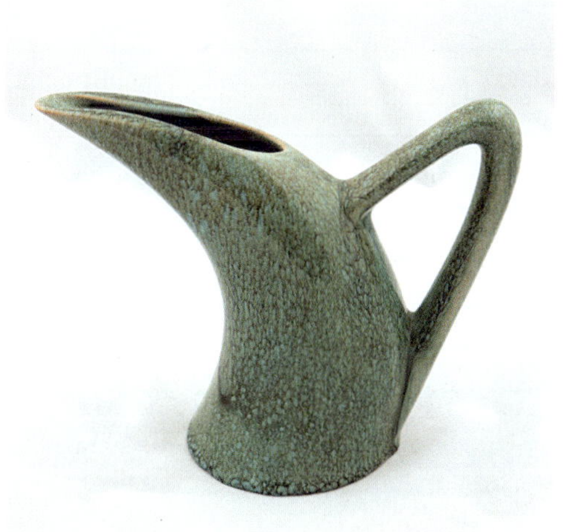

energy, as if it has drawn all of its force backward into the handle and plans to launch forward in the next instant. In general, fewer items in the 1951 collection had painted decorations; this, in addition to the heavier, more sculptural forms, meant that the animated, gestural, carefree quality of the 1950 collection was diluted. *Retailing Daily* responded with a critical eye, noting that "a more commercial, less arty feeling is in strong evidence in the new line, as compared with the earlier offerings."[56]

In 1952, AAA decided to coordinate the new additions to the Stonelain line with the launch of its textile designs for Riverdale Fabrics. Small plates, bowls, and vases in forms that carried no special distinction were decorated with illustrations that complemented the patterns in the fabrics. These decorations were not as idiosyncratic or emphatically gestural as those that appeared on the original objects. The overall character of the Stonelain line seemed diminished, reduced to a supporting role next to the fabrics, unable to command interest on its own. By 1953, new additions to Stonelain consisted almost entirely of small dishes decorated with cartoon animals drawn by Alphonse Shum and Laura Jean Allen; a few designs could be personalized by the purchaser. These items had no pretensions—admirable or otherwise—to the world of fine art and fairly can be described as kitsch.

Given the multiple aesthetic connections to Modern art examples, stylistically Stonelain could be classified as Modernist. However, it is worth noting that its marketing rhetoric differed substantially from that used to promote Modernist household wares as seen elsewhere in this book. Modern furniture, as I discussed in chapters 2 and 3, was often promoted to audiences of diverse backgrounds with language that emphasized its newness, rather than any ties to history: adjectives such as "fresh, free, and exciting," and "simple" appear repeatedly in marketing materials from the period.[57] Moreover, both Modern furnishings and Modern tablewares were

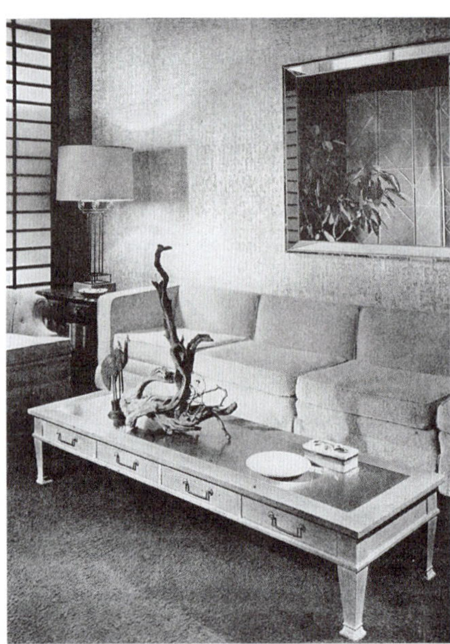

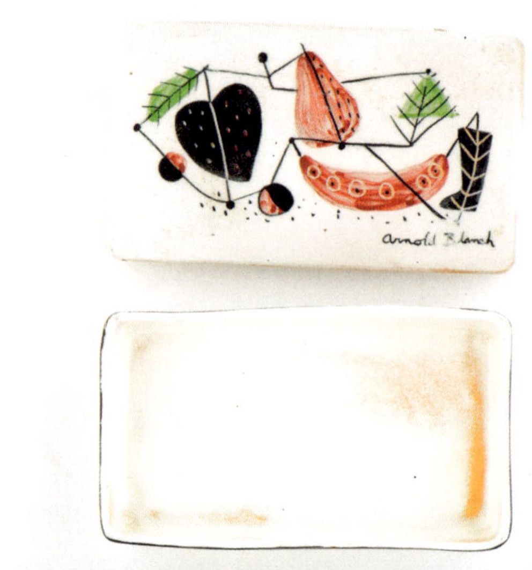

promoted for their functionality, durability, and "versatility."[58] The difference between Stonelain's promotional language, which placed the objects in a museum vitrine removed from everyday use, and the dominant rhetorical frames for Modernist wares exposes a fundamental contradiction: formally, Stonelain appears kin to Modernism, but its advertising ensconced it firmly in a world of tradition and history.

In addition to their awkward relationship to the popular promotion of Modernism, Stonelain products were an uneasy addition to mid-century Modernist interiors. In a marketing environment where Modernism was routinely described as bright and simple—and, overwhelmingly, in White-readership magazines as "clean"—the Stonelain objects may have seemed surprisingly messy: the expressive, painted decorations just a bit too casual and occasionally sloppy, the molded forms a bit soft and therefore hard to read in the details, the monochromatic glazes a bit uneven in their application. Of course, not everything in a Modern interior had to be crisp and clean-cut. One advice column appearing in *Better Homes and Gardens* in the early 1950s noted that Modernist interiors had "foibles" that were just as problematic as the decorative "knickknacks" frequently found in period-revival interiors; these foibles included "warty ceramics," "a chunk of driftwood," or "vast, squatty vases."[59] The columnist's account aptly describes not only the Herman Miller display rooms discussed in chapter 3, but also a few Modernist model interiors that featured Stonelain objects in

Fig. 130 (above left). Interior view of a living room including Arnold Blanch's *Fruit Hearts* cigarette box. *House Beautiful*, December 1950.

Fig. 131 (above right). *Fruit Hearts* (cigarette box), 1949, Arnold Blanch, designer. Stonelain, Associated American Artists, manufacturer. Glazed stoneware, 2½ × 7½ × 4½ in. (6.4 × 19.1 × 11.4 cm). Collection of Patricia Shaw.

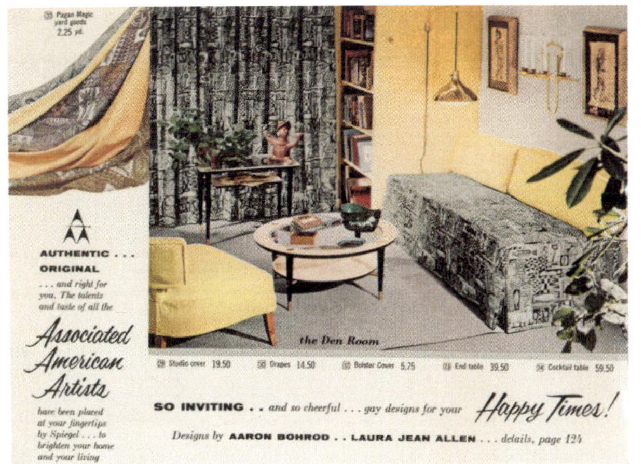

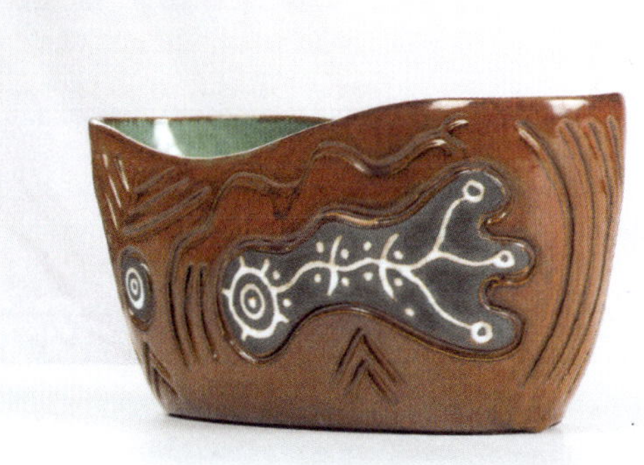

the early 1950s. In 1950, *House Beautiful* published a short article on the appeal of "furnishings in the Contemporary American style."[60] The article was accompanied by a photograph of a living room featuring an unornamented, squared sofa and a coffee table with tapered, vaguely Neoclassical legs (fig. 130). While the table itself was not Modernist, the simple contours of the sofa, table, and horizontal mullions along the back window were meant to evoke the streamlined spareness of Modernist design. The coffee table was accessorized with a massive piece of driftwood; to the left, a wooden folk sculpture of a pair of birds that is similar to Oaxacan figurines; and to the right, a Stonelain cigarette box (*Fruit Hearts*) by Arnold Blanch (fig. 131). Similarly, a Spiegel Company catalogue from 1955 showed a Modernist den decorated with Aaron Bohrod's "Pagan Magic" fabric on the daybed and as a curtain covering a plate-glass window (fig. 132). The gleaming, circular pendant lamp and the simple, tapered lines of the side and coffee tables were meant to signify Modernist interior decorating. The coffee table displayed an object that could be considered "vast [and] squatty," Julio de Diego's *Milkyway* bowl (fig. 133). On the side table, an obviously non-Western figurine, possibly Latin American, held pride of place (the catalogue described it as "Happy Feaster Sculpture: Original is in a famous Southwest Museum — this authentic reproduction is of brown and red terracotta. Unusual").[61]

As I have discussed elsewhere in this book, architectural historian Dianne Harris has argued that the rhetoric of Modern architecture in the

Fig. 132 (above left). Interior view of a showroom including Julio de Diego's *Milky Way* bowl. *Spiegel Home Shopping Book*, 1955, 4.

Fig. 133 (above right). *Milkyway* (bowl), 1950, Julio de Diego, designer. Stonelain, Associated American Artists, manufacturer. Glazed stoneware, 6 × 11¾ × 7¼ in. (15.2 × 29.8 × 18.4 cm). Collection of Patricia Shaw.

postwar suburbs was deeply embedded in a discourse of racial Whiteness, where spaciousness, openness, and crisp, clean interiors were implicitly contrasted against non-White urban environments of congestion, claustrophobia, and dirt.[62] Numerous critical theorists have also pointed to the pervasive White bias that sees Whiteness as clean and racialized others as dirty.[63] Modern furniture shared this racializing tendency with its rhetorical emphasis on "clean" lines in its advertisements for largely White audiences; the implied counterexamples were dirtiness and dinginess, qualities associated with a stereotypical urban, non-White interior. Against the presumed Whiteness of these furniture pieces, the smaller "warty ceramics" and "driftwood" in the model Modern interior provided not simply a decorative accent, but also an accent of tactile irregularity and allegedly primitive authenticity. When we consider that the "warty ceramics" and "driftwood" were often accompanied by folk artifacts of apparently non-Western origin—such as the wooden birds in fig. 130 and the terracotta sculpture in fig. 132—then we can begin to hypothesize a racialized connotation to the accessories in general. I argue that these interiors employ accessories using a rhetorical logic similar to that of the Herman Miller showrooms discussed in chapter 3. In these two examples of publications with predominantly White readerships, if the unadorned, industrially simplified Modernist furniture carries associations of Whiteness, then the handcrafted irregular forms and natural materials of the accessories signify non-White racial identities. As with the Herman Miller display spaces, in these model Modernist interiors, the relative balance between racially coded White furniture and racially coded non-White accessories is significant: the furniture defines and dominates the room, and thoroughly frames, or contains, the accents, while the accents provide variety and even a touch of curiosity, in the mode of a colonialist tourist, but they are always clearly secondary to the dominant aesthetic of simplicity and severity.

In the context of these subtle racial politics—where Modernist design is associated with the cultivation of a White racial identity, partly through the aesthetic contrast of indigenous folk artifacts used as accessories—the Stonelain ceramics were ultimately an awkward fit. Although they were the product of White artists, they attempted to be the eccentric decorative accent. Blanch's cigarette box, for example, with its irregular application of colored glazes, was not industrially Modern—"clean" and therefore racially White—but neither was it highly tactile or evocative of the natural world, and as such coded as non-White (see fig. 131). Interestingly, the brown glaze of de Diego's *Milkyway* bowl (similar to brown terracotta), along with its incised biomorphic markings, may have encouraged Spiegel catalogue readers to interpret it as a non-Western, non-White object, and thus it may have fit into the overall racialized scheme of mid-century Modernist interiors (see fig. 133). Bohrod's "Pagan Magic" textile perhaps resonated in a similar fashion: the curtains and daybed in the Spiegel catalogue feature a pattern of repeating, self-consciously primitivist motifs evocative of Native American and Mexican folk art. The title of the fabric design (given by its White designer and White commercial producers) furthered the association to stereotyped non-Western cultural traditions.

The object that was eventually used as a kind of trademark for the entire Stonelain line was profoundly indebted to the racialized politics that relegated non-Western bodies to accessory positions in the house. Gwen Lux designed a pitcher that she titled *Ubangi* in 1949 for the inaugural collection of AAA ceramics (fig. 134); in 1950, a profile rendering of it became part of the Stonelain stamp put on the bottom of each object (fig. 135). The *Ubangi* pitcher has an unusual profile, which is explained in part by its name. In 1930, as an attraction within its sideshow lineup of exotic and "freak" human specimens, the Ringling Brothers and Barnum and Bailey Circus had brought a group of women from central Africa to serve as a living display of the ritual of lip plate modifications; although they were not from the region around the Ubangi River, the circus appropriated that name for them.[64] In popular culture, a connection was forged between the name "Ubangi" and the practice of lip extensions and extreme facial modifications; examples of circus sideshow posters depicting dark-skinned women with enormous lip extensions can be found as late as 1960.[65] While there is no archival evidence to suggest why Lux gave the object its name, her *Ubangi* pitcher is distinguished by an unusually large, dramatic lip from which to pour the liquid held inside.[66] The entire object can be read as a distorted body, perhaps the body of an African woman fetishized by White, Western audiences as exotic and violently altered. Thus the pitcher that came to represent the Stonelain product line could be understood—especially in light of its title—as an abstracted female African body. The object associates people of color, once again, with accessories in the household and, in its functional role as a pitcher, metaphorically evokes the practice of limiting women of color to positions of domestic service. Of course, this design was not actually the product of non-Western craftspeople but rather was forged by a White artist. As in the American Modern advertisement that quotes W. C. Handy's "Saint Louis Blues," in this pitcher White creativity has again colonized the work of people of color, here the supposedly authentic indigenous practices from another continent.

Many other Stonelain products possessed decorative qualities that coded them, implicitly, as racially White. The historical figurines of Paul Bunyan, Ichabod Crane, and Johnny Appleseed make overt reference to a tradition of White American folk art (see fig. 126). Similarly, Doris Lee's *Winter Train* also references a tradition of White American folk art in the Grandma Moses–like primitivism of its rural, snowy landscape (fig. 136). Two objects stand out for their overt representations of racial power dynamics. Marion Greenwood designed a vase, titled *China Memory*, that is decorated in a calligraphic sketch meant to evoke Chinese ink painting (fig. 137). The figure striding across the vase wears a traditional, conical farmer's hat and carries a load in the bamboo yoke across

Fig. 134 (right). *Ubangi* (pitcher), 1949, Gwen Lux, designer. Stonelain, Associated American Artists, manufacturer. Glazed stoneware, 9½ × 7 × 3½ in. (24.3 × 17.8 × 8.9 cm). Collection of Patricia Shaw.

Fig. 135 (below). Stonelain mark, 1950. Associated American Artists.

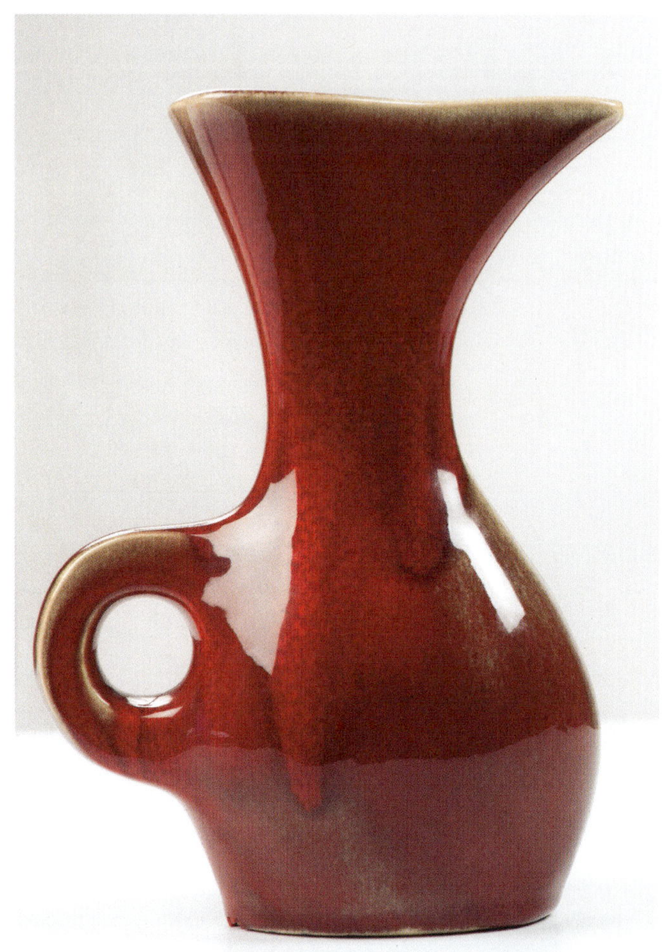

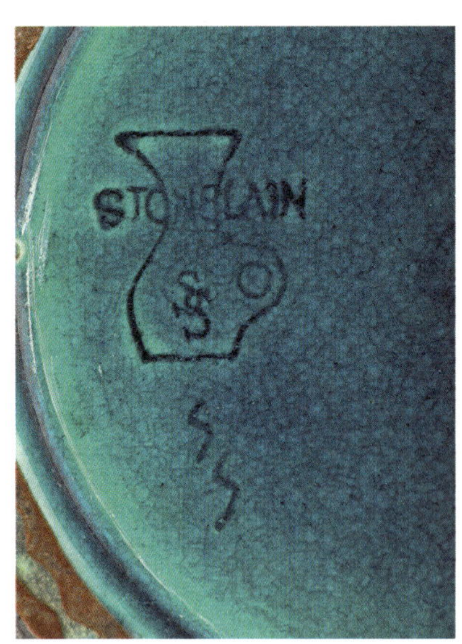

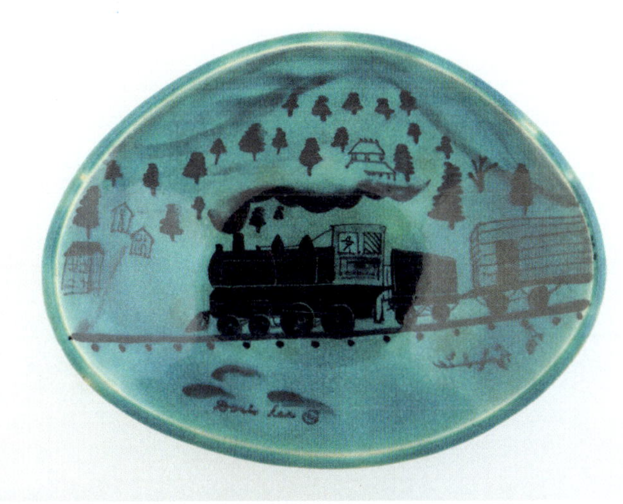

Fig. 136 (right). *Winter Train* (plate), 1949, Doris Lee, designer. Stonelain, Associated American Artists, manufacturer. Glazed stoneware, 2¾ × 10½ × 8 in. (7 × 26.7 × 20.3 cm). Collection of Patricia Shaw.

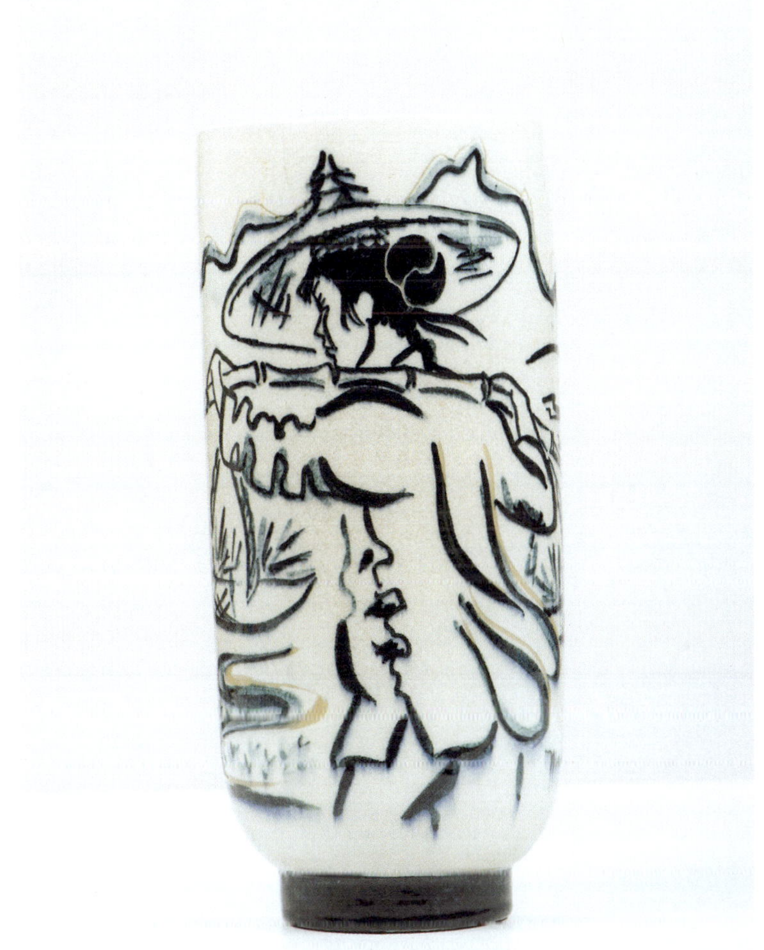

Fig. 137 (below right). Marion Greenwood, *China Memory* (vase), 1949. Stonelain, Associated American Artists, manufacturer. Glazed stoneware, 11½ × 5 × 3 in. (29.2 × 12.7 × 7.6 cm). Collection of Patricia Shaw.

his shoulders. The vase was inspired, as the catalogue explains, by "the artist's trip to China. Several coolies circle the vase in the endless procession of this mystical Oriental land."[67] Not only does the catalogue copy exoticize the subject, but it conjures the image of Chinese workers trapped on the vase, trudging forward in their labor, caught in a never-ending circle. Just as the artist is placed in a position of privileged superiority—a tourist who observes labor from a distance—so, too, the vase captures that power imbalance in its form. Greenwood is clearly quoting the aesthetic of Chinese calligraphy, but not trying too hard to give herself over to the different style; the hatching that connotes grasses by the river's edge and grains in the basket are overtly cartoonish and illustrational in a Western idiom.

Another example of a Stonelain object that clearly appropriates the identity of a non-White is a c. 1952 martini pitcher by Aaron Bohrod, intended to accompany his "Country Auction" textile design. The pitcher features, on one side only, a painting of an African American lawn jockey (fig. 138). The figure represents a shameful history of stereotyped African American figures frozen into positions of servitude for White owners.[68] In the context of Bohrod's work for AAA, there are additional points of resonance. The lawn jockey appears in his "Country Auction" textile pattern, produced as part of the AAA collaboration with Riverdale Fabrics (fig. 139). In the potentially endless run of a bolt of fabric, Bohrod's pattern features an ongoing irregular grid, each square filled with an object that could be acquired at a country auction. The jockey is merely one item out of many, merely one item to be purchased and added to the infinite array of consumer goods that define the accomplished suburban home. Its casual racism—echoed elsewhere on the fabric with a Native American cigar store statue—is clearly the purview of a privileged White buyer, one who can glance at a lamp, a weathervane, or a Black servant and consider them interchangeable. Once the figure has been isolated and transposed to the martini pitcher, it takes on an additional meaning. The jockey, whose face has been entirely abstracted into a semicircle of brown with the exception of a broad smile, becomes a friendly servant who will offer drinks inside the house as well as care for the land outside. Indeed, the high collar, vest, and breeches on the jockey recall the excessively formal outfit of the Black servant featured in numerous advertisements for Walker's DeLuxe Bourbon in 1951 and 1952 (which appeared in both *Life* and *Ebony*).[69]

While Modern interiors such as those illustrated in figs. 130 and 132 (and see also figs. 98 and 100 in chapter 3) may have incorporated indigenous non-Western artifacts, the accent pieces were supposed to be the products of racial others, demonstrating an enlightened aesthetic awareness on the part of the Cold War citizen/consumer/traveler. Indeed, handwrought expression was acceptable in a Modern interior in either a decorative object made by a racially distinct group or, alternatively, in a painting made by a White, male American fine artist.[70] Expressiveness in a racially White decorative object, however, fit into neither of these

Fig. 138 (right). Pitcher with stirring rod from the *Country Auction* collection, 1952, Aaron Bohrod, designer. Stonelain, Associated American Artists, manufacturer. The Butler Institute of American Art, Youngstown, Ohio. Gift of Dr. and Mrs. Bert Katz, given in honor of Carisa Amedia, 1997.

Fig. 139 (below right). *Country Auction* textile from the Pioneer Pathways series, 1952, Aaron Bohrod, designer. Associated American Artists for Riverdale Fabrics, manufacturer. Printed cotton, 6 ft. 5¾ in. × 46½ in. (197.5 × 118.1 cm). Cooper Hewitt, Smithsonian Design Museum, New York. American Textile History Museum Collection.

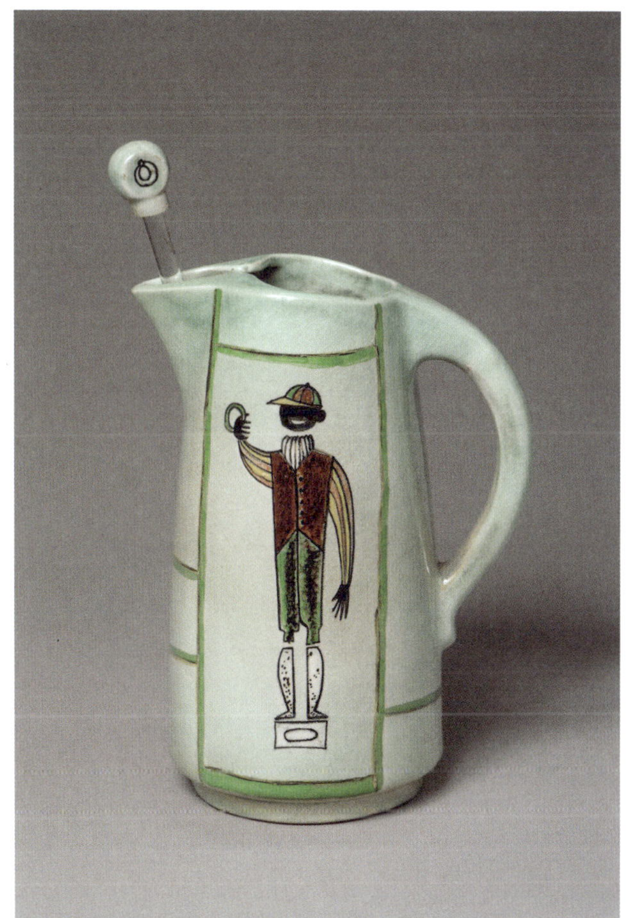

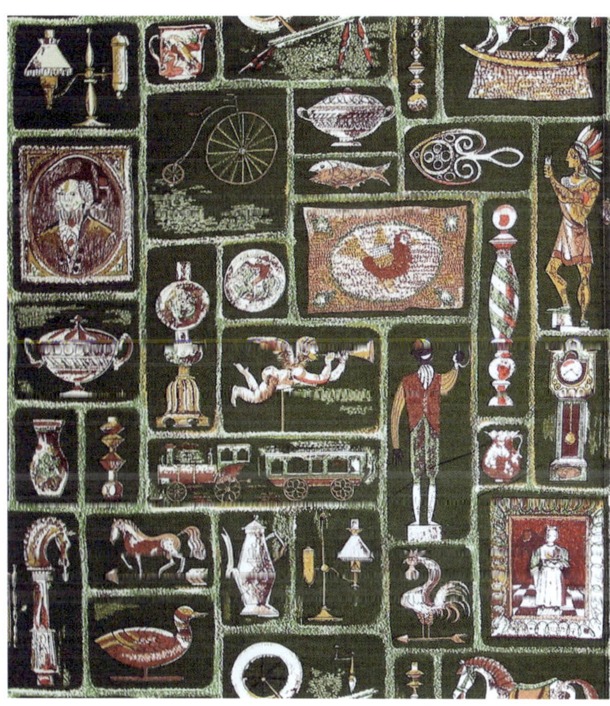

categories and was problematic. The references to racial Whiteness in the Stonelain line may have, ironically, limited its commercial appeal. Instead of being authentically "primitive" or evidence of a serious, philosophical struggle, the vase, pitcher, cigarette box, or bowl risked being diminutive, facile, or irrelevant.

Stonelain objects were likewise difficult to categorize in terms of gender. The name Stonelain itself embodied a certain gender hybridity. "Stone" referred to the strength of the material, and prompted allusions to the stereotypically masculine traits of durability and solidity. The "lain" part of the name alluded to the smooth quality of its finish, thus evoking such stereotypically feminine qualities as delicacy, translucence, and smoothness. The marketing material evidenced a similar identity split. Stonelain objects were, on the one hand, close kin to works of fine art and objects collected in museums. In this period, the gender associated with an establishment institution such as a museum might have been masculine; moreover, many of the print collectors featured in AAA's catalogues throughout the 1940s were men.[71] On the other hand, Stonelain objects were something to "'stock up' [on] now … for your own home." Stonelain was sold to the public through department stores across the country, often in the "gift" department; and AAA especially promoted the objects as gifts: "exceptional, distinctive presents in unexcelled good taste."[72] Objects for the home, or given to someone else for her home, tended to be understood as feminine: something that would be bought by, and given to, the woman of the house. By claiming that Stonelain could be both a museum-quality work of art for the ambitious collector and a tasteful gift for the socially obligated housewife, the marketing campaign blurred the gendered identity of the product. This ultimately compromised its ability to be either fine art or decorative knickknack. Its compounded gendered and racial ambiguity affected its art-world status and ultimately must have contributed to its lack of commercial success.

The Ordered Self

In its first year, the Stonelain collection featured a large number of plates and small bowls. This may have been a consequence of the artists' approach to the new line: since many of them were painters, they gravitated toward forms that would provide them a flat surface on which to paint. However, the low forms are also significant for how they function in the house. Many of the medium- and large-sized plates in the first collection seem to have been made to hang on the wall (and have holes for affixing a hanger on their backs), and several photographs in the first catalogue illustrate plates hung as works of art—that is, as items of display (fig. 140). As such, they provide a ready transition to the final section of this chapter, which examines the kinds of art consumers were encouraged to buy

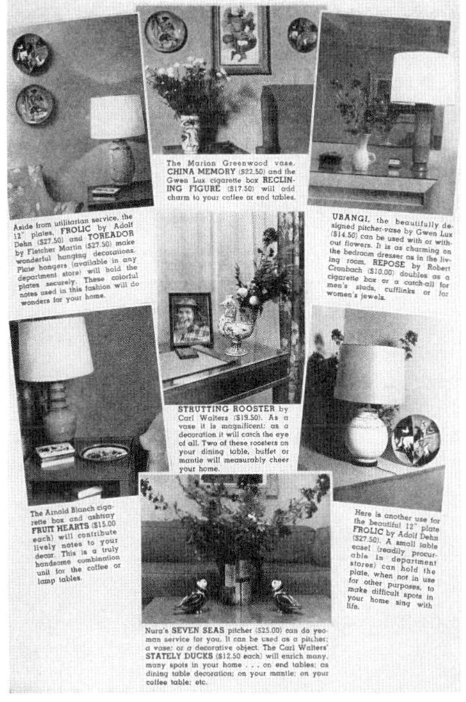

and hang on the walls of their Modern homes, as well as the formats they should follow in hanging it. For many authors writing about the construction and decoration of the postwar American home, the art that homeowners selected for their walls was freighted with particular significance. Mary Davis Gillies, a White female professional who worked at *McCall's* magazine as decorating and architectural editor from 1929 through the 1960s, authored several mid-century decorating advice books; in a 1948 publication, she offers one theory as to why many of her readers would feel less comfortable choosing art for their homes than selecting, say, sofas, wallpaper, or refrigerators.[73] "We have a poor picture tradition in this country," she ruminates in *All about Modern Decorating*. "Our slogan has been any amount for automobiles, automatic refrigerators, and glamorous cookstoves, but not one cent for art."[74] While a national tradition may be lacking in the appreciation of art, she attempts to empower her readers by explaining to them that choices in art are profoundly personal: "No one can tell you what pictures to get. Pictures are like friends. No one can pick them out for you."[75]

Another decorating advice author, Elizabeth T. Halsey, writing for *Ladies' Home Journal*, adopts a similar approach. She reminds her readers that "the choice [of art for the home] is a very personal one, so don't let art connoisseurs embarrass you into purchasing a 'good' picture because you think you should like it."[76] Her advice may seem a bit disingenuous, given that she had first entered the professional world of interior decoration as the youthful assistant to one of the most powerful "connoisseurs" and tastemakers of the twentieth century, R.T.H. Halsey, who was the esteemed collector of American decorative arts and intellectual powerhouse behind the creation of the Metropolitan Museum of Art's American Wing in 1924.[77] Indeed, in Halsey's text for *Ladies' Home Journal* readers, an ulterior logic behind the rhetoric of personal choice is revealed: because the choice of pictures in the home is deeply individual, it is also the litmus test for taste that the homeowner presents to her visitors and guests. "Pictures come under the general heading of accessories, yet must be considered separately because they play such an important decorating role," she instructs her readers. "The selection of pictures, almost more than any other furnishing, provides a clue to personality, artistic taste and individuality."[78] Similarly, in a small pamphlet devoted entirely to decorating problems in the living room, Mary L. Brandt explains to her readers the high stakes in choosing art to hang on the walls of one's home: "Pictures are one of the most revealing clues to a person's taste, and good art is not necessarily confined to oil paintings. You can find all kinds of good art in things you may never have thought of before."[79] The sense that the occasion of hanging art on the walls is the high-profile moment when one's taste—and indeed one's selfhood—is presented for judgment by others is captured in a droll anecdote by Russell Lynes in his 1950 dissection of social snobbery: "The Art Snob can be recognized in the home (i.e., your home) by the quick look he gives the pictures on your walls, quick but penetrating, as though he were undressing them. This is followed either by complete and obviously pained silence or by a comment such as 'That's really a very pleasant little water color you have there.' "[80] To the extent that the walls of one's home are a place for especially focused public scrutiny in postwar culture, the act of choosing art—and, more fundamentally, arranging it on the wall—can thus be understood as an act of putting oneself in order, configuring oneself, for public presentation.

According to Gillies, Halsey, Brandt, and other decorating advice authors, the first quandary that homemakers faced was the question of what kind of art to hang on the walls. In general, these White, female authors recommended figurative art in traditional genres and sometimes were explicitly conservative in their taste. "Pictures for the living room of the average home should not be too startling in subject, color or composition," warned Halsey. "For the living room, then, consider landscape, marines, portraits—not necessarily of family members—flower prints or figures."[81] Gillies reveals her tastes through the artists to whom she directs her readers: "Go to the Art Department of the public library and ask the librarian to give you books showing the work of Modern artists," she suggests. Her list of Modern artists largely comprises White men painting in nineteenth-century France, including Manet, Renoir, Monet, and Van Gogh, but she also highlights the American triumvirate of Regionalist painters—Thomas Hart Benton, John Steuart Curry, and Grant Wood—as worthy of attention. Indeed, she suggests that her readers "send to the Associated American Artists for catalogues," citing the business that had helped to make those three artists well-known names in many American households.[82] AAA itself stocked an almost entirely figurative catalogue of prints and color reproductions through the mid-1950s. In 1945, AAA director Reeves Lewenthal explained to a journalist that he had "not yet offered reproductions of an abstraction," and that landscape prints were vastly more popular than figure-based scenes.[83] Not every home avoided abstract art, however. It appears in occasional advertisements—including the *Life* magazine Motorola ad from 1952 (see fig. 73 in chapter 2), or a Schlitz beer ad from 1950—and in model homes featured in *Life*.[84] Brandt herself even describes one successful Modern room she had seen that contained "one wall … completely covered with Modern paintings and drawings."[85]

Homemakers were also encouraged to consider hanging items on their walls that were not paintings or limited edition prints. Gillies suggests beginning a collection by clipping pictures from magazines, and Brandt provides an extensive list of the kinds of things one might hang on her walls: "Other relatively inexpensive pictures in good taste might be an old map, framed with a colored mat and simple frame, a series of colorful prints, such as Currier & Ives prints, framed exactly alike, old botanical prints, and butterfly and bird prints. Or you may wish to have framed the pictures in an old book you have discovered."[86] Interestingly, all of these authors advise their readers that "good reproductions of fine paintings are better than mediocre originals or copies thereof."[87] They might be referring to AAA's color reproductions, which Lewenthal marketed as "gelatones" beginning in the mid-1940s, claiming that they were indistinguishable from the originals.[88] They might also be referring to subscription services such as Artifax, a Chicago-based company that sold color reproductions of European and American paintings from the fifteenth through the nineteenth centuries; Artifax sold each framed print packaged in a cardboard sleeve with a bold graphic design by George Nelson that boasted the artist's name, and some advertisements even suggested hanging the Nelson packaging design itself on the wall.[89] Consumers might also find high-quality reproductions as bonus gifts associated with the many clubs of the decade. The Heritage Club—one popular book club of the postwar period—advertised in 1955 that new members would receive a portfolio of matted and framed reproductions of Van Gogh paintings.[90] It is telling that Halsey, even as she extolls the high quality of many color reproduction services available, warns her readers to "avoid fads. In recent years, for example, Van Gogh has enjoyed such popularity that few living rooms seem to be without at least one of his paintings. This overuse detracts from the individuality of a room, makes it seem like an unimaginative copy of others."[91]

Whereas Gillies recommends that her readers go to the library to learn about art, Brandt suggests additional resources: "Acquire education and experience in art by subscribing to a good art magazine, or by going to your local art galleries or to lectures at a museum."[92] But "good art magazines" were not the only place to learn about art; as discussed in chapter 2, publications such as *Life* and *Ebony* prided themselves on regular feature articles about various aspects of the art world. While *Ebony*'s journalism tended to focus on the career and accomplishments of an individual artist, *Life*'s approach to fine art journalism in the postwar years had a distinct art-appreciation angle: its articles explained the career and work of an artist, but also introduced basic terms for formal analysis and description of paintings. Over the course of the 1950s, *Life*'s art journalism covered European Old Masters as well as a wide range of contemporary painters from both Europe and the United States. By 1958, as part of a sequence of self-promotion spots that emphasized different aspects of its editorial agenda, *Life* actually ran one advertisement for its coverage of the arts. Beneath an unattributed sketch of the *Life* presses—indebted to Diego Rivera's murals of Ford workers in Detroit—the magazine boasted of its high-quality papers and inks that made its "color reproductions the finest possible." And the personal testimony by the white-haired, pipe-smoking, White gentleman featured in the large photograph explains the educational value of *Life*'s coverage: "You'd think when a man got to be my age, he'd know it didn't pay to be pigheaded. But it took LIFE to show me how much I was missing with my 'art is for smarties' attitude. Oh, sure, I knew about the Mona Lisa's smile, but modern art was just a mess of paint to me. I really had the wrong picture before LIFE!"[93]

Many fine art articles in *Life* prominently featured full-color reproductions of paintings, whether by contemporary or historical artists. Unlike *Ebony*, whose photographic journalism emphasized the human actor and thus almost always included the artists along with their creations, *Life* published many facsimiles of works of art—which might, following Gillies's advice, be clipped from the magazine and form the basis for a homemaker's self-education on the arts.[94] Indeed, Gillies goes further and gives her readers permission to put clippings such as these directly on a wall: "Inexpensive prints may also be mounted directly on the wall like wallpaper. Arrange them in a checkerboard plan over a chest of drawers, the fireplace, or the sofa, and cover the whole collection with a single piece of glass. The glass should be at least five inches larger than the mass of pictures and may be fastened to the wall with mirror rosettes."[95]

As this last surprising bit of advice suggests, Gillies wants her readers to understand that how they arrange their art on the wall is as important as—if not more important than—the pieces that they select. She and many other decorating advice authors ultimately recommend that homeowners consider the art on their walls not as individual objects, but rather as part of a larger decorative statement that encompasses the entire room. "Pictures do not stand alone but must provide a connecting link between backgrounds and furnishings," lectures Halsey, encouraging her readers to "try to make your pictures form a unit with other furnishings."[96] Both she and Gillies guide readers to group "small pictures ... together to form a single mass," because "groupings of small pictures are sometimes more decorative than one large picture would be." In order to accomplish this, "random heights are to be avoided" and the paintings "should hang close together as a unit to avoid a helter-skelter look."[97] Brandt even suggests a hands-on approach to figuring out the best design for one's wall: "In any case, whether they [the pictures] are all the same size or of different sizes and shapes, you should first make a plan in order to get a pleasing arrangement. Measure the space you want them to fit into and then draw your plan on a large piece of wrapping paper the way you intend to group them on the wall."[98]

The mental image of someone—presumably a housewife, the target audience of Brandt's book—sketching out a plan for arranging her art on the wall on the back of a large sheet of wrapping paper brings to the surface some of the values implicit in this discussion of household art. The actual object that will be hung on the wall is revealed to be of less importance than how it is configured against other objects. The work of art that these advice authors actually celebrate is the complete arrangement designed by the homeowner, not the work of art contained within any individual frame. The housewife is the creative visionary, composing a masterpiece on her walls of sequential or mirrored elements. Her medium, so to speak, is the individual items she has selected and framed for the room. "Never hang a picture merely to fill up an empty wall space," scolds Halsey.[99] Instead, under the guidance of these books, the housewife becomes an assemblage artist, working with preexisting forms to create a statement of taste—an aesthetic statement—larger than any specific picture.

Halsey's book provides several clear diagrams to illustrate her lessons (fig. 141). In both the middle and lower pairs, the "YES" examples feature balanced arrangements of smaller works of art. These configurations play with various pendant images—sometimes a pair of related works are directly next to each other (on the left above the sofa), and sometimes they are above and below each other (over the sideboard). They might be visual puzzles, calling upon the viewer to figure out the logic of the arrangement, as they do so, they foreground the work of the homemaker who has so cleverly designed their placement on the wall. Diagrams such as these were not the only examples of arranging art that residents of suburbia might see, however. Throughout the pages of shelter magazines such as *Better Homes and Gardens*, elite magazines such as *House Beautiful*, or general-readership periodicals such as *Life*, photographs of model interiors and various advertisements provided examples of this so-called unit approach to picture hanging. Television advertisements, featuring a photograph of the prized appliance that includes just enough of the wall around it to convey a setting, were frequent exemplars of strategic, unified

Fig. 141 (right). "Picture Hanging," *Ladies' Home Journal Book of Interior Decoration* (1954), 127.

Fig. 142 (below). Advertisement for Crosley Television (detail), *Life*, January 29, 1951, 73.

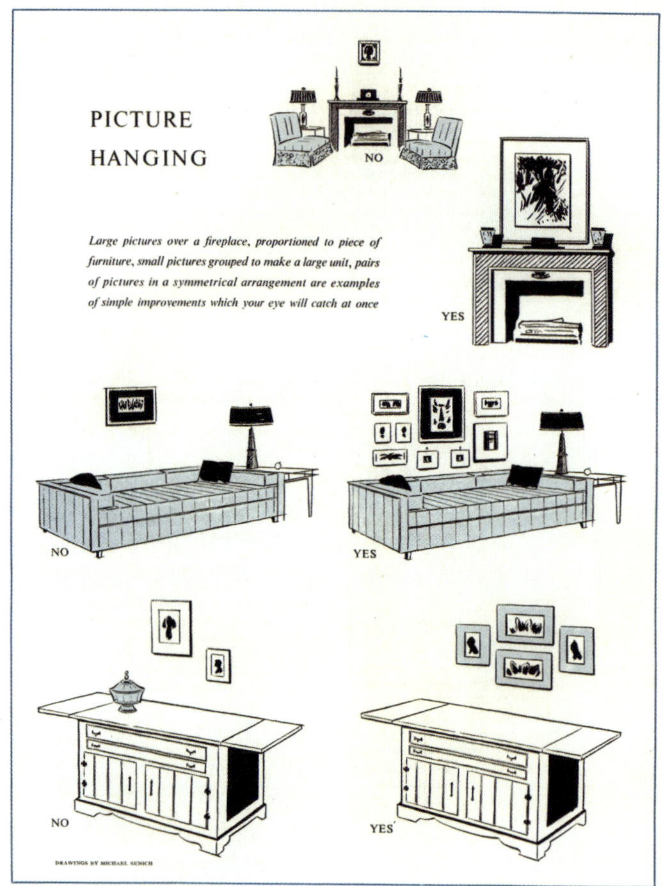

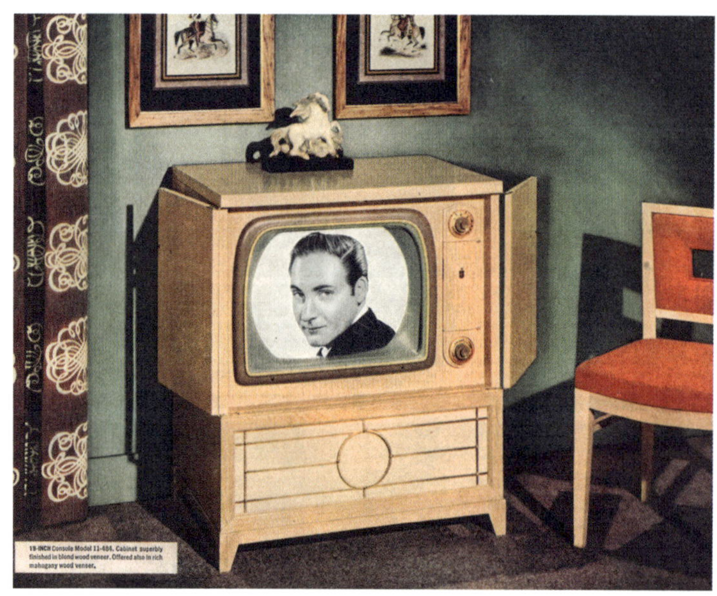

art hanging that resisted the "helter-skelter look." Crosley Television published an advertisement in *Life* in 1951 that featured two prints above the console (fig. 142). In the advertisement, the tops of the prints are cut off, but it is clear that they form a decorative pair: they are hung along a single line, framed identically, and they depict two horses, the compositions mirroring each other. Indeed, Crosley placed a ceramic sculpture on top of the television itself—the *Pacing Mustang*, designed by Gwen Lux for Stonelain—that helps to draw the art on the walls into dialogue with the furniture.[100]

Crosley was in good company in these years: advertisements for Magnavox presented a massive "television-radio-phonograph" console with four landscape paintings, framed in identical fashion, positioned in a grid directly above it;[101] GE promoted a television unit with three works of art, matted and framed to match, hung in a column next to it;[102] Zenith introduced its "Black Magic Television" with pendant landscapes positioned above it;[103] and Motorola included a trio of Modernist prints (see fig. 73). In all of these examples, the featured item in the living room is the television—source of envy, pride, and community gathering, according to countless oral histories of life in the suburbs[104]—and the art around it becomes part of that visual focus. In their depiction of art in this prime viewing location, it is significant that the advertisements routinely model the decorators' strict set of rules. The art is never uneven, irregular, or isolated; it is always part of an ordered unit that conveys abundance and forethought—there is more than one piece of art and they are carefully arranged—on the part of the family that owns the television.

Associated American Artists also promoted the coordinated-unit style of picture hanging for its prints. In catalogues from 1951 and 1954, for example, AAA illustrated a wide stylistic range of interiors with tightly scripted arrangements of prints: a centrifugal configuration of five prints over a sofa in 1951, and sofas, daybeds, fireplaces, and staircases framed by complex grids of prints in multiple sketches from 1954 (figs. 143, 144). Since AAA issued catalogues with the hope that patrons would buy more than one print—indeed, patrons were encouraged to build up a collection of prints as their financial situation allowed—model rooms like these demonstrated how one might show off numerous purchases on one wall. With the varied stylistic settings in the 1954 catalogue, especially, AAA demonstrated that orderly displays of prints were appropriate in federal-inspired living rooms, Modernist bedrooms, and Colonial Revival sitting rooms. The company also occasionally published advice on how to arrange the prints in one's home; although it has not been possible to identify the specific author of these catalogue texts, their message resonates closely with the advice offered by Gillies, Brandt, Halsey, and others. Under the heading "These Originals Can Enrich and Beautify Your Home," the author of the 1946 catalogue provided some specific directions for hanging art over a sofa: "Your sofa will also take on greater charm when complimented

Fig. 143 (right). Living room interior with AAA prints, *Patron's Supplement No. 51* (Associated American Artists, 1951), cover. Private collection.

Fig. 144 (below). Interiors with AAA prints, *Special Twentieth Anniversary Offer … Etchings and Lithographs* (Associated American Artists, 1954), 2. Private collection.

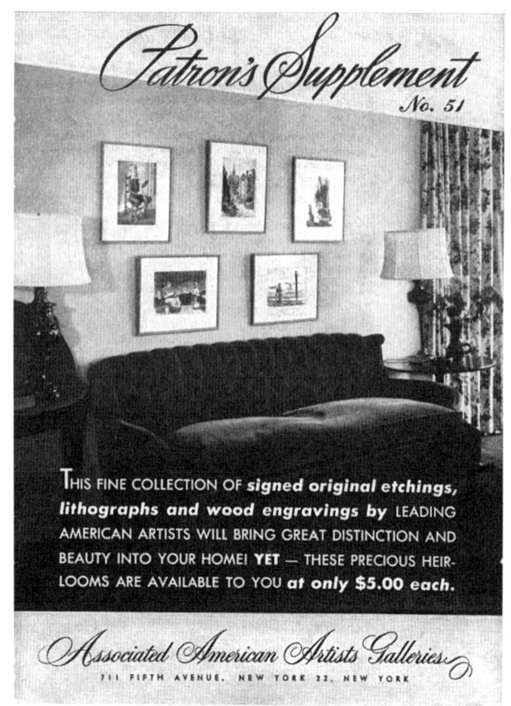

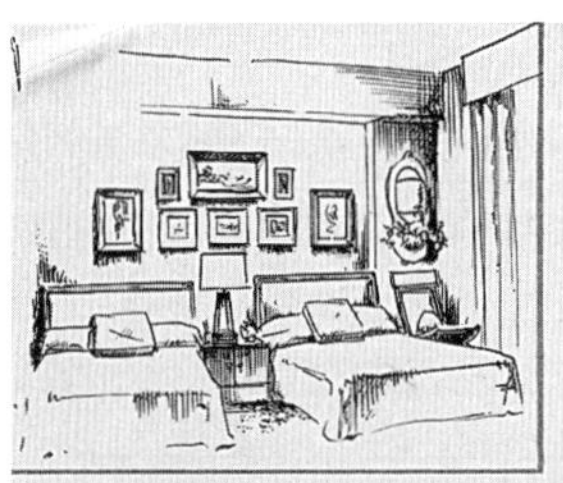
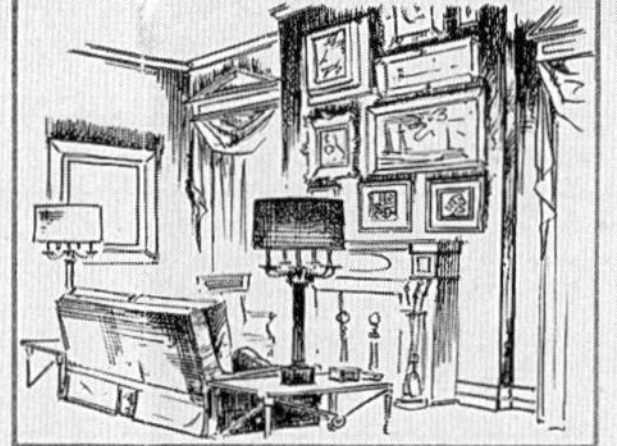

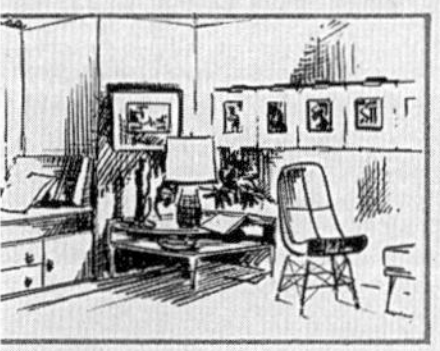
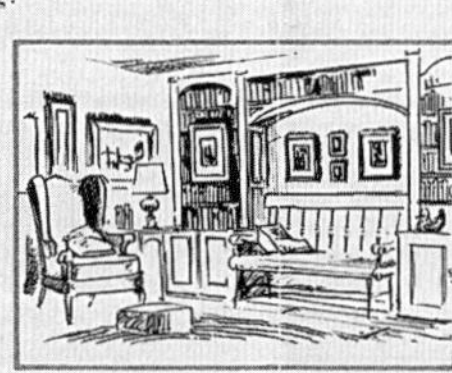
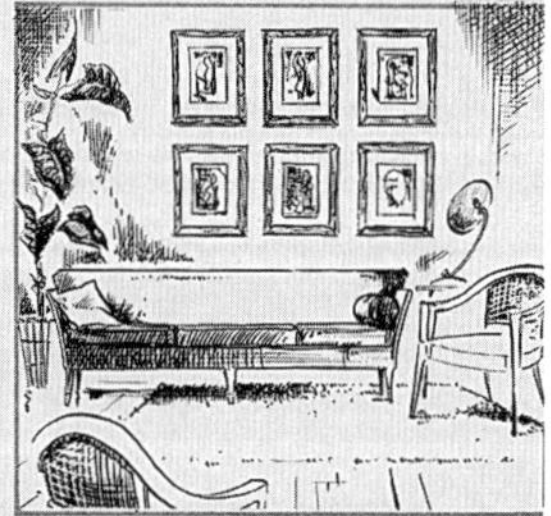

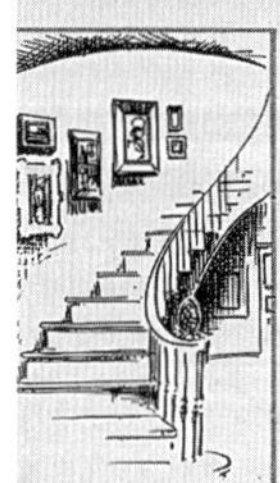
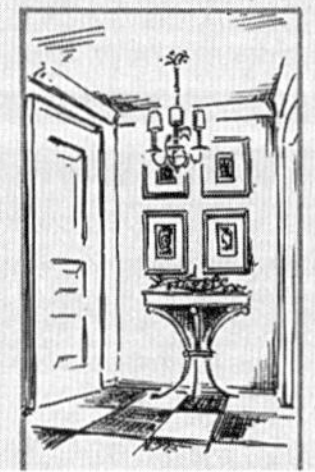
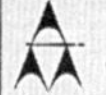

by pictures hung in good relation to it. For example, four vertical originals framed exactly alike, or three horizontal originals framed alike and hung in a single row over your sofa will produce a rectangular shape that attractively balances the sofa."[105] Around 1950, AAA boasted that a new size of color gelatone would "answer an important picture problem," which they defined as "the home decorating need of pictures 'in twos' that can be used as balancing units."[106] In this advice, as in so many others from this period, the content of the art is hardly relevant. Instead, importance is placed on the presentation: the overall visual impact of the orderly arrangement of the art in context with the furniture. With pictures arrayed across the wall, the homeowner is empowered to present an impeccably ordered self to the scrutinizing eyes of guests.

Given the range of materials that these authors encourage their readers to hang on the walls, and the time they devote to prescribing the ways those walls should be configured, it is surprising that they pay scant attention to the collection and display of non-Western objects. Gillies finishes her discussion of the kinds of objects one might display in the house with a list of seemingly random suggestions: "Maps are possibilities," she notes. "Also, I have seen mounted and pressed seaweed used. I have seen studies of Indian chieftains, costume prints of South American natives, as well as charcoal studies of hands and arms and legs by Renoir, mounted and framed, used as pictures."[107] In this list, organic materials, widely divergent populations that represent artistic traditions beyond the scope of the Western canon, and parts of female bodies are all equated. Gillies adopts for herself—and asks her readers to adopt it too—a patriarchal gaze that equates non-Western bodies with female bodies, and that reduces all of these bodies to collectible objects, no different from pressed seaweed. Brandt makes room for objects from countries outside of Europe and the United States in her book, but such objects always enter the decorating narrative as a souvenir acquired in the course of travel. She recounts in one chapter the story of "a friend of mine [who] made her husband drag a huge Persian plate all around the World's Fair on the day she found it and bought it," and of another "who brought back enough colorful fabrics and pottery from a trip to Guatemala to carry the theme throughout her whole apartment."[108] In a separate chapter she explains how one might successfully achieve the effect of a "lived-in look": "It might be a Modern room with tables filled with ceramics and *bibelots* picked up on a trip to Europe, a collection of Inca and pre-Columbian figures from Peru and Guatemala, groups of paintings and drawings of foreign lands and people on the walls, travel books and magazines piled on tables and even maybe on the floor—all indications of her interest in travel."[109] In all of these anecdotes, Brandt positions the White, Western consumer in a position of power, traveling to the far reaches of the globe (or as far as a World's Fair) and bringing back to her American home the spoils of her journey: renderings of the bodies she has seen, produced with the handicraft skills of the bodies she has seen. These objects advertise much about the journeys and self-sensibility of the White collector, but they are rarely part of a deeper examination that respects the differences, histories, and traditions of the societies from which they are taken.

If Peru and Guatemala are interchangeable in her story, Brandt's attitude toward the generic "otherness" of all non-Western traditions is reflected in a revealing anecdote in Keats's *Crack in the Picture Window*, as he describes the interior-decorating practices of the presumed-White suburb of Rolling Knolls: "Since everyone patronized the one closest shopping center, Rolling Knolls houses were furnished alike, their shelves were stocked with the same supermarket's drab fare, every woman used *The Joy of Cooking*, and everyone bought the same plastic reproduction of an African carving for the identical living-room casual table."[110] The casual racism and ignorance embodied in this "reproduction of an African carving" was only one piece of a larger consumer landscape where representations of people of African descent could be found, as critic Bernard Wolfe explains in 1955: "America is inundated with many more tangible kinds of commodities to which one stock Negroid image or another is attached. One afternoon's browsing through any fair-sized shopping center will turn up an imposing array of these mass-produced images: on food labels, wallpaper, napkins, nylon stockings, perfumes, bandanas, charm bracelets, earrings, sweaters, men's shorts, lamp shades, ash trays, figurines. ... It pleases us [White consumers] in some 'non-functional' way—amuses, titillates, entices."[111]

While the advice books are relatively silent on the role of non-Western objects (or "primitive" objects, as they are more frequently labeled in the period), the pictorial evidence of *Life* and *Ebony* suggests that they were fairly common. However, the meanings one might find in these images of Americans living with artifacts from outside the industrialized West vary considerably based on the context. Anthropologist James Clifford introduced a diagram to explain "The Art-Culture System" in his 1988 *The Predicament of Culture*, which is a helpful guide in navigating the presence of non-Western objects in these two prototypically Western periodicals.[112] In his "Machine for Making Authenticity," Clifford explains how objects acquired from beyond the traditional institutions of Western art oscillate between being valued as cultural and ethnographic artifacts, on the one hand, and being celebrated as abstract works of art, on the other. Every object contains within it the definition of what it is not—or, in the terms of the structuralist theory that guides Clifford, its binary opposite. Thus the definition of art is partly based on what is not-art (examples of not-art in his system are "tourist art, commodities, the curio collection"); similarly, what is culture is partly defined by not-culture (in his system, "fakes, inventions"). Both not-art and not-culture are removed from the realm of authenticity, which is most prized in Western society. In *Life*, as I shall demonstrate, the representations of non-Western objects tend to fall along the binary path of not-art/art. In *Ebony*, by contrast, representations of non-Western objects are more firmly situated in the realm of culture, although they occasionally seem to be positioned as not-art as well.

In its journalistic coverage of the African continent in the 1950s, *Life* tends to adopt a voice that emphasizes its exotic nature and remote difference, and frequently positions objects from Africa as collectible curios, or examples of Clifford's category of not-art. While there are some articles that cover specific political events, many of *Life*'s articles treat the continent as an undifferentiated mass, as in one 1958 article, "Rich Surprises in Africa." The photographs that accompany these articles frequently depict Africans in indigenous attire, which frames them as explicitly different from Americans; indeed, the 1958 article features more photographs of wildlife and landscapes than it does people (who are represented, in one case, by only an ornamented ankle).[113] Advertisements in *Life* betray a similar attitude. In an advertisement for Budweiser Beer, a White couple, surrounded by partially opened wedding gifts that include traditional silver candlesticks and salt and pepper shakers, unwrap a large decorative object that appears to be an incoherent assemblage of generic non-Western elements (fig. 145). The copy echoes the skeptical view of the woman as she holds the object in her lap—"Good taste? Well, sometimes there's a *wide* difference of opinion!"—and suggests that this object should be viewed as nothing more than a curiosity. Because it clearly clashes with the couple's Anglo-traditional decorating aesthetic, it is dismissed as unserious, or not-art.

A 1956 ad for Sanforized fabric from *Life* compares two White women performing in a game of charades (fig. 146). The woman who lacks the confidence conferred by the properly treated clothing, on the left, is paralyzed in front of her audience, whereas the woman who knows her clothes will not shrink, on the right, is photographed mid-pose, successfully immersed in the drama of the game. Behind the successful woman hang two framed African-styled masks. Their presence is a visual non sequitur: they are not visible in the scene on the left, and they have no aesthetic relationship to anything else in the room. However, as they are positioned in line with the model's face, they are clearly meant to represent something about her. Perhaps it is her successful abandon (she has kicked off her shoes)? On the other hand, the seeming randomness of those two objects positioned on the wall says just as much: there is no evidence that they mean anything more to the homeowners than pride in being able to surprise guests. In this, it is important to consider the possibility that for some White homeowners, the display of African art, especially, was not merely a chance to contain the exotic but was also an opportunity to articulate racist beliefs in material form. To the extent that some considered objects made on the African continent to be not just primitive, but also ugly, awkward, or monstrous, they became concrete representations of the lesser status of a supposedly different race and were related to the stereotyped artifacts

Fig. 145. Advertisement for Budweiser Beer, *Life*, November 5, 1951, 105.

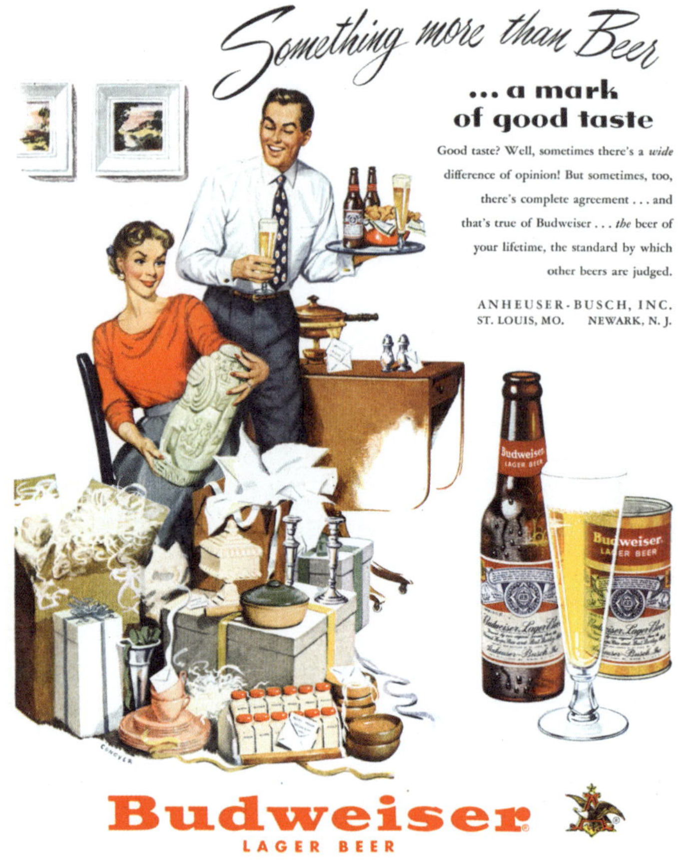

that Bernard Wolfe itemized in his account of mid-century shopping malls. David Halle proposes this logic in his 1993 study of collecting habits in the metro New York area. Although he casts his subjects in political terms that are appropriate for turn-of-the-twenty-first-century society and less apt for mid-century culture, his insight resonates for the earlier period: "Thus 'primitive' figures can also be symbols of the right, echoing and perhaps updating a long tradition (which flourished in America from the 1890s to the 1950s …) of using material objects—salt and pepper shakers, cookie jars, ashtrays, etc.—that depict black people in a degrading and stereotyped manner as subservient, powerless, and often with grossly caricatured features."[114] In a 1952 article in *Life*, one decorator orchestrated five fully conceived interiors "to match five types of women," arguing that interior design should be an act of self-portraiture. For television actor Nina Foch, he devised a "Fanciful Modern" room that features an array of masks and statuettes from various regions of Africa (fig. 147). As photographed for the magazine, Foch sits on a bench with the statuettes to either side of her and the masks floating above her head on a wall of blue. The objects seem

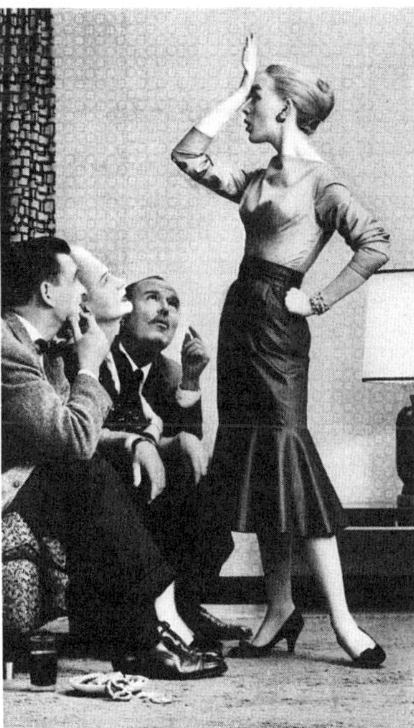
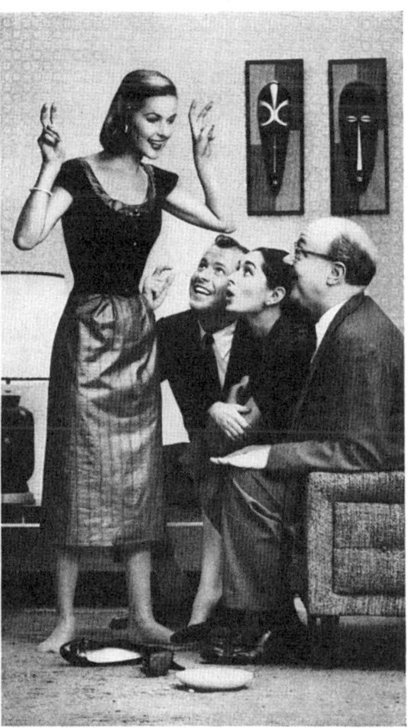

to approach her, but her white skin and vibrant red dress keep them at a respectful distance. "Miss Foch approves the color scheme," the article notes. "As a portrait background she questions the African masks, 'Maybe they are there to make me look pretty by contrast,' she says, 'but I would not use them.' "[115] In her comments, she gives voice to the casual racist bias that may have informed the display of some objects in White homes.

While non-Western art, and African art in particular, was often exoticized or even belittled in *Life*, casting it close to Clifford's not art category, there are also several examples throughout the decade of journalistic treatment of African objects as fine art. These appear in feature articles about art museum displays of African and Oceanic objects—for example, Nelson Rockefeller's Museum of Primitive Art, which he opened in New York in 1957—and the accompanying photographs convey a very different message from those that evoke the exotic other.[116] In these photographs, the individual objects of art are photographed in isolation, silhouetted against black or colored backgrounds (fig. 148). The images emphasize their contours and abstract form, and succeed in removing them physically

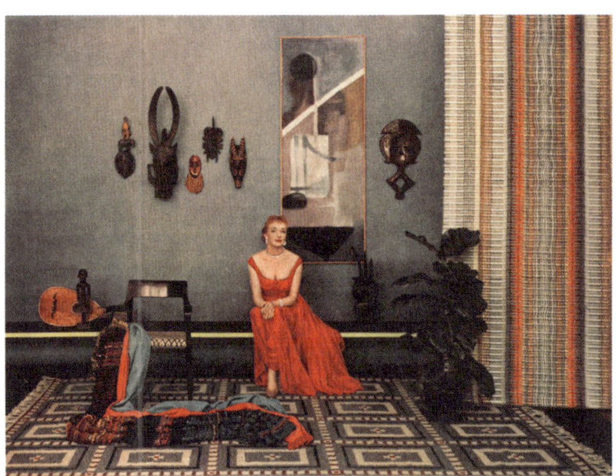

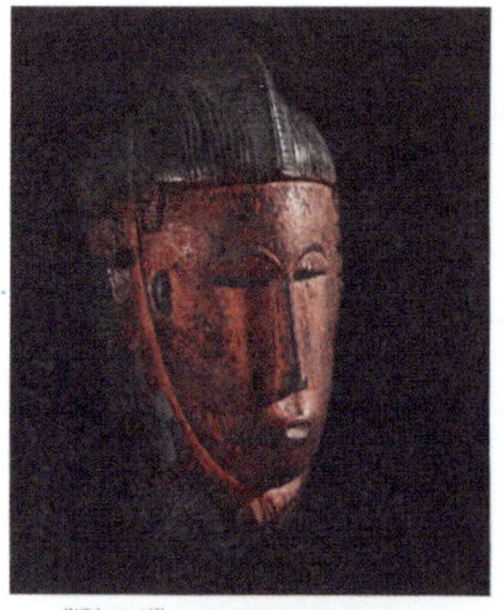

and intellectually from any cultural context. They are fully appropriated as works of art according to Western categories of aesthetics. Moreover, these actual images might be clipped from the magazine by a homemaker and then filed — or pasted up on her wall — as examples of fine art.

The treatment of artifacts and expressive works from Africa and diasporic islands in *Ebony* differs significantly from the tones that pervade *Life*, and could be better understood through Clifford's category of "culture," which he describes as "traditional, collective … material culture, craft."[117] Across a range of articles, the editorial voice in *Ebony* tends to emphasize the complex skills required to make any of these pieces, and the respect and rigor that African American scholars and practitioners bring to their study of them. In an article that highlights the work of Vernon Duncan, a dance professor at Roosevelt College in Chicago, the unsigned author explains how Duncan researched Haitian voodoo dance rituals and then introduced them to the US curriculum. Explaining that Duncan resourcefully discovered the site of "ceremonial rites" and then "studied them first hand in Haiti every night for a month," the article positions the dance tradition as a misunderstood practice: "Voodoo, a mixture of many religions and cultures, has a sharp African flavor. With its dizzy leaps and wild gyrations, it closely resembles a strenuous form of ballet. Each dancer must be able to move any part of the body independently of the rest, and muscular control of the shoulders is most important. Contrary to common belief, voodoo is not a dance of

Fig. 147 (above left). Nina Foch: Fanciful Modern. *Life*, May 5, 1952, 150. Arnold Newman, photographer.

Fig. 148 (above right). "A Prime Accumulation of Primitive Art," *Life*, May 6, 1957, 120. Nina Leen, photographer.

complete abandonment, but follows a traditional ritual prescribed for each of a number of voodoo gods."[118] Perhaps the most revealing contrast in tone between *Ebony* and *Life* can be seen in the coverage that each gave to the performance, in spring 1959, of a touring group of folk dancers, originally from French colonial Guinea, called "Les Ballets Africains." *Life's* single-page notice, titled "New York Says Tsk Tsk at African Attire," focuses on the controversy around the female dancers' topless costumes (and includes a photograph of the dancers with arms strategically positioned to cover their bare breasts).[119] *Ebony's* article, considerably longer at four pages and accompanied by eighteen photographs, seems to rejoice in the controversy while it also draws the reader's attention to the authenticity and skill of the artistic performance: "For perhaps the first time, an African dance troupe has succeeded in picturing for American audiences village life on the Dark Continent in all of its weird imagery and riotous color. Vividly costumed dancers display agile, marvelously-muscled bodies and use them with an abandon and artistry rare in the theater today."[120]

Just as articles on broader aspects of African and Afro-diasporic culture are approached with an attitude of ethnographic respect, so too the presence of African objects in *Ebony*—often seen hanging on the walls in photographs—is treated more frequently as a sign of cultured knowledge and experience, rather than exotic strangeness. An interest in African art among educated African Americans can be traced back at least to the pre-war Harlem Renaissance, when philosopher Alain Locke included his essay "The Legacy of the Ancestral Arts," complete with multiple illustrations of African masks and sculptures, in his pathbreaking 1925 anthology *The New Negro*. When Locke argued that African American artists should "receive from African art a profound and galvanizing influence," he inspired a generation of artists and intellectuals to bring examples of African art into their homes.[121] Almost three decades later, an *Ebony* profile of Perry Fuller, an industrial designer (and son of Harlem Renaissance sculptor Meta Warrick Fuller), prioritizes his skills and research in his business making reproduction African masks for the gift retail market. The author explains where Fuller sources his masks: some are from his own private collection, but he also has gained access to "rare and priceless originals that cannot be purchased" through his connections to Locke himself, as well as "officials in the Liberian embassy in Washington." The lead photograph for the article shows Fuller seated before a wall of African masks, as he holds one in his hands; the masks are at varying heights on the wall, and his own head merges with the lowest one, establishing bonds of connection, ownership, and authority between Fuller and his "valuable collection of original masks" (fig. 149).[122] The article describes how "once he secures permission of the owner, Fuller spends long tedious hours making precision rubber molds to cast the pieces in his plant."[123] A photo essay then documents the skill and attention he and his employees devote to their work, concluding with the caption "Fuller's reproductions are so accurate in form and coloring that experts cannot tell [the] difference between originals and reproductions without close study."[124] Similarly, an article on the dancer Pearl Primus (who, at the time of writing, was working toward a PhD in anthropology at Columbia University) describes her extensive fieldwork in various regions of Africa—"She saw Africa not as a tourist but as an American Negro returning to the source of her culture. In the Gold Coast, Angola, the Cameroons, Liberia, Senegal and the Belgian Congo, Pearl went native effortlessly"—and concludes with Dennis Stock's photograph of her with her "collection of African mementoes" (fig. 150).[125] The photograph captures a room where she keeps these objects, but, as she crouches in the lower left corner of the image and looks at the camera with a matter-of-fact gaze, it becomes evident that the pieces are not arranged for public display: they are not configured for orderly visual consumption, but rather cascade down the wall and almost seem to wash over her. For Primus, they represent intellectual work and travel—and perhaps, ultimately, identity—and her engagement with them seems personal and intimate, as if this room might be shared only with friends. Her connection with these objects represents her approach to dance as articulated by the article's author: in comparison with Katherine Dunham, the renowned anthropologist and dancer, "Pearl Primus is easily the more authentic of the two. The reason is that the serious 30-year-old Trinidad-born girl makes fewer concessions to commercialism in her use of the original dances of African and West Indian natives. Where Dunham stresses highly exotic costumes and sexy movement, Miss Primus approaches her primitive material with near reverence."[126]

Another example of a collection of mementos—this time, masks from a trip to Mexico—appears in an *Ebony* article on the domestic life of "wealthy heiress" Sarah Washington Hayes (fig. 151). After narrating her decision to step down from her role as a corporate president to "devote [more time] to her family and home," and documenting her Modern house and housekeeping routines, the profile concludes with a view of Hayes "alone in [the] recreation room," sitting on a Modernist couch, next to a gridded cabinet and beneath a collection of "masks, rocks, and shells" that she acquired "on tour of Mexico."[127] The bold geometric forms, large eyes, and stylized headpieces of the masks arranged along the wall mark these objects as originating from outside of Western traditions of representation. As Hayes sits below them, her relationship is clearly proprietary: they are presented to the reader, along with the other scraps of the natural world, as evidence of her worldly travels. She is following Brandt's advice, it would seem, giving us "indications of her interest in travel."[128] Yet the power dynamics in the photograph have additional, complex layers. Hayes's eyes are cast down to her knitting, in contrast to the wide, staring eyes on the masks; the masks are disembodied, but so, apparently, is she (her legs seem to be curled up beneath the drapery of her knitting). Photographer Moneta Sleet, Jr., has framed her face against the light-colored wall and her light-colored blouse and knitting so that she herself becomes a mask.[129]

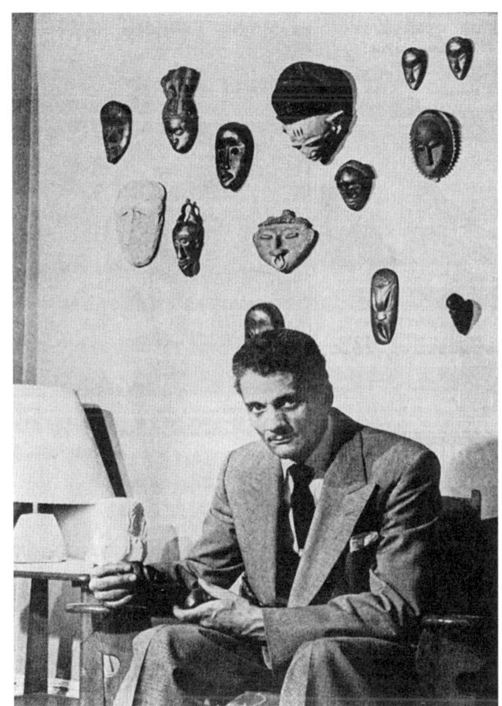

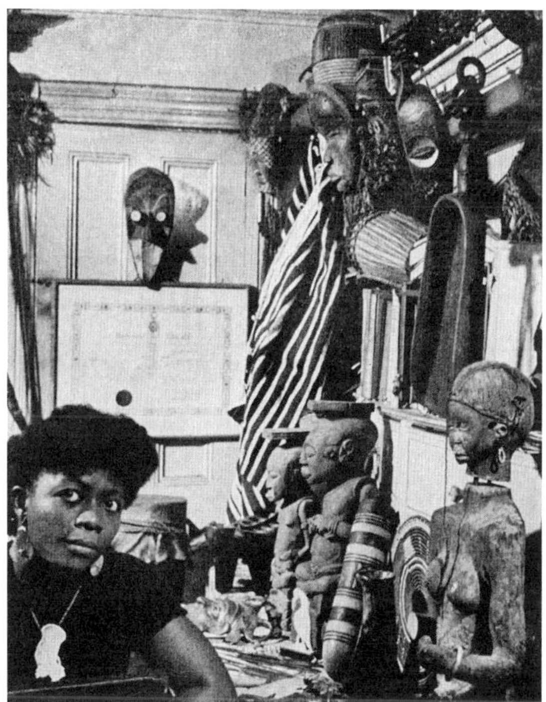

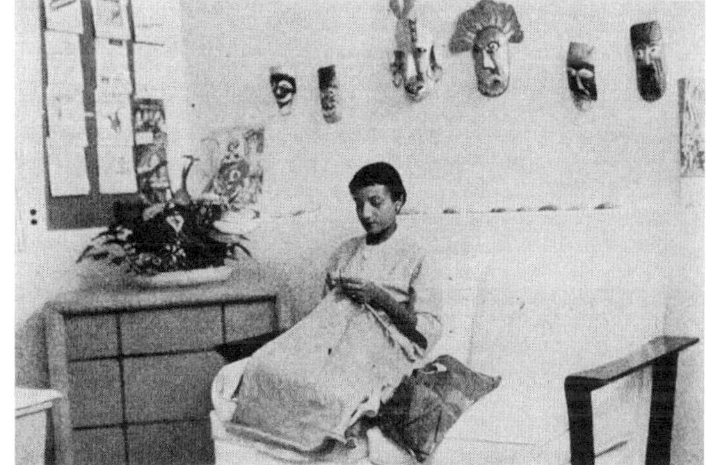

Fig. 149 (above). Perry J. Fuller
with collection of African masks,
New York, *Ebony*, December 1952,
71. Neufeld (Globe Photos),
photographer.

Fig. 150 (above right). Pearl Primus
with collection of African arts,
New York, *Ebony*, January 1951,
57. Dennis Stock, photographer.

Fig. 151 (right). Sarah Washington
Hayes with collection of masks
acquired in Mexico, Atlantic City,
New Jersey, *Ebony*, April 1957, 70.
Moneta Sleet, Jr., photographer.

Her engagement with these objects may be no more culturally sophisticated than that of the White protagonists in *Life*'s journalism, but Sleet's photograph proposes a closer kinship between the owner, sitting in her Modernist house, and her masks. That kinship echoes, however subtly, the greater respect that *Ebony* tends to show to non-Western artifacts as objects of history and collective culture.

Ebony's interest in demonstrating the cultural relevance of these objects is not uniform, however. There are, within the pages of the magazine, examples of masks used in decorating scenarios that seem more akin to the isolated exotica modeled in *Life*. On the living room wall behind Hilyard Robinson, star of the Lord Calvert Whiskey advertisement discussed in chapter 2 (see fig. 50), a large, apparently conservative seascape hangs to one side, while over his right shoulder one sees a carved profile of an African head with an exaggeratedly long neck, large painted lips, and an earring. In an article about a group of Black musicians who play bongo drums for predominantly White "swank Hollywood parties," the rhetoric veers toward the sensationalistic: "Billed as Ukonu's Afro-Californians, the drummers specialize in pulse-pounding music. Beating savagely on their drums, dancing wild native capers and shouting African jungle chants, the Afro-Californians drive listeners to wild, hysterical antics. At one recent party, a well-known movie siren worked herself into such a frenzy that she passed out."[130]

The contradictions evident within *Ebony*'s journalism—promoting African, diasporic, and other non-Western art forms with cultural respect, on the one hand, and as exotic and erotic stereotype on the other—reflect a larger tension in the magazine as a whole. Even as it relies, at times, on White models of middle-class living, it also attempts to forge an identity for its African American readership that is independent of the racist White majority culture of the country. One way it does this is through its culture-oriented approach to the art and artifacts of Africa and the diaspora, which differs from the art/not-art treatment of such objects in *Life*. As I have argued elsewhere in this book, for the White audiences of *Life* and various shelter magazines, and for the White consumers envisioned by Herman Miller, Modernism was a tool of cleanliness and control. It policed an imagined boundary between White and non-White in part by establishing the non-White as an exotic other, limited either as an isolated work of art or as a tourist curio. Alternatively, in the pages of *Ebony*, since the non-Western artifact is frequently seen as an object that is part of a larger cultural story, it is not usually reduced to an *objet* hanging on the wall or an artfully placed accessory on a side table. Because these indigenous items are not positioned as "others," but rather as part of a cultural or historical continuum, the Modernist furniture in *Ebony* does not need to stand in opposition to them and can instead occupy a different site of meaning. Put simply, when Modernism does not need to be White in *Ebony*'s interiors, it has the capacity to become something else: a style associated with Black bodily comfort and community, as I argued in chapter 2, or a style liberated from White Western history that leaves room for the deep embrace of an alternative cultural history. Through its different approach to African and diasporic art, *Ebony* suggests yet another way to approach a counter-discourse of Modernism in the mid-twentieth century.

Conclusion

The widely varying accessories discussed in this chapter—including functional cocktail glasses, semifunctional ceramic decorative pieces, and works of art to hang on the walls—were all freighted with the expectation of communicating personality in postwar decorating rhetoric. The very concept of personality was deeply wrapped up in social networks, and could be said to be defined by the judging gaze of peers and guests who drank out of glasses, tipped ashes into ashtrays, and scrutinized the order of works arranged on the walls of one's home. While I have endeavored to illuminate a presumptive, ex-nominated Whiteness that pervades many of these accessories, it is also worth considering that the very concept of "personality" is itself wrapped up in an ideological position of White privilege. Film theorist Richard Dyer argues that within the image-making industry of the West, "White people in their whiteness … are imaged as individual and/or endlessly diverse, complex and changing." From their vantage point of hegemonic power, White authors may blindly stereotype people of color as "others," but they reserve the ideological right to individuality for themselves: "White people in white culture," Dyer comments, "are given the illusion of their own infinite variety."[131] If the pursuit of personality can be understood as the pursuit of ultimate difference—distinctiveness, uniqueness—then it might be seen as a White preoccupation of the White authors like Wright, Gillies, Halsey, or Brandt who recommended that a careful selection of accessories conveys "personality." In the separate arena of *Ebony*, however, accessories are still clearly important. While many photographs in *Ebony* are too cropped to include decorative accessories (as discussed in chapter 2), some images, such as figs. 149, 150, and 151, present the accessories in intriguing dialogues with the owner. They reveal a discourse of individuality and cultural specificity that White audiences have been loath to grant to communities of color, and demonstrate that the rhetoric that equated accessories and personality translated across racial communities in mid-century America.

Epilogue
The Ubiquity of Mid-Century Modernism

The furnishing style known as "mid-century Modern" has become ubiqui-
tous in certain sectors of our twenty-first-century American landscape. It
is not only that most elementary, middle, and high schools have seats of
molded plywood—if they are very old—or molded plastic that breed a
familiarity with Eames designs so deep that children know the chairs as they
know their own bodies. Specific pockets of popular culture in the United
States have also, for the last quarter century, been inundated with increasingly entrenched visions of mid-century Modern. This recent popularity has
bred the perhaps unfounded sense that the history of these objects is just
as well known as their forms and contours. The goal of this book has been
to deepen and expand our historical knowledge about how these objects
were first marketed to consumers. My intention is to bring to light a broader
visual culture that will refocus our understanding of mid-century Modernism
and, possibly, make it look different from what we thought we knew.

The mid-century Modern revival began in the 1990s with a constel-
lation of academic books and museum exhibitions that rigorously evaluated and reinterpreted the work of the postwar generation of designers.
Pat Kirkham's *Charles and Ray Eames: Designers of the Twentieth Century*
(1995) recast the designers' work as a creative copartnership, and Stanley
Abercrombie's *George Nelson: The Design of Modern Design* (1995)
established the broad parameters of Nelson's career. Several major exhibitions put these designers' works in front of the public (not just on scholars' desks), including the Vitra Design Museum's international traveling
exhibition *The Work of Charles and Ray Eames: A Legacy of Invention* (at
multiple venues from 1999 to 2002) and the Brooklyn Museum of Art's *Vital
Forms: American Art and Design in the Atomic Age, 1940–1960* (2001).
More major traveling exhibitions on Eero Saarinen and George Nelson followed in the first decade of the twenty-first century.

Yet mid-century Modern was not merely a point of fascination for academics and curators—it was simultaneously finding audiences through commercial venues as well. After several decades focusing its product line entirely on office furniture, Herman Miller reintroduced selected home furnishings in 1994 under the line Herman Miller for the Home.[1] In 1998, Rob Forbes founded Design Within Reach (DWR; for many of us, the prices seemed hardly within reach) as a retail vendor for products manufactured by Herman Miller, Knoll, and Carl Hansen.[2] At the time, consumer access to these companies was frustratingly obscure, and one often needed a direct contact to the trade (architecture or interior design) in order to purchase products. DWR made them more broadly available, if not affordable. In the early 2000s, the visibility of mid-century Modern in popular media outlets continued to grow. A collectors' magazine, *Atomic Ranch*, began publication in 2004, and the phenomenal growth of early online auction sites such as eBay was driven by a proliferation of "Eames era" and "mid-century modern" designs.[3] If these data points reflect a subculture of collectors with dedicated interest in designs from the 1940s, 1950s, and early 1960s, then the critical success of AMC's television show *Mad Men* marks another level of growth in the audience for mid-century Modern. *Mad Men*'s first season was 2007, and it ran through 2015, charting fashion and interior-decorating trends from 1960 to 1970. The popularity of the show and its attention to aesthetic details inspired a wide range of commentary, from journalistic discussions of its approach to design to multiple scholarly treatments.[4] Contemporaneous with the *Mad Men* phenomenon, in 2012, Herman Miller relaunched its home line with a deeper excavation into its original mid-century designs, renamed the Herman Miller Collection. And, in 2014, Herman Miller acquired Design Within Reach, completing the circle of commercial access to its products.[5]

In addition to these consumer products with relatively narrow audiences, the past twenty years has witnessed the leaching-in of mid-century Modernism to varied commercial realms. Mid-century Modern architecture is regularly visible as a backdrop for contemporary fashion shoots.[6] Multiple national furniture retailers now offer a significant portion of their products designed along basic Modernist precepts such as geometric contours, lack of ornament, grid-based compositions, a distinctive accent chair to stand out in a room, and plywood, plastic, and metals as some element in an object.[7] Indeed, some readers will point to the influence of IKEA on American furniture design, which is undoubtedly accurate; when IKEA made its earliest inroads into the US market in the late 1990s, its product line was heavily indebted to the aesthetic sensibility of Scandinavian Modernism, which historically played a large part in the mid-century Modern domestic spaces of the United States.

So pervasive has some version of mid-century Modernism become in the retail and popular culture of affluent, educated consumers—which today, as in the 1950s, is still disproportionately White—that it risks being the Colonial Revival for today's generation of homeowners. The Colonial Revival was the most popular home-decorating style in the first decades of the twentieth century for White consumers, fueled by a newly established sense of pride in the history of the United States after the 1876 Centennial Exposition in Philadelphia (and receiving a reenergizing jolt with Sesquicentennial celebrations in 1926).[8] In addition to national pride, Colonial Revival furniture was often wrapped up in nostalgic myths about the piety and honesty of the generation of "founding fathers." For consumers confronting the disruptions of wars, economic depression, and controversies over immigration levels—and for those consumers who, as recent immigrants, were trying to assimilate to the dominant White, Anglo-Saxon Protestant culture—these fables about Colonial Revival furniture provided symbolic resonance to a peaceful past, free of strife, corruption, and difference. Finally, Colonial Revival furniture was frequently marketed as spare, simple, and honest, in contrast to the overbearing, cluttered, dark interiors of the Victorian era. The racialized Whiteness of the Colonial Revival style was never explicitly stated, but the history it referenced was one of White protagonists, with a default power structure of Whites above other races. Many of the qualities that made the Colonial Revival appealing to earlier generations apply to today's purchasers of mid-century Modern: the style refers to a past wrapped up in nostalgia for the "greatest generation," and it seems simpler—"cleaner"—than the gaudy excesses of interiors of the 1970s and 1980s.

The power of the mid-century Modernist aesthetic to whitewash history is explored in the work of contemporary multimedia artist Ilana Harris-Babou, and her work makes a fitting conclusion to the history traced in this book. In her sculptures, installations, and videos, Harris-Babou immerses herself in the arenas where we seek domestic advice and recipes for self-improvement. In her 2017 *Reparations Hardware* video, she re-creates the genre of promotional video that might advertise the products of a furniture company (fig. 152). As she quotes the language of contemporary home furnishings—touting products that are "tasteful and refined"—she satirizes the fashion for reclaimed materials. "There's nothing like old wood," her on-screen character intones, simultaneously mimicking advertising copy and illuminating the invisible, enslaved labor that originally worked the wood now being reclaimed. As she attempts to pound the "old wood" with a misshapen ceramic object in the form of a hammer—bearing the irregular impressions of her own fingertips and palms as she modeled the clay—the fiction of virtuous, resolute labor is turned inside out. Rather than erasing history's scars and transforming the materials into pleasurable commodities with only a decorative accent of the past, her "labor" results in a nonfunctional object that cannot serve anyone, and in which history is everywhere evident (fig. 153). The wood is splintered, weathered, and peeling, the nails irregularly driven in, the hammers themselves riddled with the marks of the hands that made them.

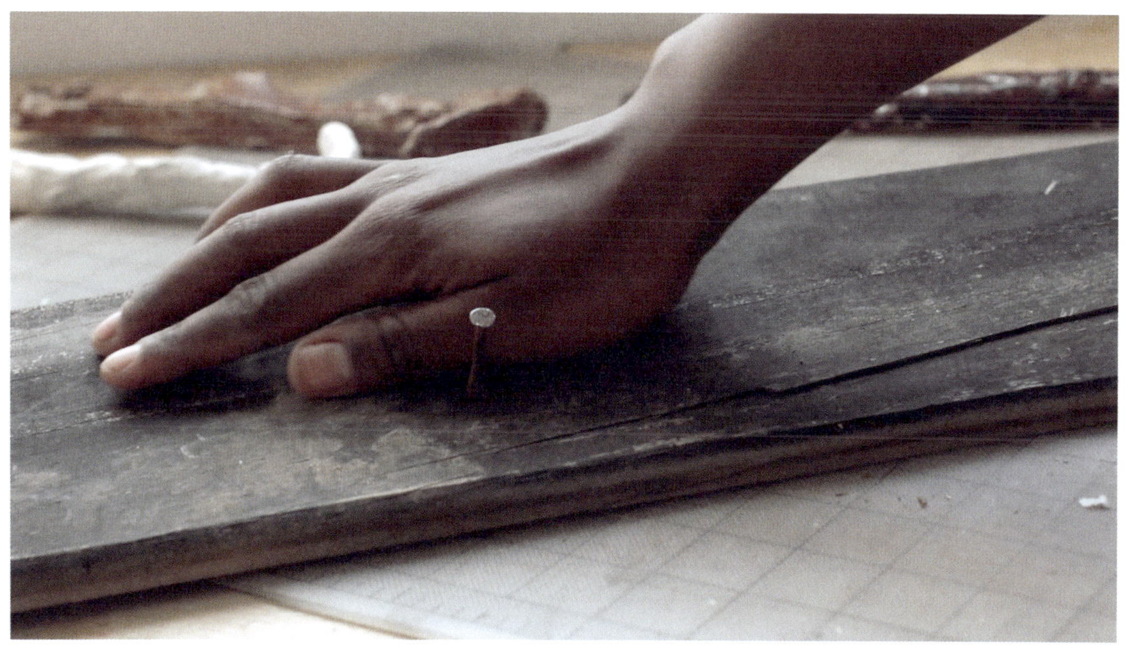

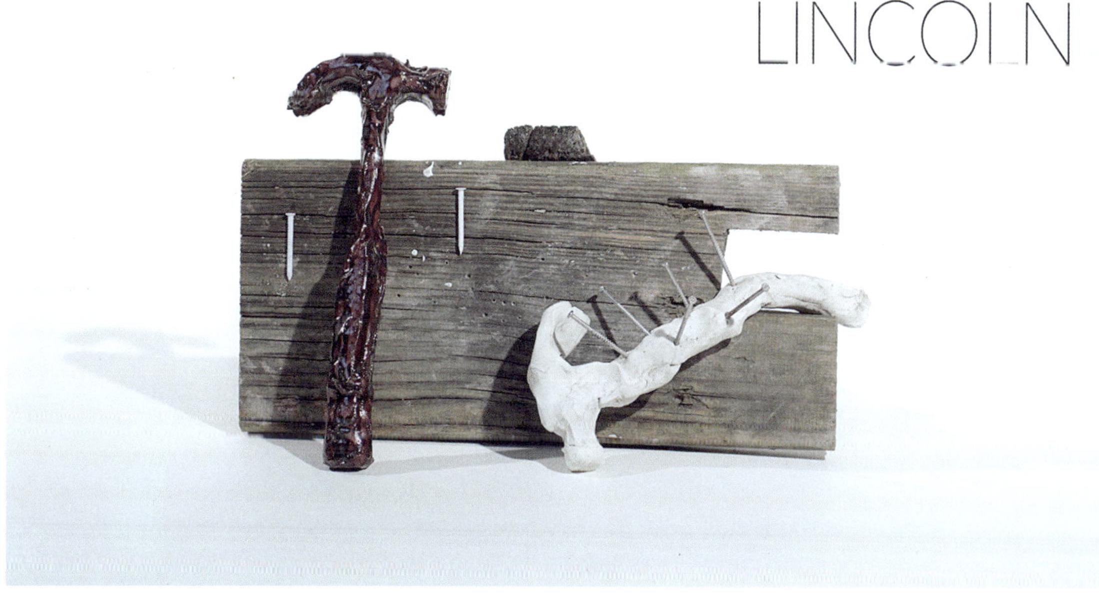

Fig. 152 (top). Ilana Harris-Babou,
still from *Reparations Hardware*
(HD video, 4:05 min., 2017). Courtesy
Ilana Harris-Babou.

Fig. 153 (above). Ilana Harris-Babou,
"Lincoln," still from *Reparations
Hardware* (HD video, 4:05 min.,
2017). Courtesy Ilana Harris-Babou.

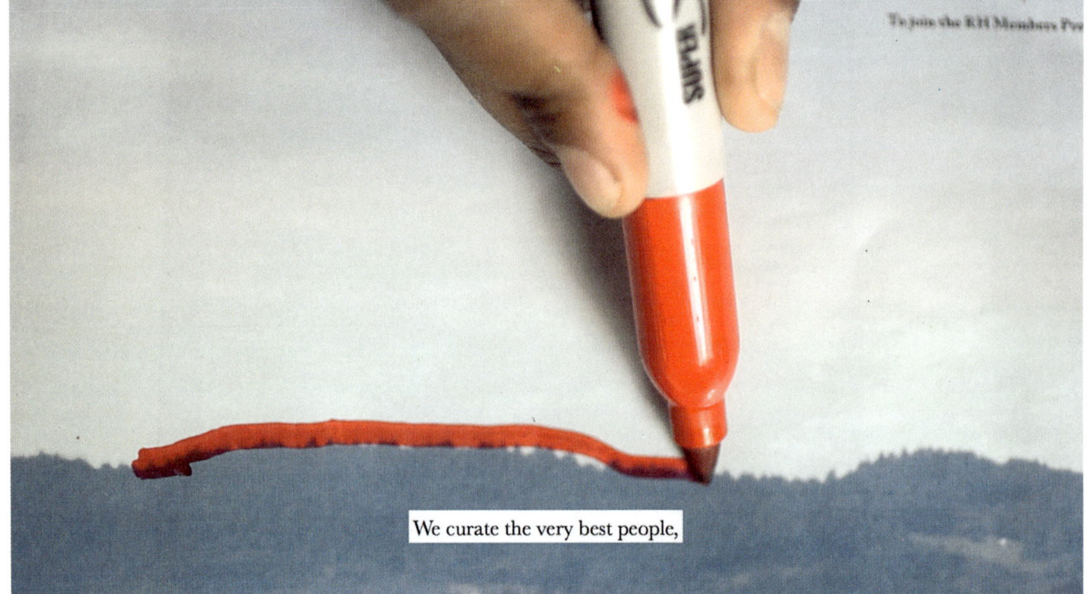

As Harris-Babou draws our attention in *Reparations Hardware* to the White privilege that allows furniture companies to rewrite history, she illuminates its contemporary presence in a 2018 video, *Red Sourcebook* (fig. 154). Turning the pages of a catalogue from Restoration Hardware—its well-known annual tome, grandly titled *Sourcebook*—she draws red lines across the pages and collages sentences from the catalogue across the screen. The White racial superiority of the language ("we curate the very best people … we hope that we, too, will ratchet up our species") is thrown into stark relief when visually paired with actual red lines, drawn as randomly across the page depicting expensive Modernist pool furniture as FHA assessors once randomly divided up neighborhoods and developments. The scars of those original red lines persist on our landscapes today, and as Harris-Babou draws across the photographed Eden of a furniture catalogue, she suggests that racial scars pervade the landscape of commercial desire as well.

Fig. 154. Ilana Harris-Babou, still from *Red Sourcebook* (HD video, 4:12 min., 2018). Courtesy Ilana Harris-Babou.

The history of mid-century Modernism that has become so popular over the past quarter century has been shaped by the powers that Harris-Babou points to: the largely White, male international commercial manufacturer, and the largely White academic establishment prior to that. What I have attempted to demonstrate, in this book, is that the cultural context of the late 1940s and 1950s—the cultural world into which these now-called mid-century Modern design objects were launched—was more complex than our latter-day histories admit. Mid-century Modernism was, at its time, invested with racialized codings for audiences who thought of themselves as White — and when audiences of the late twentieth and twenty-first centuries who also think of themselves as White look at these designs, they have largely seen them in those contexts, without noting the ex-nominated Whiteness. Tellingly, when the African American rap artist and music impresario Tyler the Creator visits Herman Miller in a 2019 video, he learns about the design innovations of Charles and Ray Eames, and then connects them to the civil rights activism of Rosa Parks: sitting in an Eames Lounge Chair, he muses, "Those guys were really innovative back in the 1940s and 1950s. I mean, who *was* innovative then and everyone was on board with it at first? Rosa Parks was innovative. I just sat in a $4000 chair and no one told me to get up. You think if Rosa Parks wasn't innovative that would be possible right now?"[9]

Just as Tyler the Creator's view of Eames innovation alters its standard (White) frames of reference, so too does Modernism of the mid-twentieth century begin to change when we interrogate its symbolic resonance for period audiences of upper- and middle-class African Americans. In the work of a Modernist designer such as Add Bates, in the work of an architect like Paul R. Williams, and in the many photographs and advertisements in *Ebony* magazine, another history of Modernist design begins to be uncovered; it is one that prioritizes bodily comfort, sociability, and community, and that allows for the deep embrace of non-White, non-Western histories. This counter-history of Modernism, as I have been calling it, is not categorically distinct from the history that permeates a White-centric Modernism. Rather, its difference lies in its emphasis, priorities, and values. Ultimately, White Americans were not the only ones making Modern design, looking at it, or consuming it in the postwar period. For other audiences — and there are more still to examine — Modernism resonated with subtly, but importantly, different meanings. My hope is that over the course of this book, mid-century Modernism has become defamiliarized for twenty-first century readers, as the objects and audiences we thought we knew begin to look different and we start to recognize that there are multiple counter-histories of Modernism throughout the twentieth century.

Notes

Introduction

1. The painting is titled *Easter Morning* in the official Rockwell catalogue but is sometimes reproduced as *Sunday Morning*. The date it appeared—May 16, 1959—was closest to the celebration of Pentecost in the spring of 1959, which is observed on the seventh Sunday after Easter. In 1959, Easter in the Roman/Western church was celebrated on March 29; Pentecost was May 17.

2. For a complex analysis of the Womb Chair, see Cammie McAtee, "Taking Comfort in the Age of Anxiety: Eero Saarinen's Womb Chair," in *Atomic Dwelling*, ed. Schuldenfrei, 3–25. See also Lutz, *Eero Saarinen*.

3. This was reportedly the view from Rockwell's own studio in western Massachusetts, underscoring the idea of the power of the gaze from the plate-glass window. Christopher Finch, *Norman Rockwell's America* (New York: Harry N. Abrams, 1975), 97. Rockwell has been the subject of much recent critical investigation. See Halpern, *Norman Rockwell*; Maureen Hart Hennessey and Anne Knutson, eds., *Norman Rockwell: Pictures for the American People* (Atlanta, GA: High Museum of Art, 1999); and Virginia M. Mecklenburg, *Norman Rockwell: From the Collections of George Lucas and Steven Spielberg* (Washington, DC: Smithsonian American Art Museum, 2010).

4. "The Cover," *Saturday Evening Post*, May 16, 1959, 3.

5. Nell Irvin Painter traces several "enlargements" of Whiteness in the history of the United States, including in the postwar period. See *The History of White People*, esp. chapters 14 and 26.

6. Blumer, "Race Prejudice as a Sense of Group Position," 3.

7. Black Hawk Hancock, "Learning How to Fiske: Theorizing Cultural Literacy, Counter-History, and the Politics of Media Events in the 21st Century," in Fiske, *Media Matters*, xx–xxv. The critical practice of storytelling and "counter-storytelling" is a central tenet of critical race theory. See, for example, Delgado and Stefancic, eds. *Critical Race Theory*, chapters 8–13; and Gloria Ladson-Billings, "Just What Is Critical Race Theory and What's It Doing in a Nice Field Like Education?" *International Journal of Qualitative Studies in Education* 11, no. 1 (1998): 8, 11.

8. Gwendolyn Wright, *USA: Modern Architectures in History* (New York: Reaktion, 2008), 167.

9. These price brackets are constructed based on the information provided in several primary documents. See Packard, *Status Seekers*, chapter 6; Whyte, *Organization Man*, chapter 24; Keats, *Crack in the Picture Window*; and "$15,000 Trade Secrets House," *Life*, January 5, 1953, 8–15. Barbara Miller Lane cites lower prices at the start of the decade for working-class homes, a $7,500–8,500 range. See Lane, *Houses for a New World*, 16.

10. Dobriner, *Class in Suburbia*; Harris, ed., *Second Suburb*; Baxandall and Ewen, *Picture Windows*; Lane, *Houses for a New World*.

11. Lane, *Houses for a New World*, 25.

12. Isenstadt, *The Modern American House*, chapter 8.

13. Lane, *Houses for a New World*, chapter 1.

14. Rothstein, *The Color of Law*. See also Jackson, *Crabgrass Frontier*.

15. Harris, *Little White Houses*, 30.

16. Pattillo-McCoy, *Black Picket Fences*; Andrew Wiese, " 'The House I Live In': Race, Class, and African-American Suburban Dreams in the Postwar United States," in *The New Suburban History*, ed. Kruse and Sugrue, 99–119.

17. Lipsitz, *How Racism Takes Place*, 54.

18. Berger, *Working-Class Suburb*, 98. Emphasis original.

19. See, for example: Walter Goldschmidt, "Social Class in America: A Critical Review," *American Anthropologist* 52, no. 4 (October–December 1950): 483–98; James A. Davis, "Cultural Factors in the Perception of Status Symbols," *Midwest Sociologist* 21, no. 1 (December 1958): 1–11; Dobriner, *Class in Suburbia*; Packard, *Status Seekers*; Berger, *Working-Class Suburb*; and Gideon Sjoberg, "Are Social Classes in America Becoming More Rigid?" *American Sociological Review* 16, no. 6 (December 1951): 775–83.

20. Painter, *The History of White People*, 371–72.

21. Goldschmidt, "Social Class in America," 493.

22. Keats, *Crack in the Picture Window*, 42.

23. Harry Henderson, "The Mass-Produced Suburbs, Part I," 28.

24. Whyte, *Organization Man*, 356.

25. Friedan, *Feminine Mystique*, chapter 1.

26. Lane, *Houses for a New World*, 195–96.

27. Meyerowitz, "Beyond the Feminine Mystique."

28. Harry Henderson notes the exclusion of "negroes" and "the poor" from suburban communities specifically: "The Mass-Produced Suburbs, Part I," 27.

29. Henderson, "Rugged American Collectivism: The Mass-Produced Suburbs, Part II," 85.

30. Packard, *Status Seekers*, chapter 5, discusses taste; he discusses housing segregation in chapter 6.

31. Warner et al., *Social Class in America*, 20.

32. Blumer, "Race Prejudice as a Sense of Group Position," 4.

33. Ibid.

34. Ibid., 3.

35. Platt suggests that most of Frazier's critiques of the Black bourgeoisie were developed in the late 1920s and had not changed significantly by the time he published the 1957 book. This gives the book, in Platt's opinion, its overly dogmatic and inflexible tone. Anthony M. Platt, "Between Scorn and Longing: Frazier's Black Bourgeoisie," *Social Justice* 20 (Spring–Summer 1993): 131–32.

36. Frazier, *Black Bourgeoisie*, 208, 230.

37. Green, *Selling the Race*, chapter 4. Brenna Wynn Greer examines the presentation of women in *Ebony*, arguing for the complexity of Black womanhood—both empowered and subjugated—in the pages of the magazine, in *Represented*, chapter 4.

38. Bernard Wolfe, "Ecstatic in Blackface." Originally published in *Commentary*, 1949.

39. Ibid., 56.

40. Castle, "I'll Take My Modern in Moderation," 9, 325.

41. Penick, *Tastemaker*, esp. chapter 7.

42. Many furniture companies advertised products in a variety of styles within a single ad in the 1950s. See, e.g., advertisement for Mongel Furniture, *Life*, April 23, 1951, 52–53; advertisement for Kent-Coffee Furniture, *Better Homes and Gardens*, April 1955, 149. Also, companies such as Kroehler Furniture advertised different-styled pieces in different months in the same magazine; compare advertisements in *Life*, April 6, 1959, 14, and October 5, 1959, 116.

43. The text that best explains the state of the field of CRAH is Holloway, "Critical Race Art History." Cheng et al., *Race and Modern Architecture*, was published as this book went to press, and is another valuable resource.

44. Frankenberg, *Social Construction of Whiteness*, 6; Roediger, *Working toward Whiteness*; Dyer, *White*; Berger, *Sight Unseen*.

45. Barthes, *Mythologies*, 138. I am grateful to Hugh Manon for conversations about Barthes's text.

46. Ibid. Emphasis original.

47. Ibid., 139.

48. Dyer, *White*, xiv.

49. Seshadri-Crooks, *Desiring Whiteness*, 3–4.

50. Harris, *Little White Houses*, 19. Emphasis added.

51. Ibid., 98, 103.

52. Sullivan, *Revealing Whiteness*.

53. Alcoff, *The Future of Whiteness*, esp. 127–28 and chapter 3. Frankenberg discusses how White women view Whiteness: a sense of blandness, and an identity pervaded by corporate brands. See *Social Construction of Whiteness*, chapter 7.

54. Harris, *Little White Houses*, 13, 3.

55. In his classic history of the Jim Crow system, C. Van Woodward points to the *Brown* decision as the legal beginning of the end of segregation. However, he also points out that residential segregation grew over the course of the 1950s, and that backlash against *Brown* led to increased racially motivated violence, especially in the South. Woodward, *The Strange Career of Jim Crow*, esp. chapters 4 and 5.

56. Stuart Hall, "What Is This 'Black' in Black Popular Culture?" in *Stuart Hall: Critical Dialogues in Cultural Studies*, ed. Morley and Chen, 474. The essay originally appeared in *Black Popular Culture*, ed. Gina Dent (Seattle, WA: Bay Press, 1992).

57. Hancock, "Learning How to Fiske," xxiii. He is referring, especially, to Fiske's article "Black Bodies of Knowledge: Notes on an Effective History." *Cultural Critique* 33 (1996): 185–212.

58. Derrick A. Bell, "Who's Afraid of Critical Race Theory?" *University of Illinois Law Review* 1995 (1995): 907; Tara J. Yosso, "Whose Culture Has Capital? A Critical Race Theory Discussion of Community Cultural Wealth," *Race, Ethnicity, and Education* 8, no. 1 (2005): 74.

59. Hancock, "Learning How to Fiske," xxiv.

60. See, for example, Kirkham, ed., *Women Designers*; Judy Attfield, "Form/female Follows Function/male: Feminist Critiques of Design," in *Design History Reader*, ed. Grace Lees-Maffei and Rebecca Houze (New York: Berg, 2010), 349–54; and Kristina Wilson, "Brooks Stevens, the Man in Your Life: Shaping the Domestic Sphere, 1934–1950," in *Industrial Strength Design: How Brooks Stevens Shaped Your World*, ed. Glenn Adamson (Milwaukee, WI: Milwaukee Art Museum; Cambridge, MA: MIT Press, 2003), 9–22.

61. A canonical text is Kimberlé Crenshaw, "Mapping the Margins: Intersectionality, Identity Politics, and Violence against Women of Color," *Stanford Law Review* 43, no. 6 (July 1991): 1241–99. See also Crenshaw et al., eds., *Critical Race Theory*, section 6.

Chapter 1
The Body in Control

1. Mary and Russel Wright, *Guide to Easier Living* (hereafter Wright and Wright, *GTEL*), 26.

2. Williams, *New Homes for Today* (hereafter Williams, 1946), 94.

3. Brandt, *Decorate Your Home for Better Living* (hereafter Brandt, *DYH*), 9.

4. For a discussion of the *Guide to Easier Living* in the context of nationalism in the 1930s and 1940s, as well as the Wrights' nationalistic appeal through their various product lines, see Lucinda Kaukas Havenhand, "Russel and Mary Wright's *Guide to Easier Living* and the 'New American Way of Life,'" *Interiors* 5, no. 2 (2014): 199–218. I discuss the invocation of the American historical past in Wright's 1930s American Modern furniture design in *Livable Modernism*, chapter 1.

5. Wright and Wright, *GTEL*, 2.

6. Williams, 1946, 94.

7. Barthes, *Mythologies*, 138.

8. Two recent studies of the genre of domestic advice are Lees-Maffei,

Design at Home, and Leavitt, *From Catharine Beecher to Martha Stewart*.

9. Lees-Maffei's study documents the wide-ranging context of domestic advice literature in the second half of the twentieth century, and her narrative weaves together periodicals and books. She draws attention to the articulation of middle-class identity as well as some of the gender expectations I examine here. See Lees-Maffei, *Design at Home*, esp. chapters 3, 4.

10. Havenhand states that the Wrights were the first married couple to publicly coauthor a domestic advice manual. See Havenhand, "Russel and Mary Wright's *Guide to Easier Living*," 201.

11. Black Hawk Hancock, "Learning How to Fiske: Theorizing Cultural Literacy, Counter-History, and the Politics of Media Events in the 21st Century," in Fiske, *Media Matters*, xx–xxv. Richard Delgado, the influential critical race theorist, argues that "stories, parables, chronicles, and narratives are powerful means for destroying mind-set—the bundle of presuppositions, received wisdoms, and shared understandings against a background of which legal and political discourse takes place." Delgado, "Storytelling for Oppositionists and Others," in *Critical Race Theory*, ed. Delgado and Stefancic, 71.

12. The tally of two thousand comes from the biographical note in Williams, *The Small Home of Tomorrow* (hereafter Williams, 1945), 6. A selected list of projects can be found in Hudson, *Paul R. Williams, Architect*.

13. The most important of these publications, arguably, was Williams's autobiographical essay, discussed further below: "I Am a Negro," *American Magazine*, July 1937, 59, 161–63. He was also referred to as "perhaps the most successful Negro artist in the U.S." in "Negroes: The US Also Has a Minority Problem," *Life*, October 3, 1938, 54. He was profiled in *Ebony*: "Designer for Living," *Ebony*, February 1946, 25–29; and in *Time*: "Something Clients Want," *Time*, January 26, 1948, 86ff.

14. This assessment is based on titles published by Murray & Gee found in WorldCat (total 275 entries, between 1932 and 1958) and the limited information available on Open Library: "Murray & Gee, Publisher," https://

openlibrary.org/publishers/Murray_& _Gee, accessed January 8, 2019.

15. For reviews of Williams's books, see "Required Reading: The Small House of Tomorrow," *Architectural Record*, July 1945, 114; "Required Reading: Houses to Build," *Architectural Record*, June 1946, 26. A 1949 article in *Ebony* referred to the popularity of his publications and quotes them extensively: Ray Duncan, "Paul Williams Tells How to Build a Home for $5,000," *Ebony*, March 1949, 42–48.

16. Williams, 1946, 4.

17. Note about publication date: the official record of the book's first publication is 1950. However, all of the publicity occurred in 1951, beginning January and February. So it is likely that the first printing happened in late 1950. See Folder: Speeches: Radio & TV shows—1950 on, Box 38, Russel Wright Papers, Department of Special Collections, Syracuse University Library, Syracuse, New York (hereafter Wright Papers).

18. For a discussion of Nelson's print career, see Stanley Abercrombie, "Nelson in Print," in *George Nelson*, ed. Eisenbrand, 18–39. Some of Nelson's writings have been collected and reprinted. See Kurt W. Forster, ed., *Building a New Europe: Portraits of Modern Architects: Essays by George Nelson, 1935–1936* (New Haven, CT: Yale University Press in association with Yale School of Architecture, 2007). For a recent assessment of Nelson's intellectual development, including his interest in Japanese design principles and humanistic mentors, see Havenhand, *Mid-Century Modern Interiors*, chapter 4.

19. Mary Largent Brandt, "Stepping Stones: To a Career in Merchandising," *The Key of Kappa Kappa Gamma*, February 1953, 34, in Mary L. Brandt Home Furnishings Training Course Materials, circa 1946, 1953. New School for Social Research Archives Collection, New York, New York (hereafter Brandt Papers).

20. She concludes her *Kappa Kappa Gamma* article by reflecting that "there was a time when men held most of the merchandising positions, but today women are replacing men." Ibid., 35. For more about the scope and stature of her career, see "Mary Brandt, 62, Decorator, Dead," *New York Times*, February 23, 1962, 29.

21. The visual aids for her lectures, as well as a spiral-bound draft of her lecture content, form the bulk of the material in the Brandt Papers.

22. Nelson and Wright, *Tomorrow's House* (hereafter Nelson and Wright, *TH*), 1.

23. Ibid., 7. Emphasis original.

24. Ibid., 9.

25. There are multiple art historical lines of analysis that connect height, vision, and power. Dianne Harris analyzes axonometric views and aerial perspective drawings and associates them with White racial power in *Little White Houses*, 89–93. Jason Weems argues for the power of aerial vision to shape identity and self-knowledge in *Barnstorming the Prairies: How Aerial Vision Shaped the Midwest* (Minneapolis: University of Minnesota Press, 2015). A canonical text on height, vision, and power is Alan Wallach, "Wadsworth's Tower: An Episode in the History of American Landscape Vision," *American Art* 10, no. 3 (Autumn 1996): 8–27.

26. Williams, 1945, 7.

27. Ibid., 8.

28. Williams does talk about remodeling and even highlights that on the cover of the 1946 book. But his advice for remodeling is so extensive and impractical (changing rooflines, changing walls and windows) that it seems mostly to be a poorly conceived rewrite of his design-from-scratch ideas. See, for example, Williams, 1946, 7–8.

29. Frank Jamison was Williams's office delineator through the 1930s and 1940s; see Henderson, "Two Case Studies," 532.

30. My thoughts on the ways that diagrams work is indebted to John Bender and Michael Marrinan, *The Culture of Diagram* (Stanford, CA: Stanford University Press, 2010).

31. Williams, 1946, 92.

32. Duncan, "Paul Williams Tells How to Build a Home," 48.

33. The c. 1946 quote is from "Mary L. Brandt Home Furnishings Training Course: Handbook of Home Furnishings," spiral-bound typed ms., chpt. 5, Brandt Papers. The 1950 quote is the title of chapter 6 in Brandt, *DYH*.

34. My assessment of the tone of her book comes from comparing the published text against the spiral-bound typed manuscript, found in her papers at the New School for Social Research, that is titled "Mary L. Brandt Home Furnishings Training Course."

35. Brandt, *DYH*, 91.

36. Marylin Hafner's papers are stored at the University of Connecticut. She was a student at Pratt in 1946, which is probably how she met Brandt and secured the commission to illustrate her training course materials; she was also art director at *McCall's* from 1950 to 1954, suggesting another important connection to magazine publishing.

37. Wright and Wright, *GTEL*, 136.

38. Ibid., 4.

39. In the archives, there is evidence that the Wrights considered a variety of candidates for the job of illustrator, wanting to find someone whose style would complement their message and not be overly individualistic. Interestingly, Kingsland's name does not appear in any of the saved notes, and it is unclear how they found him. See Folder: Mss—Book—Easier Living illustrators, Box 37, Wright Papers.

40. Wright and Wright, *GTEL*, 64.

41. Film scholar Hugh Manon has discussed the prevalence of the bird's-eye view of interior spaces in noir films of the 1940s and 1950s, and associates this surveillance with the threat of criminal activity. See Hugh Manon, "X-Ray Visions: Radiography, *Chiaroscuro*, and the Fantasy of Unsuspicion in *Film Noir*," *Film Criticism* 32, no. 2 (Winter 2007): 1–26.

42. Architecture and design critic Alexandra Lange gave a thought-provoking paper on how the Wrights marketed their heteronormativity in *GTEL* as part of the "Marketing the Future" panel at the *Visions of the Future* Flair Symposium, Harry Ransom Center, University of Texas, Austin, November 2012.

43. Nelson and Wright, *TH*, 204.

44. Williams, 1945, 8.

45. Wright and Wright, *GTEL*, 5.

46. Brandt, *DYH*, 106.

47. See, for example, the sample boys' and girls' bedrooms in Wright and Wright, *GTEL*, 80–81.

48. Nelson and Wright, *TH*, 12, 11.

49. Brandt, *DYH*, 43.

50. Ibid., 44.

51. Ibid., 45.

52. Ibid., 5–6.

53. Ibid., 13–14.

54. Wright and Wright, *GTEL*, 136.

55. Ibid., 40. Emphasis original.

56. Ibid., 158.

57. Williams, 1945, 8.

58. Ibid., 74.

59. Ibid., 90. Although both General Electric and Amana briefly promoted horizontal wall refrigerators in the 1950s, there is no evidence that the horizontal drawer model that Williams depicts was ever fabricated by an American company, lending this image a quality of future fantasy. For advertisements, see Brian Alexander, *Atomic Kitchen: Gadgets and Inventions for Yesterday's Cook* (Portland, OR: Collector's Press, 2004), 19, 72.

60. Nelson and Wright, *TH*, iii.

61. Ibid., 30.

62. Ibid., 148.

63. Ibid., 71.

64. Ibid., 75.

65. Ibid., 19.

66. Ibid., 43.

67. Ibid., 110.

68. Ibid., 147.

69. Ibid., 106.

70. *Oxford English Dictionary*, "slot, n.2." OED Online, December 2018 (Oxford University Press), accessed January 9, 2019.

71. Brandt, *DYH*, 49.

72. Ibid., 50.

73. Ibid., 47.

74. Wright and Wright, *GTEL*, 50.

75. Ibid., 82–83.

76. Unusually, the Wrights cited two sources for their guidelines for the most efficient way to make a bed. They have simplified the fifty-three steps listed in the Purdue University Bulletin (p. 22) down to thirty, but their singular pronouncement of the most efficient system contravenes the more open-ended assessment of competing bed-making methods that Marianne Muse evaluates in the University of Vermont Bulletin: "There is probably no 'one best way' of making beds under all conditions and by all types of workers." Marianne Muse, *Saving Time and Steps in Bedmaking*, Agricultural Experiment Station, Bulletin 551 (Burlington: University of Vermont and State Agricultural College, March 1949): 3. See also *Easier Homemaking*, Engineering Experiment Station in Cooperation with the Agricultural Experiment Station, Bulletin 529 (Lafayette, IN: Purdue University, 1948).

77. Wright and Wright, *GTEL*, 145.

Lees-Maffei discusses other examples of the overlapping associations between a housewife's clothing and the decorating of the house in "Dressing the Part(y): 1950s Domestic Advice Books and the Studied Performance of Informal Domesticity in the UK and the US," in *Performance, Fashion and the Modern Interior: From the Victorians to Today*, ed. Fiona Fisher et al. (London: Berg, 2011), esp. 189–93.

78. Williams, 1946, 6.

79. Williams, 1945, 7.

80. Sullivan, *Revealing Whiteness*, 73.

81. Harris explores this issue in commercial media surrounding the suburban home. See *Little White Houses*, esp. chapters 2 and 3.

82. See, e.g., Bhabha, *The Location of Culture*, chapter 3; and Said, *Orientalism*. For a critical interrogation of the intertwined nature of gender and race, see Anne McClintock, *Imperial Leather: Race, Gender and Sexuality in the Colonial Contest* (New York: Routledge, 1995).

83. Brandt, *DYH*, 102.

84. Ibid., 100.

85. Sullivan, *Revealing Whiteness*, 73.

86. Wright and Wright, *GTEL*, 50, 67. Ellipses original.

87. Wright and Wright, "Life without Dorcas," carbon copy typed manuscript, c. 1946, p1, Folder: Mss-Manuals-Life Without Dorcas-complete, Box 37, Wright Papers. The earlier drafts of this manuscript are written in Russel's hand, suggesting that he is the original author.

88. Ibid., 3.

89. Williams, 1946, 7.

90. Industrial designer Norman Bel Geddes popularized the concept of streamlining in design. See Norman Bel Geddes, "Streamlining," *Atlantic Monthly*, November 193, 553, 556–58. For a critical view of the racial implications of the 1930s obsession with streamlining, see Christina Cogdell, *Eugenic Design: Streamlining America in the 1930s* (Philadelphia: University of Pennsylvania Press, 2004).

91. "I Am a Negro," *American Magazine*, reproduced in Henderson, "Two Case Studies," 534.

92. Williams, 1945, 8.

93. Sullivan, *Revealing Whiteness*, 73.

94. In addition to Henderson, "Two Case Studies," see David Gebhard, "Paul R. Williams and the Los Angeles

Scene," introduction to Hudson, *Paul R. Williams, Architect*, 19–29; and Garnett, "Paul Revere Williams: Innovator, Achiever, Architect."

95. "Something Clients Want."

96. Henderson "Two Case Studies," 231.

97. Williams, 1945, 14.

98. Ibid., 24.

99. Ibid., 34, 44.

100. Reprinted in Henderson, "Two Case Studies," 533.

101. Ibid, 534. Emphasis original.

102. In the 1949 article for *Ebony*, Williams even talks about exterior house designs as a metaphor for racial diversity in a given neighborhood, which he suggests is a positive thing. Duncan quotes him: "Variation of window space and of exterior wall facing, and imaginative use of color and of painted bricks, for instance, give life and variety to a neighborhood even where the floor plans are very much alike." Duncan, "Paul Williams Tells How to Build a Home," 44.

103. Williams, 1945, 8.

104. Williams, 1946, 55; Williams, 1945, 78. There is an additional use of the term "rambling" in 1946, 49, for a country house designed by A. Quincy Jones.

105. As C. Van Woodward notes, the lunch-counter sit-ins of 1960 precipitated nonviolent tactics to integrate other public spaces in the South, including "theaters, hotels, public parks, swimming pools, and beaches, as well as in churches, courtrooms, libraries, and art galleries." Woodward, *The Strange Career of Jim Crow*, 171.

106. Nelson and Wright, *TH*, 5.

107. Williams, 1946, 5.

108. Nelson and Wright, *TH*, 181.

109. Lipsitz, *How Racism Takes Place*, 29.

110. Williams, 1946, 90.

111. Brandt, *DYH*, 11.

112. Ibid., 12.

113. On MacAlister, see Danielle Charlap, "Demonstrating the Profession: Interior Decorating Instruction on Early Television," in *Shaping the American Interior: Structures, Contexts and Practices*, ed. Paula Lupkin and Penny Sparke (London: Routledge, 2018), 107–24. The Herman Miller ad appeared in the *New Yorker*, June 9, 1956, 46.

114. Brandt, *DYH*, 12.

115. Williams, 1946, 8.

Chapter 2
"Modern Design? You Bet!"

1. For a history of the Chicago Metropolitan Assurance Company, see Robert E. Weems, Jr., *Black Business in the Black Metropolis: The Chicago Metropolitan Assurance Company, 1925–1985* (Bloomington: Indiana University Press, 1996).

2. To conduct research for this comparison, I looked at every issue of *Ebony* (published monthly) from November 1949 to November 1959. *Life* was published weekly, and I looked at a minimum of one issue per month of *Life* in same period, often more.

3. The history of *Ebony* has been documented by those inside the publication as well as scholars from the outside. Some of the most important texts are Johnson, *Succeeding against the Odds*; Burns, *Nitty Gritty*; Green, *Selling the Race*; Chambers, "Presenting the Black Middle Class"; Stange, " 'Photographs Taken in Everyday Life' "; and Greer, *Represented*. As Greer notes, Johnson was not copying the Whiteness of *Life* so much as he was copying "methods that produced commercially successful publications" (150).

4. For a thoughtful assessment of *Life's* reach, see James L. Baughman, "Who Read *Life*? The Circulation of America's Favorite Magazine," in *Looking at* Life *Magazine*, ed. Doss, 41–51. He advises scholars not to replicate *Life's* own mythology by overstating its impact and influence.

5. Burns states that newsstand sales, prior to the mid-1950s, constituted "about 90 percent of our total circulation" and were "primarily in big urban areas." Burns, *Nitty Gritty*, 120. Johnson describes a dip in newsstand sales in one month during the 1954 recession from 500,000 copies to 400,000, and explains the strategies he implemented to move to a larger subscriber base. Johnson, *Succeeding against the Odds*, 234–35. Contemporaneously, the change to a larger subscription-based business is discussed in "Negro Progress Spells Success for 'Ebony'—Mirror of the 'Bright Side,' " *Advertising Age*, October 24, 1955, 49. In *Ebony* itself, there is evidence of the change in editorial comments in "Backstage," *Ebony*, April 1958, 14. Greer cites

monthly circulation figures just under 500,000 in 1955. Greer, *Represented*, 186.

6. Information derived from the 1950 census and used by *Ebony* for advertising. Chambers, *Madison Avenue and the Color Line*, 46. The 1959 statistics are from "Backstage," *Ebony*, February 1959, 16. A scholarly study of advertising in *Ebony* from 1963 described the magazine as the "chief medium" by which advertisers could "address the national Negro market," further testimony to its stature as the preeminent publication for the African American marketplace. See Berkman, "Advertising in 'Ebony' and 'Life,' " 53.

7. "Current Population Reports: Consumer Income," Series P-60, No. 24 (Washington, DC.: US Department of Commerce, Bureau of the Census, April 1957), 13. Indeed, Berkman's comparison of ads in *Life* and *Ebony* is largely focused on what he perceives as the class differences that are a consequence of the overall lower incomes of African American families. Berkman, "Advertising in 'Ebony' and 'Life,' " 57–58.

8. Stein, "The Graphic Ordering of Desire."

9. "The Philadelphia Museum: Created by Main Line families, it brings great art to the public," *Life*, September 3, 1951, 66ff.; "What Do U.S. Museums Buy?" *Life*, July 31, 1950, 40ff.; "The Metropolitan and Modern Art: Amid brickbats and bouquets the museum holds its first U.S. painting competition," *Life*, January 15, 1951, 34ff.

10. "Supple Sculpture: Chaim Gross makes lively figures of lithe nudes and agile acrobats," *Life*, January 8, 1951, 63–67; "Marion Perkins: Talented Chicago sculptor wins top art prize but still works as freight handler," *Ebony*, October 1951, 107–12. Although it does not directly fall under the category of professional art practice, both magazines published articles about Modernist "push-button" houses: "Push Button Home: Michigan physician's plush estate almost runs by itself," *Ebony*, November 1954, 42–48; and "McCulloch's Push-Button Paradise: A millionaire manufacturer builds a mechanical dream house," *Life*, May 7, 1956, 71ff.

11. "Speaking of Pictures: Hardware

Sculpture," *Life*, March 3, 1952, 6ff.; "Janitor Genius: Admirers call John Dunn a 'modern Leonardo da Vinci,'" *Ebony*, December 1952, 140ff.

12. "A Designer's Home of His Own: Charles Eames builds a house of steel and glass," *Life*, September 11, 1950, 148–52; "Furniture Designer: Add Bates makes custom-built designs in East Harlem shop," *Ebony*, February 1951, 70–73.

13. Peter Stackpole was a California-based photographer who worked for *Life* in the 1950s. He had also known the Eameses since the early 1940s, when he documented their experiments with molded plywood machinery. See Neuhart with John Neuhart, *The Story of Eames Furniture*, 291.

14. The article was published August 8, 1949; photographs by Martha Holmes.

15. The photograph appears on 150–51.

16. "Furniture Designer," 73.

17. Bates appears numerous times in the *New York Amsterdam News*, the leading African American newspaper in New York. Most of the citations are social notes, but they provide basic information about his life: he appeared regularly onstage as a dancer and actor in the 1930s, although by February 1940 a gossip columnist noted that he "had not been seen in a long time." In 1942, he returned safely from a stint in the merchant marine in Africa; in July 1943, the "big surprise was the quiet marriage" of Bates and Julia Baxter of Newark. The *News* has no information about his design career. Confusingly, his name appears as both "Add" and "Ad." His full name was "Addison." For a more comprehensive discussion of his career, see Kristina Wilson, "Add Bates, 306, and Interlocking Modernisms in Mid-Century Harlem," *American Art* 35, no. 1 (Spring 2021).

18. Susan Manning, *Modern Dance, Negro Dance: Race in Motion* (Minneapolis: University of Minnesota Press, 2004), 56–57.

19. For information about the 306 group, see Schwartzman, *Romare Bearden*, 79–85; Fine, ed., *Procession*, 248; and Romare Bearden, "A Tribute to 'Spinky' Alston," *New York Amsterdam News*, June 18, 1977, A1. Bearden later explained that in 1940, Bates gave him his first solo show in his second-floor studio space at 306. Romare Bearden, "The 1930s—An Art Reminiscence," *New York Amsterdam News*, September 18, 1971, D24; Schwartzman, *Romare Bearden*, 112; and Perry, "Cultural Identity in African-American Art, 1900–1950," 13.

20. "He, his white wife, Ellen, and their skillful, pretty brown skin daughter, Julia, now 3, live in a six-room Brooklyn apartment. … His house is equipped with custom-built furniture made by Ad Bates, famed Harlem furniture maker. Wright, his wife, and Bates designed the furniture." Michael Carter, "Book-of-the-Month Author Talks for AFRO," *The Afro-American* (Baltimore), January 13, 1945; reprinted in Keneth Kinnamon and Michel Fabre, eds., *Conversations with Richard Wright* (Jackson: University of Mississippi Press, 1993), 54.

21. Bearden and Harry Henderson, *A History of African-American Artists from 1792 to the Present* (New York: Pantheon Books, 1993), 305, 312.

22. "A Designer's Home of His Own," 147, 152.

23. "Furniture Designer," 73.

24. Given the artistic practice of the Eames studio as documented by Pat Kirkham, it is extremely unlikely that Charles and Ray would have allowed anyone to photograph them and their work without significant input; and, as in n13 above, Stackpole already knew the Eameses and their work. Indeed, Charles's blurred head in a Stackpole photograph on page 151 in the article is reminiscent of the photographic tricks that Charles and Ray experimented with. See Kirkham, *Charles and Ray Eames*, 150–57, 311. Colomina also emphasizes the importance of the Eames's constructed photographs in how scholars and the public came to understand the Eames house. See Colomina, *Domesticity at War*, chapter 3.

25. "A Designer's Home of His Own," 152.

26. "Furniture Designer," 70.

27. Ibid., 73, 72. In addition to William Morris, Jr., the patrons mentioned in the article were Joseph Kalmanoff, a Russian Jewish immigrant and founder of Metropolitan News Company, originally a distributor of Yiddish newspapers; and Clarence A. Isaac, his son in law. See "Joseph Kalmanoff, 83, Is Dead," *New York Times*, November 6, 1968; and "Kalmanoff-Isaac," *New York Times*, April 23, 1944.

28. "A Designer's Home of His Own," 152.

29. "Furniture Designer," 70.

30. "Nineteen Young Americans: *Life* presents a selection from the country's best artists under 36," *Life*, March 20, 1950, 83ff.

31. "Leading Young Artists: Group of emancipated Negro painters is making notable contribution to U.S. art," *Ebony*, April 1958, 33ff.

32. Gibson, *Abstract Expressionism*, 76. Emphasis original.

33. "Nineteen Young Americans," 83.

34. Ibid., 84. *Room No. V* is now in the collection of the Museum of Fine Arts, Boston, acc. no. 2007.2.

35. Ibid.

36. "Leading Young Artists," 33.

37. Ibid.

38. Ibid., 36–37.

39. Ibid., 37.

40. Folder: Barbara Chase, Box 91; Folder: Paul Keene, Jr., Box 96; Folder: Charles W. White, Box 101, Courtesy of the John Hay Whitney Foundation Papers, MS 1952, Manuscripts and Archives, Yale University Library.

41. Transcript of Oral History interview with Merton D. Simpson, November 1968, Archives of American Art, Washington, DC; Bruce Weber, "Merton D. Simpson, Painter, Collector and Dealer in African Art, Dies at 84," *New York Times*, March 14, 2013.

42. Debate over the *Ebony* editorial philosophy happened in the 1950s and is evident in some editorials. Several scholars have examined this, including Green, *Selling the Race*; Chambers, "Presenting the Black Middle Class"; and Berkman, "Advertising in 'Ebony' and 'Life.'"

43. Brief biographies of Bailey and Morehead can be found in Deborah Willis, *An Illustrated Bio-Bibliography of Black Photographers, 1940–1988* (New York: Garland, 1989), 11, 104. White was clearly an interesting subject for photographers, as his portrait by Bob Moore is included in Willis, *Reflections in Black*, 129. White was also a photographer, as Willis discusses in "In Search of Beauty: Charles White's Exposures," in *Charles White*, ed. Oehler and Adler, 85–93.

44. My analysis of these photographs in the context of Black agency and action is inspired, in part, by Leigh Raiford and Martin A. Berger's scholarship on photography and racial activism. See Raiford, *Imprisoned in a Luminous Glare*; Berger, *Seeing through Race*; and Berger, *Freedom Now! Forgotten Photographs of the Civil Rights Struggle* (Berkeley, CA: University of California Press, 2013).

45. The canonical source of this interpretive rubric is Harold Rosenberg, "The American Action Painters," *Art News*, December 1952, 22–23, 48–50.

46. See these advertisements for Lord Calvert Whiskey: Hedrick in *Life*, March 13, 1950, 138; Williams in *Life*, January 22, 1951, 54; Nash in *Life*, January 16, 1950, 53; Caldwell in *Life*, October 30, 1950, inside back cover; Hammond in *Life*, February 1, 1954, inside back cover.

47. See these advertisements for Lord Calvert Whiskey: Robinson in *Ebony*, February 1952, 47; Olden in *Ebony*, October 1951, 43; Edwards in *Ebony*, November 1951, 49; Carter in *Ebony*, January 1952, 47.

48. There is one exception to this: Hammond is captured in four photographs: one portrait and three showing him with his maps, horses, and drinking with a colleague. See Hammond in *Life*, February 1, 1954, inside back cover.

49. Moreover, many of the ads illustrated their subjects with White colleagues, suggesting that they cultivated professional respect across racial lines, although this never transferred to the hosting photographs at home, which depicted exclusively African American gatherings.

50. This potential for confusion between advertising and editorial content has ramifications for today. Some digital archiving databases that document the contents of *Ebony* include the Lord Calvert advertisements as articles, for example.

51. Ad for Lord Calvert Whiskey, *Ebony*, October 1951, 43.

52. Wright and Wright, *GTEL*, 19.

53. Stange analyzes *Ebony*'s approach to the photography of individual subjects and offers a taxonomy of its photographic language slightly different from mine. Central to her thesis, however, is the importance of the human subject and the idea of identification between reader and photographic subject. See Stange, " 'Photographs Taken in Everyday Life,' " 208.

54. John H. Johnson, "A Message from the Publisher," *Ebony*, November 1955, 121.

55. Willis, *Reflections in Black*, xvii. Stange describes the effect of *Ebony*'s photographic project: "*Ebony*'s images would detach, or disarticulate, racialized icons—that is, the recognizable black face and body—from the familiar markers of degradation, spectacle, and victimization to which they had always been linked if represented at all; the pictures would, instead, reproduce iconic blackness articulated to equally naturalized and sanctioned symbols of class respectability, achievement, and American national identity." Stange, " 'Photographs Taken in Everyday Life,' " 208. See also Raiford, *Imprisoned in a Luminous Glare*, esp. 12–16. Although she focuses on photography's role in social activism, she notes the importance of photography in the cultivation of a normative, positive group identity: "The process of black visual self-representation also produced public documents of African American citizenship and middle-class belonging. In the century after Emancipation these images of uplift functioned as constructions of identity. They were at once performances of idealized identity and documents of dignified lifestyles" (15).

56. "Redcap Interpreter: Negro who speaks 11 languages is guide for displaced persons," *Ebony*, March 1952, 72.

57. Winthrop Sargeant, "New Life at the Old Met: Rudolph Bing's recipe for opera is part Vienna, part Broadway, part Mr. Bing," *Life*, February 12, 1951, 75ff. Eileen Darby is credited as working for Graphic House.

58. Sandy Isenstadt discusses the centrality of spaciousness in middle-class concepts of home in *The Modern American House*. For the power of a panoramic gaze, see Alan Wallach, "Wadsworth's Tower: An Episode in the History of American Landscape Vision," *American Art* 10, no. 3 (Autumn 1996): 8–27; and Jason Weems, *Barnstorming the Prairies: How Aerial Vision Shaped the Midwest* (Minneapolis: University of Minnesota Press, 2015). Harris also discusses the power of elevated sight in *Little White Houses*, 89–93.

59. Readers of *Life* had already been introduced to Herman Miller's products as affordable. See a 1951 feature article on new designs by Charles and Ray Eames and George Nelson for the reader who self-identified as a "less affluent modernist." The "bargain-priced" objects included the fiberglass armchair designed by the Eameses. "Four Rooms: $1,800. Modern furniture comes in a bargain-priced package," *Life*, May 14, 1951, 89ff.

60. "$15,000 'Trade Secrets' House," *Life*, January 5, 1953, 13, 8.

61. Ibid., 12.

62. "The U.S. Need for More Livable Homes," *Life*, September 15, 1958, 70.

63. Ibid., 63.

64. "Push Button Home," *Ebony*, November 1954, 42.

65. Ibid., 43. The sofa is credited as "custom-made," but no designer is listed. The only recognizable design in the house is an Eames fiberglass-reinforced plastic armchair in the bathroom.

66. Painter describes the postwar period as the "third enlargement of American whiteness" in *The History of White People*, chapter 26.

67. "Four Rooms: $1,800."

68. The *Ebony* photographic studio possessed a Butterfly Chair, as documented in the tenth-anniversary issue: a photo essay celebrating the extensive amenities in the Johnson Publishing Company headquarters included an image of David Jackson and Isaac Sutton preparing to photograph a female model on a Butterfly Chair. See "Johnson Magic Casts Spell over Three More Magazines," *Ebony*, November 1955, 124.

69. A model leaning into an undressed Butterfly Chair is also included in "Fashion Fair," *Ebony*, September 1951, 81. For a comprehensive discussion of how the Johnson Publishing Company promoted Dandridge as a celebrity and sex symbol, see Greer, *Represented*, 177–82.

70. Black Hawk Hancock, "Learning How to Fiske: Theorizing Cultural Literacy, Counter-History, and the Politics of Media Events in the 21st Century," in Fiske, *Media Matters*, xx. See also Delgado and Stafancic, eds., *Critical Race Theory*, chapters 8, 9, 10.

71. Burns, *Nitty Gritty*, 120–28. See also Chambers's discussion of Johnson's successful approach to selling advertising, *Madison Avenue and the Color Line*, 42–45.

72. Johnson recounts his pitch to the

head of Zenith Radio in *Succeeding against the Odds*, 185–88.

73. Chambers, *Madison Avenue and the Color Line*, esp. chapter 2; Weems, *Desegregating the Dollar*, chapters 2 and 3; Greer, *Represented*, esp. chapter 5.

74. "The Brown Hucksters," *Ebony*, May 1948, 28–33.

75. Johnson, *Succeeding against the Odds*, chapters 21, 22, 28, 30. Also, see Chambers, *Madison Avenue and the Color Line*, chapter 1.

76. Elspeth Brown discusses the identity politics of African American modeling agencies after World War II in "Black Models and the Invention of the US 'Negro Market,' 1945–1960," in *Inside Marketing: Practices, Ideologies, Devices*, ed. Detlev Zwick and Julien Cayla (Oxford: Oxford University Press, 2011), 185–211.

77. "Negro Progress Spells Success for 'Ebony,'" 50.

78. Ibid.

79. Chambers, *Madison Avenue and the Color Line*, 66. Greer discusses the way public relations professionals such as Moss Kendrix cultivated their racial identity as a mark of experiential expertise using Gayatri Chakravorty Spivak's term "strategic essentialism." Greer, *Represented*, 211–12.

80. "Negro Progress Spells Success for 'Ebony,'" 50.

81. Fiske, *Media Matters*, 43.

82. Chambers, "Presenting the Black Middle Class," 67–68; Green, *Selling the Race*, chapter 4; Burns, *Nitty Gritty*, 94, 102; Frazier, *Black Bourgeoisie*, chapter 9.

83. John H. Johnson, ghostwritten by Burns, "Why Negroes Buy Cadillacs," *Ebony*, September 1949, 34.

84. Greer, *Represented*, 228–32, 241. In her detailed study of Coca-Cola's advertising campaigns in the "Negro market," she writes, "Taken on their own, the black Coke ads pictured African Americans doing things, wearing things, and styling themselves in ways that many blacks in America did, or aspired to do, which had nothing to do with a desire to appear or be white" (241).

85. Harris, *Little White Houses*.

86. Ibid., 30.

87. Barthes, *Mythologies*, 138–40.

88. For "clean lines," see advertisement for Lincoln, *Life*, February 7, 1955, 82–83; for "clean, functional lines," see advertisement for Oldsmobile, *Life*, July 2, 1956, 44; for "clean, crisp fashion," see advertisement for Buick, *Life*, April 5, 1954, 154.

89. Ad for Gleem toothpaste, *Life*, January 6, 1958, inside front cover.

90. Ad for Bruce Floor wax, *Ebony*, November 1952, 39.

91. Modess, *Ebony*, May 1950, 11; see also ad for Kotex, *Ebony*, May 1955, 29. However, a 1954 Hoover vacuum cleaner advertisement portrays an African American housewife pushing her machine on a carpet next to an austere, rectangular chest of drawers on metal legs, details that would signify as Modern. This is, by my reckoning, the only advertisement that appears in *Ebony* in the 1950s that explicitly connects Modernism and cleanliness with African American protagonists. See advertisement for Hoover, *Ebony*, December 1954, 11.

92. "U.S. Housing Part II: More Livable Homes: Bold New Plan for Best Land Use: Row houses give indoor spaciousness, outdoor privacy and even a park," *Life*, September 22, 1958, 72ff.; see also "U.S. Housing III: Homes That Achieve Most in Livability: Tailored to fit owners, houses suit families' ways, whims and budgets," *Life*, September 29, 1958, 54ff.; "Part IV: More Livable Homes: More Space Upstairs and Down: Two houses designed for LIFE gain comfort, save money with more floors," *Life*, October 6, 1958, 82ff.

93. Edward Durell Stone, "A Gracious Home Shapes the Family," *Life*, September 22, 1958, 81.

94. Dyer, *White*, 31.

95. Greer discusses Coca-Cola's ads that interchange models of different races, and suggests that one possible way to interpret them is as a metaphor for how racial integration was conceptualized in the 1950s. See Greer, *Represented*, 141.

96. Ad for Schlitz, *Ebony*, February 1951, 14; ad for Schlitz, *Life*, February 5, 1951, 36.

97. The ad appeared in *Life*, January 21, 1952, 57; and *Ebony*, March 1952, 73.

98. These appeared in *Life*, May 4, 1953, 40; *Ebony*, July 1953, 43.

99. These appeared in *Life*, July 19, 1954, 81–83; *Ebony*, September 1954, 45. The *Life* ad included a two-page silhouette-style spread, the first page of which was replicated in *Ebony*; in *Life*, an additional White model appeared in the second page.

100. *Life*, July 29, 1957, 48–49; *Ebony*, August 1957, 54.

101. *Life*, April 14, 1952, 111; *Ebony*, May 1952, 31.

102. The three thousand per month figure, as well as the nickname "the Eames chair," comes from "Eames's House," *Life*, September 11, 1950, 152.

103. My reading here is indebted to the observations Greer makes about how women are represented in *Ebony* in her book, *Represented*, chapter 4.

104. "Modern Designs for Negro Dolls," *Ebony*, January 1952, 50, 46.

105. Ibid., 46.

106. Ibid., 50. The quote is actually from Zora Neale Hurston, commenting on the new dolls.

107. Chambers, *Madison Avenue and the Color Line*, 82; see also 86.

108. Ad for Ballantine Ale, *Life*, November 1, 1954, 133.

Chapter 3
Like a "Girl in a Bikini Suit" and Other Stories

1. Neuhart, with John Neuhart, *The Story of Eames Furniture*, 491–97; Abercrombie, *George Nelson*, 84–92; DePree, *Business as Unusual*.

2. Makovsky and Lanks, "Nelson and Company"; Michael Maharam, ed., *Irving Harper: Works on Paper* (New York: Rizzoli, 2013), 21–31; Michael Darling, "Bringing Home a Revolution: The Domestic Furniture of the George Nelson Office," in *George Nelson*, ed. Eisenbrand, 66–89; Abercrombie, *George Nelson*, chapter 5.

3. Neuhart's text is exhaustive in its documentation of the collaborative design process in the Eames studio. See, in particular, Neuhart, with John Neuhart, *Story of Eames Furniture*, 64–243, 530–678. See also Joseph Giovannini, "The Office of Charles Eames and Ray Kaiser: The Material Trail," in *The Work of Charles and Ray Eames*, ed. Albrecht, 44–71; and Kirkham, *Charles and Ray Eames*, chapter 5.

4. May, *Homeward Bound*; Clifford Clark, "Ranch-House Suburbia: Ideals and Realities," in *Recasting*

America, ed. May, 171–93; Cohen, *A Consumer's Republic*.

5. In 1957, a list of retail prices was included in "Holiday Handbook of Chairs." The Nelson Coconut ($272) and Eames Lounge Chair ($368) were among the most expensive listed, but the Barcelona Chair by Ludwig Mies van der Rohe (retailed by Knoll) was the most costly ($825) and could be considered an example of luxury-level pricing. Eero Saarinen's Womb Chair ($270) and an armchair by Finn Juhl ($240) were comparable in price to the Coconut and Eames Lounge. Conversely, the Eames plywood chair was among the least expensive at $48. George Nelson, "Holiday Handbook of Chairs," *Holiday* 22, no. 5 (November 1957): 141. Interestingly, in only six years, the price of the Eames plywood chair had apparently been raised 60 percent. In 1951, *Life* magazine promoted Herman Miller's designs as "Bargain-priced" with the Eames chairs being the most affordable items listed: the plywood chair with metal legs was $29, and the plastic chairs were $33. See "Four Rooms: $1800. Modern furniture comes in a bargain-priced package," *Life*, May 14, 1951, 89ff.

6. George Nelson (hereafter GN) to D. J. DePree (hereafter DJD), February 26, 1947. Correspondence with George Nelson, 1945–47, Ref copy file 2, Corporate Archives, Herman Miller International, Zeeland, Michigan (hereafter HMI).

7. DJD, "Comments on Forecast factors of September 24, 1956," typed ms., 2, 5. Gray Box Series, HMI.

8. An industry editorial about the 1951 Good Design exhibition, cosponsored by the Merchandise Mart in Chicago and the Museum of Modern Art in New York, offers some additional perspective about the market for Modernist design at the start of the decade. In an analysis of how the Chicago department store Carson, Pirie, Scott capitalized on the 1951 Good Design exhibition, the reporter described the limits of the consumer market for Modernist wares: "acceptance" of Modernist home designs "is steadily growing, especially among young people. But, since this element that most appreciates what Good Design has to offer falls within the lower income bracket, the high prices of the merchandise—particularly furniture—is said to narrow its market. The increasing public readiness for Good Design in all categories of home furnishings—furniture, decorative textiles, lamps and accessories—could be translated into actual sales if prices were lowered 'considerably' on the majority of items offered, it is felt, or, to look at it another way, there is a market (albeit limited at the moment) for merchandise of Good Design standards but at lower prices." Hortense Herman, "Carson's Finds 'Good Design' Pays Off," *Retailing Daily*, April 19, 1951, Folder 21, Box 2, Freda Diamond Collection 1945–1984, Archives Center, National Museum of American History (hereafter Diamond Collection).

9. Whyte, *Organization Man*, 320.

10. Ibid., 312–15.

11. Frazier, *Black Bourgeoisie*, 208.

12. Packard, *Status Seekers*, 63.

13. Lynes, *The Tastemakers*, 307.

14. Ibid., 308.

15. Lizabeth Cohen's masterful history of the rise of a consumer society in the postwar era helps to contextualize the marketing logic that simultaneously exhorts consumers to buy so as to fit in, and also to buy in order to stand out. In chapter 7 of her book, she examines the move within the advertising industry away from "mass" marketing and toward "market segmentation," which we ultimately know as niche marketing. Cohen, *A Consumer's Republic*.

16. Whyte, *Organization Man*, 317.

17. Keats, *Crack in the Picture Window*, 18.

18. Ibid., 45.

19. For *Life*, see "Four Rooms: $1800." For the *New Yorker*, see Promotional brochure for Executive Office Group, c. 1954, NEE2, HMI. Although far from exhaustive, my research in the archival discourse of Herman Miller in the 1940s and 1950s reveals no other references to general interest publications for advertising spots; *House Beautiful*, *Interiors*, *Progressive Architecture*, *Arts & Architecture*, and other publications focused on architecture and interior design are the magazines that are mentioned. An unpublished manuscript on the history of Modern furniture in HMI from 1958 or 1959 quotes DePree on his desire that Herman Miller would ultimately become a company "attractive to the average buyer." The author writes: "[DePree] would like to meet the challenge contained between the lines of a statement made by a California school teacher. 'I have chosen my way of living,' this teacher declared, 'and I know the objects that will support this way of life. Most of them are in the Herman Miller line, but I cannot afford them.' " A footnote for the quote: "As quoted by D. J. DePree from memory during an interview, May 15, 1958." "Evolution of Furniture By William S. Gamble 1958 or 1959," p. 6, Folder: "D J DePree's Papers on HM History, Folder 9, Box 81," Gray Box Series, HMI.

20. "Herman Miller Objectives," undated ms., probably c. 1956, Gray Box series (Acc #10, Box #12), HMI.

21. Whyte, *Organization Man*, 306.

22. Darling, "Bringing Home a Revolution," 76.

23. The chart appeared in the April 11, 1949, issue, 100–101.

24. The model of the avant-garde as cultural resistance is discussed in a variety of texts. See, among others, Renato Poggioli, *The Theory of the Avant-Garde* (Cambridge, MA: Belknap Press of Harvard University Press, 1968); Thomas Crow, "Modernism and Mass Culture in the Visual Arts," in *Modern Art in the Common Culture* (New Haven, CT: Yale University Press, 1996), 3–38.

25. Harvey, *The Fifties*, 127. See also Nickles, "More Is Better."

26. "There's a New Pattern in Furniture Behavior," *House Beautiful* 89, no. 6 (June 1947): 115.

27. "Herman Miller Furniture Company and Stormy Petrel George Nelson Team Up to Prove Handsome Furniture Can Be Had," *Interiors* 106, no. 10 (May 1947): 107.

28. *The Herman Miller Collection* (Zeeland, MI: Herman Miller Furniture Company, 1950). Reprinted in L. Pina, *Herman Miller: Interior Views* (Atglen, PA: Schiffer Publishing, 1998), 131. Herman Miller's 1950 product catalogue is almost identical to the 1948 catalogue, and this quote appears in 1948 as well as 1950.

29. "There's a New Pattern," 111. Another article commented on how easily the various modular units could appear uniformly identical: "When closed, the desk resembles other storage units." Ethel Brostrom, "New

Family of Furniture," *Better Homes and Gardens* 25, no. 8 (August 1947): 99.

30. Storage furniture, as a specific type, raises larger interpretive issues in the postwar home than can be addressed in this book. See, for example, Hine, *Populuxe*, 72; Harris, *Little White Houses*, chapter 6.

31. For a broader account of the role of color in design marketing, see Blaszczyk, *The Color Revolution*.

32. Darling, "Bringing Home a Revolution," 84.

33. My thanks to Davis Baird for pointing out the significance of tripods in scientific research. See E. Bright Wilson, *An Introduction to Scientific Research* (New York: McGraw Hill, 1952).

34. The Hilda Stories, http://www .hermanmiller.com/why/the-hilda -stories.html, accessed June 17, 2014.

35. Darling, "Bringing Home a Revolution," 87.

36. Darling reports that Herman Miller sold only thirty-seven units per year in the sofa's first six years of manufacture. Ibid.

37. Jackson Pollock Interview with William Wright, 1950, reprinted in *Art in Theory, 1900–1990*, ed. Charles Harrison and Paul Wood (New York: Blackwell, 1992), 576.

38. Adolph Gottlieb and Mark Rothko with Barnett Newman, "Statement" to the *New York Times*, June 13, 1943, reprinted in *Art in Theory, 1900–1990*, ed. Harrison and Wood, 562.

39. Clement Greenberg, "Abstract, Representational, and So Forth" (orig. 1954), in *Art and Culture: Critical Essays* (Boston: Beacon Press, 1961), 136–37.

40. Gibson, *Abstract Expressionism*; Leja, *Reframing Abstract Expressionism*; Craven, "Abstract Expressionism and Third World Art."

41. Gibson, *Abstract Expressionism*, 86.

42. Barthes, *Mythologies*, 139.

43. Quoted in Darling, "Bringing Home a Revolution," 72.

44. Nelson, "Holiday Handbook of Chairs," 142.

45. Another example of a dog interacting with Nelson's designs can be found in "Modern Living: Low Down Furniture," *Life*, December 27, 1954, 73; and a dog is depicted posed in an Eames plastic armchair in "Four Rooms: $1800," *Life*, May 14, 1951, 89.

46. I'm indebted to the late Bob Viol, corporate archivist at Herman Miller, for these insightful critiques of the Marshmallow Sofa design. My own household experience with the Nelson platform bench has demonstrated similar risks of the object tipping over when human weight is not evenly positioned.

47. For an extensive discussion of the Eames Lounge Chair, see Eidelberg et al., *The Eames Lounge Chair*.

48. Lyford, *Isamu Noguchi's Modernism*, 139.

49. Robert Vischer, "On the Optical Sense of Form: A Contribution to Aesthetics" (1873), in *Empathy, Form, and Space: Problems in German Aesthetics, 1873–1893*, ed. Harry Francis Mallgrave and Eleftherios Ikonomou (Los Angeles: Getty Center for the History of Art and the Humanities, 1994), 104.

50. Gibson, *The Ecological Approach to Visual Perception*, 129, 134. A thoughtful assessment of the current state of design research and the conceptual importance of Gibson's term "affordance" can be found in Almquist and Lupton, "Affording Meaning."

51. Jason Weems discusses the development of the plywood splints, and also uses the term "empathy" in his analysis, in "War Furniture," 46–48. Ultimately his assessment of empathy in these designs differs from mine.

52. Elizabeth Guffey has documented the design of the modern wheelchair in the years immediately following World War II, when it was developed as a response to the needs of disabled war veterans. See *Designing Disability*, chapter 2.

53. Ibid., 64.

54. Ibid., 9.

55. Weems notes that the leg splints were modeled on Charles's own leg. Although there is no evidence to suggest that an adult White man modeled the Eames chair body, the leg splint precedent is suggestive. Weems, "War Furniture," 47.

56. Almquist and Lupton note that in the recent turn toward studies of "users" in design research, the result is not a " 'humanist' subject; he or she is an 'engineered' subject, who responds correctly to stimuli and thus can be shaped into a reliable member of mass society." Almquist and Lupton, "Affording Meaning," 9.

57. Harris, *Little White Houses*, 30.

58. Ibid., 19. Emphasis added.

59. This assertion is based on my own reading of the magazine from 1950 to 1959. An Eames plastic chair appears in the bathroom of Dr. Howard McNeil's "Push Button Home," *Ebony*, November 1954, 48; and an Eames Lounge Chair is shown in a study in S. B. Fuller's home: "Suburban Showplace," *Ebony*, February 1959, 40. These would appear to be the only examples in the decade.

60. For examples of featured homes, see "Here's a Private World on a City Lot," *Better Homes and Gardens* 30, no. 3 (March 1952): 60–61; John Normile, "House for a Family That Does Things," *Better Homes and Gardens* 33, no. 1 (January 1955): 51, 57; "How to Build a Good, Low-Cost House," *Woman's Day*, June 1957, 27–29. The last example does not include White inhabitants in its photographs, but the presence of only White people in all other editorial and advertising images in the magazine strongly implies White inhabitants. For an example of fashion images, see "At Home—and at Ease," *Woman's Home Companion*, August 1952, 108–11.

61. Advertisement for Masonite Corporation, *House and Garden* 105, no. 2 (February 1954): 111.

62. Sullivan, *Revealing Whiteness*, 73; Dyer, *White*, 76.

63. Castle, "I'll Take My Modernism in Moderation," 6.

64. The showrooms themselves are important source material for historians and have been studied. See Petty, "Attitudes towards Modern Living." Characterizing the differences between Herman Miller's and Knoll's showrooms, Petty suggests that the former possessed an "eclectic approach," whereas Knoll's was more luxurious (195). Knoll's newest New York showroom was featured in *Life* in 1953, and the lack of any kind of non-Western accessory in the multiple photographs is notable. "Drum Beaters for Modern," *Life*, March 2, 1953, 72–76.

65. Abercrombie, *George Nelson*, 107. Internal correspondence suggests that Nelson was involved with photographing the collection in the late 1940s and staging its showrooms. See, for example, GN to DJD, January 1, 1947; GN to DJD, March 17, 1947.

Correspondence with George Nelson, 1945–47, HMI.

66. Kirkham, *Charles and Ray Eames*, 193–99.

67. *The Herman Miller Collection 1952* (orig. Zeeland, MI, 1952; reprint, New York: Acanthus Press, 1995), 73.

68. Leslie Piña, ed., *The Herman Miller Collection 1955/56* (orig. Zeeland, MI, 1955; reprint, Atglenn, PA: Schiffer, 1998), E5.

69. *Herman Miller Collection 1952*, 43.

70. Ibid., 14; this image was an original publicity photograph for Nelson's new work in 1947 and was published in Brostrom, "New Family of Furniture," 49, where the caption states that it depicts a display at Kresge Department Store in New Jersey. Nelson mentions staging a department store display in Hartford, Connecticut, in late 1946, raising the possibility that he staged the Kresge photograph as well. GN to DJD, December 16, 1946. Correspondence with George Nelson, 1945–47, HMI. Slides of the Herman Miller New York showroom from the early 1950s show a very similar wicker-wrapped glass jug used as an accessory. New York Showroom c. 1951–1954, HMI.

71. *Herman Miller—Interiors* (Zeeland, MI, 1961), n.p.

72. *Herman Miller Collection 1952*, 103.

73. The date of this photograph is 1960–62; it was published in an expandable, loose-leaf dealer catalogue dated to these years. HMI. In the Nelson Papers, this catalogue is dated c. 1961. George Nelson Papers, Archives and Library, Vitra Design Museum, Weil-am-Rhein, Germany (hereafter Nelson/Vitra).

74. Herman Miller began to sell folk art objects directly to the public in the commercial venture directed by Alexander Girard, known as the Textile and Objects Shop (T&O), in 1961. The T&O was a combination showroom (for textiles) and retail store (for the folk art objects). Because the photographs studied here predate the T&O, and because Herman Miller's showrooms were not retail stores, the accessories depicted in these photographs are unlikely to have been for sale. Herman Miller repeatedly emphasized the importance of accessories in staging its showrooms in its sales reports from the mid-1950s but never suggested

that the accessories were for sale. See, for example, Sales Department Handbook, Herman Miller Furniture Company, January 1956, HMI. For Girard, see Kiera Coffee, *Alexander Girard* (Los Angeles: Ammo Books, 2011), 200–214, 238–51; and Obniski, "Selling Folk Art and Modern Design."

75. Indeed, there is a history of putting laboratory flasks in domestic settings as a kind of Dada gesture. See the 1932 exhibition at the Museum of Modern Art, *Machine Art*.

76. Sullivan, *Revealing Whiteness*, 122. See also her discussion on 174–77 about the "'museumification' of ethnic cultures … for the purposes of white middle-class consumption, pleasure, and profit."

77. See p. 205, Herman Miller loose-leaf dealer catalogue, 1960–62, HMI.

78. Colomina, *Domesticity at War*, chapter 3.

79. Kirkham, *Charles and Ray Eames*, chapter 4, esp. 174–88.

80. See Reynolds-Kaye, *Small-Great Objects*.

81. Advertisement for Herman Miller Furniture Company, *New Yorker*, May 12, 1956, 29.

82. Bali and Java are two different islands in Indonesia, which had been established as an independent country in 1949 after centuries of Dutch colonial rule. Evidence of this superior attitude toward non-Western objects persisted throughout Nelson's career. In his 1977 *How to See*, one of the few passages that includes images of non-Western art is a discussion of the "four hundred faces" he found in his own living room. As he explains: "Can you describe the colors and patterns of any run in your dwelling? … The pictures in the front hall? When were they last looked at? Right here it occurred to me that I might try this game myself and I scored very badly. In the course of trying to see our living room with a fresh eye, I noticed some faces, and was presently involved in an inventory. … As it turned out there were some four-hundred-plus faces, visible and waiting to be counted in that one room." His living room contained faces—figurines and objects—from a wide variety of artistic traditions that he clearly had not looked at for quite some time. But as he concluded, "Seeing things is an intellectual-aesthetic exercise which increases

one's inalienable capital: riches that can be accumulated without cost and, once acquired, cannot be lost or stolen." George Nelson, *How to See* (1977; reprint, Oakland, CA: Design Within Reach, 2003), 128, 132. For a very different interpretation of the value of non-Western art as a source of inspiration for Western artists, see John MacKenzie, *Orientalism: History, Theory and the Arts* (Manchester: Manchester University Press, 1995), chapter 5.

83. Gibson, *Abstract Expressionism*, 76.

84. "Evolution of Furniture by William S. Gamble 1958 or 1959," 6, HMI.

85. Nelson, "Holiday Handbook of Chairs," 139.

86. Bhabha, *The Location of Culture*, chapter 3; and Said, *Orientalism*. For an example of how race and gender are conflated in the art world—and can be used to critical effect in art history—see Anna Chave, "New Encounters with *Les Demoiselles D'Avignon*: Gender, Race, and the Origins of Cubism" (1994), in *Reclaiming Female Agency*, ed. Norma Broude and Mary D. Garrard (Berkeley: University of California Press, 2005), 301–24.

87. Nelson, ed., *Chairs*, 7.

88. Nelson, "Holiday Handbook of Chairs," 138–40.

89. Ibid., 142.

90. Advertisement for Herman Miller Furniture Company, *New Yorker*, May 12, 1956, 29. An internal memo indicates that Nelson was responsible for advertising copy in the spring of 1956. Memo from DJD to Max DePree, Hugh DePree, and Vernon Poest, January 4, 1956, ACCN 10 1955–1956, HMI.

91. Longinotti's oral histories of the office have helped to expand historians' understanding of the design process. See The Hilda Stories, http://www.hermanmiller.com/why/the-hilda-stories.html, accessed June 17, 2014; Makovsky and Lanks, "Nelson and Company."

92. Pat Kirkham, "The Evolution of the Eames Lounge Chair and Ottoman," in Eidelberg et al., *The Eames Lounge Chair*, 59; Hine, *Populuxe*.

93. Neuhart with John Neuhart, *Story of Eames Furniture*, 651. In the 1980s, because it was not sustainable, Herman Miller changed production, and the chair is now available in cherry

or walnut. My thanks to Thomas Kuehne for pointing this out to me.
94. Pat Dalton, "'Places Like Park Forest Are Unreal,'" undated clipping c. January 1960, Folder 10416: Nelson Scrapbook 8, 1956–61, I, Nelson/Vitra.
95. Slavoj Žižek, introduction to Žižek, ed., *Mapping Ideology*, 10.

Chapter 4
"The Quick Appraising Glance"

1. Manufactured by Steubenville Pottery from 1937 to c. 1960. See Ann Kerr, *Collectors' Encyclopedia of Russel Wright* (Paducah, KY: Collector Books, 2002), 127–40.
2. Russel Wright, "Accessory Pieces: Some Rules for Choosing Tableware, Lamps, Vases and Pictures," *New York Times*, October 3, 1948.
3. Gillies, *All about Modern Decorating*, 137.
4. Brandt, *Decorate Your Home for Better Living* (hereafter Brandt, *DYH*), 185.
5. Seeley et al., *Crestwood Heights*, 48.
6. Kennedy, *The House and the Art of Its Design*, 235.
7. Walter Browden, "Liquor, Bar Accessories, and Home, Sweet Home," *Crockery and Glass Journal* 148 (March 5, 1951): 5. *Better Homes and Gardens* offered corroborating data in 1952 when its public relations office claimed that six out of ten families who read the magazine "entertained in their homes last week, and nine million guests were involved." Letter from *Better Homes and Gardens* Vice President and Advertising Director to G. Fox and Company, Hartford, CT, 1952, in Folder 2, Box 2, Freda Diamond Collection 1945–1984, Archives Center, National Museum of American History (hereafter Diamond Collection)
8. "Showers of Good Gifts for the Bride," *House and Garden*, May 1954, 188.
9. Mary and Russel Wright, *Guide to Easier Living* (hereafter Wright and Wright, *GTEL*), 184.
10. Keats, *Crack in the Picture Window*, 118
11. Ibid., 118 and 89. Russell Lynes offered a more G-rated critique of cocktail parties in a 1951 article for *Life*: "The cocktail party is not, of course, the only social device for

gathering bores together, but it is one of the most common." Lynes, "Bores," *Life*, September 3, 1951, 117.
12. "Survey Reveals Buyers' Pre-Show Interest," *Crockery and Glass Journal* 149 (December 1951): 90–96.
13. Kerr, *Collectors' Encyclopedia of Russel Wright*, 222. See also labels and samples found in Envelope: Morgantown Glass Samples, c. 1948, Box 21, Russel Wright Papers, Department of Special Collections, Syracuse University Library, Syracuse, New York (hereafter Wright Papers).
14. Regina Blaczyzk has traced Wright's decidedly mediocre success with glass design in "The Wright Way for Glass."
15. Wright and Wright, *GTEL*, 185.
16. Robert Fetridge, "Along the Highways and Byways of Finance," *New York Times*, June 10, 1951, F11. Box 5, Folder 13, Diamond Collection. Diamond and Libbey quoted this article countless times in the following decades as evidence of the vast reach of her influence. For a more complete account of Diamond's design career, see Kirkham, ed., *Women Designers*, 279–280.
17. See Freda Diamond's oral history interview in Paul Avrich, *Anarchist Voices: An Oral History of Anarchism in America* (Princeton, NJ: Princeton University Press, 1995), 51–54.
18. Marilyn Hoffman, "Designer Plans Practical Ensemble Furnishing for Typical U.S. Homes," *Christian Science Monitor*, September 5, 1951, clipping, Folder 20, Box 1, Diamond Collection.
19. Freda Diamond, "From the Designer's Point of View," *China, Glass, and Decorative Accessories*, August 1951. 18. clipping, Folder 16, Box 1, Diamond Collection.
20. "One and only" is from the advertisement for the Libbey Circus line (see fig. 113). A photograph of Diamond in her studio is in "Designer for Everybody," *Life*, April 5, 1954, 70.
21. Although Diamond's name does not appear in ads for Aqua Ripple, she donated examples of the design to the Smithsonian National Museum of American History and named herself as the designer. My thanks to Bonnie Campbell Lilienfeld for sharing with me Diamond's donated glassware to the NMAH. In addition, primary documents attribute the design to her. See "Elegant New Designs Seen in Pittsburgh Table Show," *Coshocton*

(Ohio) Tribune, January 6, 1955, reprinted in Felt, "Freda Diamond," 12; and "Tableware on Display," *New York Times*, January 7, 1955.
22. Keats, *Crack in the Picture Window*, 86.
23. "Best Buys for a Cupboard Cellar," *House and Garden*, May 1954, 163.
24. "House and Garden's Complete Summer Cook Book," *House and Garden*, June 1954, 70.
25. Glassware Merchandise Data, Box 14, Wright Papers.
26. "Cupboard Cellar," 164. Also, Mary Davis Gillies says that the "checklist of basic requirements" for glassware includes six different types; and a "complete assortment of wine and liquor stemware would include" eleven additional shapes and sizes. Gillies, *All about Modern Decorating*, 172.
27. These various drawings, and many others, can be found in Box 21, Wright Papers. See Kerr, *Collectors' Encyclopedia of Russel Wright*, 226–27.
28. "Man in the Kitchen," typed ms., October 28, 1954, folder Articles: Man in the Kitchen, Women's Home Companion, Box 38, Wright Papers. The article eventually ran, with an entirely different text, as "Any Man Can Keep House," *Women's Home Companion*, September 1956, 50–51.
29. "April 23, 1954 (Notes for Caroline Bird) What I Don't Like About American Women/ Russel Wright, Industrial Designer," typed ms., Folder: Articles by RW—pending, Box 39, Wright Papers.
30. The photographs are labeled VB-14 and VB-17, Folder: American Modern Dinnerware I, Box 1, Wright Papers.
31. Labeled VB-10, Folder: American Modern Dinnerware I, Box 1, Wright Papers.
32. Labeled VB-8, Folder: American Modern Dinnerware II, Box 1, Wright Papers.
33. "Talk to Employees," undated typescript, c. 1952, p. 3, Folder: American Modern Tour—Slide Lecture, Notes, and Talk to Store Employees, Box 38, Wright Papers. In these lecture notes, he refers to television dining, outdoor dining, and children's tablewares as areas of expansion.
34. The advertisement featuring *Moby Dick* is *House and Garden*, March 1952, 5; others are *House and Garden*, January 1952, 1; *House and Garden*,

June 1952, 3; *House and Garden*, October 1952, 9; *House and Garden*, November 1952, 1; *House Beautiful*, April 1952, 16; *House Beautiful*, May 1952, 1; *House Beautiful*, August 1952, 1; *House Beautiful*, September 1952, 8; *House Beautiful*, December 1952, 6. Havenhand discusses this advertising campaign as an example of American nationalist identity formation (without specific discussion of race) in *Mid-Century Modern Interiors*, 15–17.

35. Advertisement for American Modern, *House and Garden*, June 1952, 3.

36. W.E.B. Du Bois connected the erasure of Black creativity from American history with the history of slavery and White ownership of the Black body. Philosopher Sullivan comments on Du Bois's *The Gift of Black Folk: The Negroes in the Making of America* (New York: Washington Square Press, 1970) when she writes, "By treating black folk as property to be bought and sold, white people are able to graft the contributions of black people onto themselves, transforming, by means of a racist alchemy, black contributions into white contributions." Sullivan, *Revealing Whiteness*, 124.

37. Regina Lee Blaszczyk, "'We Must Create Demand by Advertising': Carl U. Fauster, Libbey Glass, and Postwar America," *Glass Club Bulletin* (1993), in Folder 13, Box 5, Diamond Collection. See also Ardelle Coleman, company history of Libbey Glass, typed ms., c. 1951, Folder 1, Box 2, Diamond Collection.

38. Advertisement for Currier and Ives Libbey Glass, *Life*, November 14, 1949, 147.

39. Gaynor Maddox, "New Glassware Practical," *Reno Evening Gazette*, July 9, 1953, quoted in Felt, "Freda Diamond," 9. See also Edna Miles, "All-Purpose Glassware Is Popular," *Boyden (Iowa) Reporter*, March 18, 1954, quoted in Felt, "Freda Diamond," 11–12. Diamond had been arguing for fewer, multifunctional glass forms as early as 1951, in an article she published in the *Crockery and Glass Journal* titled "The Trend to All-Purpose Glassware," 149 (July 1951): 100, 136. See Folder 13, Box 5, Diamond Collection.

40. Press release glued to a press photograph, c. July 1953, Folder 40, Box 2, Diamond Collection.

41. Trade press release on Steve Hannagan Associates stationery, by Mary Appel, c. July 1953, Folder 40, Box 2, Diamond Collection; see also advertisements for Highlander Libbey Glass, in Felt, "Freda Diamond," 74; also *Life*, November 2, 1953, 70.

42. Advertisements for Currier and Ives Libbey Glass, Felt, "Freda Diamond," 32; also *Life*, November 14, 1949, 147; Advertisements for Curio Libbey Glass, Felt, "Freda Diamond," 52.

43. In 1947, Libbey introduced an "Americana" set of decorations, likely created by Diamond, that included a water glass with a "Southern Hospitality" decoration that included a White woman in a large hoopskirt and a parasol. See "Looking through the Ads with Virginia Scott," *Glass Review*, January 1979, 30, in Folder 1, Box 2, Diamond Collection. A later Libbey design, currently undated but printed on a different glass form from those depicted in the 1947 ad, includes a suite of "Plantation Scenes," and one, labeled "Southern Hospitality," shows an enslaved butler serving drinks to a White woman in a hoopskirt with a Rhett Butler–type admirer looking on. These glasses can be found on websites such as Etsy and eBay, where dating is approximate at best.

44. On ex-nomination, see Barthes, *Mythologies*.

45. In "Date with a Dish," *Ebony*, March 1952, 100, and December 1952, 88, the dining table set as part of the *Ebony* test kitchen appears to have Heisey's New Era glasses (introduced in 1934). You can also discern their distinctive contours in a photograph of the test kitchen and dining room in "New Home Service Units Are Unique," *Ebony*, November 1955, 128. For more on the New Era design, see Wilson, *Livable Modernism*, 76–77. There are ads for Heisey in *Ebony*, December 1952, 61; *Ebony*, May 1953, 8.

46. Halsey, *Ladies' Home Journal Book*, 77.

47. For a comprehensive history of AAA, see Seaton and Myers, eds., *Art for Every Home*. The content in this section is indebted to my own essay in that publication, which was originally published with the title "'Ceramic Pieces in the Mode of Our Day': Stonelain and Decorative Taste in the American Home, 1950–54."

48. "Available now to our patrons before public presentation," AAA product pamphlet (New York: Associated American Artists, summer 1950), n.p. [1].

49. "With Stonelain in your department you hold a winning sales hand!" AAA retailers' manual (New York: Associated American Artists, 1950), 3. Reel D256, frame 308. Associated American Artists records, circa 1934–1981. Archives of American Art, Smithsonian Institution (hereafter Associated American Artists Papers, AAA-SI).

50. Advertisement for Hudson's department store, *Detroit News*, October 8, 1950. Reel D256, frame 259. Associated American Artists Papers, AAA-SI.

51. Advertisement for Rich's department store, *Atlanta Journal and Constitution*, September 17, 1950. Reel D256, frame 261. Associated American Artists Papers, AAA-SI.

52. "And now we bring you the unprecedented opportunity ..." AAA product pamphlet (New York: Associated American Artists, 1950), n.p. [4].

53. My thanks to Ellen Denker for explaining the technical aspects of de Diego's ceramic construction.

54. "Fall 1951 Collection: Stonelain," AAA press release, July 1951, 2. Reel D256, frame 328. Associated American Artists Papers. AAA-SI.

55. "Ceramics Marked by Note of Whimsy," *New York Times*, August 23, 1951, 19.

56. "Stonelain Fall Ceramics," *Retailing Daily*, August 27, 1951. Reel D256, frame 326. Associated American Artists Papers. AAA-SI.

57. Advertisement for Hudson's, Reel D256, frame 259. Associated American Artists Papers, AAA-SI; advertisement for Kent-Coffey Manufacturing Company, *Better Homes and Gardens*, April 1955, 149; advertisement for Mengel Furniture Company, *American Home*, October 1953; advertisement for Heywood-Wakefield Furniture, *House and Garden*, April 1954. For additional examples of the use of "simplicity," and arguments for functionality, see "Furniture Designer," *Ebony*, February 1951, 73; "Paul Williams Builds His Ideal Home," *Ebony*, September 1953, 48.

58. Advertisement for Selig Manufacturing Company, *House and*

Garden, May 1954, 192; advertisement for Melmac, *House and Garden*, May 1954; advertisement for Harker Pottery Company, *House and Garden*, May 1954, 175.

59. Castle, "I'll Take My Modern in Moderation," 325.

60. "The American Marriage of Elegance and Easy Upkeep," *House Beautiful*, December 1950, 142–45.

61. *Spiegel Catalogue* (Chicago: Spiegel, 1955), 124.

62. Harris, *Little White Houses*, esp. chapters 1 and 3.

63. See Sullivan, *Revealing Whiteness*; Dyer, *White*; Alcoff, *The Future of Whiteness*.

64. Robert Bogdan, *Freak Show: Presenting Human Oddities for Amusement and Profit* (Chicago: University of Chicago Press, 1990), 192–95. For an additional photo of the Ringling Brothers 1930 circus performance, see Joe Nickell, *Secrets of the Sideshows* (Lexington: University Press of Kentucky, 2005), 189–90.

65. There are three posters showing lip-extended figures from 1960 to 1965 in Randy Johnson et al., *Freaks, Geeks, and Strange Girls: Sideshow Banners of the Great American Midway* (Honolulu, HI: Hardy Marks, 1996), 72, 110, 127.

66. A rockabilly song titled "Ubangi Stomp" was written by Charles Underwood and first recorded in 1956 by Warren Smith. The lyrics narrate a trip through "Africa" where the singer sees "natives" doing an "odd" dance that is called "the Ubangi Stomp." It has become a standard rockabilly song, covered by many recording artists over the past sixty years.

67. "And now we bring you," AAA product pamphlet, n.p. [13].

68. Harris discusses the prevalence of Black lawn jockeys on White suburban lawns in *Little White Houses*, 298–302.

69. See, e.g., advertisement for Walker's DeLuxe Bourbon, *Ebony*, November 1951, 14; and *Life*, November 5, 1951, 140.

70. For discussion of the construction and presentation of the concept of self in Abstract Expressionist painting, see Leja, *Reframing Abstract Expressionism*; and Gibson, *Abstract Expressionism*.

71. See, e.g., the four men profiled in "Catalogue: Signed Original Etchings," AAA product catalogue (New York: Associated American Artists, 1939), 60.

72. "And now we bring you," AAA product pamphlet, n.p. [5].

73. Gillies also authored *Popular Home Decorating* (New York: Wise, 1940); and *McCall's Book of Modern Houses* (New York: Simon and Schuster, 1951, 1959). She originally published *All about Modern Decorating* in 1942, then published a revised and enlarged version (quoted here) in 1948. Under the auspices of McCall's, in the late 1940s she pioneered a plan in Philadelphia to repurpose abutting fenced-in yards for collective use as children's play spaces and community gardens called "Yardville." The "Yardville Project" eventually spread to more than three hundred cities in the United States. See *McCall's Book of Modern Houses*, 193; and Department of State, "Air Bulletin," 3, no. 47 (July 12, 1949): 8–9.

74. Gillies, *All about Modern Decorating*, 141.

75. Ibid., 142.

76. Halsey, *Ladies' Home Journal Book*, 123. Halsey authored additional volumes under this title in 1957 and 1959.

77. Elizabeth Tower was the third wife of Richard Townley Haines Halsey and was thirty-nine years his junior. She was twenty-one when she collaborated with him on the book that explained the history of the American Wing in depth, *The Homes of Our Ancestors* (Garden City, NY: Doubleday, Page, 1925). For a thoughtful discussion of the intellectual origins of the American Wing and the anti-immigration, pro-White nationalism of the 1920s, see Wendy Kaplan, "R.T.H. Halsey: An Ideology of Collecting American Decorative Arts," *Winterthur Portfolio* 17, no. 1 (Spring 1982): 43–53. See also "Elizabeth Tower Halsey, Educator on Euthanasia, 72," *New York Times*, April 9, 1976.

78. Halsey, *Ladies' Home Journal Book*, 123.

79. Mary Brandt, *How to Plan Your Living Room* (New York: Greenberg, 1955), 69.

80. Russel Lynes, *Snobs* (1950; reprint, New York: HarperCollins, 2008), 36–37.

81. Halsey, *Ladies' Home Journal Book*, 123, 124.

82. Gillies, *All about Modern Decorating*, 142.

83. Walter Adams, "No Body Too Poor to Buy a Masterpiece," *Better Homes and Gardens*, December 1945, 33.

84. Advertisement for Schlitz beer, *Life*, April 3, 1950, 60; "Modern Living: A Carport Converted," *Life*, October 4, 1954, 52–53.

85. Brandt, *DYH*, 185.

86. Brandt, *Living Room*, 69.

87. Brandt, *DYH*, 220.

88. "Around Associated American Artists they still tell the story that Luigi Lubioni couldn't pick out his original water color, 'Sunlit Patterns,' from the gelatones of it. And that Raphael Soyer was so certain that a gelatone of his 'Modern Tempo' was the original pastel that he rubbed it and then examined his finger tips for chalk marks." Adams, "No Body Too Poor," 62.

89. See Artifax brochure and clipping, "Packaging Makes the Picture," *Business Week*, December 3, 1949, Folder 10412: Scrapbook 4, 1947–54 III, George Nelson Papers, Archives and Library, Vitra Design Museum, Weil-am-Rhein, Germany.

90. Advertisement for The Heritage Club, *Life*, June 6, 1955, 7.

91. Halsey, *Ladies' Home Journal Book*, 123.

92. Brandt, *DYH*, 220.

93. Advertisement for *Life* magazine, *Life*, April 7, 1958, 114–15.

94. *Life* ran many articles with full-color art illustrations that seem ready for clipping. A very brief list includes "The Sad Men [Stephen Greene]," *Life*, October 23, 1950, 64ff.; "Raoul Dufy in America," *Life*, January 22, 1951, 62ff.; "The Artists Look at U.S. Industry," *Life*, January 5, 1953, 78ff.; and "Painter of Protest Turns to Reflection: Ben Shahn," *Life*, October 4, 1954, 96ff.

95. Gillies, *All about Modern Decorating*, 141.

96. Halsey, *Ladies' Home Journal Book*, 125.

97. Quotes are from Gillies, *All about Modern Decorating*, 145 and Halsey, *Ladies' Home Journal Book*, 126, alternating.

98. Brandt, *Living Room*, 70. Brandt also provided advice about hanging pictures in her *DYH* that closely mirrors the directives of Halsey and Gillies: "Small pictures can be grouped and arranged over a sofa, desk or table, as an integral part of the furniture, providing the grouping forms a definite block pattern. Don't ever stagger pictures along a wall." Also: "In hanging a group of small pictures of different sizes (but, we hope, of related interest), it is best to keep the lower edges of the frames at the same level. Grouped in this manner, small pictures which would look silly individually achieve a lovely pattern and an attractive decorative effect." Brandt, *DYH*, 189.

99. Halsey, *Ladies' Home Journal Book*, 125.

100. Lux's *Pacing Mustang* was featured on the cover of a preview catalogue of the Stonelain line: "Available now to our Patrons Before Public Presentation: Original Creations from the Ceramic Collection," AAA product catalogue (New York: Associated American Artists, c. 1950), cover and 4.

101. Advertisement for Magnavox, *Life*, February 2, 1952, 45.

102. Advertisement for GE TV, *Life*, December 6, 1954, 24.

103. Advertisement for Zenith TV, *Life*, November 27, 1950, 17.

104. See Harvey, *The Fifties*; Keats, *Crack in the Picture Window*, 70; and Lynn Spigel, *Make Room for TV: Television and the Family Ideal in Postwar America* (Chicago: University of Chicago Press, 1992).

105. "Catalogue of Signed Original Etchings and Lithographs by Leading American Artists," AAA product catalogue (New York: Associated American Artists, 1946), 27.

106. "It's no great trick to find a *single* picture that has the proper spark and quality—but it's very difficult to secure two pictures by the same artist dealing with related subjects … with related color harmony … of the same size and shape … where both are equally satisfying. After much search we *did* succeed in finding these three pairs of magnificent paintings by three great artists—paintings which fill every creative art requirement … as well as the home decorating need for pictures 'in twos' that can be used as balancing units." "Associated American Artists Present a New Idea in Full Color Paintings That Answers an Important Picture Problem," AAA product pamphlet (New York: Associated American Artists, c. 1950).

107. Gillies, *All about Modern Decorating*, 143.

108. Brandt, *DYH*, 195.

109. Ibid., 219.

110. Keats, *Crack in the Picture Window*, 58. He further describes these houses: "Each Rolling Knolls

home, decorated by a female do-it-yourself on advice from television, magazines and the Sunday papers, came in time to sport the same trivet on the wall, the same cardboard mobile, the same TV hassocks, the same plastic primitive bookends." Ibid., 80.

111. Wolfe, "Ecstatic in Blackface," 53.

112. Clifford, *Predicament of Culture*, 222–26.

113. "Rich Surprises in Africa," *Life*, December 1, 1958, 88ff. Also, the article on Queen Elizabeth's assumption of the crown of England, which happened during a trip to Kenya, includes eight different photographs of Africans, wearing tribal outfits, and Indians, dressed traditionally, to celebrate her coronation. See "Elizabeth Goes as a Princess, Returns as a Queen," *Life*, February 18, 1952, 28ff.

114. Halle, *Inside Culture*, 157.

115. "Portrait Backgrounds: Decorator chooses settings to match five types of women," *Life*, May 5, 1952, 150–51.

116. "A Prime Accumulation of Primitive Art," *Life*, May 6, 1957, 119. See also "Speaking of Pictures: Candid artists in old Africa," *Life*, November 3, 1958, 10–11; and the incongruous appearance of an African statuette in a silhouette photograph of an amaryllis in "Foolproof Indoors: New method helps home gardens," *Life*, December 7, 1959, 114–15.

117. Clifford, *Predicament of Culture*, 224.

118. "Voodoo Goes to College: Classes in primitive dance highly popular with students at Chicago's Roosevelt College," *Ebony*, July 1952, 78.

119. "New York Says Tsk Tsk at African Attire," *Life*, March 2, 1959, 78.

120. "African Ballet Upsets New York: Authentic African dance troupe, pounds drums, bares breasts, and unnerves police," *Ebony*, May 1959, 37.

121. Locke, "The Legacy of the Ancestral Arts," 256. Although Palmer Hayden did not entirely agree with Locke, an example of an interior that includes African art from the prewar period is Palmer Hayden's *Fêtiche et fleurs* (c. 1931–32; Museum of African American Art, Los Angeles).

122. The photograph is attributed to Neufeld, Globe Photos.

123. "African Mask Maker: Brooklyn artist Perry Fuller successfully produces and sells primitive sculpture," *Ebony*, December 1952, 71.

124. Ibid., 75.

125. "Pearl Primus: Foremost dancer to unveil new, exciting work based on year-long study of African peoples," *Ebony*, January 1951, 54, 57. Primus ultimately earned her doctorate in anthropology from New York University in 1978. Jennifer Dunning, "Pearl Primus Is Dead at 74; A Pioneer of Modern Dance," *New York Times*, October 31, 1994.

126. "Pearl Primus: Foremost dancer," 56.

127. "Life of a Wealthy Wife: Successful business woman finds her niche: at home," *Ebony*, April 1957, 65, 70.

128. Brandt, *DYH*, 219.

129. Moneta Sleet, Jr. would become one of the most famous photographers working at *Ebony*, known for his generation-defining images of civil rights protests and winning a Pulitzer Prize for his photograph of Martin Luther King, Jr.'s widow. For a good overview of his career and relationship to contemporary art, see Smith, "Moneta Sleet, Jr. as Active Participant."

130. "Bongo Party: Wild drum music is new fad at swank Hollywood parties," *Ebony*, March 1957, 78.

131. Dyer, *White*, 12.

Epilogue

1. "Company Timeline," https://www.hermanmiller.com/about/timeline/, accessed January 5, 2019.

2. "DWR: Our Mission, Our History," https://www.dwr.com/about-us.html?lang=en_US, accessed January 5, 2019.

3. Atomic Ranch began publication in spring 2004. See "Meet Atomic Ranch's New Logo," https://www.atomic-ranch.com/architecture-design/preservation-corner/atomic-ranch-new-logo/, accessed January 5, 2019.

4. For scholarly essays on *Mad Men*, see Scott F. Stoddard, ed., *Analyzing Mad Men: Critical Essays on the Television Series* (Jefferson, NC: McFarland, 2011); and "Mad 'Men' and the Visual Culture of the Long Sixties," a panel at College Art Association, 2013.

5. "Company Timeline," https://www
.hermanmiller.com/about/timeline/,
accessed January 5, 2019.

6. Among the brands I discussed were
J. Crew and Seven for All Mankind
Jeans. "Banana Republic, Norman
Rockwell, and Mid-century Modern:
Fashioning Rebellion." Outside the
Frame: Kendall College of Art and
Design Colloquium, Grand Rapids, MI,
October 2008.

7. Among national retailers, look at
CB2, a subdivision of Crate and Barrel;
West Elm, a subdivision of Williams
Sonoma; Room and Board; and
Restoration Hardware.

8. On the Colonial Revival, see Karal
Ann Marling, *George Washington Slept
Here: Colonial Revivals and American
Culture, 1876–1986* (Cambridge,
MA: Harvard University Press, 1988);
Thomas Denenberg, *Wallace Nutting
and the Invention of Old America*
(New Haven, CT: Yale University Press,
2003); Wilson, *Livable Modernism*;
Richard Guy Wilson et al., eds., *Re-
creating the American Past: Essays on
the Colonial Revival* (Charlottesville:
University of Virginia Press, 2006);
Abigail Carroll, "Of Kettles and Cranes:
Colonial Revival Kitchens and the
Performance of National Identity,"
Winterthur Portfolio 43, no. 4 (Winter
2009): 335–64.

9. See the video at https://youtu.be
/i3zl8Jdgv7I, accessed December 20,
2019. My thanks to Autumn Perez for
directing me to this.

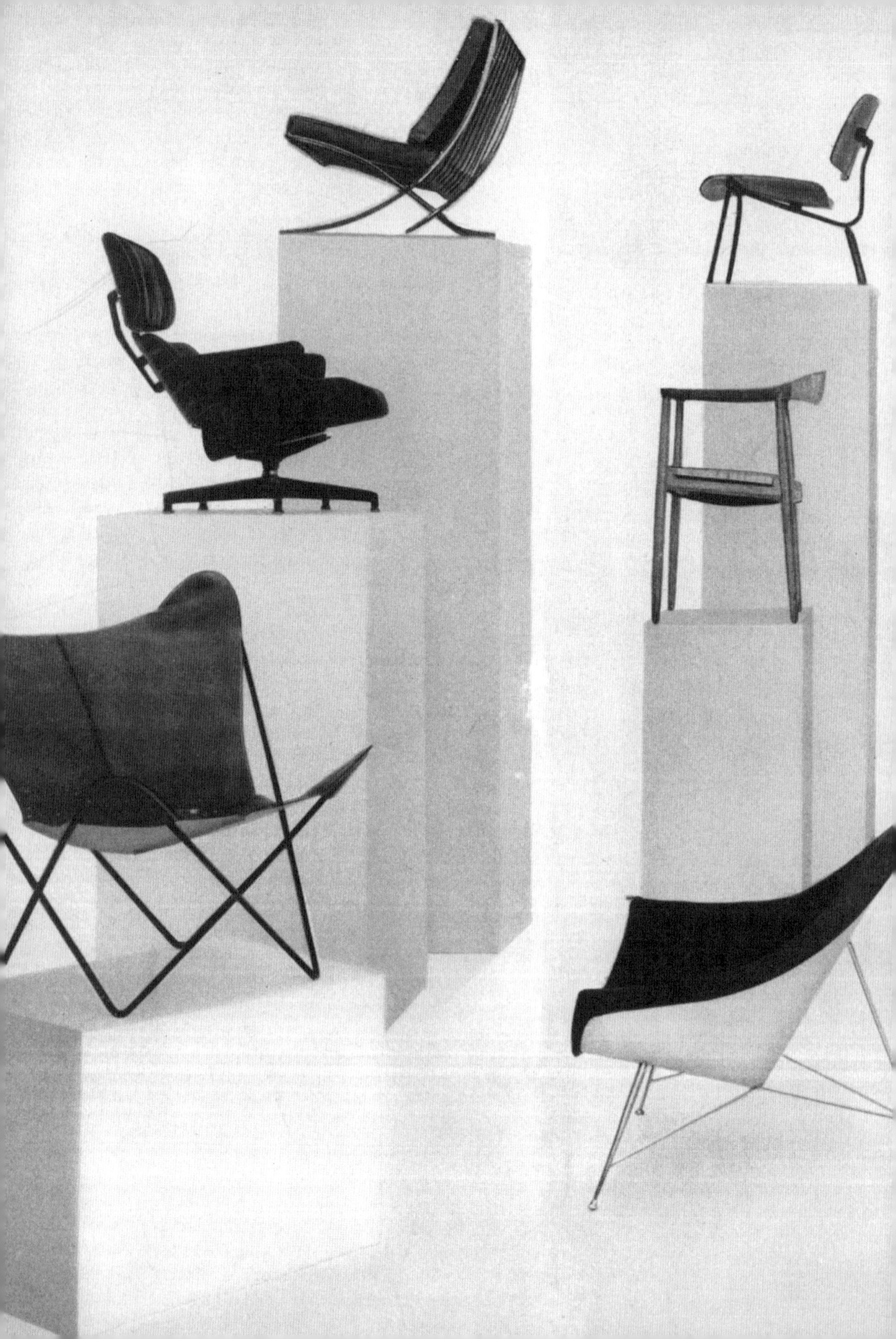

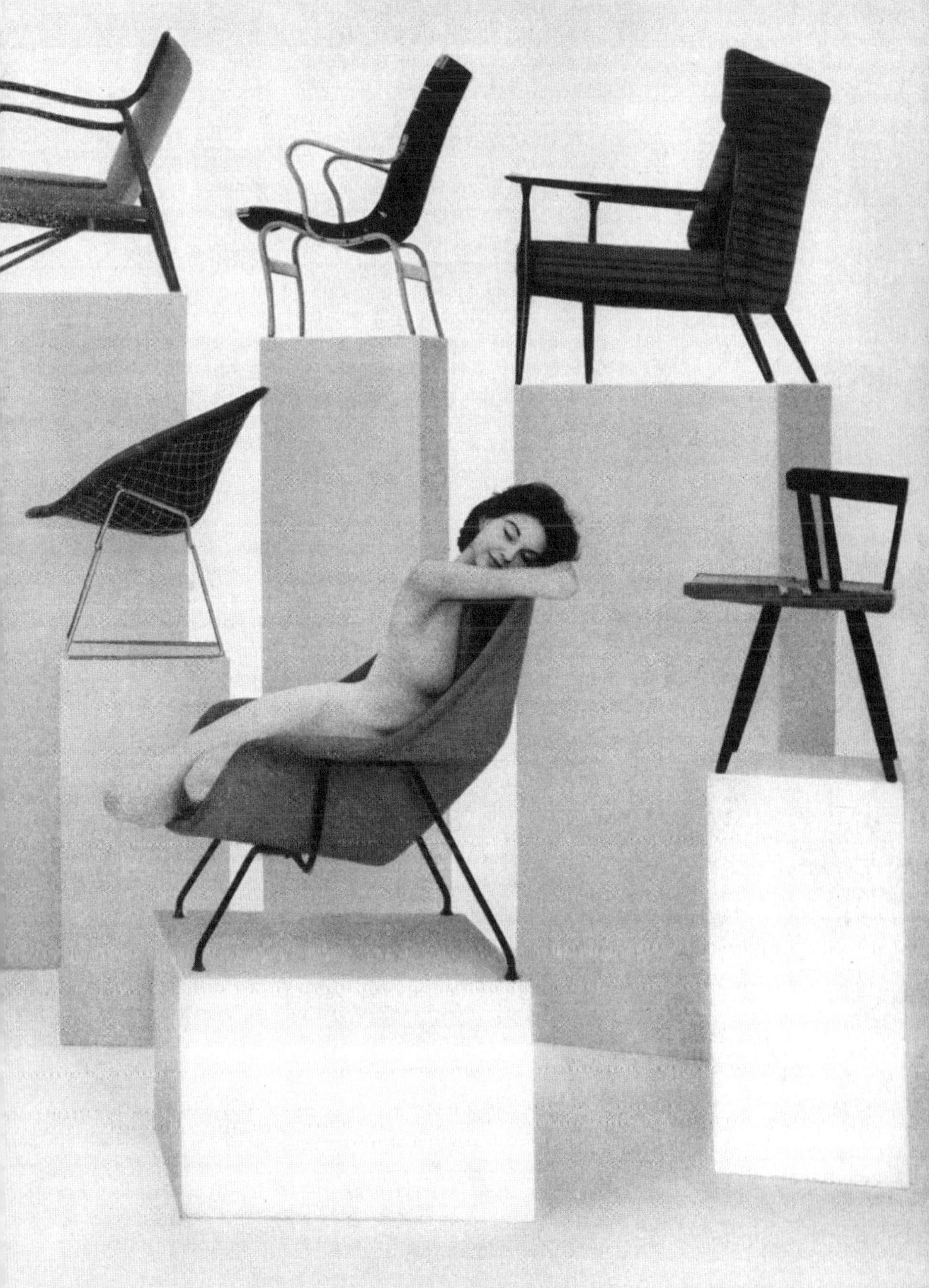

Bibliography

Archival Collections Consulted

Associated American Artists Papers, AAA-SI
Associated American Artists records, circa 1934–1981. Archives of American Art, Smithsonian Institution.

Brandt Papers
Mary L. Brandt Home Furnishings Training Course Materials, circa 1946, 1953. New School for Social Research Archives Collection, New York, New York.

Diamond Collection
Freda Diamond Collection 1945–1984, Archives Center, National Museum of American History.

HMI
Corporate Archives, Herman Miller International, Zeeland, Michigan.

Nelson/Vitra
George Nelson Papers, Archives and Library, Vitra Design Museum, Weil-am-Rhein, Germany.

Whitney Foundation Papers
John Hay Whitney Foundation Papers, MS 1952, Manuscripts and Archives, Yale University Library.

Wright Papers
Russel Wright Papers, Department of Special Collections, Syracuse University Library, Syracuse, New York.

Published Sources

Abercrombie, Stanley. *George Nelson: The Design of Modern Design.* Cambridge, MA: MIT Press, 1995.

Albrecht, Donald, ed. *Designing Home: Jews and Midcentury Modernism.* San Francisco: Contemporary Jewish Museum, 2014.

———. *The Work of Charles and Ray Eames: A Legacy of Invention.* New York: Harry N. Abrams, 1997.

Albrecht, Donald, et al. *Russel Wright: Creating American Lifestyle.* New York: Cooper Hewitt National Design Museum and Harry N. Abrams, 2001.

Alcoff, Linda Martín. *The Future of Whiteness.* New York: Polity, 2015.

Almquist, Julka, and Julia Lupton. "Affording Meaning: Design-Oriented Research from the Humanities and Social Sciences." *Design Issues* 26, no. 1 (Winter 2010): 3–14.

Archer, John. *Architecture and Suburbia.* Minneapolis: University of Minnesota Press, 2005.

Barthes, Roland. *Mythologies.* Translated by Annette Lavers. New York: Hill and Wang, 1972.

Baxandall, Rosalyn, and Elizabeth Ewen. *Picture Windows: How the Suburbs Happened.* New York: Basic Books, 2000.

Berger, Bennett M. *Working-Class Suburb: A Study of Auto Workers in Suburbia.* Berkeley: University of California Press, 1960.

Berger, Martin. *Seeing through Race: A Reinterpretation of Civil Rights Photography.* Berkeley: University of California Press, 2011.

———. *Sight Unseen: Whiteness and American Visual Culture.* Berkeley: University of California Press, 2005.

Berger, Maurice. *Revolution of the Eye: Modern Art and the Birth of American Television.* New York: Jewish Museum; New Haven, CT: Yale University Press, 2014.

Berkman, Dave. "Advertising in 'Ebony' and 'Life': Negro Aspirations vs. Reality." *Journalism Quarterly* 40, no. 1 (1963): 53–64.

Bhabha, Homi K. *The Location of Culture.* New York: Routledge, 2004.

Blaszczyk, Regina Lee. *American Consumer Society, 1865–2005: From Hearth to HDTV.* Wheeling, IL: Harlan Davidson, 2009.

———. *The Color Revolution.* Cambridge, MA: MIT Press, 2012.

———. *Imagining Consumers: Design and Innovation from Wedgewood to Corning.* Baltimore: Johns Hopkins University Press, 2000.

———. "The Wright Way for Glass: Russel Wright and the Business of Industrial Design." *The Acorn: Journal of the Sandwich Glass Museum* 4 (1993): 3–22.

Blumer, Herbert. "Race Prejudice as a Sense of Group Position." *Pacific Sociological Review* 1, no. 1 (Spring 1958): 3–7.

Brandt, Mary L. *Decorate Your Home for Better Living.* New York: Charles Scribner's Sons, 1950.

Brossard, Chandler, ed. *The Scene before You: A New Approach to American Culture.* New York: Rinehart, 1955.

Burns, Ben. *Nitty Gritty: A White Editor in Black Journalism.* Jackson: University Press of Mississippi, 1996.

Castillo, Greg. *Cold War on the Home Front: The Soft Power of Midcentury Design.* Minneapolis: University of Minnesota Press, 2010.

Castle, Marian. "I'll Take My Modern in Moderation." *Better Homes and Gardens* 30, no. 4 (April 1952): 6ff.

Chambers, Jason. *Madison Avenue and the Color Line: African Americans in the Advertising Industry.* Philadelphia: University of Pennsylvania Press, 2008.

———. "Presenting the Black Middle Class: John H. Johnson and *Ebony* Magazine, 1945–1974." In *Historicizing Lifestyle: Mediating Taste, Consumption and Identity from the 1900s to 1970s*, edited by David Bell and Joanne Hollows, 54–69. London: Ashgate, 2006.

Cheng, Irene, Charles L. Davis II, and Mabel O. Wilson, eds. *Race and Modern Architecture: A Critical History from the Enlightenment to the Present.* Pittsburgh: University of Pittsburgh Press, 2020.

Clarke, Alison J. *Tupperware: The Promise of Plastic in 1950s America.* Washington, DC: Smithsonian Institute Press, 1999.

Clifford, James. *The Predicament of Culture: Twentieth-Century Ethnography, Literature, and Art.* Cambridge, MA: Harvard University Press, 1988.

Cohen, Lizabeth. *A Consumers' Republic: The Politics of Mass Consumption in Postwar America.* New York: Vintage, 2003.

———. "A Middle-Class Utopia? The Suburban Home in the 1950s." In *Making Choices: A New Perspective on the History of Domestic Life in Illinois*, edited by Janice Tauer Wass, 58–67. Springfield: Illinois State Museum, 1995.

Collins, Bradford R. "*Life* Magazine and the Abstract Expressionists, 1948–51: A Historiographic Study of a Late Bohemian Enterprise." *Art Bulletin* 73, no. 2 (June 1991): 283–308.

Colomina, Beatriz. *Domesticity at War.* Cambridge, MA: MIT Press, 2007.

Craven, David. "Abstract Expressionism and Third World Art: A Post Colonial Approach to 'American' Art." *Oxford Art Journal* 14, no. 1 (1991): 44–66.

Crenshaw, Kimberlé, Neil Gotanda, Gary Peller, and Kendall Thomas, eds. *Critical Race Theory: The Key Writings That Informed the Movement.* New York: New Press, 1995.

Delgado, Richard, and Jean Stefancic, eds. *Critical Race Theory: The Cutting Edge.* 3rd ed. Philadelphia: Temple University Press, 2013.

DePree, Hugh. *Business as Unusual: The People and Principles at Herman Miller.* Zeeland, MI: Herman Miller, 1986.

Dobriner, William M. *Class in Suburbia.* New York: Prentice Hall, 1963.

Doss, Erika. "Catering to Consumerism: Associated American Artists and the Marketing of Modern Art, 1934–1958." *Winterthur Portfolio* 26, nos. 2/3 (Summer–Autumn 1991): 143–67.

———, ed. *Looking at Life Magazine.* Washington, DC: Smithsonian Institution Press, 2001.

Dyer, Richard. *White.* New York: Routledge, 1997.

Dyson, Michael Eric. *Reflecting Black: African American Cultural Criticism.* Minneapolis: University of Minnesota Press, 1993.

Eidelberg, Martin, et al. *The Eames Lounge Chair: An Icon of Modern Design.* Grand Rapids, MI: Grand Rapids Art Museum in association with Merrell, 2006.

Eisenbrand, Jochen, ed. *George Nelson: Architect, Writer, Designer, Teacher.* Weil am Rhein: Vitra Design Museum, 2008.

Fanon, Franz. *Black Skin, White Masks.* 1952. Translated by Richard Philcox. New York: Grove, 2008.

Felt, Tom. "Freda Diamond and the Libbey Glass Company: Advertisements, Catalog Reprints, Trade Journal and Newspaper Reports. Monograph No. 93." Weston: West Virginia Museum of American Glass, 2010.

Fine, Ruth, ed. *Procession: The Art of Norman Lewis.* Philadelphia: Pennsylvania Academy of the Fine Arts; Berkeley: University of California Press, 2015.

Fiske, John. *Media Matters: Race and Gender in U.S. Politics.* 2nd ed. New York: Routledge, 2016.

Frankenberg, Ruth. *The Social Construction of Whiteness: White Women, Race Matters.* Minneapolis: University of Minnesota Press, 1993.

Fraterrigo, Elizabeth. *Playboy and the Making of the Good Life in Modern America.* Oxford: Oxford University Press, 2009.

Frazier, E. Franklin. *Black Bourgeoisie.* New York: Free Press, 1957.

———. *The Negro Family in the United States.* Rev. ed. Chicago: University of Chicago Press, 1966.

Friedan, Betty. *The Feminine Mystique.* Edited by Kirsten Fermaglich and Lisa M. Fine. 1963. Reprint, New York: Norton Critical Edition, 2013.

Garnett, David. "Paul Revere Williams: Innovator, Achiever, Architect." In *Looking beneath the Surface: Discovering Third World Architects and Artists and Their Works,* 44–70. Berkeley: College of Environmental Design, 1991.

Gibson, Ann Eden. *Abstract Expressionism: Other Politics.* New Haven, CT: Yale University Press, 1997.

Gibson, James J. *The Ecological Approach to Visual Perception.* Boston: Houghton Mifflin Company, 1979.

Gillies, Mary Davis. *All about Modern Decorating.* Rev. ed. New York: Harper and Brothers, 1948.

Godfrey, Mark, and Zoé Whitley, eds. *Soul of a Nation: Art in the Age of Black Power.* New York: D.A.P. and Tate Publishing, 2017.

Green, Adam. *Selling the Race: Culture, Community, and Black Chicago, 1940–1955.* Chicago: University of Chicago Press, 2007.

Greer, Brenna Wynn. *Represented: The Black Imagemakers Who Reimagined African American Citizenship.* Philadelphia: University of Pennsylvania Press, 2019.

Guffey, Elizabeth. *Designing Disability: Symbols, Space, and Society.* New York: Bloomsbury, 2018.

Halle, David. *Inside Culture: Art and Class in the American Home.* Chicago: University of Chicago Press, 1993.

Halpern, Richard. *Norman Rockwell: The Underside of Innocence.* Chicago: University of Chicago Press, 2006.

Halsey, Elizabeth T. *Ladies' Home Journal Book of Interior Decoration.* Philadelphia: Curtis Publishing; Garden City, NY: Doubleday, 1954.

Harris, Dianne. *Little White Houses: How the Postwar Home Constructed Race in America.* Minneapolis: University of Minnesota Press, 2013.

———. "Making Your Private World: Modern Landscape Architecture and House Beautiful, 1945–1965." In *The Architecture of Landscape, 1940–1960,* edited by Marc Treib, 180–205. Philadelphia: University of Pennsylvania Press, 2002.

———, ed. *Second Suburb: Levittown, Pennsylvania.* Pittsburgh: University of Pittsburgh Press, 2010.

Harvey, Brett. *The Fifties: A Women's Oral History.* New York: Harper Collins, 1993.

Havenhand, Lucinda Kaukas. *Mid-Century Modern Interiors: The Ideas That Shaped Interior Design in America.* London: Bloomsbury, 2019.

Henderson, Harry. "The Mass-Produced Suburbs, Part I." *Harper's* 207 (November 1953): 25–32.

———. "Rugged American Collectivism: The Mass-Produced Suburbs, Part II." *Harper's* 207 (December 1953): 80–86.

Henderson, Wesley Howard. "Two Case Studies of African-American Architects' Careers in Los Angeles, 1895–1945: Paul R. Williams, FAIA and James H. Garrott, AIA." PhD diss., University of California, Los Angeles, 1992.

Henthorn, Cynthia Lee. *From Suburbs to Submarines: Selling a Better America, 1939–1959*. Athens: Ohio University Press, 2006.

Hine, Thomas. *Populuxe*. New York: Overlook Press, 1986.

Holloway, Camara Dia. "Critical Race Art History." *Art Journal* 75, no. 1 (Spring 2016): 89–92.

Hudson, Karen E. *Paul R. Williams, Architect: A Legacy of Style*. New York: Rizzoli, 1993.

Huppatz, D. J. "Creative Living, Ecological Design and Russel Wright's Manitoga." *Journal of Design History* 25, no. 4 (2012): 363–78.

Ingersoll, Joanne, ed. *Cocktail Culture: Ritual and Invention in American Fashion, 1920–1980*. Providence, RI: RISD Museum, 2011.

Isenstadt, Sandy. *The Modern American House: Spaciousness and Middle Class Identity*. Cambridge: Cambridge University Press, 2006.

———. "Visions of Plenty: Refrigerators in America around 1950." *Journal of Design History* 11, no. 4 (1998): 311–21.

Jachec, Nancy. *The Philosophy and Politics of Abstract Expressionism, 1940–1960*. Cambridge: Cambridge University Press, 2000.

Jackson, Kenneth T. *Crabgrass Frontier: The Suburbanization of the United States*. New York: Oxford University Press, 1985.

Jacobs, James A. "Social and Spatial Change in the Postwar Family Room." *Perspectives in Vernacular Architecture* 13, no. 1 (2006): 70–85.

Johnson, John H., with Lerone Bennett, Jr. *Succeeding against the Odds*. New York: Warner Books, 1989.

Jones, Kellie, ed. *Now Dig This! Art and Black Los Angeles*. Los Angeles: Hammer Museum, UCLA, and Prestel, 2011.

Kaplan, Wendy, ed. *Living in a Modern Way: California Design 1930–1965*. Los Angeles: LACMA; Cambridge, MA: MIT Press, 2011.

Keats, John. *The Crack in the Picture Window*. New York: Ballantine, 1956.

Kennedy, Robert Woods. *The House and the Art of Its Design*. New York: Reinhold, 1953.

Kirkham, Pat. *Charles and Ray Eames: Designers of the Twentieth Century*. Cambridge, MA: MIT Press, 1995.

———, ed. *Women Designers in the USA, 1900–2000: Diversity and Difference*. New York: Bard Graduate Center; New Haven, CT: Yale University Press, 2000.

Kozol, Wendy. *Life's America*. Philadelphia: Temple University Press, 1994.

Kruse, Kevin M., and Thomas J. Sugrue. *The New Suburban History*. Chicago: University of Chicago Press, 2006.

Lane, Barbara Miller. *Houses for a New World: Builders and Buyers in American Suburbs, 1945–1965*. Princeton, NJ: Princeton University Press, 2015.

Leavitt, Sarah A. *From Catharine Beecher to Martha Stewart: A Cultural History of Domestic Advice*. Chapel Hill: University of North Carolina Press, 2002.

Lees-Maffei, Grace. *Design at Home: Domestic Advice Books in Britain and the USA since 1945*. New York: Routledge, 2014.

Leja, Michael. *Reframing Abstract Expressionism: Subjectivity and Painting in the 1940s*. New Haven, CT: Yale University Press, 1993.

Leslie, Michael. "Slow Fade to … ? Advertising in *Ebony* Magazine, 1957–1989." *Journalism and Mass Communication Quarterly* 72, no. 2 (Summer 1995): 426–35.

Lipsitz, George. *How Racism Takes Place*. Philadelphia: Temple University Press, 2011.

Locke, Alain. "The Legacy of the Ancestral Arts." In *The New Negro*, edited by Alain Locke, 254–67. New York: Albert and Charles Boni, 1925. Reprint, New York: Touchstone, 1992.

Lutz, Brian. *Eero Saarinen: Furniture for Everyman*. New York: Pointed Leaf Press, 2012.

Lyford, Amy. *Isamu Noguchi's Modernism: Negotiating Race, Labor, and Nation, 1930–1950*. Berkeley: University of California Press, 2013.

Lynes, Russell. *The Tastemakers*. New York: Grosset and Dunlap, 1949.

Makovsky, Paul, and Belinda Lanks. "Nelson and Company: Iconic Workplace, 1947–1986." *Metropolis* 28, no. 11 (June 2009): 90–97.

Manning, Susan. *Modern Dance, Negro Dance: Race in Motion*. Minneapolis: University of Minnesota Press, 2004.

May, Elaine Tyler. *Homeward Bound: American Families in the Cold War Era*. New York: Basic Books, 1988.

May, Lary, ed. *Recasting America: Culture and Politics in the Age of Cold War*. Chicago: University of Chicago Press, 1989.

Meyerowitz, Joanne. "Beyond the Feminine Mystique: A Reassessment of Postwar Mass Culture, 1946–1958." *Journal of American History* 79, no. 4 (March 1993): 1455–82.

Miller, Laura J. "Family Togetherness and the Suburban Ideal." *Sociological Forum* 10, no. 3 (September 1995): 393–418.

Mitchell, W.J.T. *Seeing through Race.* Cambridge, MA: Harvard University Press, 2012.

Morley, David, and Kuan-Hsing Chen, eds. *Stuart Hall: Critical Dialogues in Cultural Studies.* New York: Routledge, 1996.

Nelson, George, ed. *Chairs.* New York: Whitney Publications, 1953. Reprint, New York: Acanthus Press, 1994.

Nelson, George, and Henry Wright. *Tomorrow's House: A Complete Guide for the Home-Builder.* New York: Simon and Schuster, 1945.

Nemerov, Alexander. *Icons of Grief: Val Lewton's Home Front Pictures.* Berkeley: University of California Press, 2005.

Neuhart, Marilyn, with John Neuhart. *The Story of Eames Furniture.* 2 vols. Berlin: Gestalten, 2010.

Nickles, Shelley. "More Is Better: Mass Consumption, Gender, and Class Identity in Postwar America. *American Quarterly* 54, no. 4 (December 2002): 581–622.

Obniski, Monica. "Selling Folk Art and Modern Design: Alexander Girard and Herman Miller's Textiles and Objects Shop (1961–1967)." *Journal of Design History* 28, no. 3 (September 2015): 254–74.

Oehler, Sarah Kelly, and Esther Adler, eds. *Charles White: A Retrospective.* New York: Museum of Modern Art, distributed by Yale University Press, 2018.

Ogata, Amy F. *Designing the Creative Child: Playthings and Places in Midcentury America.* Minneapolis: University of Minnesota Press, 2013.

Ott, John. "Hale Woodruff's Antiprimitivist History of Abstract Art." *Art Bulletin* 100, no. 1 (March 2018): 124–45.

Packard, Vance. *The Status Seekers.* New York: Pocket Books, 1959.

Painter, Nell Irvin. *The History of White People.* New York: W. W. Norton and Company, 2010.

Pattillo-McCoy, Mary. *Black Picket Fences: Privilege and Peril among the Black Middle Class.* Chicago: University of Chicago Press, 1999.

Penick, Monica. *Tastemaker: Elizabeth Gordon, House Beautiful, and the Postwar American Home.* New Haven, CT: Yale University Press, 2017.

Perry, Regenia. "Cultural Identity in African-American Art, 1900–1950." In *Celebration and Vision: The Hewitt Collection of African American Art,* edited by Todd D. Smith, 7–16. Charlotte, NC: Bank of America Corporation, 1999.

Petty, Margaret Maile. "Attitudes towards Modern Living: The Mid-century Showrooms of Herman Miller and Knoll Associates." *Journal of Design History* 29, no. 2 (May 2016): 180–99.

Preciado, Beatriz. "Pornotopia." In *Cold War Hothouses: Inventing Postwar Culture from Cockpit to Playboy,* edited by Beatriz Colomina, Annmarie Brennan, and Jeannie Kim, 216–53. Princeton, NJ: Princeton Architectural Press, 2004.

Raiford, Leigh. *Imprisoned in a Luminous Glare: Photography and the African American Freedom Struggle.* Chapel Hill: University of North Carolina Press, 2011.

Reynolds-Kaye, Jennifer. *Small-Great Objects: Anni and Josef Albers in the Americas.* New Haven, CT: Yale University Art Gallery, distributed by Yale University Press, 2017.

Riesman, David. *The Lonely Crowd.* 1961. Reprint, New Haven, CT: Yale University Press, 2000.

Roediger, David. *Working toward Whiteness: How America's Immigrants Became White.* New York: Basic Books, 2005.

Rothstein, Richard. *The Color of Law: A Forgotten History of How Our Government Segregated America.* New York: Liveright, 2017.

Said, Edward. *Orientalism.* New York: Vintage, 1979.

Schuldenfrei, Robin, ed. *Atomic Dwelling: Anxiety, Domesticity, and Postwar Architecture.* New York: Routledge, 2012.

Schwartzman, Myron. *Romare Bearden: His Life and Art.* New York: Harry N. Abrams, 1990.

Seaton, Elizabeth, and Jane McNamara Myers, eds. *Art for Every Home: Associated American Artists.* Manhattan, KS: Marianna Kistler Beach Museum of Art, Kansas State University; New Haven, CT: Yale University Press, 2015.

Seeley, John R., et al. *Crestwood Heights: A Study of the Culture of Suburban Life.* New York: Basic Books, 1956.

Segal, Eric. "Norman Rockwell and the Fashioning of American Masculinity." *Art Bulletin* 78, no. 4 (December 1996): 633–46.

Seshadri-Crooks, Kalpana. *Desiring Whiteness: A Lacanian Analysis of Race.* New York: Routledge, 2000.

Smith, Cherise. "Moneta Sleet, Jr. as Active Participant: The Selma March and the Black Arts Movement." In *New Thoughts on the Black Arts Movement,* edited by Lisa Gail Collins and Margo Natalie Crawford, 210–26. New Brunswick, NJ: Rutgers University Press, 2006.

Spigel, Lynn. *TV by Design: Modern Art and the Rise of Network Television.* Chicago: University of Chicago Press, 2008.

Stange, Maren. " 'Photographs Taken in Everyday Life': *Ebony's* Photojournalistic Discourse." In *The Black Press: New Literary and Historical Essays,* edited by Todd Vogel, 206–27. New Brunswick, NJ: Rutgers University Press, 2001.

Stein, Sally. "The Graphic Ordering of Desire: Modernization of a Middle-Class Women's Magazine, 1919–1939." In *The Contest of Meaning: Critical Histories of Photography*, edited by Richard Bolton, 145–61. Cambridge, MA: MIT Press, 1989.

Stole, Inger L. "There Is No Place Like Home: NBC's Search for a Daytime Audience 1954–1957." *Communications Review* 2, no. 2 (1997): 135–61.

Sullivan, Shannon. *Revealing Whiteness: The Unconscious Habits of White Privilege*. Bloomington: Indiana University Press, 2006.

Taft, Maggie. "Morphologies and Genealogies: Shaker Furniture and Danish Design." *Design and Culture* 7, no. 3 (November 2015): 313–34.

Treib, Marc, ed. *An Everyday Modernism: The Houses of William Wurster*. Berkeley: University of California Press and SFMOMA, 1995.

Venable, Charles, et al. *China and Glass in America, 1880–1980: From Tabletop to TV Tray*. Dallas: Dallas Museum of Art; New York: Harry N. Abrams, 2000.

Warner, W. Lloyd, et al. *Social Class in America*. New York: Harper & Row, 1960.

Weems, Jason. "War Furniture: Charles and Ray Eames Design for the Wounded Body." *Boom: A Journal of California*. 2, no. 1 (2012): 46–48.

Weems, Robert. *Desegregating the Dollar: African American Consumerism in the Twentieth Century*. New York: New York University Press, 1998.

Whyte, William H. *The Organization Man*. 1956. Reprint, Philadelphia: University of Pennsylvania Press, 2002.

Williams, Paul R. *New Homes for Today*. 1946. Reprint, Santa Monica, CA: Hennessey + Ingalls, 2006.

———. *The Small Home of Tomorrow*. 1945. Reprint, Santa Monica, CA: Hennessey + Ingalls, 2006.

Willis, Deborah, ed. *Picturing Us: African American Identity in Photography*. New York: New Press, 1994.

———. *Reflections in Black: A History of Black Photographers, 1840 to the Present*. New York: Norton, 2000.

Wilson, Kristina. "Like a 'Girl in a Bikini Suit' and Other Stories: The Herman Miller Company, Gender, and Race at Mid-Century." *Journal of Design History* 28, no. 2 (May 2015): 161–81.

———. *Livable Modernism: Interior Decorating and Design during the Great Depression*. New Haven, CT: Yale University Press and Yale University Art Gallery, 2004.

Wolfe, Bernard. "Ecstatic in Blackface: The Negro as a Song-and-Dance Man." In *The Scene before You: A New Approach to American Culture*, edited by Chandler Brossard, 51–70. New York: Rinehart and Co., 1955.

Woodward, C. Van. *The Strange Career of Jim Crow*. 3rd rev. ed. Oxford: Oxford University Press, 1974.

Wright, Mary and Russel. *Guide to Easier Living*. 1950. Reprint, Layton, UT: Gibbs Smith, 2003.

Žižek, Slavoj, ed., *Mapping Ideology*. New York: Verso, 2012.

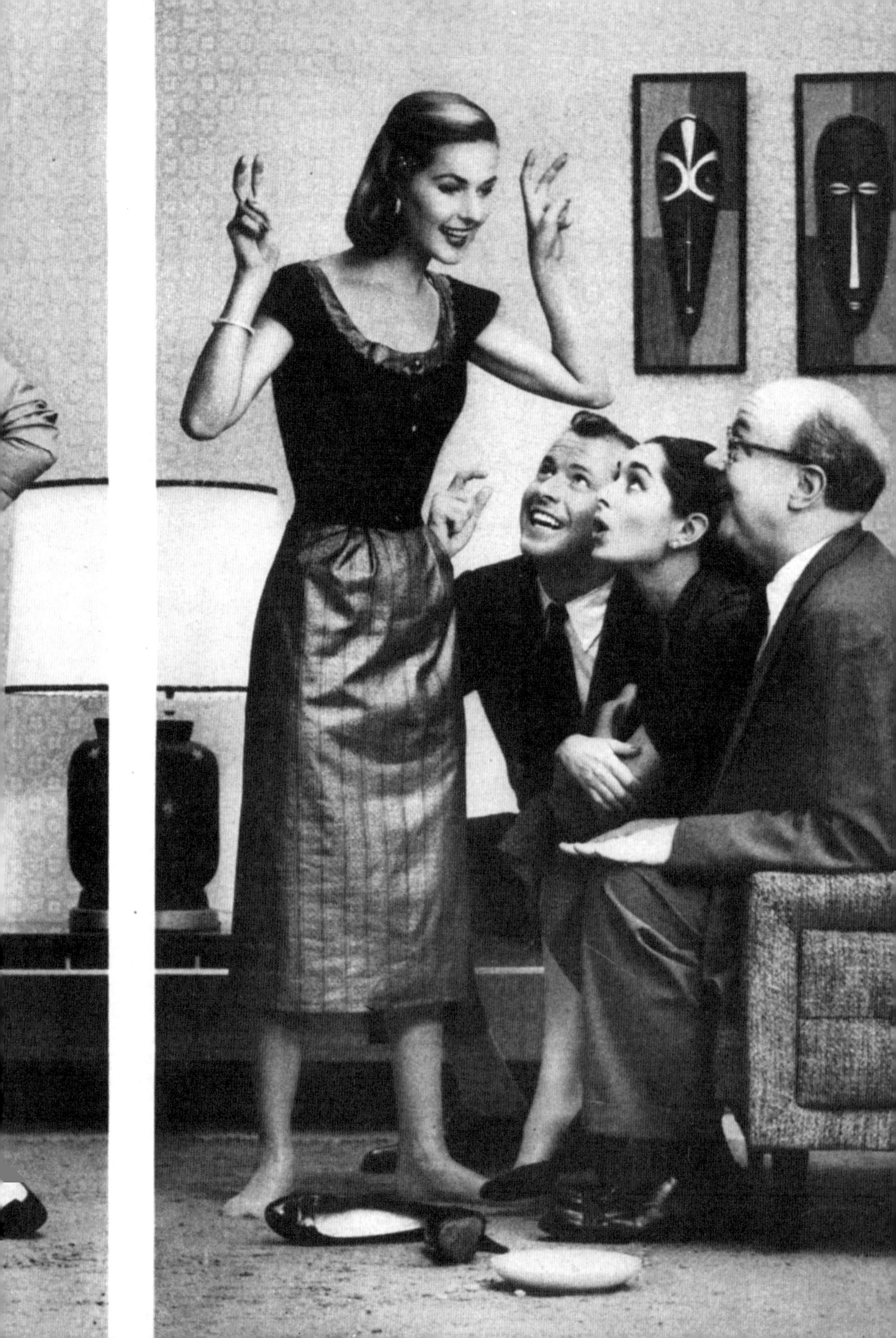

Index

Note: Page numbers in italic type indicate illustrations.

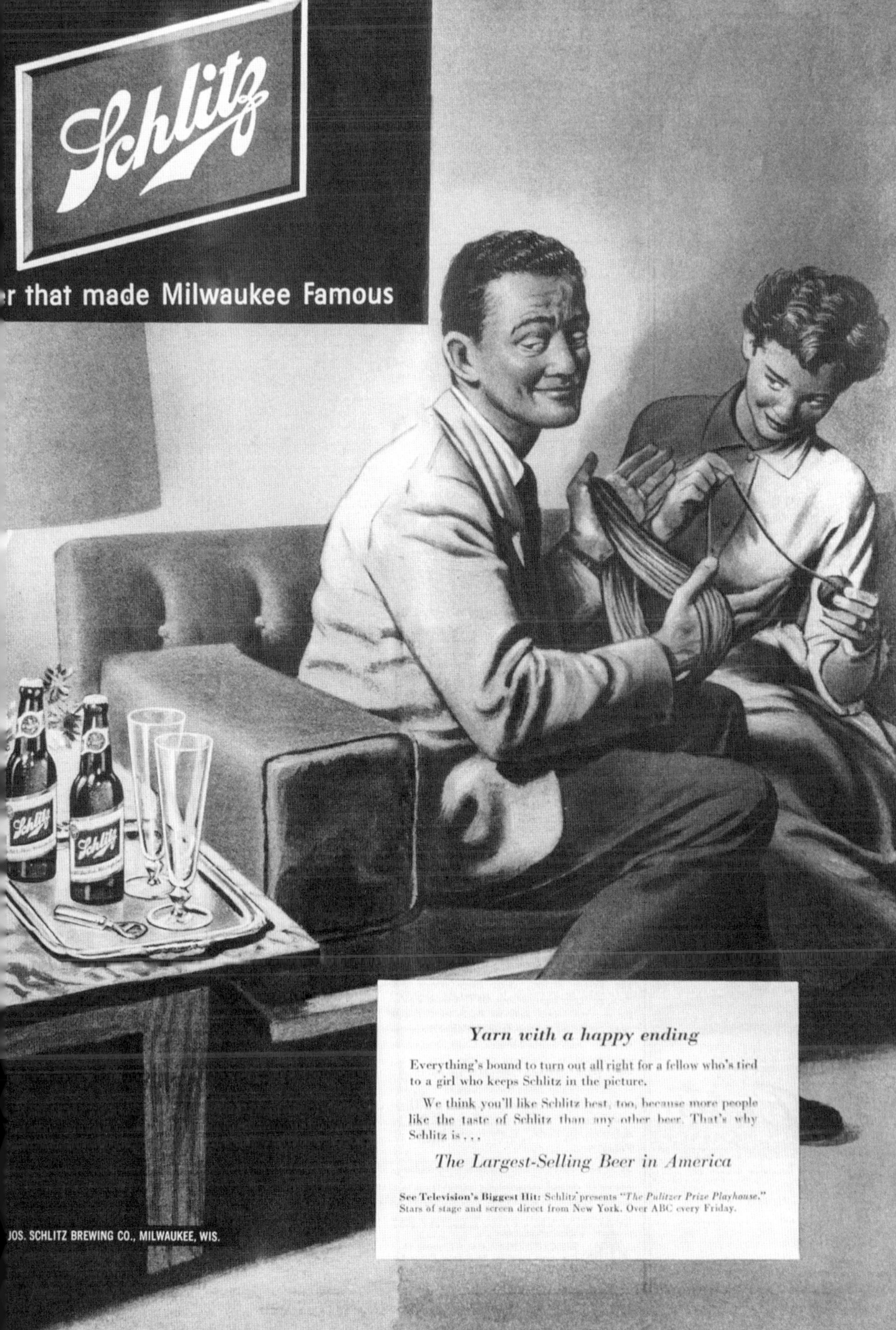

Schlitz
...r that made Milwaukee Famous
Yarn with a happy ending
Everything's bound to turn out all right for a fellow who's tied
to a girl who keeps Schlitz in the picture.
We think you'll like Schlitz best, too, because more people
like the taste of Schlitz than any other beer. That's why
Schlitz is . . .
The Largest-Selling Beer in America
See Television's Biggest Hit: Schlitz presents "The Pulitzer Prize Playhouse."
Stars of stage and screen direct from New York. Over ABC every Friday.
JOS. SCHLITZ BREWING CO., MILWAUKEE, WIS.

Photo Credits

Copyright © 1959 the Norman Rockwell Family Entities (fig. 1); Copyright © Estate of Marylin Hafner (figs. 6, 17, 18, 19, 20, 26, 34, 35); © 2019 Chicago Historical Society (figs. 8, 11); © J. Paul Getty Trust (fig. 68); © Herman Miller, Inc. (figs. 76, 78–89, 91, 96, 98–101, 104–5); © Ezra Stoller/Esto (fig. 90, 97); © Eames Office LLC (eamesoffice.com). All rights reserved (fig. 93); © The Estate of Doris Lee, courtesy D. Wigmore Fine Art, Inc. (fig. 136); © 2019 Estate of Aaron Bohrod/Licensed by VAGA at Artists Rights Society (ARS), NY (figs. 138, 139).

When deemed appropriate, every effort to contact copyright holders was made.

About the Author

Kristina Wilson is professor of art history at Clark University. She has written numerous articles on twentieth-century American art and design, and she co-curated the exhibition *Cyanotypes: Photography's Blue Period* (Worcester Art Museum 2016). She is the author of *Livable Modernism* (2004) and *The Modern Eye* (2009), which was awarded the 2011 Charles Eldredge Prize for Outstanding Scholarship from the Smithsonian American Art Museum.

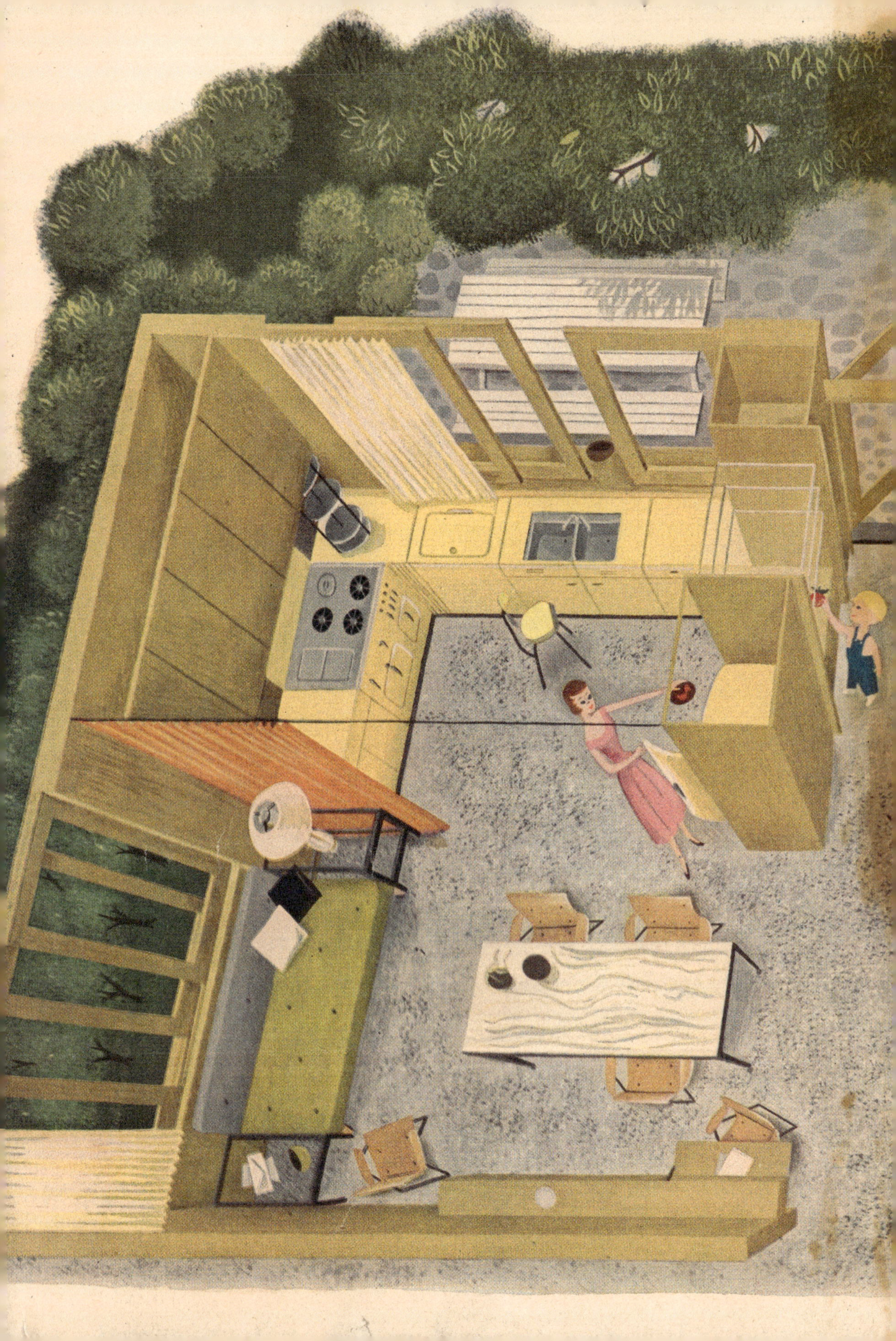